Location and Dislocation in Contemporary Irish Society

Emigration and Irish Identities

edited by
JIM MAC LAUGHLIN

CORK UNIVERSITY PRESS

First published in 1997 by
Cork University Press
Crawford Business Park
Crosses Green
Cork
Ireland

© editor and contributors 1997

British Library Cataloguing in Publication Data
A CIP catalogue record for this book is available from the British Library.

ISBN 1 85918 054 X hardback
1 85918 055 8 paperback

Typeset by Seton Music Graphics, Bantry, Co. Cork
Printed by Hartnolls Ltd, Cornwall

Contents

Notes on Contributors

Marella Buckley's work is informed by her experience of emigration, Irishness and the feminine, and by a natural spirituality. She is committed to fusing the personal and the political, the carnal and the theoretical. Currently living in Cambridge, she is writing a book about relearning how to feel at home in the body, in time and in the physical space that we inhabit.

Mary P. Corcoran is a lecturer in sociology at St Patrick's College, Maynooth. She is a graduate of Trinity College, Dublin and Columbia University. Author of *Irish Illegals: Transients Between Two Societies* (Greenwood Press, 1993), she is also a contributor to *The New York Irish* (The Johns Hopkins University Press, 1996). Her research has focused on issues of identity and ethnicity as manifested among the Irish community in New York City.

Breda Gray is currently researching gender, emigration and Irish identities in the Department of Sociology at Lancaster University. She has written on displacement and emigration with particular reference to Irish women in Britain. Her chapter, 'Nation, Diaspora and Irish Women' appears in Mary Maynard and June Purvis (eds.) *New Frontiers in Women's Studies* (Taylor and Francis, 1996).

Liam Greenslade is a researcher, teacher and broadcaster who focuses on the Irish in Britain. He has published widely on aspects of the mental and physical health of Irish immigrants. He is currently secretary of the Liverpool Irish Centre and Director of Féile, the Liverpool Irish Cultural Festival.

Gerard Hanlon works at the Management Centre, King's College, London. He completed his Ph.D. in the Sociology Department of Trinity College, Dublin and has worked at the London School of Economics and at Sheffield University. Author of *The Commercialisation of Accountancy* (Macmillan, 1995), his current research interests are the changing nature of expert work and the growth of managerialism within professional services.

Kieran Keohane is a lecturer in sociology at University College, Cork. He obtained a Ph.D. from York University, Canada and his current research interests are social theory and cultural analysis in the interpretative tradition. He has published in the area of popular culture, immigration policy and the philosophy of contemporary social theory. His book *Symptoms of Canada* is published by University of Toronto Press.

Eithne Luibheid is working on a Ph.D. in ethnic studies at the University of California, Berkeley. Her current research interests are women's sexuality as a site through which immigrant communities negotiate cultural betrayal, resistance and accommodation.

Jim Mac Laughlin is a political geographer at University College, Cork. He is on the editorial board of *Migration: A European Journal of International Migration and Ethnic Relations* and has published widely on nationalism, racism, emigration, state-formation and the philosophy of the social sciences. He is also a member of the editorial board of Cork University Press's 'Undercurrents' series. He has contributed to *Ireland and Cultural Theory*, edited by Colin Graham and Richard Kirkland (Macmillan, 1997), and to *The Political Geography of the New World Order*, edited by Colin H. Williams (Belhaven Press, 1993). He is the author of *Ireland: The Emigrant Nursery and the World Economy* and *Travellers and Ireland: Whose Country, Whose History?*, both published by Cork University Press. He is currently working on a volume dealing with multiculturalism and minorities in contemporary Irish society.

Fintan O'Toole is a journalist with *The Irish Times*, and also writes regularly for *The Guardian*, *The Observer* and *The Independent on Sunday*. He frequently broadcasts on BBC television and radio. His books include *The Politics of Magic*, on the playwright Tom Murphy, *Meanwhile Back at the Ranch: The Politics of Irish Beef*, and two volumes of essays and journalism, *A Mass for Jesse James* and *Black Hole, Green Card*. A third volume of essays, *The Ex-Isle of Erin* was published in 1997.

Ian Shuttleworth was educated at the University of Leicester and at Trinity College, Dublin. He has been a lecturer in social geography in Queen's University, Belfast since 1993. His main research interests include migration, urban change, the educational and economic fortunes of young people, employment equality issues in Northern Ireland, and census analysis. His work on these themes is to be published in the *Economic and Social Review* and in the *International Journal of Population Geography*.

Bronwen Walter is senior lecturer in geography at Anglia Polytechnic University, Cambridge. She has a longstanding interest in Irish emigration to Britain with particular reference to Irish women emigrants. She has co-authored a recent report for the Commission for Racial Equality on anti-Irish discrimination in Britain. Her research on Irish women and emigration has been published in *Society and Space* and in *Feminist Review*.

Introduction

JIM MAC LAUGHLIN

As a social scientist and political geographer with an interest in the role of place in structuring social processes and influencing the ways in which ideas are formulated and decision-making is conditioned, I have long been curious about the 'birthplaces' of books, intellectual debates and traditions. The idea for this particular collection of essays came to me in Todos Santos in northern Guatemala in the autumn of 1988. This scattered village is located just across the border from Chiapas in south Mexico, high up in some of the highest mountains in Central America. I had been travelling and working my way through Nicaragua, El Salvador and Guatemala for three months and had arrived in Todos in mid-November of that year. Shortly after my arrival, I joined up with a team of *campesinos* who were building a dirt road north of Todos Santos to link it with a neighbouring village some fifteen miles away. In the course of the two weeks that I spent working on the road alongside these villagers, I was constantly asked two questions. Firstly, everyone wanted to know where I had come from, or more precisely, how many hours did it take to get to Guatemala from Europe. Guatemalan Indians regularly cover huge distances in search of work and to trade their tiny surpluses of crops and crafts. They consequently have a very practical attitude to the measurement of distance. It is measured in terms of hours spent in buses. When I told these particular villagers that Ireland was thirteen hours by aeroplane from Guatemala city, they were astounded. The second question usually followed directly on from the first. The village men especially wanted to know if I could get them a job in this place called 'Ireland', or at least in Europe, of which they had heard more.

Some years later in an even smaller village in south Colombia, I was struck by the inter-relatedness of seemingly isolated villages in South America and centres of employment in the world economy. Three men in the remote Colombian village that my partner and I stumbled across in the high summer of 1994 worked on oil-rigs off the east coast of Scotland and returned 'home' once every two or three years. Like Todos Santos, this Colombian village also was a place that people regularly left, in this case *campesino* men, in search of work and a supplementary source of income in the city. They were also places to which they regularly returned, usually in the spring, to work the land and to put in a crop which kept poor families fed throughout the winter months.

Both places brought to mind towns and villages all along the west and north-west coast of Ireland in the late nineteenth and early twentieth century. These were also places that regularly sent migrant workers to Scotland and England where they were often at the outer edges of an expanding world of commercial agriculture and industrial capitalism. As I watched truckloads of Guatemalan *campesinos* heading south out of Todos Santos, I was reminded of the world out of which my parents had grown. I was also reminded of the very real trauma that Irish young adults must have undergone when they too were wrenched from hearth and home to labour – in conditions not that different from those experienced by chain gangs in the American South well into this century – for long hours on farms and in factories from the lowlands of Scotland and England to the industrial cities of North America. The poignancy of the scenes of departure that I witnessed in Todos Santos in the late 1980s must have been multiplied a thousand times over in late nineteenth- and early twentieth-century Ireland. It certainly brought home to me that emigration is not just about movement and travel in any narrow geographical sense. It is first and foremost about movement in a socio-economic, ethnic and cultural sense. This latter form of movement literally takes emigrants far away from 'home' and drops them into alien and often deeply-alienating, environments to etch out a living in the strictest competition with other workers who often see them as their social inferiors. As David Fitzpatrick recently argued in a Thomas Davis lecture on the massive post-Famine emigration from Ireland in the 1850s and 1860s, the trauma of this type of emigration may have been every bit as disorienting as the Famine itself was for those directly caught up in both events.

Emigration certainly was a traumatic and wrenching experience for the villagers of Todo Santos. They, too, had to leave the easy familiarity of their village to seek work in Guatemala city and elsewhere where they had to live out part of their lives on the mean streets of the capital city and in places that could not be further from life as they knew and made it in Todos Santos.

When I returned 'home' to Ireland just before Christmas in 1988, I was once again struck by the many similarities between Irish towns and villages, on the one hand, and those that I had come to know in Guatemala, Nicaragua, El Salvador and Peru, on the other. Here, too, in the late 1980s large numbers of young adults were snatching a few days – the lucky ones sometimes got a week or two – back 'home' before having to return to work, more often than not on building sites, in pubs, in offices and in hospitals in England, the United States, Germany and France. Like villagers from Todos Santos who made it across the border into Costa Rica or Mexico, many of the young Irish in America were also 'illegals'. They, too, were often entangled in 'emigrant traps'. They had to put up with the situations in which they found themselves and over which they had no control. They were very often afraid to return home because this involved running the gauntlet of immigration authorities who have always policed the borders between 'home' and 'abroad' in an effort to keep the 'foreigner' out.

Thus, the idea for this collection was born between two worlds that only *appeared* to be worlds apart. From the point of view of the Irish emigrant, Ireland still has many of the features of a Third World country. Like Guatemala, it was, and still is, what I categorised in the late 1980s as 'an emigrant nursery'. Like Central American countries, and like ex-colonial societies scattered across north Africa, it supplies cheap and abundant labour to the core areas of the world economy.

However, this volume was also born out of a deep suspicion of increasingly sanitised views which suggested that today's Irish emigrants were moving to benign taxfields and fields of opportunity in Europe. This was what political leaders in particular suggested after they 'rediscovered' the reality of emigration as they canvassed for political support in the run-up to the general election at the end of the 1980s. Some politicians indeed professed themselves startled by the embeddedness of emigration in working-class and rural families at this time. In many parts of the country, and not just in the imaginary world of 'the west of Ireland', it was now common to find three or four family members working and living abroad, chiefly in England, but also in the United States, in mainland Europe and even further afield in countries like Japan and Australia. In other words, families here, like so many of the families I had come to know in Morocco, in Egypt, in Palestine, in the Caribbean basin and in Central and South America, were truly multinational institutions. Only the nucleus of the family was 'at home'. The rest, like my own, were scattered elsewhere.

The next stage in the evolution of this volume involved the bringing together of contributors from across gender divisions and political boundaries who could critically and authoritatively discuss the most salient features of what was increasingly categorised as 'new wave' Irish emigration. This was not an easy task and it was made all the more difficult by the very 'scatteredness' of this new Irish diaspora. I had already labelled Ireland an 'emigrant nursery for the world economy'. I now had to locate contributors who could write about the experience of Irish emigrants wherever they were in the global economy. Because so many recent emigrants were still flocking to England, especially to London and the south-east of England, considerable coverage is still devoted here to what is in effect a modern expression of a very deep tradition in Irish emigration. Next came the problem of how to provide coverage on the new Irish Americans and the even newer 'continental Irish'. Filling the many gaps in our information about emigration to continental Europe proved especially difficult because of the dearth of substantial research material on recent Irish emigration to countries like France, Germany, Holland and Denmark. As a number of essays in this volume testify, it was not quite so difficult to find good writers who could cover the American scene. Finally came the problem of how to deal with the effects of emigration on Ireland itself. This proved even less difficult, although I was concerned to measure the impact of emigration, not only in narrow demographic effects or in simple economic terms, but also in socio-cultural and political terms. The resulting volume is multidisciplinary in perspective and as near to global in focus as has been possible. It is global also in the wider sense in that it focuses on the socio-economic status, the mental and physical health, the racial victimisation (and victimising) and the contested and gendered identities of the Irish in Ireland's new world order. Thus it brings together geographers, social scientists, economists and contributors from women's studies and literary criticism who have established reputations in writing on the theme of 'new wave' emigration. More importantly still, however, it also includes new arrivals to the field of emigration and what I call 'diaspora studies', budding writers and researchers who are doing so much to challenge and broaden the staid traditional views on Irish emigration that have characterised the hegemonic discussion on recent 'new wave' Irish emigration.

1. Emigration and the Construction of Nationalist Hegemony in Ireland
The Historical Background to 'New Wave' Irish Emigration

Jim Mac Laughlin

BEHAVIOURAL VERSUS STRUCTURAL ACCOUNTS OF IRISH EMIGRATION

'New wave' emigrants from Ireland today are portrayed as a people set apart from their predecessors by their professional and other educational qualifications, and from their peers by their spirit of adventure and enterprising spirit. This acceptance of emigration as both *natural* and *traditional* indicates a profound devaluation of nationalism as a political philosophy informing social and economic policy, not just constitutional debate, in modern Ireland.[1] It also reflects the hegemonic status of behavioural and geographical explanations of Irish emigration which lack any critical analysis of its social class impact and its structural causes and consequences within Irish society. Only rarely has emigration been treated as a *functional relationship* which has linked Ireland to overseas labour markets and reflected the country's peripheral status, not just its peripheral location in the world economy.[2] Long considered by nationalists in particular as a 'blight' on Irish society, emigration has attracted surprisingly little theoretical attention from Irish historians, or from contemporary Irish social scientists. Most historical accounts suffer from an excess of nationalism and national exceptionalism. Ever since the 1960s, most theoretical accounts have been tainted through a narrowing association with behaviouralism and modernisation theory. This has hindered the development of cross-cultural and transnational perspectives on Irish emigration. Framed in the narrow logic of core-periphery theorising, another literature, heavily influenced by revisionism, has treated historic and recent Irish emigration as an inevitable response to the process of modernisation of an island economy on the edge of Europe. Most of these accounts are framed in the narrow logic of costs-benefits analysis. They simply provide atheoretical descriptions of the impact of emigration on Irish society and its contribution to the Irish 'diaspora' overseas.[3] Moreover, the dominance of historical studies of Irish emigration has meant that we now know more about its pre-Famine trends, including the status of Irish emigrants in Victorian Britain and in the United States in the nineteenth century, than

we do about young Irish school leavers and college graduates in the international labour market today.[4] This is not simply a reflection of the hegemonic
status of history within the social sciences in Ireland. It reflects a long-
standing tendency in Irish society to view emigration as a historical tradition
which began in 'the past' and continues to work itself out today.[5]

The national exceptionalism in many historical studies of nineteenth-
century emigration is now also evident in accounts of recent Irish emigration. It
continues to influence official interpretations of 'new wave' emigration. Thus,
the tendency today is to explain emigration away in terms of Ireland's unique
location, or to treat it as a cultural tradition and a 'peculiarity' of the Irish.
Emigration is therefore viewed simply as an expression of an institutionalised
ideology which encourages young adults to seek *lebensraum* – or 'living space' –
abroad because, it is argued, Ireland is too small a country to provide work for
everyone at home. In a pioneering study of the Irish in Britain in the 1960s,
J.A. Jackson wrote:

> The habit of emigration has become incorporated into Irish life; it is an institu-
> tionalised feature of existence and represents, in the assertion of independence
> involved, a part of the rites de passage for many young people in both parts of
> Ireland.[6]

According to this fatalistic perspective, emigration simply reflects a historical
tradition so deeply ingrained in the Irish psyche that Irish young adults are
perceived as naturally and culturally predisposed to emigrate well before they
think of entering the home labour market.[7] Unlike their nineteenth-century
predecessors, the purveyors of this new conventional Irish wisdom trace emigration to the social psychological attributes and aspirations of Irish young adults.
They portray 'new wave emigration' as a welcome development in Irish youth
enterprise culture because it encourages young adults to think in terms of
geographical mobility when thinking about work and lifestyles.[8]

Viewed over the long term, emigration was not simply a behavioural trait of
the Irish. Neither was it solely a mechanism for resolving regional inequalities
in income, employment and standards of living between Ireland, on the one
hand, and Britain, North America and Australia, on the other. Emigration has
long been inextricably linked to the process of class formation and capitalist
development in Ireland. It has also been a component of class development,
and class struggle, in that emigration has long been a 'hidden injury' of class
which has affected the sons and daughters of small farming and working-class
families more than other sectors of Irish society.[9] Since at least the nineteenth
century, it has contributed to the maintenance of a bourgeois hegemony and
fostered the emergence of a petty bourgeoisie by dispatching large numbers of
young adults abroad, thereby creating political and economic space for both
these sectors at home. Thus, there are many parallels between nineteenth-

century labour migration from Ireland and contemporary migration flows which link north Africa, the Caribbean and eastern Europe to the core areas of the European and global economy.[10]

This chapter focuses on Irish emigration in the late nineteenth and early twentieth century, the period when modern Irish emigration began. It contrasts throughout the differences between a world-systems approach and more conventional core-periphery and behavioural explanations of Irish emigration. It suggests that Irish emigration is an intrinsically geographical phenomenon linked to processes of core-formation and perihperalisation at national and international scales. As such it has clearly had geographical causes and consequences. Thus, for example, large-scale emigration in the late nineteenth and early twentieth century was responsible for the construction of new lived-in environments which extended the frontiers of the global economy, especially in North America and Australia, and contributed to the transformation of lived environments and social space within Ireland. This does not mean that Irish emigration can be explained away in simple geographical terms, which is precisely what conventional core-periphery theorising does. This latter approach also reifies place. It treats exploitative relationships in spatial rather than social class and political terms.[11] In so doing, it de-nationalises the causes and consequences of Irish emigration and treats it as something that is socially and politically dysfunctional. It also uses national categories and spatial abstractions like 'Britain' and 'Ireland' to explain away the regional diversity of Irish emigration since the nineteenth century. The continued use of these categories in the study of Irish emigration betrays a profoundly underdeveloped geographical and indeed sociological imagination. Whatever is thought about Ireland's status as a uniform field of emigration today, this chapter argues that the regional, social, and economic geography of Ireland in the nineteenth and twentieth century was far too complex for the country to be treated as a featureless isomorphic plain over which the currents of emigration flowed evenly. It further suggests that large scale emigration since pre-Famine times has reduced the socio-regional diversity of Ireland to a 'blandscape' of rich agricultural heartlands ringed by a relic landscape of small to medium farmsteads and declining rural communities.[12] Finally, it shows how world-systems theory avoids the pitfalls of voluntarism in behavioural accounts, and the problem of reification in traditional core-periphery models of Irish emigration, by tracing it back to *structural processes* operating within Irish society and operating also at the level at the level of the international economy.

TOWARDS A WORLD-SYTEMS PERSPECTIVE ON IRISH EMIGRATION

World-systems theory offers entirely different meanings to the terms 'core' and 'periphery' from those used in conventional core-periphery theorising. It treats these terms as historical and geographical 'happenings', not just as spatial categories which geographers and historians can impose at will upon reality in order to better explain patterns of emigration.[13] Thus, it insists that places do not become 'cores' or 'peripheries' through the acquisition of locational features. They become such through the operation of the structuring processes underlying development and underdevelopment. As Taylor has shown, world-systems theorists use these categories to refer to complex processes and not directly to areas, regions or even nations. From this perspective, regions and states become cores through the predominance of core processes operating within them, just as other regions and states are peripheral because of the peripheral processes which operate there.[14] The categories 'core' and 'periphery' do not exhaust world-systems concepts for structuring space. One of the most original elements in this approach is the concept 'semi-periphery'. This is neither core nor periphery. It combines a mixture of both processes and can be directly applied to zones, areas or states when they exhibit a predominance neither of core nor peripheral processes. As Taylor has also shown, this means as well that the 'overall social relations operating in such zones involve exploiting peripheral areas while the semi-periphery itself suffers exploitation by the core'.[15] This distinction between 'cores' and 'peripheries' as processes and not simply places is neither semantic nor trivial. As Agnew has shown, it is related to the way in which the world economy has been structured since the nineteenth century, not least through the structuring forces of migration and emigration.[16] This also means that there are important distinctions between conventional core-periphery and world-systems explanations of emigration. Due to the high level of 'locationalism' in the former, for example, 'cores' and 'peripheries' become agents of social change. They act as substitutes for social agency in that they explain emigration away in terms of simple geographical 'push' and 'pull' factors operating at the level of the international economy. 'Cores', in this mode of theorising, attract emigrants, just as 'peripheries' produce them. Cores are also 'activated' to such a degree that they exploit peripheries.

This is quite unlike the usage of 'core' and 'periphery' in world-systems theorising about development, underdevelopment and emigration. Here locational factors facilitate, but do not constitute, explanations for social phenomena.[17] Thus, a world-systems approach to Irish emigration suggests that the proper starting point for nineteenth-century Irish emigration is less 'English misrule' in Ireland than the wider structural forces and the narrower local worlds where national and international forces contributing to emigration intersected and lifted young adults from familiar surroundings and deposited them in unfamiliar environments. Therefore, world-systems theory differs from more conventional core-periphery explanations of Irish emigration in a variety of ways. Firstly, it argues that emigration was not caused by locational factors, or by any heightening of the geographical mobility of Irish young adults consequent upon transformations in transportation and communication networks.

Secondly, it traces emigration less to the peripheral location of Ireland in the international economy than to the peripheral status of the Irish state. This meant that, even if they wished to do so, successive administrations in the late nineteenth and early twentieth century were unable to halt involuntary emigration from Ireland. Thirdly, it suggests that Irish emigration has long had its roots in the interface between an agricultural/export-led Irish economy and an international economy that placed new values on rural and working-class communities in Ireland because they constituted 'emigrant nurseries' which supplied the world economy with reserves of cheap and adaptable labour.[18]

Viewed thus, export-led rural capitalism outside the north-east of Ireland generated huge surpluses of labour, as well as surpluses of agricultural commodities, and compelled large numbers of young adults to seek opportunities abroad that were not available within the narrow parameters of rural capitalism in post-Famine Ireland. Finally, unlike revisionists and modernisation theorists, world-systems theory refuses to reduce emigration to simple cultural and historical 'causes', or to treat it simply as a behavioural phenomenon. World-systems theorists trace it, instead, to the political and economic structures of nineteenth- century Ireland, including those social and economic structures which fostered the emergence of a native bourgeois and petty bourgeois nationalist ruling class. World-systems theory, therefore, shows that Ireland was far from being peripheral to the process of capitalist industrialisation. Since at least the nineteenth century, it is argued, revolutions in transportation forced even the most remote pockets of rural Ireland into the world economy and transformed small-farming communities into 'emigrant nurseries' by annihilating the spatial barriers to the circulation of commodity labour as well as the commodities of labour. Thus, nineteenth-century emigration from Ireland contributed to the economic and political peripheralisation of large parts of rural Ireland while facilitating core-formation both within Ireland and in the world economy. Ireland, in other words, became a cla; economy. It exploited and exported cheap labour and, in s core-formation in its rich agricultural heartlands, while simu exploitation by the core areas of the British and the world economy.

Focusing on these links between indigenous rural capitalism and large-scale emigration in the nineteenth century, this chapter offers a critique of those nationalist interpretations which trace emigration to 'English misrule' in Ireland. It also suggests that a structuralist perspective avoids the pitfalls of behaviouralism and voluntarism that have characterised 'modernisationist' and cost-benefit analyses of historical and recent Irish emigration. Rather than treating emigration as something caused by the fatal attractions of foreign fields of opportunity, or by the adventurous spirit and 'individualism' of Irish young adults, it portrays it instead as a *social response* to structuring and restructuring processes operating at the levels of local and national society and at the level of the international economy. The section that follows examines political attitudes to Irish emigration in the nineteenth century. This includes a discussion on the relationship between emigration and the construction of petty bourgeois nationalist hegemony in Ireland in the late nineteenth and early twentieth century.

POLITICS AND EMIGRATION IN NINETEENTH-CENTURY IRELAND

Political attitudes towards Irish emigration have long been refracted through social class, and particularly through ethnic lenses.[19] These, in turn, have shaped, and have been shaped by, prevailing political orthodoxies, particularly by attitudes towards nationalism and Ireland's place in the international economy.[20] Thus, for example, Malthusianists on both sides of the Irish Sea portrayed Irish emigration in the nineteenth century as an inevitable response to the process of rural modernisation. By the middle of the century they were advocating selective state support to facilitate emigration. They also contributed to an early sanitisation of Irish emigration by suggesting that those who left Ireland fared well outside of it. They attributed the widespread emigration of the post-Famine decades to revolutions in transportation which drew Ireland closer to Britain and North America where, more radical Malthusianists suggested, the 'troublesome Irish' properly belonged.[21] Viewed thus, emigration was a necessary social evil because it facilitated the transition from 'tradition' to 'modernity', both in the Irish countryside and in the Irish psyche.

Irish nationalists were among the first to attack as erroneous this naturalisation and sanitisation of Irish emigration. They systematically refuted each assimilationist premise underlying the anglicisation of post-Famine rural Ireland through the operation of *laissez faire* policies there, including *laissez faire* attitudes towards large-scale rural emigration. They attributed emigration to 'landlord rule' and 'English misrule' in Ireland, and insisted that Malthusian defences of Irish emigration contained a hidden political agenda which suggested that the Irish could be ruled more effectively if only the rural and urban poor could be encouraged to emigrate. Rudimentary though it was, this essentially *historicist* reaction to Irish emigration problematised a whole range of related socio-economic issues that were supposed to have been resolved through the operation of *laissez faire* principles of political economy in colonial Ireland.[22] Discussing the role of historicism on Celtic critiques of English political economy on Celtic agrarian legislation and on attitudes towards nation-building in Scotland and Ireland at this time, Clive Dewey has argued that historicists shifted the entire cause of agrarian social and political conflict from population pressure, on the one hand, to a conflict of laws and a conflict between advocates of national self-determination and defenders of colonial rule in the Celtic fringe of Britain, on the other.[23] They portrayed it, instead, as a conflict between *Celtic* custom and *English* commercialism. Medium to large tenant farmers in post-Famine Ireland particularly attacked an underlying assumption in agricultural policy in colonial Ireland which suggested that rancherism was necessarily more productive than 'petite culture'. This was especially the case in rural Catholic Ireland where local historians and antiquarians came of political and intellectual age just as the hegemonic status of the beleaguered Anglo-Irish aristocracy was under attack from an emergent Catholic petty bourgeoisie.

The Italian Marxist, Antonio Gramsci, used the category 'hegemony' in a socio-historical sense to define 'the moment when objective and subjective forces combine to produce a situation of revolutionary change'.[24] This is the moment when the economic and political structures of the old order are collapsing and when new social forces emerge which have the will, determination and historical insight to take advantage of changing developments in national and international society. This precisely describes socio-political developments in Ireland in the aftermath of the Famine. That was when a challenging collectivity comprising substantial Catholic tenants and the middle class came of political age and established for themselves a position which enabled them to dominate small farmers and the 'respectable poor' outside the north-east of Ireland.[25] Writing in an Italian context in the 1920s and 1930s, Gramsci recognised that a 'hegemony' had distinctive geographical correlates and that it was rooted to particular places.[26] He particularly emphasised the role of rural-to-urban migration in the consolidation of the power basis of the petty bourgeoisie in the south of Italy. Thus the manner in which the largely peasant Mezzogiorno had been integrated into an Italian state dominated by northern industrialists especially attracted Gramsci's attention. The latter, he argued, in alliance with southern landowners and an intelligentsia which operated as intermediaries between peasants and landowners, established hegemonic control over all of Italy in the late nineteenth century. In so doing, they laid the basis for a continuous depletion of the south of Italy through the migration northwards of the sons and daughters of the rural poor who were redundant to the nation-building needs of the bourgeoisie in the south, but were crucial to the success of industrial capitalism in the north of Italy.

Gramsci's approach is particularly suited to an analysis of class configuration, state-formation and emigration in post-Famine Ireland for a number of reasons. Firstly, Gramsci recognised the rural poor as important actors in the political arena who contributed, through emigration, to class formation and industrial development in the late nineteenth and early twentieth century. In particular, he showed how, through their links with the petty bourgeoisie, the substantial peasantry and small-farming communities had a debilitating effect on working-class politics and on radical movements for agrarian reform. Secondly, he showed how regionally powerful groups (e.g. northern industrialists in the case of Italy) exerted control over society at large by forming inter-regional and intra-national class alliances. Thirdly, Gramsci explained the anomaly of subordinate social classes being led by a middle-class intelligentsia in terms of the latter's social class origins, particularly their close links with the rural poor and with the 'respectable' working class. He showed, therefore, that the intelligentsia, especially the clergy, functioned as social mediators between dominant and subordinate classes in regionally-differentiated and stratified nation-states. Peasants and small farmers, he argued, frequently also regarded priests, teachers and others set above them in a deeply ambivalent manner. On the one hand, they looked up to them as their political 'betters' and 'natural' leaders because so many of them were their own flesh and blood.[27] This was especially the case in the south of Italy and in the west of Ireland where priests, teachers and other petty officials acted as social intermediaries between the rural poor and nation-building classes. Their socially strategic positions also gave this group a disproportionate moral and political influence over Irish rural and working-class communities.[28]

In nineteenth-century Ireland the indigenous bourgeoisie comprised a wide range of social groups. It included large landholders, middling tenants, 'thirty acre men', the merchant class, industrialists, the shopocracy and the professions. Despite its diverse social origins, and despite also the diversity of its political outlook, this group consolidated its hegemonic control by extending its political influence beyond the rich heartlands of rural Ireland and by forming alliances with the petty bourgeoisie along the west and north-west coast.[29] In so doing, it extended the field of emigration into these areas and caused increasingly large numbers of young adults to take to emigrant trails out of Ireland in search of work and opportunity. Thus, the alliance between petty bourgeois and bourgeois class interests was predicated upon the large-scale emigration of Irish youth. It emerged from a process of land clearances and selective emigration which literally made room for viable farm units in nation-building, nineteenth-century Ireland. It owed its very existence to Ireland's status as an emigrant nursery in the world economy and to the systematic removal of Ireland's surplus sons and daughters abroad.

Irish Nation-building and Irish Emigration

In Ireland, as in peripheral and semi-peripheral economies elsewhere in the colonial world of the nineteenth century, native propertied classes did not lament the passing of 'traditional' society through emigration and capitalist modernisation. Ever since the Famine they had practiced their own crude version of rate-capping and sought to ensure that Poor Law legislation would not pose an obstacle to its programme of rural development under bourgeois and petty bourgeois nationalist hegemony. Like their peers in England and Scotland, for example, they took great care to ensure that Poor Relief would only be distributed to those who had abandoned all claims to land and property.[30] This had the effect of creating a glut of smallholdings on the property market, and these were rented or bought up by 'improving' tenants and independent farmers. Accordingly, the emptying of the countryside through poverty and emigration greatly extended the geographical range of commercial farming in Ireland and allowed those who stayed behind to add, literally, field to field. Similarly, export-led agricultural development later in the century enabled those with viable tenancies to specialise for the market in order to increase production; this in turn edged the 'surplus offspring' on family farms onto emigrant trails out of Ireland.

From as early as mid-century, the indigenous bourgeoisie had also been proclaiming Ireland's right to self-determination and gathering political control over rural Catholic Ireland through their domination of local government institutions. Catholic middling tenant farmers, merchants and large farmers in particular occupied positions of power in the Poor Law institutions established in mid-nineteenth century Ireland. These groups were among the chief bene-factors of the Famine-induced restructuring of Irish property relations and of post-Famine-induced emigration. Certainly the 'property adjustment' caused by Famine and by Famine-induced emigration extended to small-farming western counties by the closing decades of the nineteenth century. As Miller suggests:

> the structural changes in post-Famine developed *in tandem with emigration: they were mutually reinforcing as well as self-perpetuating phenomena.* For example, while it is fair to cite commercialisation of agriculture as emigration's root cause, it is equally true that process – involving the engrossment of grassland, the switch to impartible inheritance, and the proletarianisation of rural labour – could not have occurred so rapidly and thoroughly except as a result of mass emigration . . . In short, these processes were circular and interdependent.[31] (emphasis added)

But for the safety valve of emigration, the movement for agrarian reform in these districts could well have resulted in a fundamental restructuring of Irish prop-erty relations in the late nineteenth and early twentieth century (see Figs. 1–3). The takeover of this movement by larger farmers from the midlands and south of Ireland not only extended the hegemonic status of the middling tenantry. It also meant that the objectives of agrarian reform were now reduced to the transformation of existing holdings from tenancies to outright proprietorships. As the American recession of the 1870s clearly showed, when the safety valve of emigration was temporarily stopped, the resultant surplus of young adults in Ireland could fuel rural unrest and give added force to grassroots movements for agrarian and social reform.[32]

As the century progressed the substantial Catholic tenantry, cultural nation-alists, publicans, shopkeepers and the professional classes gradually dominated local government and claimed more and more of the country for nationalist Ireland. Local priests, schoolteachers and amateur historians established these 'improving farmers' as the 'natural leaders' of the local worlds of rural Ireland. Initially at least, they also sought to give the rural poor and the embryonic working class in rural Catholic Ireland a new political destiny and a national

Figure 1: Absolute Emigration per County, 1851–1880

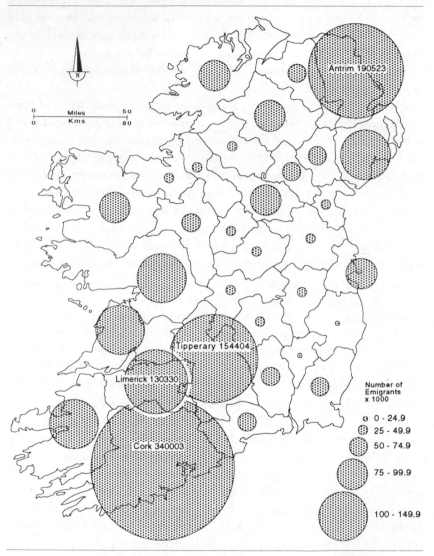

Source: Census of Population, 1851, 1881

sense of place in the international community of nation-states. What made this all the easier was the fact that, throughout 'Congested Ireland' especially, local landlords saw no solution to the massive problems of rural underdevelopment other than that of emigration. Thus, after considering the options available for the alleviation of poverty in 'Congested Ireland', one state official argued:

What seems to be needed for the relief of these districts is the establishment on a permanent basis of an emigration department, which, with a competent staff,

Figure 2: Absolute Emigration per County, 1881–1910

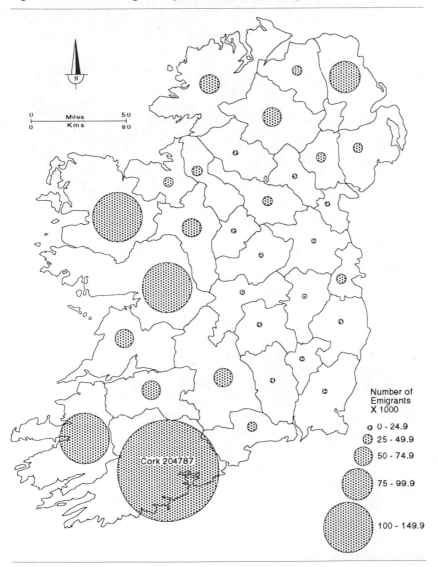

Cork 204787

Number of
Emigrants
X 1000

0 - 24.9
25 - 49.9
50 - 74.9
75 - 99.9
100 - 149.9

Source: Census of Population, 1881, 1911

and the co-operation of a voluntary committee, combined with systematic and careful oversight at ports of departure and arrival, shall from year to year, and not spasmodically, deal with all applications for <u>assisted emigration</u>, and advise or make grants in each case as may seem for the best.[33]

State and landlord support for 'assisted emigration' here showed that even the most axiomatic of *laissez faire* principles could be bent to suit the interests of

Figure 3: Population Change per County, 1851–1911

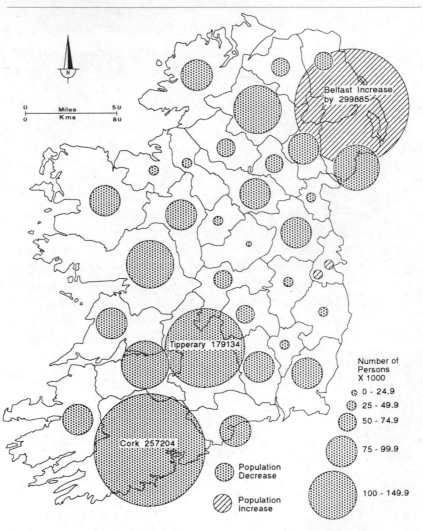

Source: Census of Population, 1911

the sate, especially if this meant a programme of assisted emigration which cleared the land of uneconomic tenancies and transformed the 'surplus' sons and daughters of small tenant farmers into a permanent proletariat in industrial Britain and North America.

Support for assisted emigration also transcended religious and ethnic division in late nineteenth-century Ireland. It particularly found advocates among the substantial Catholic tenantry and the Catholic clergy. It was especially strong in 'Congested Ireland', that is in those districts where the total

Figure 4: Population Decline in the West of Ireland, 1891–1956

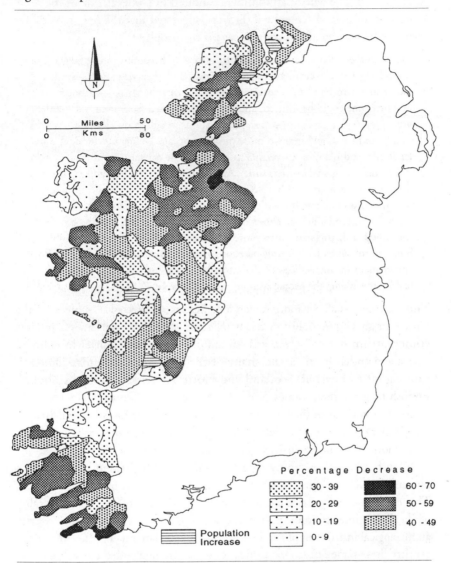

Source: Adapted from T. W. Freeman, *Ireland: A General and Regional Geography* (London: Methuen, 1965), p. 124.

rateable valuation of the land divided by the number of inhabitants amounted to less than thirty shillings per person (see Fig. 4).[34] In the early 1890s, this categorisation of 'congestion' defined an area of land of just over three-and-a-half million acres with a population of almost half-a-million inhabitants spread across counties Donegal, Leitrim, Roscommon, Sligo, Mayo, Galway, Kerry and Cork. By 1910, the frontiers of 'Congested Ireland' extended to twice that acreage and the Congested Districts Board ministered to more than one million rural dwellers. The wife of a prominent landlord in Donegal, one of the more 'congested' of Ireland's congested districts, suggested that the only remedy for the endemic poverty of this county was for the people:

> to rely on their own industry and efforts, instead of becoming public beggars, or beseeching the Government to help them – in other words requesting the Government to hand over to them the result of other people's labours. If a healthier tone could be infused, and the people roused from their old indolent ways, Donegal's great curses – misrepresentations, beggings, and laziness – would vanish, and we should hear no more pitiable appeals. Doling out meal, abusing landlords, and blaming Government can never be the cure for the evils from which these congested districts suffer. At present there is neither industry nor the desire for improvement. When seasons do not fail the people can exist, and are happy, and do not care for settled work. They have their warm cabins, and all the winter the men lounge about doing nothing. To get the people away from the crowded districts and into more profitable fields of labour, if possible at home, if not, abroad, is the only cure for Donegal. Thousands of girls could find employment in the factories of Belfast and vicinity, but as long as meal can be had for the asking, the people will not exert themselves.[35]

This statement is all the more remarkable because it referred to subjects of the Crown in an Ulster county in terms redolent of the paternalism, racism and ethnocentrism normally reserved for subordinate communities in colonial Africa and India. In the event, many of the poor 'vanished' from Donegal, running off to England, Scotland and North America with hardly enough English to write their names (see Figs. 5 and 6).[36] Nationalists made huge political capital out of these attempts to transform large parts of rural Ireland into 'emigrant nurseries' which 'banished' the 'troublesome Irish' abroad to make more room for Anglo-Irish 'graziers and their bullocks' in rural Ireland.[37]

English political economy in nineteenth-century Ireland clearly was a powerful secular discourse which justified the 'kulakisation' of Irish agriculture. This encouraged large-scale emigration under the guise of scientific neutrality while all the time economic policy in colonial Ireland was covertly and overtly an ideological instrument of Anglo-Irish rule. By the latter half of the nineteenth century these same *laissez faire* principles were often defended by Irish nationalists because they bolstered the economic structures of nation-building Ireland. Whelan has argued that 'political economy' here was:

> . . . an establishment discipline geared to supporting the status quo. Its claims to be founded on natural – and hence universal – laws were bogus; its abstract generalisations involved a denial of Irish difference, falsely arguing that a political economy appropriate to England applied with equal force in Ireland.[38]

Like most commentators, however, he fails to show how *laissez faire* policies were also supported by indigenous elites and by an emergent native ruling class.

Figure 5: The Irish-born Population in 'Principal Towns' in Britain in 1851

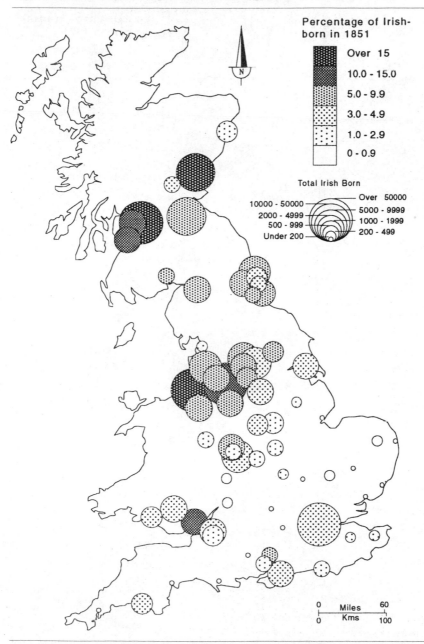

Source: Colm Pooley, 'Segregation or Integration? The Residential Experience of the Irish in Mid-Victorian Britain', in Roger Swift and Sheridan Gilley (eds), *The Irish in Britain, 1815–1939* (London: Pinter, 1989), p. 64.

Figure 6: The Irish-born Population in 'Principal Towns' in Britain in 1871

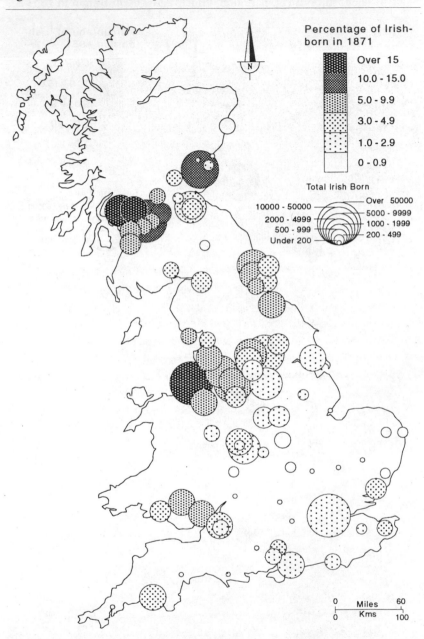

Source: Adapted from Colm Pooley, 'Segregation or Integration? The Residential Experience of the Irish in Mid-Victorian Britain', in Roger Swift and Sheridan Gilley (eds), *The Irish in Britain, 1815–1939* (London: Pinter, 1989), p. 65.

With the post-Famine emergence of an organic Irish intelligentsia, subjectively and objectively related to the dominant sectors of a modernising Irish society, *laissez faire* policies in Ireland had developed an Irish strain. In attacking an Anglo-Irish hegemony, this same intelligentsia ensured that confident and rational nationalist conclusions were embodied across a wide spectrum of topics subsumed under the discourse of English political economy in Ireland. Now, however, Irish nation-builders, most notably the Catholic church and cultural nationalists, tended to Anglicise the causes of problems like rural poverty and large-scale emigration and nationalised their solutions. As the century drew to a close, however, it was clear that the Malthusian acceptance of emigration as a 'natural' phenomenon had transcended ethnic divisions and taken root in a bourgeois Irish nationalist ideology. By this time, therefore, English political economy in Ireland had spawned an Irish variant of free market economics which suited the specific interests of medium to large Irish tenant farmers. This was an instrument of bourgeois and petty bourgeois rule which justified the scattering of the sons and daughters of the rural poor and the working class in the interests of modernising Irish society and Irish agriculture in particular. The rural bourgeoisie, particularly the petty bourgeois 'thirty acre men' who were the backbone of the Home Rule movement, now looked on emigration as a hedge against land sub-division, the bane of good farming practices in late Victorian Ireland. Like 'progressive landlords' elsewhere in the country, they suggested that any curtailment of the voluntary emigration of this sector of Irish society ran counter to the principles of political economy and the 'natural' principles of *laissez faire* capitalism.[39]

In Ireland, as elsewhere in Europe, nationalism also stressed the organic links between 'the people', or 'volk', and their homeland, or 'heimat'. The very idea of a 'volk' conjured up images of a people with a strong territorial imperative, a people linked to the national territory through a 'blood and soil' racism that fused them with their homeland in one organic whole. Indeed, nationalists suggested that the link between the 'volk' and their 'heimat' was an entirely 'natural' even quasi-sacred relationship.[40] From the start, however, categories like 'volk' and 'the people' were entirely exclusionist, and nationalism, as in Irish nationalism, did not fulfil an anchoring or 'territorialising' function for many of the rural poor, including large numbers of young women who were 'banished' from Mother Ireland's farms through emigration. Unlike in late nineteenth-century France, for example, where the sons and daughters of the peasantry were transformed into Frenchmen and Frenchwomen, in other words into French *citizens*, the rural poor in Ireland were, more often than not, proletarianised into the core areas of the international, not the national, economy.[41] Here they were expected to bury an emergent nationalist identity while simultaneously preserving a Catholic sense of Irishness abroad. This meant that the new Ireland was to be built not only by, but also for, the 'stalwart, muscular, dauntless young braves' of rural Ireland. These were assumed to be 'royally endowed with every attribute that goes to make up a peerless and magnificent manhood'.[42] Their disappearance through emigration was to be prevented at all costs because it would have deprived rural Ireland of the very 'bone and sinew' needed for the construction of a healthy nation. The rural poor, on the other hand, especially the 'sad, weeping and melancholy emigrants' who had 'cast off all allegiance to the land' had no place in Irish society because they were perceived as having nothing to offer the Irish nation. Their emigration was to be tolerated, even encouraged, if it led to social mobility outside Ireland.

This conflict of attitudes towards involuntary Irish emigration was also reflected in attitudes towards Ireland's place in the global community of nations. In her *Mother Ireland,* Edna O'Brien has stated that countries 'are either mothers or fathers, and engender the emotional bristle secretly reserved for either sire'. She further suggests that:

> Ireland has always been a woman, a womb, a cave, a cow, a Rosaleen, a sow, a bride, a harlot, and, of course, the gaunt Hag of Beare . . . She is thought to have known invasion from the time when the Ice Age ended and the improving climate allowed deer to throng her dense forests.[43]

This chapter suggests that it has always been Ireland's misfortune – more precisely the misfortune of young Irish women emigrants and young emigrants in general – to have been numbered among the Motherlands, not the Fatherlands, of the world.[44] Feminists have shown how nationalist characterisations of Ireland as a suffering, self-sacrificing mother have promoted sexist stereotypes of Ireland and the Irish which served the interests of the coloniser in the fifteenth and sixteenth century and those of Irish political leaders in the nineteenth and early twentieth century.[45] These same stereotypes have served the political and economic agendas of Irish political leaders since at least the nineteenth century. Nationalists condemned the haemorrhaging of Mother Ireland through emigration, arguing that England condoned Irish emigration because it was depriving Mother Ireland of her sons and, more especially, her daughters. The tragedy of large involuntary emigration and the marginalisation of women in Irish society is intimately related to this image of Ireland as a mother, more precisely to constructs of Ireland as a *poor* mother. While feminists have shown how images of Ireland as a suffering and self-sacrificing mother have obscured the realities of most women's lives by writing them out of Irish history, they have failed to capitalise upon a deeper mining of this imagery. This marginalisation of women, together with their symbolisation as passive mothers, ignored the very real contributions that Irish women made, not only to Irish social, political and economic life, but also to the social and economic life of whole segments of the world economy. In thus symbolising Ireland, Irish nationalists justified the political subordination and emigration of Irish women and young adults, intimating that the sufferings of Mother Ireland were externally caused, and that Irish men, not the 'fallen' Ireland-as-mother, had the answer to her problems. They at once Anglicised and feminised the causes of large-scale emigration from Ireland and proffered highly gendered, patriarchal solutions to solve this problem. In so doing, they also suggested that it was in everyone's interests, including those of women and children, that political and economic power in Ireland should pass from the hands of 'foreign' overlords to the fathers and sons of the nation. The latter were regarded as the natural leaders of the Irish nation because, it was argued, they were sprung from a virile Irish manhood which usurped English rule in Ireland.

In a highly perceptive analysis of Irish writing in the nineteenth century, Donovan shows how this marginalisation of women was also reflected in Irish writing. With the emergence of a strong nationalist movement in the post-Famine period, a new breed of Irish writers emerged who played an active self-defining and nation-defining role in nation-building Ireland. As Donovan shows, their sense of the evolution of an identity was closely linked to that of their country.[46] Not only that, the working out of an Irish male identity was widely perceived to be naturally bound up with that of the nation itself. The Irish male writer commented upon the social and political scene in Ireland with a view to altering it. Irish women writers, for their part, by and large stayed *within* the narrower space occupied by the *individual*, or, more typically, by the *couple of individuals*, and stressed the *specificity* of the female experience and female sensibilities. Their characters are often as not what she terms '*passive sufferers* in the grip of [a] life-denying morality'. Their creators do not see themselves as 'toppler[s] or re-inventor[s] of the world through the machinations of their craft'.[47] Unlike their male counterparts, for example, who used landscape and history to actively comment upon the state of an entire society, they used these same effects to passively reflect the fleeting moods of individual characters. They also used them to present individuals who work towards a vision of selfhood within the given limits of society. Many of the characters in Irish women's writing at this time stay inside established conventions of form and narrative and highlight private, as opposed to public and political, journeys towards self-definition. Irish male writers, on the other hand, many of them from the urban middle class, wrote of a quite different world from that of their female counterparts. Unlike the latter, who were largely content to remain within structures increasingly now laid down by Irish men, and not just by the Anglo-Irish ascendancy, these male writers rejected existing political, moral and social structures. In an effort to consolidate their own identity, they ended up creating a new moral system and literary form within which an Irish *nationalist* identity struggled into existence. Women writers were literally pushed to the edges of this literary world-in-the-making. Irish male writers tested the very limits of artistic forms and structures laid down by the writers from the landed aristocracy and by British poets and novelists. With few exceptions, Irish women writers focused in upon the narrow world of relationships, feeling and sentiment, while their male counterparts ranged out across the public world of class conflict and political strife in a nation-building Ireland. In the event, nation-building became a predominantly male project, something to which Irish women, including women writers, often passively submitted.

If the middling tenantry and the emergent bourgeoisie did not loudly lament the passing of traditional Ireland through emigration, the Catholic Church and cultural nationalists certainly often did so. They specifically stressed the destructive effects of emigration on the religious life of rural Ireland and on the social and cultural landscape of rural society. In so doing, they revealed the clash of interests between Catholic nation-builders and cultural nationalists, on the one hand, and those of rational rural capitalists, on the other. The attitudes of the latter had to consider the countervailing, often conflicting attitudes of the Catholic Church towards involuntary, large-scale emigration. Church leaders and cultural nationalists in particular feared that emigration had become so far advanced by the late nineteenth century that it was fast becoming a voluntary activity attracting not only the rural poor, but also 'hale and hearty' young boys and the athletic male population. The Church was also equally concerned with the volume and the quality of Irish emigration. Cultural nationalists, for their part, suggested that the widespread emigration of young Irish women was depriving the country of its 'breeding stock'. Young women, it was argued, were sacrificing 'their dowries and a certain prospect of marriage for the pleasure of serving in a business house in New York or even going into a situation as housemaids in American families'.[48]

These conflicting attitudes of the Catholic Church and the emergent bourgeoisie point to the divisions in hegemonic attitudes towards Irish emigration. They also suggest that the nation in Ireland, as elsewhere in Europe, denoted a process of *moral* development and fostered the growth of an organic national identity. Both developments implied a prioritisation of the material and political interests of the bourgeoisie over the rural poor and the embryonic working class. Accordingly, bourgeois concern for the economic viability of the new Irish nation-in-the-making frequently conflicted with the wider social and cultural ideals of the Catholic Church and cultural nationalists. Whole sections of the rural poor, therefore, were considered redundant to the nation-building project as Irish nation-builders and entrepreneurs staked their claim to self-determination on a vehement disavowal of the Irish as an impoverished and 'barbarous' race. This was especially important given that racial discourse in Britain depicted Ireland as an ungovernable and impoverished country and equated the Irish with animals and 'sewer rats' who, through their association with squalor and 'dirty work' in England, were considered beyond the pale of civilised Victorian society.[49]

Milan Kundera has claimed that 'the struggle of man against power is the struggle of memory against forgetting'.[50] The middling tenantry and petty bourgeoisie
of late nineteenth-century rural Ireland successfully struggled against the power of
landed ascendancy by 'forgetting' their plebeian origins, and forgetting especially
the emigrant poor. Discussing the 'grandiose programme' of the Communists
in post-War Czechoslovakia, Kundera further argued that their opponents:

> . . . had no great dream; all they had was a few moral principles, stale and lifeless,
> to patch up the tattered trousers of the established order. So of course grandiose
> enthusiasts won out over the cautious compromisers and lost no time turning
> their dream into reality: the creation of an idyll of justice for all. Now let me
> repeat: an idyll, for all. People have always aspired to an idyll, a garden where
> nightingales sing, a realm of harmony where the world does not rise up as a
> stranger against man . . . From the start [however] there were people who realized
> they lacked the proper temperament for the idyll and wished to leave the
> country. But since by definition an idyll is one world for all, the people who
> wished to emigrate were implicitly denying its validity.[51]

This also describes the relationship between Irish emigrants and the Irish
diaspora since the nineteenth century, on the one hand, and Irish nation-
builders, on the other. Excluded from Irish society and denied a place in the
nationalist idyll, emigrants expressed their denial of an Irish nation constructed
under bourgeois nationalist hegemony by emigrating. They were scattered over
the four corners of the world, at least to the English-speaking world, according
to the dictates of a threatened Anglo-Irish ascendancy and an emergent indigenous rural bourgeois hegemony. They were a scattered people who entered
diaspora time, and their lives and histories were no longer charted in Irish time
or Irish history.[52] Leaving a country that literally had no time for them, they left
behind the timeless world of peasant life and entered the precise world of commodified labour and factory time. Like the offspring of African slaves and black
minorities who inhabit Gilroy's 'Black Atlantic', Irish emigrants increasingly
now lived in a 'Green Atlantic', a world constituted as:

> a non-traditional tradition, an irreducibly modern, ex-centric, unstable, and
> asymmetrical cultural ensemble that cannot be apprehended through the
> manichean logic of binary coding.[53]

EMIGRATION, NATIONALISM AND THE GEOGRAPHY OF EXCLUSION

For Irish nationalists 'culture,' and cultural practices, were refining and
elevating forces which contributed to the peripheralisation of the rural poor
through emigration.[54] Thus, 'culture' in nation-building Ireland was not only
perceived as a combative source of identity that was different to 'Englishness', it
was also a protective enclosure which differentiated respectable 'insiders' from
'outsiders' in Irish society. As a result, emigrants, and whole sections of the

labouring and travelling poor, were 'outsiders' in this increasingly commercialised, settled and sanitised society. Moreover, they were 'outsiders' in a dual
sense. As emigrants, they were geographically beyond the pale of nation-building
Ireland but were, nevertheless, expected to help the nation-building drive back
home through political lobbying and financial support from abroad. As the
sons and daughters of the rural poor and the 'travelling Irish', they were also
outside the nation-building agenda of the national bourgeoisie. This meant that
the Irish nation was forged as a historical system of exclusions and dominations.
It excluded whole sections of the rural poor and large numbers of young adults
from its moral and political structures. The more Ireland sought to 'showcase'
itself as a progressive modern nation in a nineteenth-century world of powerful
nation-states, the more impoverished small farmers and the travelling poor were
treated as a blemish on the social and political landscape of the struggling
nation. They did not fit into the hegemonic image of Ireland which nationalists
had invented in order to counteract colonial constructs of the Irish as an
'unmanageable' and 'barbarous race'.[55]

Thus, there was a marked overlapping between the involuntary emigration
of the rural poor, on the one hand, and Irish nationalism, on the other, which
goes back to the circumstances in which the Irish nation was conceived as
a cradle for bourgeois Irish respectability. As representatives of a counter-
hegemonic culture buried under an individualistic and materialistic culture of
the rural bourgeoisie, the rural poor were considered 'masterless vagabonds'
who could wreck Ireland's image as an emergent European nation. An
estimated 7 million people left Ireland for North America alone between the
beginning of the seventeenth century to the foundation of the Irish state.
Between 1851 and 1921, just under 4.5 million Irish emigrants settled in
North America, Australia and New Zealand. An estimated 4 million Irish
moved to the United States between 1846 and 1925. A similar number is
estimated to have left Ireland between 1855 and 1914. As the century
progressed, the exodus gradually became an irrevocable one towards countries
from which there was little prospect of return.[56] By way of comparison, the
corresponding figures for the number of emigrants from the United Kingdom,
Germany and Scandinavia who moved to the United States at this time were
3.97, 5.41 and 7.6 million respectively. Similarly, an estimated 3.5 million
Russians, two thirds of them Jews, and 12.23 million Italians settled in the
United States between the mid 1860s and the mid 1920s.[57] Miller has argued
that this vast outflow:

> was at once a barometer of the social and economic changes taking place on both
> sides of the Atlantic and itself a major determinant of the modern shapes of North
> American and Irish societies. In spite of the diminutive size of their homeland,
> the Irish played an important role in the commercial and industrial revolutions
> that transformed the North Atlantic world.[58]

Fitzpatrick has shown that the scale of the flight from Ireland was 'unprecedented in the history of international migration'. Focusing more narrowly upon the demographic effects of the Famine than upon the significance of indigenous processes of rural capitalist modernisation in explaining large-scale emigration, he further elaborates:

> Even in the period of heaviest Famine-induced mortality, emigration was equally important as a source of the decline in Ireland's population. About a million people left the country between 1846 and 1850, and emigration was still greater over the following five years. The total loss of over two million amounted to about a quarter of Ireland's highest recorded population of 8,175,000 in 1841. Yet the Famine 'exodus' was neither the beginning or the end of large-scale emigration . . . The effect of the Famine was to extend massive emigration to every county and parish of Ireland. . . The patterns established during the crisis were perpetuated, Connaught and Munster remaining the most important sources of emigration throughout the following century. Already in 1855, as the Poor Law Commissioner Edward Senior remarked with wonder 'everybody has one leg over the Atlantic'.[59]

Widespread emigration on this scale certainly linked the peripheralisation of peasant Ireland to the growth of industrial and agricultural cores in the international economy. Moreover, Irish migration to Britain and North America at this time was probably as bewildering and disorientating an experience as the Famine itself was for large numbers of young adults who were systematically forced to emigrate because of lack of land, opportunity and work at home. Far from being peripheral to the process of capital accumulation and capitalist production, workers from Ireland were central both to the process of core formation at home and abroad, and to frontier expansion in the world economy. They occupied a central position in the international labour market. As we have already seen, revolutions in transportation forced the integration of rural Ireland into the world economy by annihilating the spatial barriers to the circulation of commodities, capital and labour throughout the nineteenth century.[60] In so doing, they contributed to the commodification and internationalisation of Irish labour. Because they were a major source of cheap and adaptable labour for the world economy, new values were consequently placed on rural and working-class communities so that by the close of the century Marx's fatalistic prediction that Ireland's destiny was to become 'an English sheepwalk and cattle pasture', her people 'banished by sheep and ox', had largely come true.[61]

Emigration on this scale also placed Ireland among the leading European exporters of labour throughout the nineteenth and the early twentieth century. Given the size of the country, and the intensity of the rural exodus, Irish emigration was at least on a par with some of the greatest migratory movements in modern history, including the shipment of approximately 9.5 million live African slaves to the Americas between 1450 and 1871.[62] Given the fact that

TABLE 1: *Population of Ireland (Republic), 1841–1989*

Year	Population (000s)	Year	Population (000s)
1841	6,529	1926	2,972
1851	5,112	1936	2,968
1861	4,402	1946	2,955
1871	4,053	1951	2,961
1881	3,870	1961	2,818
1891	3,469	1971	2,978
1901	3,222	1981	3,443
1911	3,140	1989	3,515

Source: *The Social and Economic Implications of Emigration*, National Economic and
Social Council, March, 1991, p. 48.

the Irish not only gravitated to the urban centres of the east coast of North
America but also played a significant role in clearing native Americans from the
interior, they were among the chief benefactors of white colonial and capitalist
expansion in North America. Irish involvement in these bitter 'race wars'
against Native and Black Americans is a forgotten chapter in current debates
around Ireland's internationalist and anti-colonial legacy.

The entire history of Irish emigration points to its intrinsic geographic
nature and stresses the symbiotic relationship between processes of core formation
and peripheralisation operating in the Irish countryside and the contribution of
Irish emigrants to core-formation and colonial expansion abroad. Indeed, in his
analysis, Jackson suggested that 'the experience' of Irish migration was 'deeply
rooted in the soil of Ireland itself'.[63] The processes which contributed to it in
the nineteenth century were clearly still at work well into the twentieth century.
Thus, Jackson argued:

> While there has been a considerable change in some respects in the degree of
> deprivation felt in Ireland, the principal and immediate cause of emigration
> remains economic. The rural areas have demonstrated a decreasing ability to sus-
> tain even a declining population wile the urban areas, with few exceptions, have
> failed to maintain industry and commerce commensurate with their increased
> population.[64]

Many historians have commented on the fact that the volume of emigration
from nineteenth-century Ireland was such that labour, not the produce of the
land, constituted the country's major export. Others traced Irish emigration to
the disintegration of peasant society and the development of bourgeois values.
Accordingly, Lyons interpreted the 'headlong exodus' of one million people from
Ireland between 1845–1851 as 'the *instinctive* reaction of a panic-stricken people

to the spectacle of their traditional way of life breaking into pieces before their very eyes'.[65] Modern Irish emigration dates from this period. This was because, as Kerby Miller suggests, Ireland by the middle of the nineteenth century:

> was little more than an inferior appendage of British capitalism and imperialism . . .
> This was the crucial, colonial context in which Irish modernization occurred,
> determined and distorted by the priorities and tastes of the sister island.
> Consequently, Ireland's economic development, its further integration into world
> capitalism, was highly uneven, specialized, and dependent . . . In fact, Ireland's
> social adjustments to the exigencies of colonialism and world capitalism – adjust-
> ments dictated by external pressures and internal inequities – mandated massive,
> sustained emigration. Put bluntly, emigration became a societal imperative of
> post-Famine Ireland: in reality less a choice than a vital necessity both to secure
> the livelihoods of nearly all who left and most who stayed and to ensure the
> relative stability of a fundamentally 'sick' society which offered its lower classes
> and most of its young people 'equal opportunities' only for aimless poverty at
> home or menial labour and slum tenements abroad.[66]

A structural approach shows that nineteenth-century Irish emigration was not caused by locational factors, or by any raising of the geographical consciousness of Irish young adults. Neither was it 'caused' by what Marx calls 'the idiocy of rural life' or the disenchantment with rural life consequent upon exposure of young adults to the fatal attractions of 'foreign fields' of opportunity. These factors, we have seen, contributed to, and facilitated emigration but did not account for its volume or social composition. Neither do they explain the social or geographical patterns in Irish emigration. Emigration on the scale experienced in Ireland in the nineteenth and early twentieth century had its roots in the interface between Ireland and the international economy. It was rooted in a colonial land structure and in an indigenous rural capitalism which linked Ireland to the world economy. Export-led capitalist development in the latter half of the nineteenth century generated *labour surpluses* as well as *commodity surpluses* and this compelled Irish young adults, particularly the 'unwanted' sons and daughters of small to medium farmers, to seek employment opportunities abroad that literally were not available at home. Contrary to Lyons, large-scale emigration on this scale was not just the 'instinctive' reaction of a 'panic-stricken' people who saw their traditional way of life breaking to pieces before their very eyes. It was also the rational response of the sons and daughters of small farmers to structural changes in Irish agriculture and to new opportunities in the global economy. As such it was a continuation of trends dating from at least the eighteenth century when Ireland was integrated into an evolving world capitalist order under the hegemony of Great Britain.[67]

Between the late eighteenth and mid-nineteenth century, famines and famine-induced emigration transformed the geolinguistic map of Ireland by greatly reducing the number of peasants and Irish-speakers in the country. It facilitated the eastward drift of the geographical pivot of political power in nation-building Ireland. It fundamentally altered power relations in rural society and dampened the class conflict in rural Ireland by removing Ireland's 'surplus' sons and daughters abroad.[68] By the mid-nineteenth century, improving landlords and the indigenous middling tenantry were already exerting hegemonic control well beyond the heartlands of commercial farming. As we have already seen, the latter constituted a new challenging collectivity in late nineteenth-century Irish society and forged a class alliance with the small farmers and the petty bourgeoisie in peripheries of rural Ireland.[69] Emigration here clearly facilitated the emergence of these social classes and added to the survival of their social and political hegemony. After the Great Famine, emigration eased class conflict in the Irish countryside. It also contributed to a reduction of tension within families by easing pressure on land and family resources in the agricultural heartlands of the country and in the developing peripheries of the west of Ireland. Between one-third and a half of those who left between 1855–1914 were aged 20–24 years old, and a significant number of the remainder were teenagers.[70] The number of family farms certainly increased dramatically at this time. By 1901, the socially-strategic 'thirty acre men' amounted to one-third of all Irish farmers in the country. They were particularly well-organised in the agricultural heartlands of the midlands and the south of Ireland. In the nation-building half of the nineteenth century, the focus of their political agitation had switched from civil rights and the right to property to national issues and the right to national self-determination.[71] The political clout of family farmers also increased throughout this period and the movement for agrarian reform, which originated in small-farming districts in the west of Ireland after the Famine, was now taken over by the rural bourgeoisie of the midlands and south-east of the country. As a result, Breathnach argues, its aims were:

> . . . reduced to seeking the transfer of existing holdings to outright proprietor-ship. As a result, the eventual resolution of the land question did nothing to resolve the economic problems of the bulk of Irish farmers, who continued to occupy tiny holdings on which they produced young cattle for sale, via an unequal exchange relationship, to cattle fatteners elsewhere. However, it did have the effect of creating a mass of conservative property-owning peasants who have dominated the Irish political scene until recently.[72]

By the 1920s, these socially-strategic farmers dominated the Irish state while whole sections of rural Ireland had literally moved to Britain, the United States, Canada and Australia.

Finally, it would be wrong to suggest that Irish young adults were passively raised alongside established emigrant trails that linked rural Ireland to the established labour markets of Britain and North America. They also forged *new* trails to the expanding frontiers of the world economy, and their going literally

Figure 7: Regional Patterns of Seasonal Migration from Ireland, 1841

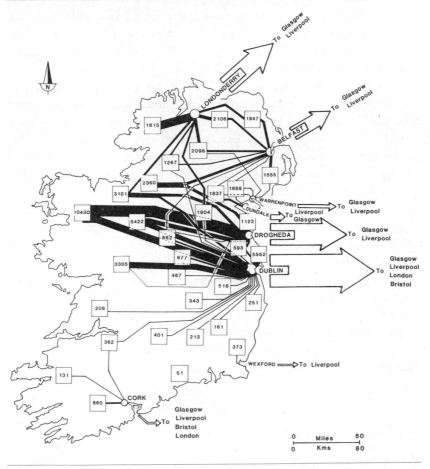

Source: Adapted from T. W. Freeman, *Pre-Famine Ireland* (Manchester University Press, 1957).

drained youth from many Irish rural communities. This contributed to political stability at home by channelling young adults abroad just as they came of political age. It marked the onset of a senilisation of Irish politics and contributed to the consolidation of patriarchal values in urban and rural Ireland. It also shifted the focus of power in Ireland from the Big House and the colonial 'Pale' to the highways and byways and contested terrains of the country's agricultural heartlands. Migrants from Ireland not only resolved regional deficits in the supply of labour in Britain, North America and Australia at crucial periods in the development of global capitalism, but they also provided families at home with cash. This contributed to the survival of peasant, small-farming and working-class communities well into the twentieth century. Handley estimated that between 1880–1900 almost 38,000 seasonal migrants were annually leaving Ireland for Britain.[73] An estimated 18,000 seasonal migrants from the west and north-west of the country were still moving between Ireland, Scotland and the north of England on the eve of World War I (see Fig. 7). Many of these engaged in 'tattie-hoking' and other unskilled harvest work, and their destinations reflected a need to locate in regions accessible to the rural poor, including poor 'tinkers' and Irish Travellers. Many of the former would have been indistinguishable from the latter, and may, in fact, have been considered as 'tinkers' by their Scottish and English employers. Many more 'settled' seasonal migrants may have regarded seasonal work in lowland Scotland or the north of England simply as a geographical extension of 'hiring out' practices that were customary among impoverished rural and working-class families throughout late nineteenth-century Ireland.[74] The Irish poor at this time commonly 'hired out' young children, some of them as young as 10 years of age, to local farmers and other employers in an effort to supplement meagre family incomes in districts where opportunities for paid employment for adults were few and far between. Their poverty, and their survival strategies, tended to identify them with, rather than distinguish them from, 'tinkers' who similarly looked on the 'travelling life' as a strategy for survival that was infinitely preferable to the impoverishment of rural sedentarism.[75] This meant that emigration was not just a structural feature of Irish society. As this chapter has shown, it fulfilled a wide range of important social, political and economic functions in Irish society and in an evolving new world order.

NOTES AND REFERENCES

1 Jim Mac Laughlin, 'Social Characteristics and Destinations of Recent Emigrants From Selected Regions in the West of Ireland' *Geoforum*, vol. 22, no. 3, 1991, pp. 319–31; Jim Mac Laughlin, *Historical and Recent Irish Emigration: A Critique of Core–Periphery and Behavioural Models*, Irish Studies Occasional Paper Series, No. 5 (University of North London Press, 1994).

2 P. Breathnach, 'Uneven Development and Irish Peripheralisation', in P. Shirlow (ed.) *Development Ireland* (London, Pluto Press, 1995); R. Munck, *The Irish Economy: Results and Prospects* (London, Pluto Press, 1993).

3 Kenneth Connell, *The Population of Ireland* (1756–1845 (Oxford University Press, 1950); James H. Johnson, 'Harvest Migration from Nineteenth Century Ireland', Institute of British Geographers, *Transactions and Papers*, XLI, 1967, pp. 97–112; James H. Johnson 'The Two Irelands at the Beginning of the Nineteenth Century' in N. Stephen and R.E. Glascock (eds.), *Irish Geographical Studies in Honour of Estyn Evans* (Blackstaff, Belfast, 1970), pp. 224–243.

4 H. Diner, *Erin's Daughters in America* (Baltimore, Johns Hopkins University Press, 1983); M. Lennon et al., *Across the Water* (London: Virago Press, 1988); Cormac O Grada, 'Seasonal Migration and post-Famine Adjustment', *Studia Hibernica*, vol. xxxiii,1973, pp. 48–76; Ruth Ann Harris, *The Nearest Place That Wasn't Ireland* (Ames, Iowa, Iowa State University, 1994).

5 Joseph Lee, *The Modernisation of Irish Society*, 1848–1918 (Dublin, Gill and Macmillan, 1981).

6 J. A. Jackson, *The Irish in Britain* (London, Routledge and Kegan Paul, 1963), p. 63.

7 Damian Hannan, *Rural Exodus: A Study of the Forces Influencing the Large-Scale Migration of Irish Youth* (London, Chapman, 1970); D. Hannan, J.J. Sexton, B. Walsh and D. Mc Mahon, *The Economic and Social Implications of Emigration* (Dublin, National Economic and Social Council, 1990); P. Vaughan and David Fitzpatrick, Irish Historical Statistics (Dublin, Gill and Macmillan, 1978).

8 R. Foster, 'Young Emigrants Still Looking West', *The Irish Times*, 14 April, 1987.

9 R. Sennet and R. Cobb, *The Hidden Injuries of Class* (New York, Vintage Books, 1973).

10 Jim Mac Laughlin, ' Defending the Frontiers: The Political Geography of Race and Racism in the European Community' in C. Williams (ed.), *The Political Geography of the New World Order* (London, Bellhaven, 1993).

11 Richard Peet, 'Spatial Dialectics', *Geographical Viewpoint*, vol. 35, no. 3, 1982.

12 K. Whelan, 'The Bases of Regionalism', in P. Ó Drisceóil (ed.) *Culture in Ireland: Regions: Identity and Power* (Belfast, Institute of Irish Studies, 1993).

13 Immanuel Wallerstein, *The Modern World System* 1, (New York, Academic Press, 1979); F. Braudel, *The Perspective of the World* (London, Collins 1987).

14 Peter Taylor, *Political Geography* (London, Longmans, 1985), p. 16.

15 ibid., p. 21 .

16 J. A. Agnew, 'Sociologizing the geographical imagination', *Political Geography Quarterly*, vol. 1, 1982 p. 162.

17 Jim Mac Laughlin, 'Emigration and the Peripheralization of Ireland in the Global Economy', *review, Journal of the Fernand Braudel Center*, vol. xvii, no. 2, 1994 pp. 253.

18 Jim Mac Laughlin, *Ireland: The Emigrant Nursery and the World Economy* (Cork University Press, 1994).

19 S. Giley, 'Catholics and Socialists in Scotland, 1900–30', in R. Swift and S. Gilley (eds.), *The Irish in Britain, 1815–1939* (London, Barnes and Noble, 1989), pp. 212–38.

20 R. Black, *Economic thought and the Irish Question, 1817–1870* (Cambridge University Press, 1960); T. H. Boylan, T.H. Foley, T.P. Foley *Political Economy and Colonial Ireland* (London, Routledge, 1990).

21 G. Dangerfield, *The Damnable Question: A Study in Anglo-Irish Relations* (London, Barnes and Noble, 1979), p. 47.

22 Boylan and Foley, *Political Economy*, p. 47.

23 Clive Dewey, 'Celtic Agrarian Legislation and the Celtic Revival', *Past and Present*, vol. xxii, no. 3, 1974 pp. 30–69.

24 Antonio Gramsci, *The Prison Notebooks* (London, Lawrence and Wishart, 1971), pp. 124–6; Antonio Gramsci, *Selections from Political Writings, 1910–1920* (London, Lawrence and Wishart, 1977), pp. 147–50.

25 Sam Clark, 'Agrarian Class Structure and Collective Action in Nineteenth Century Ireland', *British Journal of Sociology*, vol. 29, 1978, pp. 27–45.

26 Jim Mac Laughlin and J. A. Agnew, 'Hegemony and the Regional Question: The Political Geography of Regional Industrial Policy in Northern Ireland, 1945–1972', *Annals*, Association of American Geographers, vol. 76, no. 2, 1986.

27 Antonio Gramsci, *The Modern Prince and Other Writings* (New York, International Publishers, 1957), pp. 45–52; C. Buci-Glucksmann, *Gramsci and the State* (London, Lawrence and Wishart, 1980), pp. 96–107; Carl Boggs, *Gramsci's Marxism* (London, Pluto Press, 1980), pp. 36–55.

28 Jim Mac Laughlin, 'Place, Politics and Nation-building Ulster', *Canadian Review of Studies in Nationalism*, vol. xx, no. 4, 1991, pp. 319–31; Jim Mac Laughlin, 'The Politics of Nation-building in Post-Famine Donegal', in W. Nolan et al. (eds.), *Donegal: History and Society* (Dublin, Geographical Publications, 1995), pp. 583–625.

29   M. Higgins and J. Gibbons, 'Shopkeepers-graziers and land agitation in Ireland, 1895–1900', in P. J. Drudy, (ed.), *Ireland: Land, Politics and People* (Cambridge University Press, 1982).

30   Jim Mac Laughlin, *Travellers and Ireland: Whose Country, Whose History ?* (Cork University Press, 1995).

31   Kerby A. Miller, *Emigrants and Exiles* (New York, Oxford University Press, 1985), p. 424.

32   Breathnach, 'Uneven Development', p. 85.

33   J. H. Tukes, *Donegal, Suggestions for Improvement of Congested Districts and Expansion of Railways, Fisheries etc* (London, Ridgway and Picadilly, 1889), p. 44.

34   F. S. L. Lyons, *Ireland Since the Famine* (London, Fontana, 1982), pp. 205–6.

35   Cited in J. Maurice (ed.), *Letters from Donegal in 1885* (London, Richard Clay, 1886), p. 70.

36   David Fitzpatrick, *Irish Emigration, 1801–1921* (Dundalk, Dundalgan Press, 1984).

37   Jim Mac Laughlin, 'Ireland: The Emigrant Nursery', p.155.

38   Kevin Whelan, review, 'Political Economy and Colonial Ireland', *Irish Reporter*, no. 6, 1992, pp. 35–6 .

39   Fitzpatrick, *Irish Emigration*; P. M. Mayhew, *London Labour and the London Poor* (New York: Academic Press, 1836).

40   Benedict Anderson, *Imagined Communities* (London, Verso, 1983); Jim Mac Laughlin, 'Reflections on Nations as Imagined Communities', *Journal of Multilingual and Multicultural Matters*, vol. 9, no. 5, 1988.

41   Mac Laughlin, *Emigrant Nursery*, p. 74; E. Weber, *Peasants into Frenchmen* (Stanford University Press, 1976).

42   B. M. Kerr, 'Irish Seasonal Migration to Britain', *Irish Historical Studies*, no. 3, 1943 pp. 34–5.

43   G. O'Brien, *Economic History of Ireland from the Union to the Famine* (London, Routledge, 1921).

44   Mac Laughlin, *Emigrant Nursery*, p. 3.

45   G. Meaney, 'Sex and Nation', in A. Smyth (ed.), *Irish Women's Studies Reader* (Dublin, Attic Press, 1991), p. 232.

46   Katie Donovan, 'Irish Women Writers: Marginalised by Whom', in Dermot Bolger (ed.), *Letters from the New Island* (Dublin: Raven Press, 1991), p. 126.

47   ibid., p.126.

48   G. R. C. Keep, 'Official Opinion on Irish Emigration in the Later Nineteenth Century', *Irish Ecclesiastical Record*, LXXXI, p. 432.

49   Jim Mac Laughlin, 'The Evolution of Anti-Traveller Racism in Ireland', *Race and Class*, vol. 37, no. 3, 1996, pp. 51–2; David Sibley, *Geographies of Exclusion* (London, Routledge, 1992), pp. 45–6.

50   Milan Kundera, *The Book of Laughter and Forgetting* (London, Faber and Faber, 1980), p. 3.

51   *ibid.*, pp. 8–9.

52   Daniel T. Rodger, *The Work Ethic in Industrial America, 1850–1920* (Chicago University Press, 1979), p. 56.

53   P. Gilroy, *The Black Atlantic* (London, Verso, 1993), p. 198.

54   Edward Said, *Culture and Imperialism* (London, Verso, 1994), p. xiii.

55   L. P. Curtis, *Apes and Angels* (London, David and Charles, 1971).

56   Lyons, *Ireland Since the Famine*, pp. 44–5.

57   M. A. Jones, *Destination America* (London, Weidenfeld and Nicholson, 1976), p. 17.

58   Miller, *Exiles and Emigrants*, p. 7.

59   David Fitzpatrick, 'Flight from Famine', in C. Porteir (ed.), *The Great Irish Famine* (Cork, Mercier, 1995), p. 175.

60   Karl Marx, *Capital* (Moscow, Progress Press, 1956), p. 262.

61   ibid., p. 288.

62 B. Davidson, *The African Slave Trade* (Boston, Little Brown, 1980), p. 68.

63 Jackson, *The Irish in Britain*, p. 24.

64 ibid., p. 27.

65 Lyons, *Ireland Since the Famine*, p. 44.

66 Miller, *Exiles and Emigrants*, p. 362.

67 K. Bottigheimer, *English Money and Irish Land* (Oxford University Press, 1971); C. Reagan, 'Economic Development in Ireland', *Antipode*, vol. 11, no. 2, 1980.

68 Mac Laughlin, 'The Politics of Nation-building'.

69 Clark, 'Agrarian Class Structure', p. 27.

70 Fitzpatrick, *Irish Emigration*, p. 17.

71 K.T. Hoppen, *Elections, Politics and Society in Ireland, 1832–85* (Oxford University Press, 1985).

72 Braudel, *The Perspective of the World*, p. 130.

73 J. E. Handley, *The Irish in Modern Scotland* (Cork University Press, 1947), p. 213.

74 Mac Laughlin, 'Social Characteristics of Recent Emigrants'.

75 Dympna Mc Loughlin, 'Irish Travellers and Ethnicity' in M. Mc Cann et al. (eds.), *Irish Travellers: Gender and Identity* (Belfast, Institute of Irish Studies, 1994), p. 55.

2. The Blackbird Calls in Grief
Colonialism, Health and Identity Among Irish Immigrants in Britain

LIAM GREENSLADE

> The blackbird calls in grief
> I know what harm has happened
> Someone has broken his home
> and killed his little birds.
> (Anonymous twelfth-century Irish poet)

THE HEALTH OF IRISH MIGRANTS IN BRITAIN: THE PERSONAL CONTEXT

I come from a family of Irish migrants which is characterised by high male mortality outside of Ireland. Of my mother's four migrant brothers, three died before the age of 60. These were men who left Ireland to participate in the post-war reconstruction of Britain in the 1950s and 1960s. They came to work on building sites and in factories. While their level of formal education was not high, they were by no means illiterate or uneducated. Skilled, semi-skilled and unskilled manual workers at different times in their lives, depending where the work or the money was to be found, these men settled in England and brought up their families here. They did not see their families grow much beyond late adolescence. These were men who, from the epidemiological viewpoint, would be regarded as having higher than average risk of premature mortality. They smoked and drank more than they knew to be good for them. They worked hard under often appalling conditions and took great pride in their role as earners or providers. For them, not being able to work through either illness or unemployment was a kind of living death. But as is the case with many, if not most male Irish manual workers, it would be a mistake to think of them as the stereotypical earth-shovelling, hod-carrying automata drowning their sorrows and boosting their joys in pints of porter and noggins of whiskey. They were cultured people who read voraciously, could debate politics, religion or history with anyone (as, when an undergraduate, I often found out to my cost). They knew the words to hundreds of songs and as many poems. They could play musical instruments and hold conversations in two languages, sometimes simultaneously.

36

But here they were in exile in England, not just far from home, but far from what they might perhaps have expected from life in Ireland. For all their culture and intelligence, for all their dignity and self-respect, in England they were just more Paddy work-horses come to do the jobs that the natives refused. Every day spent in England was a reminder of that.

I believe that the gap between ability, expectation and desire, on the one hand, and daily experience, on the other, proved too frustrating to bear. With nothing to go home for or to, they tolerated their lives in England as best they could, killing the pain and dealing with the stresses in the ways their circumstances permitted. Sometimes it would be too much to bear and they would vent their frustrations on each other, or on those nearest them. More often than not, they would take it out on themselves, self-destructively working harder or drinking more than was ever justifiable in any obvious way.

As both a child and an adult, these men represented a conundrum to me, one I have come across many times in my own work. Their early deaths were not brought about by a deficient genetic heritage, poor constitutions, or simple over-indulgence in tobacco and alcohol. That is not to discount the possible contribution of all of these factors in explaining their premature deaths. What contributed most, I believe, was the driven nature of their existence. The cause of their 'drivenness' was to be found in the socio-historical conditions which surrounded them. This constrained their life choices in England, limited their freedom to manoeuvre and led to their sacrifice of long-term advantage on the altar of day-to-day survival, both psychic and economic. Theirs was a kind of madness whose well-springs were not to be found 'inside' them in any meaningful sense of the word. It permeated the very social context in which they originated and subsequently found themselves. That it did not lead to breakdown in the psychiatric sense was no accident, but neither was it merely fortuitous that it did result in premature death.

This chapter examines data on the health of Irish migrants in Britain and seeks to contextualise this data within the concrete experience and life activities of Irish migrants in Britain and their social and historical relationship to the society in which many of them will live for most of their adult lives. It suggests that high rates of premature mortality, as well as physical and mental illness that emerge in studies of the Irish community in Britain, are not explicable through the use of orthodox medical, epidemiological and socio-behavioural models of morbidity. Taking as my starting point the work of Fanon on medicine and colonialism, I shall argue that such models are inadequate to the extent that they overlook key factors in the socio-historical experience of Irish migrants to Britain, factors which first of all bring Irish people to the shores of Britain and subsequently condition their behaviour with regard to health. This chapter is restricted largely, but not exclusively, to the issue of physical health and mortality rates among the Irish in Britain. I shall also argue that the long-standing economic and cultural effects of the colonial experience exert an important impact upon health-related behaviour of Irish migrants to Britain.

IRISH MIGRANTS IN BRITAIN IN THE 1990S

Irish migrants make up the largest ethnic minority group in Britain. Numbering some 837,000 at the 1991 census, first-generation Irish migrants constitute nearly 1.6 per cent of the total population.[1] Due to anomalies in the way in which the British census records ethnicity, it is impossible to state precisely the size of the total Irish ethnic group which would include those born in Ireland, those of Irish parentage and those claiming Irish ethnicity due to descent.

A number of estimates have emerged in recent years however. Greenslade based his calculations on the 1988 General Household Survey and estimated that first and second generation Irish people (i.e. those born in Ireland and those of Irish parentage) numbered approximately 3 million people or approximately 7 per cent of the total population of Britain.[2] Worcester in a survey conducted for MORI and the *Irish Times* identified first-, second- and third-generation Irish people and, by extrapolation, estimated that Irish people made up some 14 per cent of the British population and number just over 6 million people here.[3] On the basis of these estimates, Irish people in Britain make up the largest migrant group in Europe.

Despite the size of this group, the Irish in Britain have remained, as Pearson and his colleagues point out, 'for generations an invisible minority'.[4] Until very recently, almost no research had been conducted into their circumstances and conditions in Britain. The most recent and most comprehensive survey of Irish communities in Britain was that published by Jackson in 1963.[5] Since then, most published research has emerged in a piecemeal fashion and has focussed upon basic questions of demography and on specific aspects of ethnic identity, the historical experience and the religious practices of Irish migrants in Britain.[6] In the small amount of research on the demographic and socio-economic status of Irish communities in Britain which has emerged over the past decade, a fairly dismal picture of Irish migrant life emerges. Greenslade and others found that the Irish in Britain had a disproportionately large elderly population, they suffered higher than average rates of unemployment and had lower than average incomes and earnings.[7] Other indices of socio-economic deprivation in his study showed that the Irish-born and their children in Britain were less likely than their British counterparts to own their own home or to own a car.

A similar picture of deprivation and vulnerability emerges in other contemporary studies based on Census data. In London, Connor found, amongst other things, that Irish people were proportionately more likely than the UK-born population to experience unemployment, to live in overcrowded housing and to be living in housing with shared basic amenities.[8] These patterns are repeated in studies of Sheffield, Liverpool, Birmingham and Manchester.[9]

Compared to the UK population as a whole, the Irish in Britain were over-represented among the unemployed and economically inactive. They were also over-represented in the more vulnerable areas of the housing market and tended to do worse than average in the level of housing amenities to which they have access. Owen's analysis of the 1991 census data re-affirms these local findings. He found that the rate of male unemployment among the Irish in Britain, estimated at 19.3 per cent, was nearly twice that of the UK white population. Migrants from the Irish Republic also had a lower rate of home ownership (55.4 per cent) than the latter (66.6 per cent).[10] Owens' overall findings concur with those of Greenslade and his colleagues who suggest that the pattern of economic and social experience amongst Irish people in Britain is closer to that of the non-white ethnic minorities than it is to that of the population as a whole.[11] In the absence of systematic research on Irish migrants, the causes of relative deprivation and economic disadvantage among the Irish in contemporary Britain are still subject to speculation. Nonetheless, the invisibility of the Irish communities both in research findings and in areas of social policy, social welfare and socio-economic disadvantage gives some cause for concern.

THE PHYSICAL HEALTH OF IRISH MIGRANTS IN BRITAIN

If the socio-economic profile of the Irish in Britain in the late 1980s and early 1990s presents a less than rosy picture, the vista becomes gloomier still when we examine their health status. In an analysis of data from the 1991 Census of population Greenslade and Kneafsey found that, compared to the UK population, the Irish-born were more likely than the population to be suffering from a limiting long-term illness and displayed higher than average rates of permanent adult sickness.[12] While the former can perhaps be accounted for by the age profile of the Irish population, the latter cannot so easily be accounted for since it excludes those under 16 years and those above pensionable age.[13]

Studies of mortality amongst migrants to Britain during the 1970s and 1980s showed that Irish migrants in particular have a considerably poorer health profile than most other migrant groups. This research makes use of the Standardised Mortality Rate (henceforth SMR) to identify the mortality characteristics of sub-groups within the UK population. The SMR for a sub-population is based on the ratio of the observed number of deaths to the statistically-expected rate in a given population. It is standardised to allow for differences in age structure among different social or ethnic groups, and is computed separately for men and women. SMRs can be calculated for specific causes of death and identify differences of incidence of mortality across different sub-populations. The standard mortality rate for the UK population is set at 100 and any excess may be expressed directly as a percentage. Anything above this figure represents a worse than expected mortality rate; anything below it is better than the average rate. The SMRs for Irish-born men in the 15 to 64 age group in England and Wales between 1970 and 1978 were 22 per cent higher than the average rate for men. They were 16 per cent higher than average for women. Moreover Irish-born men were the only migrant group whose life expectancy disimproved on moving to Britain.[14] This is significant and atypical in a general and on-going discussion which suggests that the health of migrants improves as a result of emigration.

When Balarajan and Bulusu conducted a similar investigation for the period 1979 to 1983 they found that age-adjusted mortality rates for both Irish-born men and Irish-born women were significantly higher than those of the host population. They were also higher than those found among other migrant groups.[15] In this period, excess mortality for those in the 20–69 age group stood at 28 per cent for men and 20 per cent for women. Their findings are summarised in Table 1 below. In addition to experiencing excess mortality in every age grouping relative to the total population of England and Wales, Irish people in Britain also had the highest excess mortality rate of any migrant group. More disturbing still are the levels of excess mortality amongst the younger age groups. Irish men in the 20–49 age group especially showed a very high level of excess mortality (47 per cent). Excess mortality amongst Irish women in the same age group (23 per cent) was exceeded only by that found among women born in Africa.

TABLE 1: *Age-adjusted all Cause Standardised Mortality Rates (SMRs) Amongst Irish-born Residents in England and Wales 1979–1983 (England and Wales SMR = 100)*

	Irish-born	
	Males	Females
Age Group		
20–29	145	110
30–39	162	124
40–49	143	124
50–59	132	121
60–69	122	118
70 plus	116	115
All 20–49	**147**	**123**
All 20–69	**128**	**120**

Source: Balarajan and Busulu 'Mortality Among Immigrants in England and Wales 1979–1983', M. Britton (ed.), *Mortality and Geography: A Review in the mid-1980s of England and Wales* (London, HM50, 1990)

Balarajan and Bulusu also analysed differential trends in mortality amongst non-native groups in England and Wales between 1970–1972 and 1979–1983.[16] They found that the percentage decline in 'all cause' mortality for the population as a whole fell by 13 per cent for men and 9 per cent for women in this period. For Irish men and Irish women, on the other hand, the decline was only 8 and 7 per cent respectively. For the larger ethnic/migrant minority groups, only men born in the Indian sub-continent experienced a lower rate of decline than that experienced by Irish men. Amongst the female population, only Scottish and Italian women fared worse than the Irish-born. The authors of this study concluded that mortality levels were highest for Irish men and Irish women, and were certainly higher than those recorded for host populations in England and Wales.[17] This survey showed that the physical health profile of the Irish-born in England and Wales worsened in the seventies and early eighties.

TABLE 2: *Standard Mortality Rates (SMRs) by Degree of Irishness Longitudinal Survey (LS) 1% Sample of British population (LS SMR = 100)*

	Males	Females
Born Northern Ireland	117	132
Born Republic of Ireland	117	114
Born rest of world:		
Both parents Irish	115	174
Mother only Irish	121	76
Father only Irish	107	111

Source: Raftery et al. (1990)

Another study conducted by Raftery and his colleagues used the Longitudinal Survey (henceforth LS), a 1 per cent sample of the entire British population based on successive censuses, in order to establish levels of morbidity amongst the Irish-born and their children in Britain.[18] A variety of studies of migrant health have shown that patterns of morbidity and mortality amongst migrants tend to adjust over time and begin to resemble those of the host population the longer they reside in the host society.[19] Thus, they suggest that over a generation or so, both the overall mortality rate and the cause-specific patterns of death amongst migrants shift approximate to that of the host society. Applied to the Irish migrant population, this suggests that those migrants resident the longest, and the children of Irish migrants, would exhibit mortality ratios more or less similar to those of the population as a whole. Raftery and his colleagues set out to discover whether this was in fact the case.[20] They divided the Irish populations into five groups in order to generate an 'index of Irishness' based on country of birth and parentage. They calculated standard mortality ratios for all five groups and their findings are shown in Table 2 below. Their results compare well with other findings on Irish migrant mortality and morbidity.[21] The study shows that high SMRs apply to both first and second generation Irish people. SMRs for the Irish in Britain are high regardless of county of origin of migrants. They also found that length of residence in England and Wales had an opposite effect to that predicted by other findings on migrant mortality. In the light of other studies of generational change in migrant morbidity and mortality, the study by Raftery and his associates show a persistence of high SMRs across generations. This raises significant questions about the health status of the Irish in Britain, and I shall return to this below.

EXPLAINING IRISH MIGRANT MORTALITY RATES IN THE UK

The emergence of these findings has given rise to a number of explanations of the significant differences in the mortality and morbidity rates between the Irish-born and the native-born population of the UK. There has been very little in the way of substantive theory or research to account for this. The following section discusses a number of widely-held hypotheses on this topic. Drawing upon the work of Frantz Fanon, it then offers a different, and in my opinion more plausible, explanation of high mortality and morbidity rates among Irish migrants and their children in Britain in recent decades.

'NOT THE BRIGHTEST OR BEST': THE SELECTION HYPOTHESIS

It has been suggested that Irish people differ from most other migrant groups in England and Wales because of the low 'entry barrier' on movement between Britain and Ireland.[22] Due to a number of factors, related chiefly to the difficulties of long-distance migration, other migrants tend to be fitter and are drawn from more privileged groups within their country of origin. It is suggested that Irish people suffer an 'inverse selection effect' leading the less privileged and the more unhealthy to emigrate to Britain.[23] Certainly, intuitive support for this effect of short-distance migration comes from the case of Scottish migrants to England and Wales who exhibit a similar pattern of excess mortality to that of the Irish. However, a number of facts militate against the straightforward acceptance of such an explanation. First of all, it has been noted that, unlike their Irish counterparts, male Scottish migrants actually improve their life expectancy on migration to England and Wales.[24] Secondly, the selection effect would appear to apply differently to male and female Irish migrants. While men experience a distinct disimprovement in their health on migration, the SMR profiles of Irish women in Britain exhibit little or no change in relative excess mortality on migration. Finally, as Raftery and his colleagues point out, there are novel aspects of Irish mortality patterns which render the selection hypothesis an unlikely explanation.[25] In support of their rejection of this hypothesis, they note the persistence of high SMRs across generations and the different gender pattern of mortality amongst Irish migrants to England and Wales.

'TAKE ME HOME COUNTRY ROADS': RURAL TO URBAN MIGRATION

Another commonly-held hypothesis used to explain the specificities of the health of Irish migrants relates to the transfer of Irish migrants from rural settings to predominantly urban locations in Britain. This contends that rural life is healthier than city life and that the Irish therefore suffer as a result of a shift in their living location on emigrating. It is, indeed, true that the bulk of Irish migrants who arrived during the 1950s and 1960s and formed the majority of the sample upon which the mortality data are based, originated in rural backgrounds and settled in predominantly urban areas.[26] It is also true that those areas within Ireland – in particular the western seaboard – which provided the bulk of the migrants in question are also noted for relatively low SMRs by Irish standards, especially when compared to those prevailing in urban areas in Ireland.[27] However, while moving from a rural to an urban setting may have deleterious effects upon the health of internal migrants within Ireland, the situation with regard to Irish emigrants is not at all clear. The shift from an under-developed rural economy to an urban industrial one, particularly where access to primary health care is not only markedly better, but in the case of Britain also free, lends weight to an intuitive counter-hypothesis which suggests that such a transfer would have beneficial effects on life expectancy. Certainly this seems to be the case with other migrants from outside England and Wales who have moved from the under-developed rural economies of the Third World.[28] Studies from the United States, conducted over almost a century, compared Irish and Italian migrants to urban areas and these showed that mortality rates amongst the former were significantly higher than those prevailing among the latter.[29] In Britain, as in the United States, the contrast in mortality between Irish and Italian or southern European migrants is striking. The equivalent SMRs for Italian men and women are 65 and 78 respectively.[30] This contrast in life expectancy becomes more striking when one remembers the points of similarity between these groups. Apart from being drawn from predominantly rural areas and largely sharing a common religion, namely Catholicism, they have, like the Irish, become highly urbanised in Britain and have been concentrated in the unskilled and semi-skilled sectors of the labour market. With these facts in mind, any easy acceptance of the rural-urban migration hypothesis as the principal factor in explaining the mortality of Irish migrants has to be treated with a considerable degree of scepticism.

ENGELS' PIG: THE RELATIVE DEPRIVATION HYPOTHESIS

We have already seen that the Irish in Britain are a relatively deprived minority group. They are over-represented in the vulnerable areas of the economy and often live on low incomes and in poor housing. These data aside, it has also been suggested that the over-concentration of Irish people in the lower socio-economic groups may be a contributory factor in their poor health, if only because it leads to a greater likelihood of poor diet and excess smoking and drinking.[31] However, a number of factors also militate against the acceptance of this hypothesis. First of all, in any class-by-class comparison of Irish migrants with their English-born counterparts, Irish men have higher SMRs in every class and Irish women in every class but one.[32] Secondly, while Irish men tend to be over-represented in manual and unskilled occupational and socio-economic groups, for women the class skew is in the opposite direction, with the majority falling into professional and non-manual social groups. Yet both experience markedly higher mortality rates than the UK-born population. Thirdly, while social class effects exert a powerful role in structuring the health profiles of Irish migrants, they do not account for the overall raised mortality levels amongst the second generation Irish in Britain.[33]

THE CELTIC BURDEN: GENETIC HYPOTHESES

Another argument, which most often emerges anecdotally, suggests that some-how or other Irish people suffer some form of genetic disadvantage which leads to early death.[34] In the absence of any firm evidence to back up this hypothesis, anecdotal evidence invariably relies upon stereotypes, or draws upon 'historical evidence' which assumes a homogeneity in the genetic make-up of the Celtic population of ancient Ireland and that of the modern population of the country.[35] Those who argue thus tend to focus upon the presence of relatively uncommon illnesses, such as phenylketonuria and celiac disease, in 'Celtic' populations.[36] However any acceptable genetic model that would adequately explain higher than average SMRs amongst Irish migrants has to overcome a number of difficulties. The genetic model leads one to expect clusterings of deaths around certain diseases and these are then supposed to constitute a high percentage of all deaths in the migrant population. However, when we examine 'cause-specific' mortality among Irish migrants we find that amongst men the highest SMRs are found for accidental poisoning (269), accidental falls (233), homicide (302), injuries undetermined whether accidentally or purposely inflicted (233) and tuberculosis (245).[37] Amongst women, the highest SMRs are found for accidental poisoning (177), undetermined injuries (193), tuberculosis (215), cirrhosis of the liver (159) and cancers of the trachea, bronchus and lung (159). It would be very difficult to link these to some kind of gene-causative model, particularly amongst male migrants. Furthermore, despite the high SMRs relative to the population of England and Wales, the high SMR causes account for only a tiny proportion of all the deaths within the Irish migrant population. Indeed, they accounted for only 3 per cent of male deaths and 5 per cent of all female deaths.[38] Irish migrants die of pretty much the same causes, and in similar proportions, as the population of England and Wales as a whole. They just do so at younger ages and in proportionately higher numbers. It would appear then that, like other one-dimensional accounts of high mortality amongst Irish migrants, the genetic hypothesis fails to fully account for the latter.

CIGARETTES AND WHISKEY: THE LIFESTYLE EXPLANATION

Like genetic hypotheses, explanation in terms of the Irish migrant lifestyle tend to crop up most often anecdotally. And, like the genetic hypothesis, is it most often supported by simplistic stereotypes unsupported by evidence. The image of the Irish navvy with a pint of stout in one hand, twenty Major Extra Length in each pocket, and a diet consisting entirely of fried food, is often drawn upon to validate such anecdotal explanations.[39] Not only is such an anecdotal account demeaningly stereotypical, it is also deeply sexist because it fails to address the high mortality rates amongst Irish migrant women.

However, if we return to the high SMRs cited above then there is a sense in which the above stereotype is supported by data on drinking behaviour and smoking, at least for men, and to a lesser extent for women. The homesick drunk who neglects his or her health, smokes excessively, falls off tall buildings or under trains, gets into fights and is murdered or who accidentally imbibes from the wrong bottle one day – this stereotype does exist, to an extent, in reality. However, as I have already pointed out, the high SMR attributable to these quite specific causes of death account for only a tiny proportion of all Irish migrant deaths. Furthermore, when we examine the few studies available of Irish drinking behaviour and smoking habits, then the stereotype supporting such accounts can itself be called into question. In their analysis of Irish drinking patterns based on the General Household Surveys (GHS) of 1984, 1986 and 1988, Pearson, Greenslade and others found that the Irish in Britain were more likely to be abstainers from alcohol and, when the data were standardised for age and social economic group (SEG), no more likely than their British-born counterparts to consume alcohol at all.[40] This is in keeping with data from Ireland, a country which has the highest rate of lifetime abstention in Europe and has one of the lowest rates of death by cirrhosis of the liver in the developed world.[41] However, the data on levels of alcohol consumption seems to suggest that there is a connection between levels of alcohol consumption and the health problems of the Irish in Britain. Thus, Greenslade and his colleagues found that Irish GHS respondents who drank were more likely to do so at levels above the limits recommended as safe at that time (14 units per week for women, 21 per week for men).[42] These findings, however, do not support the stereotypical image of the Irish drinker as a stereotypical drunk. Age-adjusted rates of alcohol consumption can be calculated for both manual and non-manual SEGs and these indicate the tendency to consume alcohol above safe levels for both groups and for men and women. Harrison and Carr-Hill found that the level of alcohol consumption among Irish men in Britain was higher than that of their British counterparts, while that of Irish women tended to be lower than the British average. They also noted that heavy drinking amongst Irish men in Ireland approximated to that found in a 'high consumption' area of England, such as Yorkshire. In the case of Irish women in Britain, their drinking corresponded to that of British women in a 'low' consumption area like the West Midlands. It is not, however, possible to translate these comparisons meaningfully into a model which would enable us to assess the effect upon migrants in terms of their overall health.

On smoking, the evidence is less clear. Balarajan and Yuen found that, compared to the UK-born population, the Irish in Britain were more likely to be heavy smokers.[43] Pearson and his colleagues found that, compared to the British-born population, first- and second-generation Irish people in Britain were more likely to have been smokers at some time in their lives and, with the exception of first-generation Irish of Northern Irish extraction, they were also more likely to be smokers.[44] However, since neither of these studies was adjusted for social class (and smoking behaviour is known to be closely linked to socio-economic status), it is difficult to draw any precise conclusions from these findings. Nonetheless, it is clear that, of all the hypotheses so far examined, the 'lifestyle'-related one stands up the best in accounting for high rates of mortality of Irish migrants in Britain, provided, of course, that we dispense with the stereotypical image of the Irish migrant that underpins many simplistic explanations of the health status of the latter. If excess alcohol consumption and cigarette smoking are attributable to the high mortality rates among Irish migrants, we must then ask what factors cause the latter to smoke and drink heavily in the first place. Since both behaviours are known responses to stress, it behoves us to interrogate why such 'coping strategies' are adopted by the Irish in Britain, rather than, as seems to be the case at present, simply use such characteristics in and of themselves to explain away the poor health profile of the Irish in Britain.[45]

THE MENTAL HEALTH OF THE IRISH IN BRITAIN

If the data on physical morbidity amongst Irish migrants make depressing reading, then the psychiatric data complement this. As I have dealt with this more extensively elsewhere, I shall restrict myself here to summarising already-available analyses.[46] Throughout the 1970s and 1980s, Irish-born people in Britain were between two-and-a-half and three-and-a-half times more likely to be hospitalised for some kind of psychiatric disorder than the English-born.[47] In fact, people born in the Irish Republic had the highest rate of both all and first admissions to psychiatric hospital. Those from Northern Ireland had the second highest rate. Irish men and women in Britain also had the highest cause-specific rates of entry in every diagnostic category, except schizophrenia, where those of Caribbean and Polish origin had rates that were even higher than the Irish.

For Irish men, the highest cause of admission were alcohol-related disorders. Here rates of admission were between seven and nine times higher than those recorded for the English-born population. For Irish women, depression was the largest single cause of admission, with rates between one-and-a-half and two-and-a-half times that of English-born women. In addition, a number of studies have shown that Irish-born people in Britain have amongst the highest rates of suicide and parasuicide.[48]

One might suppose that such high and persistent rates of suicide and admission to psychiatric hospital would have stimulated further research in this area. This has not been the case. Only a handful of studies have emerged over the course of the past twenty years purporting to explain rates of admissions to psychiatric institutions by ethnicity, and none of these have looked at the issue of suicide and ethnicity in contemporary Britain.[49] In the key teaching texts on ethnicity and mental health, Irish migrants rate barely a mention, despite their over-representation as an ethnic group amongst health service users.[50] In these texts, little more than a paragraph is devoted to discussion of the high rates of psychiatric admission amongst Irish people in Britain. It is as if the pervading stereotype of 'Irish madness' acts as an explanation for their over-representation in admission to psychiatric institutions. Irish people here are portrayed as inherently mad, case closed. This aside, as in the case of physical morbidity, a similar set of anecdotal and intuitive hypotheses have emerged which purport to explain away the data. Inherent instability, the Celtic temperament, culture shock and relative deprivation are amongst the principle components of such ad hoc explanations. No studies of incidence or prevalence in the non-hospi-talised communities have as yet emerged to provide evidence in support of any of these hypotheses. Interestingly enough, one community-based study of the prevalence of 'mental disorder' found that Irish migrants to Britain exhibited better psychological adjustment on a series of measures than either matched populations of Irish people in Ireland and British people in Britain.[51]

HEALTH AND ILLNESS IN A SOCIO-CULTURAL CONTEXT

In any discussion of health and illness, the first thing that must be remembered is that such concepts like 'health' and 'illness' are not 'natural' or readily opera-tionalised in any scientific sense. As many writers have pointed out, even the identification of health and illness cannot be simply taken for granted. The identification of illness itself cannot be divorced from social and historical conceptions of what 'normal' or non-pathological functioning might be.[52] In nature, for example, the punctuation of a continuum between life and death, between pathology and normality, cannot be said to occur. This entails a human intervention, and beyond the significance attached to certain states of body and mind, there are no diseases or illnesses in nature. This is not to say that the biological or physical phenomena that we use as a basis for identifying and/or explaining illness and disease do not exist. It is simply to stress that they are not all that there is to say on the question of health and illness. Concepts like illness, sickness, disease and even health itself are social constructs. Our interpretations and actions in response to these are conditioned by the socio-historical circumstances in which they emerge. How we understand and deal with the issue of sickness depends upon a whole array of extra-medical considerations; the dominant forms of knowledge in society at any given time, available technology and authorised procedures for treating disease, to name but a few. This is true of both physical and 'mental' illnesses.

If illness is difficult to conceptualise, then health is even more so. We can understand it both culturally and subjectively in a number of ways. It can, for example, be the simple absence of symptoms preventing usual functioning. Alternatively, it can be much more than this. It may be a lifestyle orientation to the prevention of pathology and the extension of life-span through diet, exercise and the avoidance of certain stimulants damaging to health. As anyone with even the slightest knowledge of contemporary health issues is aware, none of these polarised alternatives is simple or context-free. How we conceive of personal or collective health, how we construct it and how we seek to improve it – these are all subject to a whole range of economic, political and socio-cultural constraints which may vary from group to group and from individual to individual in any given society at any one time. For example, to the starving society or a famished individual, levels of cholesterol in food are unlikely to be a significant issue in dietary selection. Similarly, our toleration of symptoms, like our health-related behaviour, will vary as a function of our needs, circumstances and experience. Sometimes we simply cannot allow ourselves to engage in 'illness behaviour' because of the relative costs and disadvantages of doing so. If we have others depending upon us, then we are likely to define both our health and our symptoms and construct our behaviour in terms of these impacts on other areas of our social and economic life. In short, we may 'grin and bear it' until such symptoms become disabling rather than merely present. Nevertheless, illness behaviour is always more than merely a response to symptoms. It is also a response to the circumstances in which those symptoms occur, circumstances related to such issues as access to services, availability of resources and the balancing of conflicting demands on time, energy and money. All of these shape the construction of relative health and pathology.

In addition to these conceptual and material factors, there is also a 'meta-physical' dimension which must be considered when discussing notions of health and illness. We live in a culture which, generally speaking, places a split between body and mind right at the centre of its metaphysical thinking. So central is this divide to our way of thinking about health, that our common-sense language permits very few ways of talking our way around it. When we attempt to bridge this gap in Western society we are invariably forced to reduce one to the other, or borrow some 'holism' from cultures whose circumstances bear little relation to our own. Equally invariably such reductions, whether idealistic or materialistic, become self-defeating and the borrowings which they encourage usually fail to survive the translation from one cultural context to the other.

With regard to the Irish in Britain, it is my contention that their historically long-standing, poor physical and mental health experience reflects a unity which implies a circumvention of this culturally conditioned, metaphysical disjunction. That is, both their experience of physical and mental health are conditioned, and ultimately explained, by the same set of underlying historical, social and political factors which they share with other groups, but whose combination is perhaps historically unique in the case of the Irish. In other words, the health of Irish people in Britain is not simply an issue of medical and/or psychiatric concern. It goes beyond that and requires a consideration of the fundamental construction of Irish identities and Irish culture as social and historical facts. Implicit in the argument adopted in this chapter is the view that the psycho-physical health experiences of the Irish in Britain are inextricably related to a basic socio-historical relationship. They are not tied to the genetic structure of Irish people, to micro-organisms, or to lifestyle behaviours. They are linked, instead, to the historical relationship between a colonising culture and a fundamentally different colonised one.

COLONIALISM AND EMIGRATION: THE IRISH EXPERIENCE

Any discussion of the health of Irish people in Britain must, at some juncture, consider emigration from Ireland to Britain and its effects upon the physical and mental health of migrants. The volume of emigration over the past 150 years has not only shaped the political and economic face of Ireland. It has also had profound cultural, geographic and psychological dimensions. Whichever way we interpret the phenomenon of mass emigration in the nineteenth and twentieth centuries, and there are many contending interpretations of this, it is clear that the primary motivation for emigration is economic.[53] People have left, and continue to leave, Ireland in big numbers largely because the economy of the island cannot support them.[54] While this is transparently obvious in the case of male Irish migrants, when applied to Irish women emigrants this contention has to take into account other factors affecting their attitudes to emigration, not least patriarchal cultural values and attitudes of the Catholic Church in Ireland to a whole range of sex-related issues. Women are less likely than men to point to the economic as a factor in their migration.[55] Nevertheless, it would be impossible to dispute the importance of economic factors upon Irish female migration since partition. The position of women in the Irish economy and the labour market has been highly constrained for most of the past century. The fixing of ratios of women in certain jobs, the operation of the marriage bar and the limitation upon their ability to hold land in the rural areas all contributed to female emigration in the nineteenth and early twentieth century. Even today, Irish women have a much lower participation rate in the indigenous labour market than, for example, their British counterparts or Irish women in Britain.[56]

The inability of Ireland's economy to provide for the Irish people is, in the final analysis, a legacy of colonialism. The external domination of the Irish economy, first by British imperial interests and subsequently by transnational corporations, may be taken as causal factors in mass emigration from Ireland. The legacy of colonialism, through its systematic under-development of the productive forces, has produced an 'extroverted' development common to most former colonies.[57] This has led to a 'marginalisation of a large proportion of the population among whom very low living standards are the norm'.[58] The Irish regard emigration as a strategy for dealing with this marginalisation. Emigration, indeed, has become a dominant strategy for ameliorating the worst effects of this marginalisation at the level of the individual, the family and the community. It permits the individual to improve his/her economic prospects, to contribute to the local economy through remittances and to free scarce resources at home so that those who remain in Ireland have more to go around.[59]

A principal legacy of colonialism has been that Irish people emigrate primarily as workers, rather than, say, as refugees or political exiles. But if colonialism has exerted an economic impact, it has also had cultural and socio-psychological consequences which have influenced not merely development within Ireland, but have also shaped the 'subjective' economies of Irish migrants and influenced the physical and mental life of Irish people in Britain.[60]

INDOLENT NATIVES: IRISH MIGRANTS AS COLONISED WORKERS

The dominating feature of the colonial project since the nineteenth century has been economic exploitation, rather than military or political control. Colonialism implied territorial domination and the subordination of colonial peoples to the needs of the 'mother country'. According to Lenin, colonies existed primarily for the extraction of value and the diversion of this surplus to the metropolitan state.[61] They functioned as suppliers of raw materials, as markets for home-produced finished goods and as sources of cheap labour. Alongside this process of economic subordination have gone projects of cultural and socio-psychological domination and these reinforced the superiority of the colonist and colonial culture over the colonised. This meant that 'in the colonies the economic substructure is also a superstructure'.[62] One of the significant and recurring motifs of this process of cultural domination is the stereotype of the 'lazy native' who emerges in nearly every instance where a colonised culture confronts the people it dominates.[63] Fanon has argued that the so-called laziness observed amongst the colonised is, in fact, the pre-conscious manifestation of political resistance to a colonial labour process. It is also a social manifestation which is read back into the culture of the colonised as a quality of the individual native, as evidence of his/her inherent inferiority to the coloniser. It becomes, in short, a self-fulfilling prophesy which the native learns simultaneously to accept and to struggle against.[64] During the nineteenth century the laziness, 'ficklessness' and indolence of the Irish became almost proverbial. These attributes of the colonised were also a major mark of the distinction between them and their English colonisers. As *Fraser's Magazine* confidently asserted in 1847:

> Now of all the Celtic tribes, famous everywhere for their indolence and fickleness as the Celts everywhere are, the Irish are admitted to be the most idle and the most fickle. They will not work if they can exist without it.[65]

As with all such stereotypes, this construction of the lazy native often serves as a self-fulfilling prophesy, perverts reality, compounds the subjective struggle of the native and forces the native to constantly repudiate or accept an uncivilised, backward self-definition of themselves. Or as Brosnan put it:

> Irishness I define as the capacity of the Irish to accept and/or deliver standards which appall many of us. . . It is the antithesis of quality.[66]

This sense of inferiority surrounding the productive capacity of both society and individual is exacerbated in the Irish migrant worker. He or she leaves family and community primarily to work. But there is a price to pay for this, if only in justifying the decision to leave and subjectively rationalising the conflict that it generates. Thus, many Irish migrants to Britain undergo a reconstruction of their identity which locates their sense of self around their objective capacity to work. It is easy to see how this reconstruction comes about. To be adrift from home and family, and away from the environment in which one's personal identity and sense of self is formed and sustained, pushes the individual further towards the extreme of the colonised experience, that of being through others, towards an ontological alienation of the self.[67] This characteristic of the colonised experience is encountered by all Irish people in Britain from time to time. It causes them to wonder who they are, what they are doing and where they are going. In posing these questions the Irish in Britain look to the world around them for validation, they objectify their lives in the available narratives of 'this is my story, this is who I am'. For Irish migrants in Britain, both the availability of narratives and their social legitimacy is strictly constrained largely along the lines of British racism. They find themselves in a society where they are stereotypes, not real people; where they are required exclusively for their labour power and for little else. The most important socially validated identity for an Irish migrant in Britain is that of the worker. Its associated narrative becomes a dominant theme in their lives in Britain. In all the uncertainties and vicissitudes of the migrant experience, it is one of the few unquestionable facts, and the existential question arising from the construction of self-as-worker is fairly straightforward. It is not so much 'I am what I do' as 'I am because I do'.

But the question of Irish identity in Britain is more than simply an issue of subjective ontology. It has concrete socio-cultural implications. Over time, it has become in-built in the cultural fabric of the Irish experience in Britain. It is what distinguishes the Irish from British society and from other minority groups. It is commemorated in a multitude of songs and in the values we pass on to our children.[68] As Sykes observed in his study of social attitudes of navvies:

> One never heard complaints about men working too hard. To be known as a hard worker was something to be proud of. Men who worked hard were praised, while poor workers were regarded with contempt . . . The navvies boasted amongst themselves of the feats of hard work they had achieved or seen others achieve.[69]

Such attitudes are not restricted to male manual workers as other studies have shown.[70] They permeate the entire Irish community in Britain. They form a central component of the Irish identity which Irish people in Britain use in order to constitute themselves. The Irish may be able to do nothing about other negative stereotypes, but through hard work, which they transform into a cardinal virtue, they find a rationale for being and having pride in themselves.

There is a problem, however, associated with making work, or any single dimension of life, central to the construction of personal identity and self-esteem. When circumstances, such as illness or unemployment, deny the Irish the opportunity to work, it becomes a major problem at the level of the personal or family economy. It is an issue in the area of ego-investment. For the non-immigrant, not being able to work may be a problem also and cause serious concern. There is, however, not the same structural necessity to focus upon work in the same way that the immigrant does because work does not inexorably link personal with collective identity. The relationship between work and identity for the two groups differs in fundamental and qualitative ways.

Irish immigrants in Britain have this additional burden – in order to maintain their sense of self and their self-esteem, in order to justify their emigration and in order confront its effects, they literally *have* to work. This work, however, is characterised by the following features:

(1) Its importance and its significance for the general well-being of society is rarely, if ever, publicly acknowledged or economically rewarded. This is true of both navvies and nurses.
(2) The Irish are typically still employed below the level of their abilities, intelligence and qualifications.
(3) They frequently have to face confidence-undermining remarks and racist behaviour in the work place.

Having made work central to their being, it remains in many senses a physically and emotionally impoverishing aspect of their experience. One result of this is that when they get sick (i.e. experience symptoms) they tend not to do anything about it, until, that is, those symptoms become actually disabling and prevent them from working. They engage in acts of denial, because to admit of illness would severely undermine their identities. In a study of ethnic groups presenting for treatment at a Massachusetts hospital, Zola found clear evidence of this phenomenon.[71] Irish patients were more likely to deny the presence of pain in their current illness and to report fewer bodily symptoms. Zola characterised the Irish handling of illness in the following way ;

> While in other contexts the ignoring of bodily complaints is simply descriptive of what is going on, in Irish culture it seems to be the culturally prescribed and supported defense mechanism – singularly most appropriate for their psychological and physical survival.[72]

Zola also noted that Irish patients tended to put off seeking medical advice until symptoms began to impede the ability to work.[73]

RESISTING ARREST: COLONIALISM IN THE SURGERY

There is an added twist to this story which also stems from the historical experience of colonialism. In his study of colonialism in Algeria, Fanon showed how medicine becomes imbricated with colonial power over the native. In the case of medicine and the colonial subject, the former 'becomes one of the most tragic features of the colonial situation'. It is so, he contends;

> because . . . the colonial constellation is such that what should be the brotherly and tender insistence of one who only wants to help me is interpreted as a manifestation of the conqueror's arrogance and desire to humiliate.[74]

Fanon here describes a tragic and total breakdown of communication, a complete divergence in understanding of the nature of the therapeutic relationship. For the colonised subject, a visit to the doctor is always an ordeal to be escaped with the integrity of the body intact. The colonised patient resists not merely treatment from, but also contact with, the coloniser. In its standardisation and normalisation of the power relationship between doctor and patient, between the representative voice of colonial technical authority and a subject of that authority, the consultation is an immediate personalisation of the political fact of power and domination which may be felt but not easily articulated. Fanon argues that it is 'not a systematic opposition, but a "vanishing" on the part of the patient'. [75] In virtually every other situation, the colonised can preserve or salvage some pride or self-esteem from his or her contact with the official faces of colonialism. The manifest prescriptive power of the doctor and the admission of weakness or need on the part of the patient which the medical situation entails, renders such a 'salvage' operation difficult, if not impossible. In putting off the moment of contact with the medical services, the colonised subject avoids the short-term consequences of misunderstanding and humiliation implicit in the consultation. However, he or she also sacrifices his or her long-term chances of survival by neglecting 'their' health.

Some of Fanon's contentions are borne out in observation of the socio-medical behaviour of Irish people in Britain. Donal Mac Amhlaigh has given us an account of his experience while working as a ward orderly in Northampton during the 1950s. He noted the tension which Irish patients displayed in periods of consultation. As he put it:

> they go into the doctor as they used to go in to the aristocrats or landlords long ago – shaking with humility.[76]

Now it might be argued that Mac Amhlaigh's experience would be less likely to be true today. However, in a comparative study of Irish and Italian migrants in the United States one decade later, Zola found that Irish patients were more likely to have put off presenting for treatment than the Italians and, compared to their counterparts in the host society, were more likely to be in urgent need of treatment. He also found that 'sanctioning', i.e. the practice whereby one individual takes the primary responsibility for reporting another's symptoms in the light of their resistance, to be 'the overwhelming favourite (sic) of the Irish'.[77] More recently still, Greenslade and his associates found that while Irish migrants in Britain were more likely than the British to report acute recent illness (i.e. illnesses which had forced them to cut back on their activities), they were less likely than the latter to have consulted a doctor.[78]

THE IRISH MIGRANT HEALTH EXPERIENCE: SOME VIGNETTES

The complexity of the Irish migrant health experience is difficult to encapsulate in any simple economic model. This section gives some flavour of the forms that experience takes in vignettes drawn from observations, interviews and conversations conducted in Irish migrant communities of Britain over the last five years. I make no claims for their representativeness, but hope they will illustrate adequately the issues I have touched upon in this chapter.

A is a widow in her late 60s. Apart from short periods when her children were young, she has been in constant full- or part-time employment since her arrival in Britain. At the time of our meeting, she was working part-time as a cleaner and had recently taken a fall at work which left her with minor but painful injuries to an arthritic knee. Although this accident left her confined to her house for three days, she refused to allow her adult daughter to make a doctor's appointment or take her to a casualty department for X-rays. Her days of confinement were normal days off and, despite stiffness and swelling, she returned to work on the next normal working day.

B is a bar manager in his 50s and suffers from circulatory illness in both legs. Despite the obvious pain his present job causes him, he has refused to retire on an invalidity pension. Although his illness has been long-standing, it was only persistent family and medical pressure which forced him to have an operation on the veins in his legs. In fact, as he readily admitted, it was the sanction of potential amputation which persuaded him to admit to surgery. He discharged himself from hospital the day after the operation and was back on his feet at work a few days later.

C is a married man in his mid-30s and works as a manager for a large construction firm. Having joined the firm during the boom years of the early 1980s, he found himself in the position of having for the first time to lay off considerable numbers of a predominantly Irish workforce due to a recession in the building trade. He was deeply conscious that some of the older men would be unlikely ever to work again. During this period, he has begun to suffer from a series of 'psychosomatic' and stress-related illness: psoriasis, frequent colds and migraine headaches.

D is a single man in his 60s. He suffers from angina. Despite this condition, he regards himself as available for work and will take any job offered. On one such job, a loaded pallet was dropped from a crane injuring his foot. He continued to work until it became so swollen that he could no longer put on his working boots. Despite this, he did not seek medical attention for a further three days until a relative insisted that he went to the local casualty department. He had suffered a severe fracture.

E is a single woman in her mid-20s. A university graduate who emigrated in the 1990s, she confided that she was being treated with radium for cervical cancer. She discussed with detailed knowledge both the unpleasantness of the treatment and the symptoms. In the same conversation, she observed how much the illness had changed her for the better, having released her from significant, but now to her clearly trivial, worries about her body image and appearance. She was in fact lying and had no such condition.

F is a former university lecturer in his 40s, married with children. He described himself as someone who would put off going to the doctor until the last possible moment, irrespective of the symptoms. He also described himself as having a complete lack of confidence in professional medical remedies.

G is a widower in his 80s. Having worked as a hospital porter for many years, he was compulsorily retired at the age of sixty five. However, he did find another job and continued to work until he was seventy, when he was made redundant. He then signed on as available for work at an Unemployment Benefit Office for six months until it was discovered that he was beyond the retirement age and benefit was withdrawn. He still regards himself as available for work and would take any job he was offered.

We see in each one of these vignettes indicators of the complex response to the matrix of health, illness, work and identity characteristic of Irish migrants in Britain. We also see factors which potentially explain why the individuals in question suffer such excess levels of mortality; the significance of work in their lives, the toleration of pain and discomfort; the unwillingness to seek medical attention, and the readiness to resume work without adequate recovery time.

THE MYTH OF THE HEALTHY MIGRANT: CONCLUDING COMMENTS

This chapter has argued that colonialism, the same historical force which has made emigration a ubiquitous feature of Irish life for generations, has also produced amongst the Irish in Britain a cultural approach to health and illness characterised by denial, on the one hand, and doctor avoidance, on the other. The former derives from the central fixation on worker identity which emigration brings about, the latter from the unarticulated, perhaps inarticulable, experience of domination which medical intervention implies and to which the colonised subject would be sensitive. This cultural-historical matrix forms the background to the health experience of Irish migrants. It becomes part of their cultural practice and is transmitted across generations to their British-born children. Moreover, it renders them a unique group and, I believe, accounts for much of their poor health profile. The evidence, such as it is, given the stark neglect with which Irish health issues have been treated in Britain, does not conflict with this contention. Moreover, it provides a far more useful model for exploring the existing data than any of the uni-dimensional hypotheses so far considered.

The persistence of high levels of excess mortality and mental illness, and the extension of the former into second-generation Irish people, does not, on the face of things, suggest an optimistic prognosis. The changing of cultural practices, particularly ones so deeply ingrained, is not easily accomplished. However, we can begin to take steps to understand the problem of Irish migrant health and the context surrounding it, and in so doing bring about change. Clearly, the first issue which must be addressed is that of emigration itself. If the foregoing teaches us anything at all, it is that emigration exerts harmful effects on the health of Irish people in Britain, if only because it forces them into a context in which health takes second place to other priorities. While their departure from Ireland may reduce economic and political tensions within

Ireland, it is a reduction bought through the sacrifice of the physical and mental health of large numbers of Irish emigrants.[79]

In the short term, bringing a halt to emigration from Ireland constitutes an impossible task. Conditions in Ireland are such that emigration will remain the only viable economic option for many people for years to come. We can, however, acknowledge the realities of emigration and the implications it holds for the emigrant. Rather than see emigration as some benign form of international labour mobility, we should see it for what it is, namely as a short-term survival strategy with long-term counter-survival implications for both the individual and the economy. Within the communities of the Irish diaspora, change has already begun to take place. As the children of those emigrants of the 1950s and 1960s have come of age and have been joined by new first-generation emigrants in the 1980s, a raising of cultural consciousness and self-confidence has begun to occur. Irish communities have started to emerge from the socio-psychological ghettos into which British racism forced them, and are beginning to mobilise around significant issues of survival. Borrowing and adapting their strategies from the struggles of other oppressed groups within British society, they have set off on the long road of confronting and eradicating the institutionalised racism and injustice facing Irish people in that society. By raising awareness within their own communities and that of the wider society, by allying themselves to other groups in struggle, they are slowly but surely eroding the constraining links in the chains of dependency and inferiority which a colonial history imposed upon them.

So there is some cause for optimism after all. But, like charity, it is a process which begins at home. Until a change in the attitudes and behaviour of Irish society towards both emigration and emigrants occurs, the tragedy of Irish migrant health in Britain is likely to continue to play itself out with appalling consequences. As President Robinson pointed out in her speech, 'Cherishing the Irish Diaspora', to the Oireachtas in February 1995;

> The men and women of our diaspora represent not simply a series of departures and losses. They remain, even while absent, a precious reflection of our own growth and change, a precious reminder of the many strands of identity which compose our story . . . They know the names of our townlands and villages. They remember our landscape or have heard of it. They look to us anxiously to include them in our own sense of ourselves and not to forget their contribution while we make our own.

If the present chapter serves any purpose, it should add weight and additional meaning to these words.

ACKNOWLEDGEMENTS

Some of the research included in this paper was funded by Declan Kelly plc and the Economic and Social Research Council to whom grateful thanks are extended. My gratitude is also offered to the Irish communities of Birmingham, Liverpool, London, and Manchester, to Janet Ditchfield, Rosemary McGill, Tim Lynn, Neil Doolin and the staff and customers of Liverpool Irish Centre, for their help, co-operation, and patient toleration. Responsibility for errors is my own.

NOTES AND REFERENCES

1   L. Greenslade, *The Irish in Britain in the 1990s: A Preliminary Analysis*, Reports on the 1991 Census no. 1 (Liverpool, Institute of Irish Studies, 1993).
2   ibid.
3   R. Worcester, *The Irish in Britain* (London: Market and Opinion Research International Ltd, 1993).
4   M. Pearson, M. Madden, and L. Greenslade, *Generations of an Invisible Minority*, Institute of Irish Studies, Occasional Paper, no. 2 (Liverpool, Institute of Irish Studies, 1991).
5   J. A. Jackson, *The Irish in Britain* (London, Routledge and Kegan Paul, 1963).
6   M. Hickman, *Religion, Class and Identity: The State, the Catholic Church and the Education of the Irish in Britain* (Aldershot, Avebury, 1995); S. Fielding, *Class and Ethnicity: Irish Catholics in England* (Milton Keynes, Open University Press, 1993); D. Owen, *Irish-born People in Great Britain: Settlement Patterns and Socio-economic Circumstances*, 1991 Census Statistical Paper, no. 9 (Warwick, Centre for Research in Ethnic Relations, 1995).
7   L. Greenslade, M. Pearson, and M. Madden, *Irish Migrants in Britain: Socio-economic and Demographic Conditions*, Occasional Papers in Irish Studies, no. 3 (Liverpool, Institute of Irish Studies, 1991).
8   T. Connor, *The London Irish* (London Strategic Policy Unit, 1987).
9   L. Greenslade, 'Issues in the Health of Irish People in Sheffield', paper presented at National Conference on Irish Issues, University of Sheffield (Sheffield, 1994).
10 Owen, *Irish in Britain*.
11 L. Greenslade, M. Pearson, and M. Madden, 'From Visible to Invisible: The "Problem" of Health and Irish People in Britain', in L. Marks and M. Warbouys (eds.), *Migrants, Minorities and Medicine* (London, Pluto Press, 1996).
12 L. Greenslade, and M. Kneafsey, *The Irish in Britain in the 1990s: A Comparative Study* (Liverpool, Institute of Irish Studies, n.d.).
13 Owen, *Irish in Britain*.
14 A. M. Adelstein, et al., 'Comparison of Mortality of Irish Immigrants in England and Wales with that of Irish and British Nationals', *British Medical Journal*, vol. 79, 185–89.
15 R. Balarajan, and L. Bulusu, 'Mortality Among Immigrants in England and Wales 1979–1983', in M. Britton (ed.), *Mortality and Geography: A Review in the mid-1980s of England and Wales* (London, HMSO, 1990).
16 ibid.
17 ibid.
18 J. Raftery, D. Jones, and M. Rosato, 'The Mortality of First and Second Generation Irish Immigrants in the UK', *Social Science Medical Journal*, No. 31 (1990), pp. 577–584.
19 S. L. Syme, et al., 'Epidemiologic Studies of Coronary Heart Disease and Stroke in Japanese Men Living in Japan, Hawaii and California', *American Journal of Epidemiology*, vol. 102, 1975, pp. 477–480.

20   Raftery, Jones and Rosato, *Mortality of Irish Immigrants*, p, 581.
21   M. G. Marmot and R. M. Adelsten and L. Bulusu, *Immigrant Mortality in England and Wales*, 1970–1978. Studies of Merical & Population Ruam, no. 47, London HMSO 1984.
22   ibid.
23   ibid.
24   ibid.
25   Raftery, Jones and Rosato, *Mortality of Irish Immigrants*.
26   Greenslade, Pearson and Madden, *Irish Migrants in Britain*, 1991.
27   D. Bell, 'Premature Mortality in the Republic of Ireland 1971–1981', *Irish Geography*, vol. 19, 1986, pp. 33–40.
28   Marmot et al., *Immigrant Mortality*.
29   I. Rosenwaike, and K. Hempstead, 'Differential Mortality by Ethnicity: Foreign-born Irish, Italians and Jews in New York City 1979–1981', *Social Science Medicine*, vol. 29 1985, pp. 885–889.
30   Balarajan and Bulusu, *Mortality Among Immigrants*.
31   Marmot et al. *Immigrant Mortality*.
32   ibid.
33   Raftery, Jones and Rosato *Mortality of Irish Immigrants*.
34   L. Greenslade, 'Lightning in the Blood: Identity and Health Amongst Irish People in Britain', paper presented at 11th national Conference on Irish Dimensions in British Education, Soar Valley College, Leicester (Leicester, 1994).
35   M. W. P. Carney, *Celts and Mental Disorder: A Preliminary Investigation* (London, Northwick Park Hospital, 1992).
36   P. S. Harper, 'Genetic Variation in Wales', *Journal of Royal College of Physicians*, no. 10, 1976, pp. 321–32.
37   Marmot et al., *Immigrant Mortality*.
38   Raftery, Jones and Rosato, *Mortality of Irish Immigrants*.
39   Greenslade, *The Irish in Britain*.
40   Pearson, Madden and Greenslade, *Generations of an Invisible Minority*.
41   M. Webb, 'Alcohol Excess – the Curse of the Drinking Classes', in C. Keane (Ed.), *Mental Health in Ireland* (Dublin, Gill and MacMillan, 1991).
42   L. Greenslade, M. Pearson, and M. Madden, 'A Good Man's Fault: Alcohol and Irish people at Home and Abroad', *Alcohol and Alcoholism*, no. 30, 1995, pp. 23–34.
43   R. Balarajan, and P. Yuen, 'Smoking and Drinking Habits: Variations by Country of Birth', *Community Medicine*, vol. 8, pp. 237–39.
44   Pearson, Madden and Greenslade, *Generations of an Invisible Minority*.
45   M. Blaxter, *Health and Lifestyles* (London, Tavistock, 1990).
46   L. Greenslade, 'White Skins, White Masks: Psychological Distress and the Irish in Britain', in P. O'Sullivan (ed.), *The Irish in the New Communities* (Leicester University Press, 1992).
47   R. Cochrane, and S. Bal, 'Mental Hospital Admission Rates of Immigrants to England : A Comparison of 1971 and 1981' *Social Psychiatry*, No. 24, 1989, pp. 2–11.
48   A.W Burke, 'A Five Year Follow-up Study of Attempted Suicide Amongst the Irish-born Population in Birmingham', unpublished report, St Georges Hospital Medical School, London, 1986.
49   Carney, *Celts and Mental Disorder*.
50   P. Rack, *Race, Culture and Mental Disorder* (London, Tavistock, 1982); S. Fernando, *Race and Culture in Psychiatry* (London, Croom-Helm, 1988); R. Littlewood, and L. Lipsedge, *Aliens and Alienists* (Harmondsworth, Penguin, 1989).

51 R. Cochrane, 'Mental Illness in Immigrants to England and Wales: An Analysis of Mental Hospital Admissions', *Social Psychiatry*, vol. 12, 1977, pp. 23–35.

52 D. Mechanic, *Medical Sociology* (New York, Free Press, 1978).

53 Mac Laughlin, J., *Historical and Recent Irish Emigration: A Critique of Core – Periphery and Behavioural Models*, Irish Studies Occasional Paper, no. 5 (University of North London Press, 1994).

54 P. Breathnach, 'Uneven Development and Irish Peripheralisation', in P. Shirlow (ed), *Development Ireland* (London, Pluto Press, 1995).

55 B. Walter, 'Gender and Recent Irish Migration to Britain', in R. King (ed.), *Contemporary Irish Migration*, Special Publication no. 6 (Dublin, Geography Society of Ireland, 1991).

56 P. Jackson, *Migrant Women: The Republic of Ireland 1987*, Document no. V/139/89-EN, Employment, Social Affairs and Education, Commission of the European Communities, 1987.

57 R. Crotty, *Ireland in Crisis: A Study in Capitalist Colonial Underdevelopment* (Dingle, Brandon, 1986).

58 Breathnach, 'Uneven Development'.

59 Crotty, *Ireland in Crisis*.

60 L. Greenslade, '(In)dependence Development and the Colonial Legacy in Contemporary Irish Identity', in P. Shirlow (ed.), *Development Ireland* (London, Pluto Press, 1995).

61 V. I. Lenin, *Imperialism: The Highest Stage of Capitalism* (Moscow, Progress Press, 1967).

62 Fanon, F. *The Wretched of the Earth* (Harmondsworth, Penguin, 1967).

63 Albert Memmi, *The Colonizer and the Colonized* (New York: Orion, 1965).

64 Fanon, *Wretched of the Earth*.

65 Cited in N. Lebow, *White Britain and Black Ireland* (Philadelphia, Institute for the Study of Human Issues, 1976).

66 Cited in J. Lee, *Ireland 1912–1985: Politics and society* (Cambridge, Cambridge University Press, 1989).

67 F. Fanon, *Black Skin, White Masks* (London, Paladin Books, 1970).

68 U. Cowley, *A Tribute to the Navvies* (Manchester, Irish World Heritage Centre, 1995).

69 A. J. M. Sykes, 'Navvies: Their Work Relations', *Sociology*, vol. 3, pp. 21–35.

70 M. Daniels, *Exile or Opportunity: Irish Nurses and Midwives in Britain*, Occasional papers in Irish Studies no. 5 (Liverpool, Institute of Irish Studies, 1992).

71 I. K. Zola, 'Culture and Symptoms – Analysis of Patients Presenting Complaints', *American Sociological Review*, no. 31, 1966, pp. 615–30.

72 ibid.

73 I. K. Zola, 'Pathways to the Doctor – from One Person to Patient', *Social Science Medicine*, no. 7, 1973, pp. 677–89.

74 F. Fanon, *A Dying Colonialism* (Harmondsworth, Penguin, 1970).

75 Ibid.

76 D. Mac Amhlaigh, *An Irish Navvy* (London, Routledge and Kegan Paul, 1964).

77 I. K. Zola, 'Pathways to the Doctor'.

78 Greenslade, '(In)dependence, Development and Colonial Legacy'.

79 Mac Laughlin, J., 'Social Characteristics of Recent Emigrants from Selected Regions in the West of Ireland', *Geoforum*, vol. 22 no. 3, 1991; R. Munck, *The Irish Economy: Results and Prospects* (London: Pluto Press, 1993).

3. Contemporary Irish Settlement in London
Women's Worlds, Men's Worlds

BRONWEN WALTER

London remains the major destination of Irish emigrants in the 1990s. About three quarters of those leaving Ireland moved to Britain, and half of these settled in London alone.[1] This chapter examines the contemporary situation of Irish people in London, their patterns of movement, areas of settlement, work profiles and housing conditions. It draws particular attention to the different experiences of women and men, and also 'places' the Irish community in London within a broader framework of ethnic groupings, including the white British-born collectivity.

Irish people's lives are strongly influenced by the distinctive gendering of their 'roots', overlaid by interaction with varieties of British gender relations encountered in London. These have important material consequences. For example, Irish women have outnumbered Irish men in London throughout this century, arrived at younger ages than men and participated in a common narrow range of 'women's work'. Men, on the other hand, have shown a much stronger tendency to remain single and continue to occupy an 'ethnic niche' in the construction trade.

Irish migrants include those originating both in the Irish Republic and in Northern Ireland. The two parts of the island are examined together here since both experience high levels of emigration to Britain. Moreover, they are often amalgamated for statistical purposes in published tables of the 1991 Census, and cannot be separated. In many respects, the two groups of people are also treated similarly in Britain. The 1948 Ireland Act declared that the new republic was 'not a foreign country' from Britain's point of view, so that immigration is not monitored and Irish citizens are entitled to vote as soon as they choose to register on the electoral roll. Northern Irish people discover that they are regarded as 'Irish' by the British in Britain, regardless of their own feelings of allegiance or identity.[2]

However, there are important differences in the experiences of people from Northern Ireland, which shares state systems of the United Kingdom such as education, health and welfare, and the Republic which is an independent state. Separate forms of identification are demanded from migrants from the Republic claiming the benefits to which they are entitled. Moreover, profound feelings of difference from each other are expressed by Irish people originating in the two parts of the island and now living in London.[3]

LONDON AS A FOCUS OF IRISH SETTLEMENT

London has attracted Irish migrants in large numbers for centuries. Clusters of Irish people were noted in Saint Giles-in-the-Fields in the early seventeenth century and in the eighteenth century groupings in Saffron Hill, Wapping, Shoreditch, Bloomsbury, Whitechapel and Poplar formed the nuclei for the development of the 'rookeries'.[4] By the time of the first Census count by birthplace in 1841, 75,000 Irish-born people were recorded there, 25.9 per cent of the total living in England. During the nineteenth century, Irish settlement consolidated in the centre and spread east along the docks. The main area of origin of Irish-born migrants was Munster in the south of Ireland, migrants arriving in from Bristol and other ports in south-west England and travelling overland to London. Irish vagrants in the West London Union in 1848 came from Limerick, Galway and Tipperary, whilst in 1854 many of those located in Saint Giles Rookery came from Cork.[5] In her detailed examination of Irish settlement in London in the middle of the nineteenth century, Lees showed how

> the Irish produced a remarkably resilient, tenacious subculture that not only sheltered but bound its members, not only strengthened but limited their ability to adapt to urban life.[6]

London's proportion of the total has increased steadily so that, by 1991, 32.5 per cent of the Irish-born in England lived in London (Figure 1). Although London shared in the overall decline in the size of the Irish-born population of Britain after a peak in the middle of the nineteenth century, the rate was slower (Figure 2). The decline had halted in London by 1911, whereas it continued in the rest of Britain until 1931. The 'third wave' emigration of the 1980s was experienced mainly in London and south-east England, the total in Britain continuing to fall after a second peak in 1971. Between 1981 and 1991, London's share of new arrivals increased sharply, the proportion of young Irish-born people (20–24) in Britain as a whole living in London rising from 32 per cent to 47 per cent.[7]

When the most recent arrivals are studied, however, the attraction of London becomes even more marked (Table 1). In 1991, 60.5 per cent of Irish Republic-born women and 59.3 per cent of men, living outside the United Kingdom one year previously, were located in London. This is a substantial increase on proportions of 44.8 per cent and 40.5 per cent, respectively, in 1981.[8] The age group constituted over half of all one-year Republic-born Irish

Figure 1: Proportion of the total Irish-born population of Britain living in London, 1861–1991

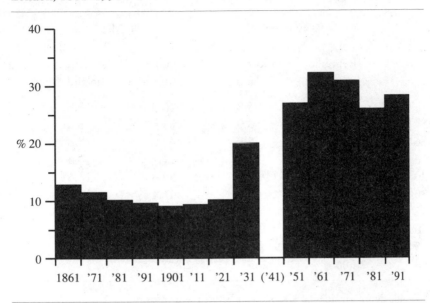

Note: No census in 1941 due to World War II

Source: Census of G.B., 1851, vol. II, preface pp. 14–16; 1851 Pop Tables II, vol. 1, Tables XXXIX, XL; Census of England and Wales, 1921. Gen. Tables, Table 52; 1951, Gen. Tables, Table 39; 1961 Birthplace and Nationality Tables, Table 1; Census of Scotland, 1951, vol. III, Table 31; 1961, vol. V, Table I; Census 1971, G.B. Country of Birth Tables, Table 3; Census 1981, Country of Birth Tables, Table 2; Census 1991, Ethnic and Country of Birth Tables, Table 1

migrants in Britain (Table 2). Interestingly, London was much less popular amongst one-year migrants in their 20s from Northern Ireland. Only just over one quarter located there, 28.9 per cent of women and 26.4 per cent of men. The age group was also less dominant in the overall pattern of one-year migrants from Northern Ireland. A substantial number of young middle-aged people, constituting 31.8 per cent of all Northern Irish-born women and 28.8 per cent of men, was presumably accompanied by the larger proportions of Northern Irish-born children.

More women travelled as young independent people, the gender ratios of one-year migrants being particularly high amongst 18–19 year-olds from the Irish Republic (Table 3). There was a also a clear majority of women in the 20–29 year-old age group, especially in London, and again amongst older people aged over 60, though men predominated in the 30–59 working-age groups. The small inflow of older women probably comprised widows moving to live with married children in Britain.

TABLE 1: *One-year Migrants* from Ireland Living in London, Proportions of Total in Britain by Age Group, 1991*

	% Women		% Men	
Age	Republic of Ireland	Northern Ireland	Republic of Ireland	Northern Ireland
1–4	36.9	5.8	26.9	13.5
5–15	37.8	6.9	35.4	8.8
16–17	37.9	5.9	42.2	15.8
18–19	61.2	33.3	21.2	46.4
20–29	60.5	28.9	59.3	26.4
30–44	43.6	15.0	41.4	17.2
45–59	32.0	16.0	38.5	17.6
60–64	25.4	27.7	17.2	25.0
65+	27.1	16.0	28.1	16.0
N	2,506	253	2,827	253

* People living outside the UK one year before the Census.
Source: 1991 Census, Ethnic Group and Country of Birth, Table 4.

TABLE 2: *One-year Migrants from Ireland Living in Britain, Proportions by Age Group, 1991*

	% Women		% Men	
Age	Republic of Ireland	Northern Ireland	Republic of Ireland	Northern Ireland
1–4	3.4	6.4	4.8	5.6
5–15	6.7	13.1	7.8	12.0
16–17	1.4	1.3	1.9	1.4
18–19	9.8	1.7	6.2	3.5
20–29	55.1	36.4	50.5	37.6
30–44	14.7	31.8	19.1	28.8
45–59	5.4	6.0	7.2	8.1
60–64	1.0	1.3	1.0	1.2
65+	2.5	1.9	1.5	1.9
TOTAL	100.0	100.0	100.0	100.0
N	6,652	1,339	5,777	1,330

Source: 1991 Census, Ethnic Group and Country of Birth, Table 4.

Figure 2: Total Irish-born population in Britain and London, 1861–1991

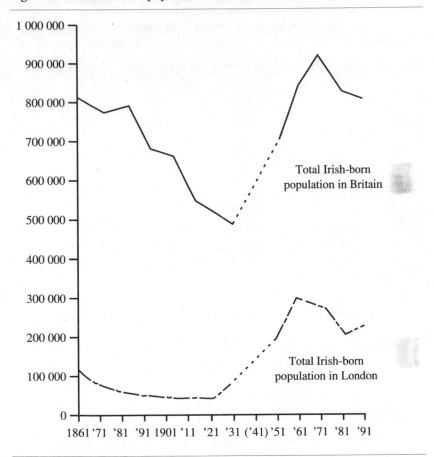

Source: As for Figure 1.

A distinctive feature of Irish settlement in London since 1861 has been the greater number of women than men recorded in each Census (Figure 3). More women than men have emigrated from Ireland in most decades since 1861.[9] However, the south-east region is the only one in Britain where this gender balance has occurred consistently in the Irish-born population.[10] The ratio was highest in the first half of the twentieth century, peaking in 1921 when there were 1,630 women for every 1,000 Irish-born men in London. By 1991, it had risen from a low in 1961 of 1,116 to 1,148 overall, though the ratio was higher for Republic-born women (1,160) than for those from Northern Ireland (1,055). The pattern of women significantly outnumbering men echoed that of the total London population, but was even more pronounced. It indicates the high demand for women's labour in London, particularly as clerical and personal service workers.

TABLE 3: *Gender Ratios¹ of one-year Migrants from Ireland, 1991*

	% Women		% Men	
Age	Republic of Ireland	Northern Ireland	Republic of Ireland	Northern Ireland
1–4	818	1,162	1,122	500
5–15	989	1,100	1,056	857
16–17	870	895	783	333
18–19	1,816	500	2,395	800
20–29	1,256	976	1,281	1,068
30–44	885	1,112	932	969
45–59	862	750	718	684
60–64	1,155	1,125	1,700	1,250
65+	1,865	1,000	1,800	1,000
Average	1,168	958	1,310	829

¹ Women per 1000 men

Source: 1991 Census, Ethnic and Country of Birth, Great Britain, Table 4

Figure 3: Gender ratios of Irish-born and total population of London, 1861–1991

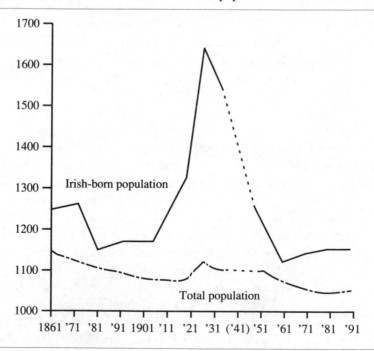

Source: As for Figure 1.

The Census of Great Britain constitutes the most important source of statistical data about the Irish population in London. However, care must be taken in interpretation of the figures, especially those collected in 1991. There was serious under-enumeration of the population as a whole, amounting to a 'missing million'.[11] This is thought to be related to fears, both of casual callers by flat-dwellers and of identification by those avoiding the community charge or poll tax introduced by the Conservative Government under Margaret Thatcher in 1990.[12] It had differential effects by age group, gender, place and ethnic group, and was particularly marked in Inner London boroughs where the charges were highest, including Camden, Haringey and Lambeth. Estimates have been produced to allow correction factors to be used.[13] These show that the under-enumeration was most severe amongst young men in the non-white population living in inner cities. Specific calculations have not been produced for the Irish-born, but the rates for migrants are likely to be high. Moreover, young Irish people are clustered in inner cities where completion of census forms was lowest. If rates for young Irish-born men are similar to those of the Black Caribbean community, the under-enumeration may be as high as 15–20%.[14]

DEMOGRAPHIC STRUCTURE OF THE LONDON IRISH POPULATION

The character of contemporary Irish settlement in London is strongly influenced by its demographic structure. Age, gender and generation affect all aspects of people's lives, including employment and, therefore, standard of living, as well as housing need and leisure patterns. It is thus necessary to identify the broad outlines of demographic structure and examine the processes of their construction and change. For those born in Ireland, this structure mainly reflects waves of immigration, tempered to some extent by subsequent moves out of London and differential mortality.

It is important to set the experiences of 'new wave' migrants in the context of previous generations. Not only have patterns of Irish community life been established over considerable periods of time, but new arrivals themselves frequently contribute directly to continuity by living with relatives for their first few weeks, months or even longer.[15] During the twentieth century, the Irish community in London has become increasingly clustered on the west side of inner London and immediately adjoining outer London boroughs. Location quotients of the Irish-born population in London in 1991, which measure the amount of clustering in a particular area compared with the pattern of the total population, show very high levels in certain boroughs (Figure 4). In Brent, for example, clustering of the Irish-born is 136 per cent above average, followed by Islington 86 per cent, Camden 68 per cent and Ealing 55 per cent.

Four age groups are now examined in greater detail. Differences relating to gender and Northern/Republic Irish origin will be highlighted.

Figure 4: Location quotients of the Irish-born population in London, 1991

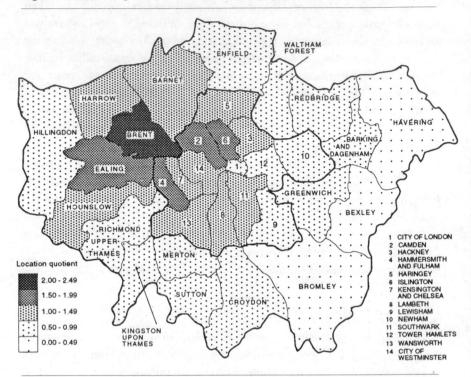

Note: A value of 1.0 shows clustering of the Irish-born sub-group is the same as in the total population. Higher values show greater clustering e.g. 1.5 shows 50% greater clustering than in the total population.

Source: 1991 Census, Local Base Statistics.

AGE AND GENDER PATTERNS

The age structure of the London Irish-born population is younger than that of the total Irish-born population of Britain (Table 4). Young people (16–24) and younger middle-aged adults (25–44) are relatively more numerous. Together these age groups comprise 43.0 per cent of the Republic Irish-born (34.0 per cent in Britain) and 57.3 per cent of the Northern Irish-born (48.4 per cent in Britain).

Compared with the total London population, however, the Irish-born population is weighted towards the older groups, especially those aged 45–64, who comprise 38.2 per cent of the Republic-born population aged 15+, but only 25.6 per cent of the total in London. The 'bulge' in this age group is clearly brought out in Figure 5. The Northern Irish-born population pyramid, by contrast, follows a declining pattern by age, more similar to that of the London total.

TABLE 4: *Irish-born and Total Populations in London and Britain by Age Group, 16+, 1991, %*

Age	LONDON			BRITAIN		
	Republic of Ireland	Northern Ireland	Total	Republic of Ireland	Northern Ireland	Total
16–24	9.9	12.6	16.6	6.2	10.5	15.9
25–44	33.1	44.7	40.5	27.8	37.9	36.5
45–64	38.2	27.3	25.6	42.1	32.2	27.4
65+	18.6	15.4	17.9	24.0	19.4	20.1
Total	99.8	100.0	100.6	100.1	100.0	99.9
N	206,868	40,776	5,375,652	573,131	231,804	4,3865,121

Source: 1991 Census, Ethnic Group and Country of Birth, Table 2.

Overall, therefore, the Irish in London are young compared to the Irish-born in Britain but old for London as a whole. The 'new wave' arrivals in the 1980s rejuvenated the Irish-born population after a low period in the 1970s, but the very large numbers arriving in the 1950s and 1960s continue to have a marked impact on the Irish-born population structure.

Young people

Numbers of young Irish-born people in London increased sharply between 1981 and 1991 (Table 5). Even allowing for greater under-enumeration of men, both numbers and rates of growth were higher for young women. Between 1981 and 1991, there was an 81.5 per cent increase in the age group 15–24 for women (1981: 8,323, 1991:15,107) compared with an increase of 65.4 per cent for men (1981: 6,566, 1991: 11,060).[16]

TABLE 5: *Change in the Irish-born Population in London by Age Group, 1981–91*

Age group	Women	Men
	% change	% change
0–14	+105.6	+79.9
15–24	+81.5	+65.4
25–44	-8.9	-0.8
45–64	+1.5	-0.2
65+	+32.5	+22.2
Total	+8.6	+8.8

Source: Connor, 1987; 1991 Census, Ethnic Group and Country of Birth, Table 2.

Figure 5: Age-sex pyramids of (a) Republic Irish-born, (B) Northern Irish-born and (C) total population in London, 1991

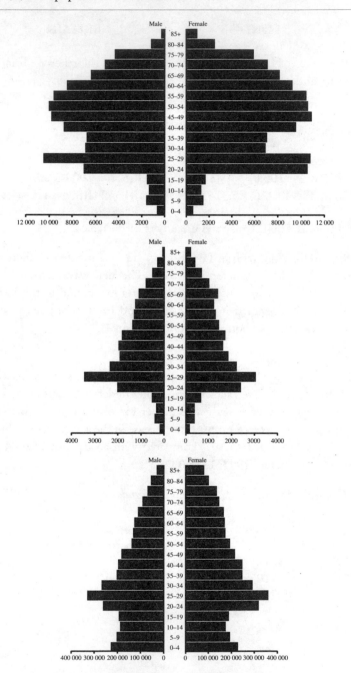

Source: 1991 Census, Ethnic Group and Country of Birth, Table 2

Figure 6: Young people aged 16–24 as a percentage of total Irish-born population in London, 1991

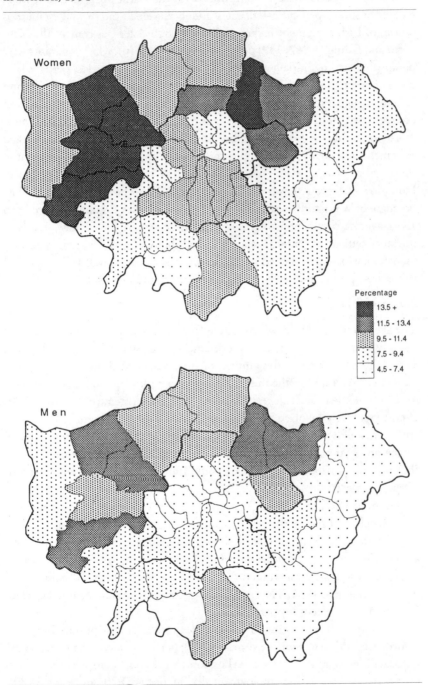

The distribution of young people in London has two distinct elements (Figure 6). The first reflects continuity with the traditional pattern of Irish settlement shown by Figure 4. Greatest numbers were found in well-established centres of Irish settlement including Brent (2,829: 12.9 per cent of the Irish-born) and Ealing (1,947: 11.9 per cent of the Irish-born). Many migrants were presumably settling initially where they had relatives and friends, perhaps later moving out to independent rented accommodation. However, the second feature is high growth rates of young Irish-born people in outer London boroughs, which have had quite low Irish-born populations in the past. This is most noticeable in boroughs adjoining the western 'core' of established settlement. In Harrow, for example, there was an increase of 432.8 per cent in the number of Irish women aged 20–24 (1981: 125; 1991: 666) and in Hounslow the growth was 297.0 per cent (1981: 134; 1991: 532). The boroughs of Waltham Forest and Redbridge in north-east London also recorded above-average proportions of young women and men. These new trends in migrants' settlement patterns reflect the availability of privately rented accommodation, which has declined sharply in inner city areas, as well as the arrival of young Irish people in higher-earning categories than in the past.

Early middle age

The age group 25–44, in which family formation is a prominent feature for many, was the only one in which a decline was registered between 1981 and 1991 (Table 5). Whereas the number of men remained almost unchanged at 42,644 (1981: 42,988), the number of women declined by 8.9 per cent from 48,226 to 43,941. This suggests that the 'new wave' migration in the 1980s almost exclusively involved young people, though the doubling in numbers of Irish-born children (0–14) during the decade indicates an upturn in the rate of migration of young families. When the group is disaggregated, it can be seen that a disproportionate number of young families originated in Northern Ireland (Table 2).

The overall decline in this age group mainly reflects return migration to the Irish Republic in the 1970s which involved a significant number of families. Together, married men, married women and children under 15 accounted for almost 68 per cent of the total returning.[17] The peak age groups for return in this group was 25–29 for women and 30–34 for men, which has reduced the totals remaining in 1991. The largest proportion of returnees recorded Greater London as their area of former residence.

By contrast, highest growth rates in the total London population were recorded by this age group (women +22.9 per cent, men +18.6 per cent) reflecting the expansion of jobs in London in the later 1980s.[18] This was an unexpected reversal of the employment decline of the 1970s and early 1980s, and related to the growth of jobs in the financial sector.[19]

Higher rates of Irish-born people in this age group have remained single than in the population as a whole (Table 6). Amongst those aged 35–44, for example, 11.6 per cent of Republic-born and 11.9 per cent of Northern Irish-born women had never married, compared with 8.0 per cent of the total population. For men, the rates are 18.3 per cent for the Republic-born, though only 8.4 per cent for Northern Irish-born, against 8.7 per cent overall. These rates have implications for housing needs within the group, suggesting that rented and hostel accommodation may be in greater demand than in the total population.

Later middle age

Numbers in the older working-age group 45–64 changed very little during the 1980s (women +1.5 per cent, men -0.2 per cent) (Table 5). The Irish-born age group is much more substantial than in the adult population as a whole (Table 4), resulting from high levels of immigration from Ireland during the 1950s when this group was young. Stability over time indicates the settled nature of the community, many of the group being parents to second-generation children firmly established in Britain. Most have now lived in London for at least 30 years.

Many people in this age group are aunts and uncles of the 'new wave' migrants and often provide an initial point of contact for them. They also create a strong demand for a distinctive kind of Irish social life in London which involves traditional cultural activities such as music and dancing. These are often based around the Catholic Church which has provided support and continuity of aspects of Irish life in the the 1950s.[20]

TABLE 6: *Never-married People in London Irish-born and Total Populations, 1991, %*

	Women			Men		
	Republic of Ireland	Northern Ireland	Total	Republic of Ireland	Northern Ireland	Total
16–19	96.8	97.6	97.8	100.0	98.9	99.3
20–24	88.0	88.5	76.9	93.00	93.4	88.9
25–34	46.7	39.6	28.9	57.1	50.1	41.7
35–44	11.6	11.9	8.0	18.3	13.5	13.7
45–54	7.1	4.8	5.1	13.0	8.4	8.7
60–64	8.6	7.7	6.0	14.3	10.1	8.1
65–74	11.1	9.0	7.3	11.3	5.7	7.5
75+	14.0	8.7	10.6	11.7	9.3	6.5
N	1,179	730	418,011	1318	671	131,124

Source: 1991 Census, 2% Individual Samples of Anonymised Records.

Older people

There was a large increase in proportions of the Irish-born population aged 65 and over between 1981 and 1991, reflecting the generation who came to Britain during World War II, after a low period of emigration in the 1930s and especially following the lifting of travel restrictions in 1946. The presence of a sizeable group of Irish-born pensioners is a new trend in the Irish community. People in this age group were born before 1926 and grew up in an isolated, economically stagnant Ireland which contrasted with the British past of their present neighbours:

> Until the 1940s the horizons of country life were generally very narrow. The daily tasks were predictable and routine, and people's lives were closely structured by religion. Few houses had radios or took newspapers, transport was limited and television not yet available. For many families the only contact with the wider world was the occasional letter from relatives in America.[21]

Irish pensioners in London vividly recall the hardships of those times.[22] Many prefer separate pensioners' groups which can take account of these cultural differences, which have often become magnified by the ageing process:

> Elderly immigrants also share a tendency to re-experience the "culture shock" of adapting to life in an alien environment when encountering the losses and social isolation of ald age; to lose learned language skills (Gaelic was the mother tongue of many people in this generation); and to become conscious of the depth of the cultural gap between themselves and their British-born children and grandchildren.[23]

Higher proportions of women in older age groups have remained single (Table 6). Amongst those aged 75 and over in 1981, for example, 14.0 per cent of Republic-born women never married, compared with 10.6 per cent of the total population, though the Northern Irish total was lower at 8.7 per cent. The difference is even greater for men. Only 6.5 per cent of all men aged 75+ in London had never married, but the proportions were 11.7 per cent for Irish Republic-born men and 9.3 per cent for those from Northern Ireland. Many women had worked as domestic servants or nurses, occupations where live-in accommodation had been one of the attractions to single migrants. Such women now find it difficult to obtain adequate housing, especially without support from children in their old age.[24] Single older Irish men are over-represented in inner city hostels and amongst those sleeping rough. Often these men were peripatetic building workers who never established permanent homes and failed to learn domestic skills.[25] Their employment 'on the lump' has made their entitlement to state benefits uncertain and, therefore, avoided.[26]

A larger total of older Irish people live alone, including those whose partners have died. In a sample of one hundred Irish people aged over 60 in Haringey,

Figure 7: Older people aged 65+ as a percentage of total Irish-born population in London, 1991

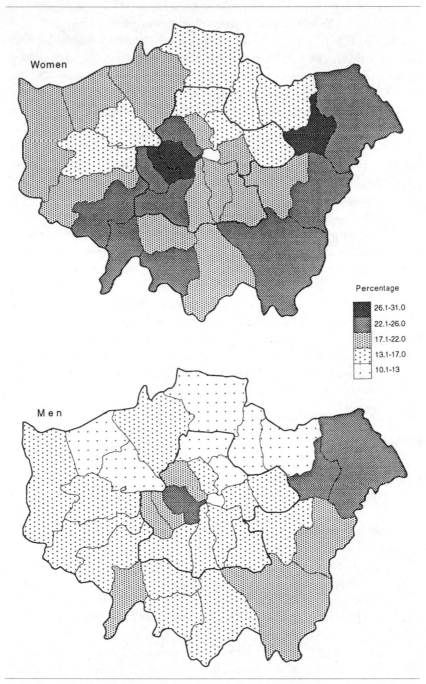

Key to boroughs. See Figure 4

Source: 1991 Census, Local Base Statistics

68 per cent lived alone and 33 per cent had no other relative living in London.[27] This represents a higher rate than amongst other groups in London and reflects independent migration in young adulthood, traditions of low marriage rates in Ireland in the past and the work patterns of labour migrants in Britain.[28]

Older Irish-born women are disproportionately located in particular inner London boroughs, notably Westminster, where in 1991 they comprised nearly a third of all Irish women (31.0 per cent), Kensington and Chelsea (29.1 per cent), Camden (25.3 per cent) and Hammersmith and Fulham (23.7 per cent) (Figure 7). They form a significant proportion of the total elderly population in these boroughs, for example 10.6 per cent in Hammersmith and Fulham, and 9.8 per cent in Westminster. Older Irish men are similarly concentrated into the boroughs of Westminster, Kensington and Chelsea, but comprise a much smaller proportion of the Irish male population because of higher mortality.[29] These boroughs have well above-average proportions living in the furnished private rented sector, which is associated with the worst housing characteristics.[30]

Older Irish people are also relatively more numerous in outer London boroughs as a result of suburbanisation. Both women and men are over-represented in easterly boroughs, including Barking and Dagenham and Havering where inner city inhabitants were rehoused in local authority housing in the 1950s. This distribution may reflect outward movement from the easterly spread of Irish settlement along the docks at the beginning of the century. Older Irish women are also clustered in south-western sections of outer London, including Kingston-on-Thames, Richmond-on-Thames and Sutton. These areas extend beyond the central clusters of Ealing and Brent and reflect upward mobility into owner-occupation of migrants from the 1950s.

SECOND-GENERATION IRISH PEOPLE

Children of Irish-born parents are often known as the 'second generation'. Although not all would identify themselves as Irish, there are many reasons why they should be included in discussions of the Irish community in London. Since migrants are usually young adults, children are born within a few years of their arrival when their parents' Irish past is still fresh. The majority are brought up, at least nominally, in the Catholic religion which to some extent cuts them off from full identification with non-Catholic neighbours. Hickman found that all London-born children of Irish parents in her sample of Catholic pupils regarded themselves as Irish.[31] Moreover Ullah found that contrary to British assumptions, anti-Irish prejudice was widely experienced by a sample of second-generation Irish adolescents in Birmingham and London.[32] Questions relating to identity formed a major issue in these young people's lives.

In other, recognised, 'ethnic groups' it is assumed that children take on their parents' ethnicity, so that for example the 1991 Census figures usually include people of African Caribbean origin born in Britain (53 per cent born in the

UK). In order for numbers of Irish people to be considered on the same basis, it is important to attempt a recognition of Irish upbringing and cultural backgrounds. However, in the absence of an 'Irish' category in the 1991 Census, no count exists of those identifying themselves as Irish who were born outside Ireland. Such a category would, of course, exclude people with Irish-born parents who chose not to identify themselves in this way. But it would indicate the size of the group who did not feel part of the white British majority.

Indicative evidence is available from statistical surveys which include parental birthplace. In 1983, the Labour Force Survey collected this data which gave a weighted total of 223,492 people who were born in the United Kingdom to parents originating in the Irish Republic and living in London. This increased the size of the Irish community to 408,822, a factor of 1.2, though it omitted those born to Northern Irish parents. The Irish thus constitute the largest ethnic group by migration in London, comprising at least 10 per cent of the total population.

Clearly the size of the second generation is related to variations in the flow of immigration. In 1983, the most numerous age group was 15–24 who formed 32.6 per cent of the total (Figure 8). These were the children of the 1950s and 60s 'second wave' migrants, which still forms the largest part of the London-Irish community. By contrast the older cohort of 25–34 year olds, whose parents would have arrived in the War and early post-War period, constituted only 16.8 per cent.

The growth in demand for Irish studies courses in London during the 1980s can been ascribed in part to the large numbers of second-generation children

Figure 8: Age-sex pyramid of population born in the United Kingdom to Irish-born parent/s and living in London, 1983

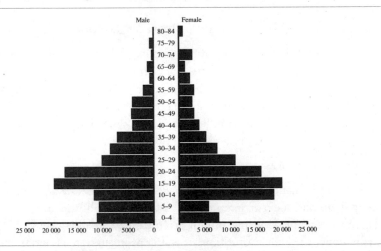

Source: Labour Force Survey, 1983

Figure 9: Occupational groupings of Irish-born and total populations by gender and age, Britain, 1991

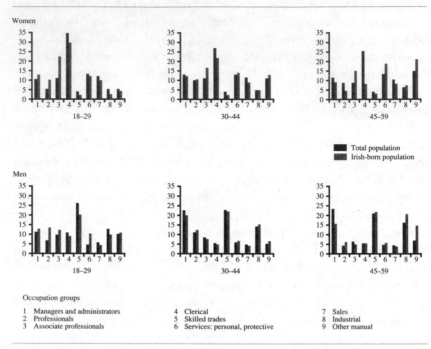

Occupation groups

1   Managers and administrators
2   Professionals
3   Associate professionals

4   Clerical
5   Skilled trades
6   Services: personal, protective

7   Sales
8   Industrial
9   Other manual

Source: 1991 Census, 2% Individual Samples of Anonymised Records

coming of age in a period of expanding numbers entering higher education. It also reflects the need to confront issues of Irish identity when negative images have a high political profile.[33]

SOCIO-ECONOMIC POSITION OF IRISH PEOPLE IN LONDON

Irish-born people in London are overwhelmingly labour migrants.[34] Most have come to find a paid job, to seek better opportunities or to advance their careers. Their moves are highly responsive to vacancies in Britain.[35] An analysis of Irish people's place in the socio-economic structure is thus a measure of the demand for their labour as well as an indication of the skills with which they arrive. There may not necessarily be a match between the two.

OCCUPATION PROFILES

Evidence at the national level suggests marked differences by age group in the occupations and socio-economic status of the Irish-born in Britain in 1991 (Figure 9). Sample sizes in London are too small to allow age to be disaggregated, but the known weighting of young people towards London makes it reasonable to infer that the characteristics of the 18–29 group as a whole is more influenced by the London component than are those of other British regions.

A striking feature of Figure 9 is the strong representation of Irish-born people aged 18–29 in higher status occupations demanding advanced qualifications. The proportions of both women and men in managerial and professional categories is clearly well above the national average. Nearly half (45.4 per cent) of all Irish-born women are in these groups compared with 26.5 per cent of all women. For men, the figures are 39.0 per cent and 26.5 per cent respectively. Nurses account for an important part of this group and explain the higher representation of women in these occupations. If non-health occupations only are considered, 29.7 per cent of Irish-born women (18.9 per cent of the total population) and 36.3 per cent of Irish-born men (24.2 per cent of the total population) are included. Even without an important 'niche' occupation, therefore, there is still a substantially greater than average proportion of young Irish people in higher level managerial, administrative and professional work, evidence of a 'brain drain' from Ireland in the 1980s.[36]

At the same time, however, other young Irish people remained concentrated in manual, often casual work. Although the largest proportion of the male age group was still categorised in the traditional area of skilled construction trades (20.1 per cent), unusually for the male Irish-born population as a whole this was lower than average amongst the total population (25.2 per cent). It was in the personal service category that young Irish-born men were concentrated more distinctly (10.4 per cent, compared with 4.1 per cent average). By contrast, the pattern of employment of middle-aged working men (30–44) was quite close to the overall average. That of older men (45–59), however, diverged quite strongly with clearer concentrations in the traditional industrial and general labouring categories.

Amongst women, the persistence of nursing as a distinct category of work can be traced throughout the age range. A survey of Irish nurses in 1988 showed that the women came from all parts of Ireland, particularly from rural backgrounds.[37] The great majority gave desire to enter nursing as their main reason for emigration, and most felt that their stay would be quite short and that they would prefer to return home if a job became available. It would appear that Ireland has an oversupply of well-educated girls who aspire to become nurses. Since Britain has a shortage in this area, their skills are in demand.[38] Very unusually, fewer than average Irish-born women were in domestic service jobs in the youngest working age group, though as with men, the proportions in 'unskilled' work increased sharply with age.

These generational trends point to dual strands in the labour patterns of 'new wave' Irish migrants. On the one hand, there are clear continuities, with nursing remaining an important area for women and the building trade attracting about one third of men. On the other hand, below average proportions both of women in personal services and men 'on the buildings' represent significant changes. A further new element is the greatly strengthened managerial and professional category. It appears that young Irish people filled a much higher level skills gap in London in the 1980s than they had done in the past.[39] This reflects the high demand for professional, technical and managerial employees in London and south-east England during the 1980s.[40] It also suggests a lack of opportunities in Ireland for young people with higher educational qualifications.[41]

Some pointers to the employment profiles of second generation Irish people in London can be drawn from the 1983 Labour Force Survey (Table 7). The figures suggest that those with Irish-born parents occupied an intermediate position between the Irish-born and other white UK-born populations. For women, the most noticeable change was the decline in proportions in the health professions and the increase in clerical workers. There was also a sharp drop in the domestic service category, though the younger age profile must be taken into account. Similarly for men, the proportion in managerial and professional categories had risen steeply and might rise further as the main cohort reached middle age. A small concentration in the construction industry could still be discerned, perhaps as sons followed fathers in family trades or businesses. These findings generally support Hornsby-Smith and Dale's findings that English-born second-generation Irish people from the Republic had attained higher educational and occupational status than an English control group.[42]

The socio-economic position of the Irish-born populations in London from both the Republic and Northern Ireland can be placed in a broader comparative context by using the Registrar General's social class categories based on occupation (Table 8). Although these are based on a two per cent sample and thus small numbers, they bring out clearly the continuing concentration of Republic-born migrants in the lowest socio-economic categories, despite recent changes in qualification levels. Amongst women, 29.9 per cent were in the semi-skilled and unskilled categories IV and V, well above the city's average of 19.0 per cent and higher than any other group in the table. They were closest to Black Caribbean women, whose total was 26.4 per cent. But women from Northern Ireland had below average proportions in these categories, only 16.2 per cent which was similar to the English-born (16.8 per cent). Irish Republic-born men also had the highest representation in groups IV and V (28.5 per cent), strikingly higher than the average of 18.9 per cent and almost identical with the Black Caribbean proportion of 28.2 per cent. Again, this contrasted with the situation of men from Northern Ireland who had only 18.0 per cent in these groups.

At the other end of the scale, Irish Republic-born women had average proportions in the highest social class categories, I and II (33.5 per cent), but the figure for Northern Irish-born women was well above this (50.0 per cent). This remarkably high figure mirrored that of Welsh (47.9 per cent) and

TABLE 7: *Occupational Categories (KOS groupings) in London by Birthplace/ethnic group; Irish Republic, UK of Irish Parents, other White UK-born, 1983, %*

		IR-born	UK-born/IR parents	Other white UK
Women				
ii	Prof., ed., welf., health	21	13	13
v	Managerial	3	7	5
vi	Clerical and related	22	37	40
vii	Selling	6	12	8
ix	Catering, cleaning, persl.	39	21	17
xiii	Printing, assembling	2	2	2
	TOTAL	51,455	43,172	906,280
Men				
i	Prof. management/admin	1	6	10
v	Managerial	8	12	12
vi	Clerical and related	7	12	12
ix	Catering, cleaning, personal	1	8	6
xi	Processing, non-metal	11	3	4
xii	Processing, metal	11	13	14
xiii	Printing, assembling	7	5	3
xiv	Construction	26	10	5
xv	Transport	11	13	10
	TOTAL	55,574	55,458	1,257,701

Source: Labour Force Survey 1983 (from Walter 1988)

Scottish women (44.8 per cent) and was sharply above that of the English (32.0 per cent). It presumably reflects the in-migration of highly qualified women from outlying parts of the United Kingdom, not counterbalanced as in the case of the Republic-born by those filling unskilled jobs. This pattern of movement supports the idea of an 'escalator region' in the south-east of England, especially for women who had exceptionally high rates of transition from white-collar to managerial positions.[43]

Republic-born men's occupational groupings did not replicate this pattern. The proportion in classes I and II (25.1 per cent) was well below average (31.5 per cent) though above that of Black Caribbean men (16.0 per cent). Again Northern Ireland-born men were considerably above average (41.8 per cent), though lower than Welsh (57.5 per cent) and Scottish men (46.4 per cent).

TABLE 8: *Social Class by Birthplace/ethnic Group in London, 1991, %*

Registrar General's social class	England	Scotland	Wales	NI	RI	Black Caribbean	Indian	Total
Women								
i	2.7	3.8	4.2	6.4	2.8	1.0	3.8	3.1
ii	29.3	41.0	43.7	43.6	30.5	28.1	21.7	30.4
iii n	45.5	36.3	34.4	29.7	29.9	37.7	42.8	41.8
iii m	5.6	3.9	3.6	4.1	6.9	6.7	4.9	5.7
iv	11.4	10.8	9.1	11.5	16.8	17.0	21.6	13.0
v	5.4	4.2	4.9	4.7	13.1	9.4	5.2	6.0
Total %	99.9	100.0	99.9	100.0	100.0	99.9	100.0	100.0
Total	25,400	768	471	296	1,372	1,663	1,549	35,703
Men								
i	7.5	10.5	15.0	10.2	4.3	2.0	10.9	8.3
ii	31.3	35.9	42.5	31.6	20.8	14.0	30.3	31.1
iii n	15.3	13.3	11.4	10.5	8.0	14.3	19.4	14.9
iii m	27.5	21.7	17.3	29.5	38.4	41.6	22.0	26.8
iv	12.9	13.1	9.4	10.8	16.0	19.3	14.1	13.4
v	4.8	5.4	4.3	7.2	12.5	8.9	3.2	5.5
Total %	99.3	99.9	99.9	99.8	100.0	100.1	99.9	100.0
Total	28,356	907	508	332	1,524	1,466	2,016	40,045

Key:
i   Professional etc. occupations
ii   Managerial and technical occupations
iii n   Skilled occupations – non-manual
iii m   Skilled occupations – manual
iv   Partly-skilled occupations
v   Unskilled occupations

Source: 1991 Census, 2% Individual Samples of Anonymised Records.

These results underline the need to disaggregate the 'Born in Ireland' category of the 1991 Census, which disguises important differences in the experiences of people from the two parts of Ireland. Despite the high proportion of graduates amongst recent arrivals which have captured the headlines,[44] there is still a larger number of poorly qualified migrants, mainly from the Republic, whose employment patterns are even less favourable than those of a community widely recognised to suffer job discrimination, the Black Caribbean group.

UNEMPLOYMENT

Rates of unemployment amongst the Irish population in London are a measure of the demand for their labour and an indication of the proportion experiencing hardship through low income. It is well known that the statistics on unemployment reflect increasingly stringent criteria for eligibility as well as positive presentation, so that they substantially underestimate the true numbers out of work. In addition, married women have consistently been excluded from the totals, both because of inadequate insurance cover and because they can be classed alternatively as full-time domestic workers.

Statistics on unemployment are therefore best used as a comparative measure showing the position of the Irish-born relative to other groups, rather than as absolute indicators (Table 9). They show that in 1991 Irish-born men aged 16+ had markedly higher rates of unemployment (17.1 per cent) than other white men (11.6 per cent). However, the rates were substantially higher again for most other ethnic groups. Perhaps surprisingly the rate for men under 25 appeared to be marginally lower (17.9 per cent) than in the non-Irish white population (18.5 per cent). But the under-enumeration in this age group is a very important factor here. It is possible that a high proportion of the missing 15–20 per cent of the young male Irish-born age group was unemployed and thus homeless. On the other hand, it may be a measure of the demand for migrant labour to fill low-paid service jobs, which this age group of Irish men is now entering (Figure 8).

TABLE 9: *Unemployment in London by Ethnic/birthplace Group, 1991*

	% Economically active population 16+		% Exonomically active population 16–24	
	Women	Men	Women	Men
Irish-born	8.1	17.1	9.6	17.9
White non-Irish	7.5	11.6	12.1	18.5
Indian	11.7	12.0	16.8	20.3
Black Caribbean	13.9	24.2	24.4	38.6
Black African	26.9	32.0	38.9	46.0
Pakistani	22.9	24.2	29.6	31.2
Bangledeshi	35.2	36.0	38.6	26.0
Black other	19.9	28.3	26.8	37.9
Other ethnic	13.5	17.9	21.6	30.2

Source: 1991 Census, Local Base Statistics.

The highest rates of unemployment amongst men under 25 were in boroughs with long-established Irish communities where fewer new migrants had settled (see Figures 4 and 6). These included Hackney (37.0 per cent), Camden (32.2 per cent) and Southwark (28.9 per cent). Each of these boroughs had below the average of 9.0 per cent Irish-born males under 25. Unemployment was lowest in the outer boroughs, some of which had attracted large numbers of new arrivals. In Hounslow and Harrow, for example, young men formed large proportions of the total male Irish-born population, 13.1 per cent and 12.6 per cent respectively, and unemployment rates were well below average (7.4 per cent and 8.1 per cent). These migrants had presumably sought out jobs in new locations, rather than relying on traditional employers and forms of employment in the established areas.

Amongst women, however, the picture was different. Irish-born women had lower unemployment rates (8.1 per cent), in common with all women, but these were similar to those of the remaining white population (7.5 per cent). All other groups had higher rates. It appears, therefore, that Irish-born women found less difficulty in getting work, probably because of the wide availability of low-paid casual work in the personal services sector. Many had also been recruited in Ireland as nurses and were therefore meeting a specific shortage.[45]

HOUSING EXPERIENCE OF THE IRISH IN LONDON

It is difficult to construct an adequate picture of Irish people's housing experiences because of lack of data. Absence from ethnic monitoring categories in many cases, and recent inclusion in a few, means that the Irish are usually subsumed into the very large 'white' category. One result is to reduce the gap of advantage between the British-born white population and the recognised 'ethnic minorities'. Although the Census appears to make provision for an Irish category, its use of 'Irish-headed households' for housing statistics excludes the large number of Irish-born women living with non-Irish-born partners. The figures both understate the true size of the Irish community, though they do include part of the second generation, and omit the specific circumstances of many Irish women.

Census figures for Irish-headed households show a picture of disadvantage relative to the rest of the white population. In some respects, these Irish households occupy an intermediate position between the white majority population and the recognised 'ethnic minorities' (Table 10).

Tenure is often taken to be an indication of access to housing. The Irish have low rates of owner-occupation relative to the rest of the white population (44.0 per cent compared with 59.2 per cent). Conversely their presence in Local Authority rented housing is higher (28.9 per cent compared with 21.9 per cent), and they have moved into the Housing Association rented sector to a greater extent than the rest of the white population. A particularly distinctive feature of Irish housing patterns is the concentration in the private rented sector, which is shared only with other migrant groups. This sector has declined sharply since 1981, but remains an extremely important source of housing for single and newly-arrived Irish people. It is also the sector where poorest quality housing is found.[46]

TABLE 10: *Housing in London by Birthplace/ethnic Group of Head of Household, 1991, %*

	Irish-born	White non-Irish	Indian	Black Caribbean	Black African	Pakistani	Bangladeshi	Black other	Other ethnic
Tenure									
Owner-occupied	44.0	59.2	78.8	44.2	24.1	67.0	26.3	33.4	50.8
Rented: private	16.8	12.1	7.3	5.4	16.5	11.2	6.0	11.6	21.8
Rented: Housing Assoc.	8.0	5.1	2.6	10.5	11.7	3.5	8.3	13.6	5.9
Rented: Local Authority	28.98	21.9	9.7	39.0	46.1	16.9	57.6	40.0	19.1
Quality									
Overcrowded[1]	1.6	0.8	3.2	1.8	6.9	6.1	23.9	3.0	4.0
Lack amenities[2]	3.6	2.3	1.4	1.6	5.3	2.9	2.2	2.9	3.9
No central heating	22.0	19.8	7.6	14.8	14.8	13.5	12.1	17.9	12.8
Not self-contained	5.2	2.4	1.5	2.5	6.8	3.0	1.5	4.2	4.9

[1] 1.5+ persons per room
[2] Lack or share bath/shower and/or inside WC

Source: 1991 Census, Local Base Statistics.

Census measures of housing quality, although recognised to be inadequate indicators, also place Irish-headed households at a distinct disadvantage relative to the rest of the white population. Lack of self-contained accommodation is second only to the Black African population, and the proportion of households without central heating is highest for any group.

Because the Census is based on household addresses, no record of homelessness is made. Estimates must be made from applicants to providers of temporary accommodation. These show that disproportionate numbers of Irish-born people are involved.[47] Many newly-arrived Irish migrants find it difficult to find any affordable accommodation.[48] However a great deal of homelessness is disguised by temporary stays with friends and relatives. This is particularly true for women who are less likely to use hostels or to sleep rough.[49]

Irish travellers face the problem of inadequate site provision, though few boroughs keep records of the demand for, or use of, facilities for which they have responsibility.[50]

IRISHNESS IN LONDON: CULTURAL IDENTITY AND RACISM

Experiences of being Irish in London have undergone profound changes in the post-war period. In the 1950s and 1960s signs saying 'No Irish, no coloureds' were common, sometimes accompanied by 'No dogs'. The signs faded after the 1960s, though those announcing 'No travellers' remain. During the succeeding twenty years, the Irish have become detached from other racialised minorities as skin colour has taken on a particular salience.[51] Miles argues that the need to preserve a 'myth of homogeneity' in Britain has necessitated overt denial of difference to the Irish, even though they are implicitly inferiorised in a myriad of ways.[52]

This change has paralleled the period of the Troubles in Northern Ireland which have been brought home to Britain, and especially London, by IRA bombing campaigns. During the early years of the renewed conflict, many Irish people in London 'kept their heads down' and silenced themselves as a protection from hostility and blame.[53] However, during the 1980s a number of factors led to greater willingness to claim an Irish identity. This coincided with the upturn of 'new wave' emigration, so that the young migrants of the 1980s entered a different situation from that of their predecessors.

RECOGNITION OF IRISH IDENTITIES

An important turning point was the Hunger Strikes of 1981, which politicised many Irish people who had previously distanced themselves from the conflict.[54] One direct outcome was the formation in 1981 of the Irish in Britain Representation Group (IBRG) which provided a voice for political responses.[55] Another contingent factor specific to London was the election in the same year of a left-wing Greater London Council (GLC) with an explicitly radical anti-racist agenda. In 1982, the Council's Ethnic Minorities Committee set up a Steering Group to plan a consultation with the Irish community in London. The resulting conference, in May 1983, included representatives of over 80 of London's Irish organisations who submitted position papers on educational, cultural, political and welfare issues.[56] The 'Policy Report on the Irish Community' published a specific agenda for changes in all these areas. Particularly significant was the recommendation

> that the Committee recognise the Irish as an Ethnic Minority Group and adopt the following definition of Irish for such purposes: persons who come from, or whose forbears originate in, Ireland and who consider themselves Irish.[57]

These have become widely recognised definitions of Irish identity, with the inclusive criteria of birthplace, ancestry and personal choice. By 1995, sixteen of the thirty-three London boroughs included the Irish in their ethnic monitoring procedures, by far the largest section of all local authorities in

Britain. Yet half of all London boroughs still resist this inclusion and, outside London, recognition is extremely rare.[58]

Recognition by the GLC gave practical, financial and moral support to Irish welfare agencies which multiplied during the 1980s to meet specific needs. These included the London Irish Women's Centre, the Action Group for Irish Youth, CARA and Innisfree Housing Associations and an umbrella group, the Federation of Irish Societies. Individual boroughs established Irish centres, as in the case of Camden, and reports focussed on Irish provision at borough level, including Haringey, Ealing and Lambeth. In some cases welfare agencies for specific groups of Irish people were established at borough level including Brent Irish Mental Health Group and Lewisham Pensioners Club. A few boroughs also funded specific posts, at least for a while, including Haringey and Southwark.

Cultural activities also blossomed. Neighbourhood celebrations, which included music and dancing displays, are held annually at Roundwood Park in Brent[59] and the Fleadh in Finsbury Park.[60] Many second- and even third-generation children attend Irish dancing classes and enter competitions.

> Virtually every weekend, there's a feis somewhere in London. . . A schedule of
> feis at dancing school, national and international levels ensures that generations
> of Irish girls remain Irish about one thing – their taste for reels and jigs.[61]

Drawing attention to connections between culture and politics, the London Strategic Policy Group, a residual body from the disbanded GLC, mounted a photo-text exhibition 'Hearts and Minds Anam Agus Intinn'.[62] Information about Irish cultural life in London was displayed at a wide variety of public venues.

In London during the 1980s, therefore, a strongly Irish culture was being created in parts of London, mainly north and west of the centre. Hickman describes the clear sense of an Irish identity transmitted to second-generation Catholic schoolchildren.[63] The majority related this to family life and to being 'brought up Irish'. All the children in her London sample had visited Ireland and 69 per cent took part in Irish activities such as music and dancing lessons. This contrasted with a sample of Catholic schoolchildren in Liverpool with more distant Irish ancestry, who had never been to Ireland and only 30 per cent of whom participated in any Irish activities. She found that the London sample lived 'in a strong self-expressive Irish community' which extended across class boundaries and gave children a positive image of the Irish as a group.

ANTI-IRISH RACISM

Accompanying this higher profile and more confident assertion of Irish identity were continuing and revitalised forms of anti-Irish racism. New arrivals were sometimes sheltered from such experiences by their relative enclosure within the Irish community or the time needed to become aware of the pervasiveness and subtlety of anti-Irish racism. Many Irish people report that racism jars more the longer they stay in Britain and recognise its taken-for-granted pervasiveness.[64]

Anti-Irish racism is particularly strong in London, which represents the heartland, or 'epicentre' of Britishness.[65] The London accent was adopted as Standard English in the Middle Ages,[66] and since accent is the prime identifier of Irish people to the British, their difference is more starkly underlined in London than in north-west England or Yorkshire for example.[67] Hickman contrasts the experiences of Catholic schoolchildren in Liverpool who felt comfortable with a 'Scouse' identity.[68] The great majority (88 per cent) believed the Irish 'have mixed in well' in Liverpool, compared with only 58 per cent of the London sample.

Institutional racism is encountered when Irish people make contact with state agencies. For young migrants, this often occurs when they make benefit claims which are then subject to extra scrutiny, with the assumption that they are 'scroungers'.[69] According to a recent report

> Irish claimants' experience of the social security system is one of discriminatory and unfair treatment and racist and hostile attitudes particularly when the initial application for benefit is made or when applying for a national insurance number.[70]

The strongest and most widespread forms of racism are encountered by working-class Irish people, whom the British stereotype most virulently. The 'Paddy' caricature of stupidity, easy recourse to violence, innate predisposition to alcohol abuse and blind adherence to religious dogma is directed equally against women and men. Women may be less protected than men by Irish workplaces, pubs and clubs. Their interactions with non-Irish white society as consumers on behalf of families of goods, education, health and social services provide many opportunities for their voices to be heard and receive negative reactions. However, living in predominantly Irish areas of London cushions Irish people from racist abuse experienced in parts of Britain with smaller and more scattered Irish-born totals.

Anti-Irish racism overrides class boundaries, though middle-class people usually experience it less openly. Thus, the highly qualified section of the 'new wave' of emigrants from Ireland also encounter deeply entrenched anti-Irish attitudes. In her study of young middle-class Irish migrants in London, Kells reported that

> through direct experience of undermining incidents, or fear of what might be said, my informants experienced prejudice because of their ethnicity. They were not keen to emphasise this in most cases, however.[71]

In a survey biased towards young people in higher socio-economic groups, Randall found that half had experienced anti-Irish hostility, prejudice or racism in London, ranging from abusive 'jokes' to harassment and violence.[72] A survey of Irish nurses, again a mainly middle-class group working in a socially-approved profession, also found that more than a third reported some degree of hostility towards them as Irish people.[73]

Significantly fewer middle-class second-generation children interviewed by Hickman in London saw anti-Irish jokes as problematic, or reported having seen or heard anything about the Irish in Britain they objected to.[74] But to be excluded from acceptance within one's own class is unexpected and hurtful. Rachel Harbron, who came from a professional Protestant family in Dublin, described this:

> It's a feeling I have, especially among upper middle-class English people, that they don't regard you in the same light as themselves. We are sort of second-class citizens, which you feel strongly. They might make jokes ragging your accent or whatever but the thought is still there, that in a general way they regard themselves as better.

The experience of Protestants from Northern Ireland is particularly unsettling. Kells explains that Protestants who identify themselves as British in Northern Ireland find that in London

> the goal posts seem to have moved; their initial sense of separation from Northern Irish Catholics is challenged by people who see the two as essentially the same and as distinct from their own nationality, which is English.[76]

Moreover, middle-class Catholics and Protestants also mix together more easily in London. Over time, therefore, migrants experience a complex repositioning both inside and outside the Irish community.

Conclusion

Captured as a snapshot in the 1990s, London's Irish community has a number of distinct faces. It is by no means an undifferentiated group, despite the homogenising tendencies of British attitudes. Yet there are clear generational characteristics which are shared by large numbers of Irish people.

The migrants of the 1940s and 1950s, whose sociology was meticulously documented by Jackson in his classic work of 1963, constitute a highly visible section of the community. Women in this generation overwhelmingly entered domestic work at some period in their lives. Many were initially recruited into this area, and mothers often took up part-time caring or domestic jobs when their children were older. The Catholic Church has been a central feature of their lives. Irish men typically entered skilled trades, often in construction, working up to become foremen. Many have chosen to socialise in Irish clubs, which continue to celebrate the culture of Ireland of the 1950s. The centrality of these activities is recorded each week in reports by the newspaper of the Irish community, *The Irish Post*.

'New wave' migrants of the 1980s come from a very much changed Ireland, also experiencing high levels of unemployment but also fuller integration into the European world. Keohane describes the post-modern experiences of these young migrants, and their ambivalence about life in London:

> Three years ago I was living in London, the zillionth young Paddy to find himself at the end of a shovel on a site in the city, or behind a bar in Kilburn. Life was exciting, precarious and confusing: Shovelling muck and sharing laughs with Tamils, Malays and Geordies; boozing, getting wasted and talking about home with some lads from Cork, making just enough to get by and pay the rent with nine others on a house in South London. Some days we loved it: young internationalists with a future, making England our own. Other days we hated and despised it: peasant colonial subjects with five hundred year old axes to grind, slaving for the oppressor.[77]

He shows how the music of the Pogues captures 'fragments of the historical and contemporary experiences' of the emigrant Irish by creating pastiches which try to make sense of the fragmentation of different worlds – Ireland and Britain, the past and the present. Continuity is an integral part of 'new wave' experience, but the images are reworked to make sense of comtemporary realities.

ACKNOWLEDGEMENTS

This research was partly funded by a research grant from the Economic and Social Research Council.

NOTES AND REFERENCES

1   B. Walter, *Gender and Recent Irish Migration to Britain* (Geographical Society of Ireland Special Publications, 6, Dublin, 1991), pp. 11–20.
2   S. Pink, 'From Belfast to London: a Case Study of Identity and Ethnicity Amongst Young Migrants from Northern Ireland' (MA dissertation, University of Manchester, 1990); M. Kells, *Ethnic Identity Amongst Young Irish Middle Class Migrants in London,* Irish Studies Centre Occasional Paper Series 6 (University of North London Press, 1995).
3   Kells, ibid.
4   J. Jackson, *The Irish in London: Aspects of Urban Change,* Centre for Urban Studies (London, MacGibbon and Kee, 1964).
5   F. Wilson, 'The Irish in Great Britain in the First Half of the Nineteenth Century' (MA dissertation, University of Manchester, 1946).
6   L. Lees, *Exiles of Erin: Irish Migrants in Victorian London* (Manchester University Press, 1979).
7   OPCS 1993.
8   OPCS 1983.
9   R. Kennedy, *The Irish: Emigration, Marriage and Fertility* (Berkely and Los Anges, University of California Press, 1973); B. Walter, *Irish Women in London: The Ealing Dimension* (London Borough of Ealing, 1989).
10   Ibid.
11   Population Statistics Division OPCS, 'How Complete was the 1991 Census?' *Population Trends,* 71, 1993, pp. 22–5.

12 R. Hall and J. Hall, 'Missing in the 1991 Census: a Million Persons – and £ Millions in Grants?', *Area*, vol. 27, no. 1, 1995, pp. 53–61.

13 OPCS 1993.

14 M. Storkey, *London's Ethnic Minorities: One City, Many Communities. An Analysis of 1991 Census Results* (London Research Centre, 1994).

15 T. Connor, *Irish Youth in London* (London Irish Centre, 1985); G. Randall, *Over Here: Young Migrants in London: Education, Training, Employment, Housing, Health, Anti-Irish Racism* (London, Action Group for Irish Youth, no date).

16 OPCS 1983.

17 OPCS 1983, 1993.

17 D. Garvey, 'The History of Migration Flows in the Republic of Ireland,' *Population Trends*, 39, 1985, pp. 22–30.

18 OPCS 1983, 1983.

19 J. Hall, *Metropolis Now: London and its Region* (Cambridge University Press, 1990); M. Coombes and M. Charlton, 'Flows to and from London: a Decade of Change?' in J. Stillwell, P. Rees and P. Broden (eds.), *Migration Processes and Patterns*, vol. 2 *Population Redistribution in the United Kingdom* (London, Belhaven Press), pp. 81–99.

20 A. O'Grady, *Irish Migration to London in the 1940s and 50s* Irish in Britain Research Forum, Occasional Papers Series 3, 1988.

21 J. Beale, *Women in Ireland: Voices of Change* (London, Macmillan, 1986).

22 P. Shweitzer (ed.), *Across the Irish Sea*, Age Exchange Theatre Trust, 1989.

23 A. Norman, 'Down and Out in Britain', *Community Care*, 12 November 1987, pp. 20–1.

24 Cara Irish Housing Association, *Limited Opportunies: Economic Disadvantage and Access to Housing for Single Irish Women* (London, Cara, 1995).

25 Cara Irish Housing Association, *Access to Housing for Irish Single People: Housing Association and Local Authority Policies and Practice*, Cara, n.d.).

26 Norman, 'Down and Out in Britain'.

27 Irish Liaison Group, *The Social Situation of Irish Elderly in Haringey* (London, Haringey Council, 1987).

28 T. O'Farrell, *The Irish Elderly in London* (London, Camden Irish Elders Support Network, 1993).

29 M. Pearson, M. Madden and L. Greenslade, *Generations of an Invisible Minority*, Institute of Irish Studies Occasional Paper 2 (Liverpool, 1991).

30 B. Walter, *Irish Women in London* (London Strategic Policy Unit, 1988).

31 M. Hickman, 'A Study of the Incorporation of the Irish in Britain with Special Reference to Catholic State Education: Involving a Comparison of the Attitudes of Pupils and Teachers in Selected Secondary Schools in London and Liverpool' (Ph.D. dissertation, University of London, 1990).

32 P. Ullah, 'Second-generation Irish youth: Identity and Ethnicity', *New Community* xii, 1985, pp. 310–20.

33 N. Danaher, 'Irish Studies: a Historical Survey Across the Irish Diaspora' in P. O'Sullivan (ed.), *The Irish in the New Communities*, vol. 2, *The Irish World Wide: History, Heritage, Identity* (Leicester University Press, 1992), pp. 226–56.

34 National Economic and Social Council, *The Economic and Social Implications of Emigration* (Dublin, 1991); T. Connor, *The London Irish* (London Strategic Policy Unit, 1987).

35 F. Kirwan and A. Nairn, 'Migrant Employment and the Recession – The Case of the Irish in Britain', *International Migration Review*, 17, 1983, pp. 672–81; P. Compton, 'Migration Trends for Northern Ireland: Links with Great Britain', in J. Stillwell, P. Rees and P. Boden (eds.), *Migration Processes and Patterns* vol. 2 *Population Redistribution in the United Kingdom* (London, Belhaven Press, 1992) pp. 81–99.

36   E. Hazelkorn, '"We Can't All Live on a Small Island": The Political Economy of Irish Migration' in P. O'Sullivan (ed.), *The Irish in the New Communities* vol. 2, *The Irish World Wide: History, Heritage, Identity* (Leicester University Press, 1992) pp. 180–200.

37   B. Walter, *Irish Women in London*, op. cit.

38   Price Waterhouse, *Nurse Retention and Recruitment: Report on the Factors Affecting the Retention and Recruitment of Nurses, Midwives and Health Visitors in the National Health Service*, 1988).

39   E. Hazelkorn, *Irish Immigrants Today*, Irish Studies Centre Occasional Papers Series 1 (University of North London Press, 1990).

40   T. Fielding, 'Migration and the Metropolis: Recent Research on the Causes of Migration to Southeast England', *Progress in Human Geography* 17, 1993, pp. 195–212.

41   P. Breathnach and J. Jackson, 'Ireland, Emigration and the New International Division of Labour', Geographical Society of Ireland Special Publications 6, 1991, pp. 1–10; J. MacLaughlin, *Ireland: The Emigrant Nursery and the World Economy* (Undercurrents, Cork University Press, 1994).

42   M. Hornsby Smith and A. Dale, 'The Assimilation of Irish Immigrants in England', *The British Journal of Sociology* xxxix, 1988, pp. 519–43.

43   T. Fielding and S. Halford, 'Geographies of Opportunity: a Regional Analysis of Gender-Specific Social and Spatial Mobilities in England and Wales 1971–81', *Environment and Planning* 25, 1993, pp. 1421–40.

44   No Author. 'New Irish Bury "Paddy Myth"', *Guardian*, 24 May 1995.

45   Walter, *Irish Women in London*, op. cit.

46   Storkey, op. cit.

47   Cara Irish Housing Association, *Irish Homelessness – the Hidden Dimension: a Strategy for Change* (Cara, 1988).

48   Randall, op. cit.; B. O'Mahoney, *A Capital Offence: The Plight of the Young Single Homeless in London* (London, Routledge/Barnardo's, 1988).

49   Walter, *Irish Women in London*.

50   London Strategic Policy Unit, *Travellers and Welfare Benefits*, 1987.

51   M. Hickman and B. Walter, 'Deconstructing Whiteness: Irish Women in Britain', *Feminist Review* 49, 1995, pp. 14–21.

52   R. Miles, Racism After 'Race Relations' (London, Routledge, 1993).

53   Connor, *The London Irish*.

54   London Strategic Policy Unit 1987.

55   Haringey IBRG, *Annual Report 1986–7* (London, 1987); B. McConville, 'The London Irish', *New Society*, 16, December 1982, pp. 453–4.

56   Ethnic Minorities Unit, Greater London Council, *Report on the Prevention of Terrorism Act and Report on Consultation with the Irish Community* (GLC, 1984).

57   Ethnic Minorities Unit, Greater London Council, *Policy Report on the Irish Community* (GLC, 1984).

58   No author. 'Recognition of Irish Identity', The *Irish Post*, 3 June 1995, p. 2.

59   No author. 'The London Irish', *Independent Magazine*, 11 August 1990, pp. 22–8.

60   No author. 'So Fleadh, So Good', *Guardian* Arts, 12 June 1995, pp. 8–9.

61   No author. 'Jig', *Weekend Guardian*, 14–5 March 1992, p. 14.

62   London Strategic Policy Unit, *Hearts and Minds*.

63   Hickman, op. cit.

64   M. Lennon M. McAdam and J. O'Brien, *Across the Water: Irish Women's Lives in Britain* (London, Virago, 1988); Kells, op. cit.

65   J. Osmond, *The Divided Kingdom* (London, Constable, 1988).

66 J. Cheshire and J. Milroy, 'Syntactic Variation in Non-standard Dialects: Background Issues', in J. Milroy and L. Milroy (eds.), *Real English: the Grammar of English Dialects in the British Isles* (London, Longman, 1993).

67 B. Walter, 'Irishness, Gender and Place', *Society and Space*, 13, 1995, pp. 35–50.

68 Hickman, op. cit.

69 C. Bennett, *The Housing of the Irish*, Irish Studies Centre Occasional Paper Series 3 (University of North London Press, 1991).

70 Action Group for Irish Youth, report, 1993.

71 Kells, op. cit.

72 Randall, op. cit.

73 Walter, *Irish Women in London*, op. cit.

74 Hickman, op. cit.

75 Lennon, McAdam and O'Brien, op. cit.

76 Kells, op. cit.

77 K. Keohane, 'Unifying the Fragmentary Imaginary of the Young Immigrant: Making a Home in the Post Modern with the Pogues', *Irish Review* 9, 1990, pp. 71–9.

4. Sitting on Your Politics
The Irish Among the British and the Women Among the Irish

Marella Buckley

'I put aside all my political ideas and Irishness years ago. It gets you nowhere in this country. I just sit on it.'[1]

This chapter examines the lives of the Irish in Britain, with particular reference to the role of Irish women in generating radical discourses about their position in British and in Irish society. Using converging critiques of race, class and gender it locates the Irish woman and her community in contemporary Britain. It argues that theorising about 'Irishness' in Britain involves theorising about 'Britishness', and suggests that the emancipation of Irish femininity is inseparable from that of Irish men. It further argues that any understanding of Irish life abroad can only emerge from a grasp of the dynamics of 'Irishness' at home.

Any theoretical framework which seeks to locate the Irish woman in British society will have to be a complex one. This is because the Irish woman here stands at the intersection of many powerful political forces which contest each other across the stage of her body, her labour and her sense of self. Nevertheless, we cannot reach her through many of the theoretical discourses which have traditionally been used to discuss race, ethnicity, gender, class and identity in Britain. Thus, at least until quite recently, the race-relations debate neglected the position of the Irish in Britain. Theories of migration, on the one hand, tend to ignore the specificity of women's history and labour, keeping instead to patriarchal paradigms which fail to register woman's pivotal role in the production and reproduction of ethnicity and of racial and sexual identity. Feminists also have been at fault here. While claiming to unite all women under an anti-patriarchal banner, they notoriously excluded ethnically-defined and working-class women. Critiques of class, on the other hand, have been marked by a dry, macho syndicalism which banishes the politics of desire from the political agenda. The failure to theorise desire, in particular, naively neglects underlying networks constructed around the libido and the taboo. These in turn underlie many of the national, economic and legal structures. They also underpin much academic theorising about race, identity and gender in British society.

94

The theorising which is most relevant to the position of Irish women in Britain is probably that of Third World feminists on national social formations. Here too, however, the Irish have been noticeable for their invisibility, a fact brought home to this writer while reading the work of the African-American feminist, bell hooks. At one point in her essay 'Representing Whiteness', hooks suddenly generalises all 'whiteness' as dominant and colonising. In so doing, she ignores the Irish experience as one of several exceptions to the rule of white coloniser/coloured colonised.[2]

This chapter argues that Irish people, and Irish women in particular, must theorise their own location in political space. Surveying extreme polarisations within gender-roles, the obliteration of personal experience, the taboo on desire, the active construction of collective silences, it shows how all these strategies work together to dissolve and distance discontent, protest and desire within Irish women and Irish communities in Britain. The chapter is divided into five sections. The first looks at the low profile of the Irish in contemporary Britain. The second is a brief discussion of their representations in the media and in popular culture. Section three examines Irish social networks in Britain, paying particular attention to the role of class and gender in their formation. Section four is a brief discussion of the Irish home and family life in Britain. Section five considers the psychological health and dilemmas of the Irish under the headings of inner conflicts and migrations for abortions. The chapter concludes with discussion on the specificity of the Irish female body and suggests ways in which Irishness can generate radical discourses about 'otherness' and sexuality in national and international contexts.

THE IRISH IN BRITAIN: THE LOW PROFILE OF A LARGE BODY

Most commentators agree that the Irish community in Britain has a low profile which belies its numerical strength. This low profile in turn disguises important social class and gender divisions within this community. Divisions of class, colonial politics and sexual politics probably cut even more trenchantly within the immigrant community here than they do among the mainland Irish. Moreover, public debates around these issues are not as vocal here as they are in the Republic. In Britain, indeed, 'Irishness' could seem like an irrelevant single thread weaving through the fabric of lives which are very different in terms of privilege, gender and status.

The very status of Irishness and Irish immigrants also problematises the experience of all classes of Irish people in ways which dominant discourses often overlook. Thus, for example, representations of Irish emigration to Britain as straightforward opportunism have been common in Ireland since the early 1980s. This view presents emigrants as pursuing the capitalist dream. The much-quoted interview with Brian Lenihan covered in *Newsweek* in 1987 bears this out. Lenihan remarked:

I don't look on the type of emigration we have today as being of the same category as the terrible emigration of the last century . . . What we have now is a very
literate emigrant who thinks nothing of coming to the United States and going
back to Ireland and maybe on to Germany and back to Ireland again . . . We
regard them as part of a global generation of Irish people . . . We should be proud
of it. After all, we can't all live on a small island.[3]

Mac Laughlin and others have shown that only small proportions of Irish
emigrants in Britain end up in middle-class professional occupations.[4] The
majority, both male and female, are still in working-class and lower middle-class
jobs. This notion of economic opportunism is further undercut when we
introduce critiques of sexism and racism into debates about recent Irish emigration. These reveal the racial politics which underlie all decolonising ethnicities,
including Irishness in all its social class contexts.

Unlike in the United States, where Irish-Americans constitute a potentially
powerful political lobby of over 40 million voters, the Irish in Britain have no
such high profile. Neither do they have powerful charismatic leaders who exercise
political and financial power on their behalf. Numerically, they occupy similar
proportions in the two countries. However, the political environment within
which Irish lives are lived out in Britain and the United States is quite different.
Overt displays of Irishness around nationalism and ethnicity, commonplace in
the US, are unthinkable and dangerous in Britain. The numerical strength of the
Irish in Britain, together with their ethnically-distinct concept of themselves,
seem to be contradicted by this remarkably low profile. Moreover, the home-
based quality of Irish ethnicity in Britain, fostered also in low-key social clubs,
together with the anonymity afforded by their white skin, is in marked contrast
to the high visibility of the Afro-Caribbean community with its colourful
emphasis on street-life and youth culture. Their low profile has rendered the
racial trajectory of the Irish a relatively safer one, even as they negotiated the fall-
out of the IRA bombing campaign in Britain in recent decades.

REPRESENTATIONS

Outside negative images of Irishness constructed around notions of 'mad
bombers', the Irish community in Britain has very little contact with the British
media. There is no anti-racist organisation which patrols the national media on
their behalf. A blind eye is turned on events like the annual Roundwood Irish
Festival which can draw crowds of 100,000.[5] Although some Irish male
personalities have become minor icons of British television over the years (most
notably Gay Byrne, Eamonn Andrews, Terry Wogan, Bob Geldof and Dr
Anthony Clare), this assimilation tends to 'screen out' any specific Irishness
which could raise political anomalies to the surface of popular consciousness.

One of the most prominent Irish female voices resident in the British press is
that of Mary Kenny, columnist with the *Daily Telegraph*. Kenny articulates a

neo-conservative perspective on many issues, not least on sexual politics, and describes herself as a 'Women's Liberation Revisionist'.[6] The *Guardian* occasionally imports columns from journalists like Fintan O'Toole and Conor Cruise O'Brien. Famous Irish women who have set up permanent or temporary home in Britain, such as Maeve Binchy, Edna O'Brien and Sinéad O'Connor, are on occasion interviewed as individual artists by specialist publications initiated from Ireland. They are rarely consulted by the popular media for comment on issues such as sexual politics, Irish-British relations or immigrant life in Britain.[7]

This means that Irishness appears in British media only sporadically and problematically. Officially, Irishness is something which happens elsewhere and which periodically irrupts into British consciousness at times when Irishness, viewed like a troublesome, quirky child, is seen to demand a response from the weary, perplexed, benign elder of Britishness. These 'irruptions' range across a spectrum from – most violently – Irish paramilitary bombs exploding in England to – more meaninglessly – the quaint debates and referenda around issues like divorce and abortion which have recently featured very highly on the Irish political agenda 'back home'. From authoritarian outrage to a casual voyeurism, these journalistic moments respond to Irishness as if it called from the far, anachronistic reaches of empire and completely ignore the strong Irish presence in Britain. This active 'unseeing' is maintained very thoroughly in more popular media. In Britain, Irishness is simply not represented in advertising, pop-music, television or in computer-iconography. In terms of market forces alone, it seems strange that designers, marketers and advertisers do not 'bait' the large Irish population with images and references which mirror Irishness in a saleable fashion. In countries like France, Holland and Germany, where Irishness is a relatively neutral and even romanticised label, products such as mineral water, dairy foods, clothing, alcohol, glassware, holidays and music are all marketed from a platform of specifically Irish imagery. This promotes a mythopoetic representation of Ireland, figuring 'positive' Irish stereotypes like hospitality, beauty, artistry, naturalness and Celtic mystique. Such 'positive' Irish stereotypes do not figure in popular British media. For anyone familiar with the exigencies of Irish life in England, it is difficult even to imagine them appearing here.

This absence of the Irish face from the national marketplace cannot be simply dismissed as the avoidance of a politically-sensitive issue. The profiteering attentions of market-promoting media do not respect the boundaries around problematised collectives, or at least not without very deep reason. Instead, where profitable, consumer advertising and product marketing increasingly zone in on the ethnic in order to commodify ethnicity as a saleable, 'packagable' product. Images of Black bodies, lesbians and gay men, Native Americans and their traditions, and the people, landscapes and artifacts of the Third World are currently in wide use as ethnic or sexual 'wrapping' for the sale of anything from trinkets to cars.

The ethnic gloss in which many of these objects are packaged can also be a double investment. This is particularly so in the commodification of Black bodies and Black culture. Here certain products, like music, clothes, boots and shoes, sports gear, sound equipment, are marketed directly at young Black males. The images of Blackness which they feature serve in turn as glamourised trademarks which embellish sales among other groups, while all the time fortifying racist representations of Blacks in Britain. This repertoire keeps Blacks marginally visible in public media, but only as commodified bodies which are marketplace symbols signalling sporting, animal, unconscious, entertaining or hypersexual energies. This shows that the advertising industry and sales managers willingly risk alienating non-sympathetic customers in order to corner an expanding market. They also actively stimulate the 'lure and loathing' dynamic latent in all mainstream relations with problematised identities, teasing the desire/repulsion ambivalence in which the dominant norm and the disinherited 'other' hold each other.[8] The fact that popular and commercial media in no way engage this, or any other dynamic, between Irishness and Britishness indicates the degree to which Irishness must remain suppressed within the British political unconscious. It stands out by its absence in a cultural marketplace where other problematised identities like the black, lesbian and HIV+ are now ceaselessly and ambivalently engaged.

Of course, as immigrants, the Irish in Britain have been thoroughly commodified as labour across Britain, and across British history (see Mac Laughlin, chapter five in this volume). However, the point being made here is that British society intensely suppresses the imagery, cultural voice and subjectivity of Irishness in direct proportion to its quiet commodification of Irish labour. This analysis in no way suggests that cultural commodification of Irishness by Britain would be a welcome development. Rather, it simply highlights an utter difference, showing that instead of appearing within the arena of minority 'differences', the Irish in Britain are treated as so 'different' that they fall outside the spectrum of all hegemonic discourses in Britain.

The languages of mainland Irishness are in this decade thawing into catalytic discourses of lamentation, catharsis and reconciliation around diverse, frozen issues like the Famine and the hypocritical stance of the Catholic Church on issues like child sexual abuse, sexual abuse in general and gay and lesbian politics. These voices are energising an emergent culture which is attempting to frame new concepts for areas like divorce, gay legislation and hostilities in Northern Ireland. Around Irish people in England, however, there is a different climate which shows no particular thaw at this time. If Ireland is emerging, Britain would seem to linger still in an intensifying post-imperial crisis and is not yet ready to allow discourse around its own amnesiac numbness about the horrors of its past in Ireland.

However, the Irish Republic suppresses representations of emigrants' lives too. Audio-visual media in Ireland are flooded with fictionalised entertainment from the United States, Britain and Australia. The daily realities of Irish life in these places are never broadcast. The monocultural insularity of mainland Ireland, with its own stringent anti-immigrant policies, is largely ignored. There is a need for inclusion in the school syllabus programmes of information and debate on race relations, colour politics, migration and ethnicity. For at least a decade, host countries like Britain, France and Germany have felt obliged to include these studies in their school subjects. As the immigrants directly concerned, Irish youth needs this even more. Through video links, letter writing, holiday exchanges, electronic-mail, research projects and joint newsletters, Irish schools and colleges can link up to the racial, social and sexual realities of life for students of Irish origin in schools abroad, while Irish church communities and parishes can twin with their counterparts abroad.

We also need regular live connections on Irish television with events in Irish centres abroad, as well as regular columns in newspapers at home on life in the Irish diaspora. Such social and political links with life at home can prevent the ethnicity of the Irish in Britain from closing into a reactionary nostalgia. They can also help them reshape the country to which so many of them say they want to return. Crucially, it can open the channels of liberalising feedback as well as realistically preparing future emigrants. There is a tradition of audiovisual link-up on Irish TV and radio in a 'holiday' context, making contact with emigrants at Christmas and Saint Patrick's Day, but systematically avoiding their daily lives.

The silencing of the Irish woman in Britain is bolstered by her own government's censorship of her emigration. Irish Catholic views of femininity severely censure the mobile, independent, single or adventurous woman. State and Church collude to enshrine within the Irish Constitution the view that by her life 'within the home' woman 'gives to the state a support without which the common good cannot be achieved'. This cult of a femininity, safely gelled into a parochial and domestic context, discounts the experience of generations of Irish women who have sought their fortunes across the globe. Neither can we rely on Irish theorists for objective representations of the emigrant Irish. They frequently display an introjected anti-Irish racism where the derisive colonial discourse still speaks through their thinking. A chapter from a prominent book written in 1990 on the migrant Irish, which was hailed by another important Irish studies publication as 'a major essay', has this to say about the Irish in Britain:

> (They) may get called 'bloody Micks' or 'bog-Irish' (but) in Britain, there never has been a really rude word for the Irish . . . (With) the native cunning, all the petty prejudices and simple virtues of an island people . . ., (a) stream of irresponsible Irish people were constantly appearing before employers, landladies, welfare officers . . . (As) inadequate personalities who came looking for the 'geographical cure', something almost endemic in the Irish emigrant situation . . ., their faults were in themselves.[9]

A look at two recent British press reports about Irishness, one from the left and one from the right, further clarifies social attitudes towards the Irish in Britain. In a rare feature on Irish immigrants, the left-leaning *Guardian* echoed the Irish government's notion that Irish immigrants are assimilated into the British middle-class. In an article entitled 'New Irish Bury Paddy Myth', it was suggested that recent Irish immigrants are predominantly university-educated people who are 'twice as well qualified' as their British peers, integrating into the middle-class lifestyles of British urban centres. It was further suggested that 'wine-bar chic' is now the dominant social tone of the London Irish. This was 'supported' by remarks from one frequenter of the Irish wine-bar scene who said that 'there's very little talk ever about discrimination' nowadays. The article asserted that the phenomenon of contemporary Irish education 'debunks the racist stereotype of a thick Paddy.'[10] Printed within a new, regular section which bore the highly ambivalent title of 'Ethnic Monitoring', the feature was riddled with racist, class-prejudiced assumptions, all glossed over into the supposedly liberal sort of package which race-theorist, bell hooks, derides as 'ethnic cool'. Days later the *Guardian* published a deconstruction of their racist 'anti-racist' article by the present writer, including the reminder that:

> it is wholly congruous that 'there's very little talk ever about discrimination' among the professionals in the wine bars . . . Discrimination arises in response to display of difference. Seamless participation in the international bourgeoisie doesn't provoke it. But the merest mention of the truths of Irish/British history usually does.[11]

The paper closed the debate with a firm reassertion of its own ambivalence about Irishness. It achieved this by inventing its own title for this writer's critical text and publishing it under the title: 'Heard the one about the Irish stereotype?' This firmly relocated debate and theorising about Irishness back to the realm of the joke, while skilfully maintaining editorial ambivalence. On one hand, the 'joke' might be on the *Guardian* for having been exposed as racist within its own anti-racist feature. On the other, the title of the above article takes refuge in the stream of British discourse which characterises all Irish contestation and intervention as trivial, over-sensitive, hysterical and essentially comic.

That debate took place across the supposedly anti-racist press. On the right, however, there is no such ambivalence and the joke of Irishness can be a vehicle for more explicit violences. On learning of a proposed research project into anti-Irish racism in 1994, the *Sun* offered researchers a 'flying start' by printing 41 anti-Irish jokes lambasting the sexuality, accent, and supposed stupidity and irrationality of Irish people.[12] Importantly, the joke was used here to dismantle Irish subjectivity across all classes, targeting the doctor alongside the labourer. The jokes depicted all the pivotal experiences traditional to Irish immigrants, thus dramatising the debasement of Irish people not in a vague, hypothetical dimension but systematically, in their actual encounters with British people, with British locations and with British lifestyles. They ranged over the topics of Irish emigration, homelessness, alcoholism, the breakdown of rural Irish communities, Irish people's linguistic misunderstanding in conversation with the English and their unfamiliarity with British versions of daily landmarks like shops, lift-doors and road signs.[13]

The joke is a very significant hinge in Irish-British relations because it is one of the few locations or moments when reference to Irishness rises to the surface of British discourse. Politically, it matters because it simultaneously expresses and obscures racism, facilitating racist interaction while with the same gesture exculpating it as mere fun. When directly addressed to an Irish person, it can constitute an invitation to social bonding which rests on an oblique, mutual awareness of the uneven power-relations which the Irish person is invited to accept. The loaded dynamic typical of Irish jokes in British discourse cannot be carried over so lightly into joking with, or about, Blacks or Asians, where there is no sharing of white skin to disguise and whitewash the power-relations. As *Feminist Review* remarked about the Irish joke issue of the *Sun*, 'It is hard to think of any other group in Britain against whom such practices could go unchallenged'.[14]

SOCIAL NETWORKS AND THE IRISH IN BRITAIN

Rather than extroverted campaigns of statement, protest and agitation, the Irish community has tended instead to rely on its own informal, discreet network of self-help to resolve the problem of Irishness in contemporary Britain. Across the meeting-grounds of Church, pub and social-club, this network operates through clergy, Irish job recruiters, Irish Centre workers, housewives and volunteers. It organises the distribution of employment, the maintenance of Irish culture, language and arts, social and leisure activities as well as orchestrating the reception of fresh immigrants, helping to provide them with housing, employment, social welfare, orientation and support. This networking is, of course, a feature of Irish immigrant communities everywhere, but the difference in Britain is the fact that it may not be periodically celebrated before the host community as it often is elsewhere.

One report has recently argued that the reason for the prevalence of informal networks is 'the reluctance of Irish people to access statutory and (formal) voluntary services'.[15] This 1994 survey carried out by the Charities Evaluation Services attributed this to the:

> stigma attached to relying on the welfare system and 'anti-Irish racism' in services which fail 'to provide a culturally sensitive service'. Furthermore, it has been established that Irish women, in particular, fail to assert themselves in demanding their rights of such agencies. The 1993 London Irish Women's Centre Report

revealed that 'demands upon . . . welfare agencies in terms of gender breakdown on average show a 66% men to 33% women ratio' and in housing services, 'a startling average of 80% men to 20% women'.[16]

Irish women's contribution to unofficial services in their community is the sort of informal, unpaid social work to which patriarchy has traditionally confined women. This is also something at which they have come to excel. The London Irish Women's Centre, for example, cites as an illustration of this the 'Care in the Community' policy currently being instituted to minimise psychiatric hospitalisations under the National Health Service. It is clear that the relegation of patients to the 'community' is a euphemism for their transfer to the unpaid nursing and caring performed by women in the home and neighbourhood.[17] Their activities in these spheres leave Irish women's contribution to the maintenance of their community difficult to quantify by traditional methods.

On top of their community-centered activities, it still seems to be the norm for Irish women to shoulder most of the burden of child-rearing. For an immigrant woman, family management extends from the battle for accommodation to the negotiation of the ever-tightening National Health and social-welfare systems and on to the fielding of racist or harassing treatment of her children in Britain's huge, unfamiliar, multi-cultural schools. One might expect Irish women's single-handed parenting to be changing in the 1990s, but the pattern may actually be intensifying as the social climate allows more and more women to leave unhappy relationships, or to choose to have children alone. In 1993, 49 per cent of the Irish mothers using social services in the London area were single parents.[18] Now that divorce is instituted in the Republic of Ireland, there may well be a sharp rise in single-parent families in the Irish community in Britain.

The informal, but crucial, community-within-a-community has done its best to serve vulnerable groups like the elderly, children, the homeless, the unemployed and the newly-immigrant. However, it cannot do enough. Certain social problems such as mental illness, housing shortage, domestic violence and HIV status, all pressing problems for the general population but intensified for immigrants, need the attention of professional agencies. Such agencies have not traditionally existed for the Irish, particularly as the latter are still not recognised as a separate ethnic category. The 1994 report, 'The Service Needs of the Irish Community in Britain', declares that:

> Local authorities need to evaluate the information collected in consultation with Irish community organisations and develop an action plan to tackle anti-Irish racism . . . (They must) ensure the needs of Irish people are reflected in the community care plan and adequate resources allocated to meet the needs of Irish service users, especially older people, people with a disability, people with a mental health problem, drug users, alcohol users and Irish people affected by HIV/AIDS . . .'[19]

A major problem with the informal community networking of the Irish is that it can become a self-censoring regime which rejects certain individuals and adopts working practices according to the moral norms it is defending as traditionally Irish. This happens in other immigrant communities also. Thus, Pakistani sociologist Muhammmad Anwar identifies this conservative process as 'incapsulation' which also operates in the Pakistani community.[20] This type of conservatism can hit Irish women particularly badly as lesbianism, reproductive rights, abortion, HIV status, atheism, domestic violence, alcoholism and incest are treated as taboo topics in some or all combinations of Church, Irish social-club and Irish community media. The latter often refuse to help women with these issues. Even if they did, the need for confidentiality might well keep many women away from such networks.

Because the support of women in these neglected areas is a major function of the London Irish Women's Centre and its affiliated Irish Women's Groups around the country, the Centre 'has often evoked hostility from the general Irish community'.[21] It welcomes the tide of women who find themselves in flight from mainland Ireland, on one hand, while censored by the Irish community in Britain, on the other. The Centre organises the annual Irish Women's Conference and attempts, through publicity and cultural activities, to redress the elision of Irish culture and the Irish presence in Britain. However, it must constantly 'make sure we are not discriminated against in the Irish media as well as the mainstream British media'.[22]

THE IRISH AT WORK IN BRITAIN

SOCIAL CLASS

According to a dominant discourse in Ireland, the 'New Irish' abroad are rightful participants in an international labour market where emigration is normalised by market centralisation, by European Union, by the homogenising of global-village transport and communications networks and by non-employment in peripheralised areas.[23] Their commuting between Ireland and the professional labour markets of Europe, the United States and Australia is represented as a dance of success, a story of financial and educational prowess and an exercise of a new liberty in terms of travel, earning-power and lifestyle. Perhaps this view even includes a half-conscious revenge of the colonised as more and more young Irish people, assimilated into the professional class by state-funded university degrees, successfully plunder the job markets abroad. However, this 'New Pride' leaves many stones unturned. As Mac Laughlin argues:

> given the structure and qualifications of recent emigrants, it is difficult to account for the popular view of 'new wave' emigration as an upwardly mobile activity, chiefly attracting high achievers.[24]

In his 1989 survey of 6,000 families in the south and west of Ireland, he found that among their 1,520 emigrants to Britain, 29 per cent had third-level qualifications, 48 per cent were secondary school students with a Leaving Certificate qualification and 23 per cent had only an Intermediate or Group Certificate qualification. Furthermore, 40 per cent of all emigrants in this survey were still teenagers when they emigrated.[25]

Irish immigrant labour patterns also show that gender-stereotyping has clearly survived decades of feminist agitation and still dictates labour options today. Thus, Hazelkorn asserts that despite:

> the recent re-emergence of women into professional and managerial occupations, post-1994 female (Irish) immigrants are most heavily represented in the 'caring' professions of education, health and the welfare (16%), clerical (26%) and catering (16%) . . . Together these areas represent two-thirds of (Irish) female employment. . . While there is a greater range of employment options for (Irish) male immigrants, they are concentrated in construction (37%), metal processing (16%) and administration (13%), representing two-thirds of all Irish male employment.[26]

Her pithy conclusion is worth quoting, reflecting as it does a further complication of the Irish experience of class in Britain, namely the fundamental lack of solidarity which capitalism fosters everywhere between the middle and working classes it creates.

> Irish immigration into the UK reflects the impact of class inequalities of opportunity in line with characteristics of the indigenous society, (that is) the class structure of contemporary capitalism. It is this factor in addition to gender-stereotyping that accounts primarily for the performance of Irish immigrants in the London/UK labour market.[27]

The ties of ethnicity tend to loosen or be repressed out of embarrassment in the encounter between a homeless Irish person, or an Irish Traveller begging their way along a London Underground carriage, and the Irish financier clutching a commuter-briefcase in the seat by the window. Ireland will have to become a very much more radical society before we can assert that our sense of ethnic or cultural belonging overrides our capitalist class-interests.

Although a small proportion of Irish immigrants disperse into the British professions and others flee what they see as the Irish community's 'ghettoised' mentality, the majority continue to rely on the community's informal networks to provide them with employment contacts. In fact, this networking is often cited as an explanation for the maintenance of Irish employment within fixed patterns – in domestic service and factories for women and on the railways, docks and building-sites for men.

IRISHNESS AND GENDER ISSUES IN BRITAIN TODAY

The gender-stereotyping evident within Irish immigrant labour merits closer study. A new corpus of oral histories and documentaries is beginning to sketch out the anthropology of the Irish male labourer in Britain. These examine how the myths of the 'Paddy' have recuperated a compensatory empowerment through excellence at risky, demanding labour often eschewed by the 'natives'. Here, dislocation and discrimination are partly subverted within densely-bonded, improvised, homosocial environments. Ryan goes so far as to describe a quasi-military ethos where urban lorries transport nomadic squadrons of Irish men, loyal to their different 'captains', from site to site. This does seem to be borne out by building-site ballads such as 'McAlpine's Fusiliers' and 'Murphy's Volunteers'.[28] Irish men labour to erect the infrastructures of British cities, moving on to vacate them for the middle-class professionals – the doctors, engineers, lawyers, lecturers and business-people, some of them Irish themselves – who will use them. This pattern constitutes:

> an enduring tradition in which young men's working conditions today reproduce the pattern of their grandfathers' lives.[29]

The construction of the identity of the 'Paddy' partly mirrors the story of the Kahnawake Mohawk males who specialise in the dangerous high-steel industry in the US.[30] The Mohawks improvise within urban dislocation a similar, almost ritualistic labour pattern which maintains a positive image for them as men.[31]

The fact that Irish men in Britain have traditionally improvised the compensatory public image of a highly visible urban physicality highlights several important points about hierarchies of representation and disempowerment in contemporary Britain. Their position parallels that of the Black man in Britain and the US who is renowned for his maintenance and projection of some degree of personal power through investment in his bodily self-image. In her essay, 'Representations – Feminism and Black Masculinity', bell hooks explains this phenomenon thus:

> The concern is with the black male image, who will control it, who will represent it. A central aspect of black male aesthetics has always been the construction of an image, particularly the dissembling image.[32]

We urgently need an Irish Men's Movement which will unleash the truth of the Irish man's experience in Britain, however tormented, in the manifold dilemmas of his decolonising, erotic, emigrant, labouring, military and religious worlds. Only when the real discourse of Irish male experience is released will our men cease to punitively project their repressed difficulties onto women.

Although the disinherited male's concerns over his own image are essentially a strategy to assert a threatened virility, the concomitant relegation to the status of a visual body rings strangely of feminine experience. This 'feminisation' of ethnic men needs to be understood before their female counterparts can be drawn out of invisibility and located in political space. A growing body of theory is currently emerging around such processes, both in terms of 'the feminisation of Ireland by masculine, controlling England', and of the black male by the dominant white culture.[33] These analyses are separate rather than comparative developments.

The gendering inherent in national subordination has long been implicit in the sort of metaphors which describe colonisation as the 'rape' of a nation and the 'castration' of its autonomy. But if imperialist racism 'feminises' men, where does it leave women? I suggest that the dynamic is best understood as a three-tiered hierarchy which descends from full subjectivity down to secondary status as a commodified body-image and on down to the non-status of invisibility and non-representation. Clearly, the second tier is traditionally occupied by women as sexual objects with their male counterparts above them as whole subjects. However, where the entire collective is subordinated by a dominant 'Other' as blacks are by whites or as the Irish are in England, the disempowered male is nudged into second position. He becomes 'staged' as a flimsier object in relation to the primary, dominant male subject. When the projection of physical visibility which is the prerogative of secondary status is the only power left to access, males will occupy it. The females of the disempowered collective then slide from objectified status to complete invisibility below males. This is precisely where Black, Asian and Irish women are struggling from inside British social hierarchies and pyramids of power today. The masculine imagery of 'Paddy' 'hides the existence of Irish women in Britain'.[34]

Here we can rejoin the traditional voices of comment upon the Irish woman in Britain. All are agreed upon her invisibility, although few politically examine it. Commentators remark that she failed to gain a public profile to parallel her 'Paddy' brothers, unlike in the US where a 'Bridget' is synonymous in the public mind with a female domestic worker. Ryan attributes this to the fact that 'Irish girls [*sic*] never had quite the same working-class image in Britain as their men-folk'.[35] For one thing, chambermaids, domestic cleaners and caterers everywhere are expected to remain invisible to the users for whom they daily service buildings. Workers in the construction industry and in road-building, on the other hand, are a highly visible, nomadic presence on the urban landscape of contemporary Britain.

The invisibility of Irish women in modern Britain must be understood within its patriarchal capitalist context before specificity of the Irish experience can be discussed. The fantasy that women do not work is a fundamental construct of capitalism. Images of women as workers are rigorously censored by popular iconography. These are substituted with constructs of women as simply existing and consuming, limiting themselves to acts of sexualised labour only, ranging from the explicitly sexual to working at looking good. To fully control both genders, it is important that patriarchal capitalism 'serves' or sells women to men as luxury items in reward for male labour. Thus, women are figured as products rather than producers. The fact of their extensive, non-sexual labour is carefully suppressed in the capitalist psyche. This is one of the contexts in which the labour of the Irish woman in Britain today is ignored, although Irish women provide many of the essential services that underpin the day-to-day functioning of London.[36] However, we can look further into their invisibility. It could be suggested, for example, that the obscuring of the Irish woman in Britain has not just been incidental to her work. It has been a deliberate concern for dominant sectors of Irish society throughout this century. Her 'enclosedness' was formally engineered by a coalition of family, community, clergy and government at home, together with Catholic clergy and employers in Britain. The reason for this intense protectorate has been, predictably enough, the sexual control of the Irish woman which has always been extremely important to the fragile national psyche ever since the establishment of the Irish Republic. This concern to control women's sexualities was exacerbated for those exporting them to Britain in a way that did not apply when they headed for the United States or Australia. Throughout the colonial period, Ireland's night-marish territorial anxieties have been expressed and acted out upon the Irish female body in an elaborate theatre of containment and proprietorship. This pattern is common in other decolonising and ethnic societies also, where 'women's bodies have seemed to be a battlefield where the cultural struggles of post-colonial societies were waged'.[37] It was the emigration of multitudes of these bodies to the territory of the former coloniser which raised near-hysterical concerns to restrain the libidinous expression of the Irish female body in Britain. The insistence upon 'sheltering' poor Irish women, in particular, helped to steer their work options, limiting them to jobs which provided immediate, live-in accommodation. Up to 65 per cent of Irish nurses, for instance, have traditionally been recruited from home into pre-arranged jobs and accommo-dation.[38] In nursing, there was the additional moral 'protection' offered by hospitals overseen by nuns who would undertake the moral control of their charges as diligently as their professional training.[39] This seamless transfer directly from family and Church at home into all-female and religiously-run milieux in England was part of the 'sanitisation' and sanctification of female emigration from Ireland.

Of course, Irish women's stereotyped work environments have traditionally had certain practical benefits for them, just as invisibility can have subversive benefits for any collective. For one thing, they were used to homosocial contexts at home and often missed their mothers and sisters most.[40] They could recoup this feminine solidarity in living with work-mates. They had safe, clean accom-modation and were earning money independently now for work which often would have gone unpaid within the home in Ireland. Their public invisibility also spared them the strongly working-class image of Irish men. This meant that when a chance came for upward social mobility, some Irish women at least could readily profit. As Mac Laughlin and others have shown, one of the benefits of World War II for Irish women and their British counterparts was their wartime access to jobs which had hitherto been closed to them.[41] After the war, many managed to maintain their foothold in fields like clerical work and nursing, as well as gaining access to employment in the new social welfare bureaucracy.

Meanwhile, the 'demonisation' of Irish female emigration to Britain continued. The Catholic Social Welfare Bureau, an organ of the Catholic Church in Ireland, admonished female emigrants in its 1956 Report:

> As in other recent years, registry office marriages, laxity in attendance of religious duties and, in the case of young girls, irresponsible conduct and moral delinquency continue to provide the main case problems.[42]

This discourse around female emigration reflects the fact that the primary locus of this sanctification/demonisation dichotomy in Irishness is the female body and that body's movements, displacements or translations within the intertwining processes of desire, reproduction and emigration. The taboo on the mobile woman is, of course, universal in patriarchal society where physical mobility is damningly associated with sexual freedom in notions of the 'loose' or 'fast' woman. But, for Irish women, physical displacement in emigration does actually equate with greater sexual freedom. This, together with the related fact that Irish women travel more than most, has heightened the taboo. An emotive polarisation between purity and filth is evidently one of the most crippling dysfunctions within Irish discourse as it spreads itself across the whole field of Irish experience.[43]

The 'sanctification' of women's emigration ensured a remarkable feat, namely that the forces which colonise Irish women's sexuality could actually extend their hegemony beyond the national borders to ensure sexual control over 'their' women abroad, especially over those who were single and earning money independently and on their own account. This policing of female sexuality as a response to collective political trauma is common to many nations. In her essay 'Gender and Nation', Yuval-Davis explains how:

> often the distinction between one ethnic group and another is constituted centrally by the sexual behaviour of women.[44]

Viewed thus, women are obsessively projected as 'cultural signifiers' accorded with the task of defining boundaries around the group by the actions and messages which they do or do not engage with their bodies.[45]

The patristic urge to control adult Irish females within paradigms of immaturity and minority is reflected not only in the traditional institutions and discourses of their emigration. It is also evident in the language currently used in the literature of Irish emigration. In 1994, a major Irish studies publication characterised our emigrants in Britain as 'Irishmen' and 'Irish girls'.[46] As well as the implied seniority of the male term, its status as a single, iconic title suggests the robustness of achieved identity. The maintenance of this vigour would seem to require restraining Irish women from the full integration of gendered adulthood and ethnic identity which the potent title of 'Irishwoman' would imply. Similarly, in the statement quoted above about working-class images among 'Irish girls (and) their menfolk', Ryan relegates females to minority or child-like status while elevating males to a doubly-substantive noun which establishes them as at once male, adult and assuredly human (as 'folk').[47]

Overviewing Irish workers in Britain, we see them rigorously channelled into hypertrophied gender-stereotypes, with millions of Irish women intensely engaged in the feeding, cleaning, healing, caring and teaching of Britons and millions of Irish men focussed into clearing, constructing and fabricating the economic landscape of contemporary Britain. Their labour patterns form an exaggerated caricature of the divided gender-roles through which sexism ensures control over all individuals within patriarchal capitalism. Sexism first invades individual subjectivity, splitting off and suppressing the 'masculine' qualities within the female and the 'feminine' within the male. This half-functioning of the self facilitates control over individuals who would revolt if they were responding from the wholly-gendered self. This splitting then extends across society, guaranteeing the suppression of solidarity between the genders, who are left relating across an extreme and punitive polarisation, as they do in Ireland.

It is clear that this destruction of solidarity between the genders is necessary for the subjugation of a collective, as is the case among Blacks in Britain and the US today. As one writer argued:

> As we look at our contemporary past as black people, we see a weakening of political solidarity between the sixties and the nineties, we see a weakening of political solidarity between black men and women. It is crucial for the future black liberation struggle that we remain ever mindful that ours is a shared struggle. . .[48]

We urgently need much more analysis of the ways in which reactionary forces have institutionalised antagonisms between the genders in Irish society since the creation of the 'Free State' in order to deflect attention away from economic and territorial policy problems. Both in Irish labour patterns in Britain and in sexual mores in the Republic, it is clear that revolutionary impulses are split and defused by the repression and depression which sexism institutes.

THE IRISH HOME

WOMEN AND IRISHNESS IN FAMILIES

Why do we need an analysis of the Irish immigrant home? We need it because, both in ethnic and sexual terms, the home is fundamentally a political space.

Both the idea and the actual experience of the domestic space embody strong political dynamics for a variety of groups. For differing reasons, all women within patriarchy, and all immigrants within alien societies, stand to be strongly affected by the home. These two sensitivities coincide in the woman immigrant. For Irish women, they are layered over by the intense locus of the home and family within Irish traditions, Irish politics and within the Irish psyche.

Examining Irish home-making in Britain, we discover the path towards the establishment of 'home' to be a deeply gendered trajectory. Standard analyses of the migration patterns of women tend to expect and find that women 'follow' their men in emigration. The home is seen as a naturally-existent entity which passively follows the earning power of the male, with wife and children being sent for and imported once the male can finance them. This perspective, while acknowledging some link between women and the physical, social, emotional, educational and cultural entity that is the domestic home, ignores the almost single-handed physical and social labour of females in the construction of it.

Any exploration of this unpaid, uncredited labour of females in turn exposes the sexist underpinning of our whole society and economy. For the immigrant woman, her labour in the construction of domestic space and the production of citizens will go unacknowledged, as will the home-labour of women of all classes. However, her labour in the socialisation of children will be further problematised by the dilemmas of assimilation. If she chooses to transmit ethnicity to her children, her labour will no longer just pass unacknowledged but may be seen as actively subversive. In Tory Britain, for example, the dominant discourse calls unabashedly for assimilation of immigrants into mainstream society. Here the ethnic woman may be labouring, not just on behalf of the national mores, as do native women, but against them as they present themselves in school subjects the media, legislation, sexual politics and popular opinion. In educating children, she must 'counteract the devaluation of Irish culture in the mainstream media' and 'the total exclusion of any Irish material in the education system'.[49] She also confronts the more general problem of cultural imperialism inherent in school subjects and in the media.[50] Furthermore, the strategies of racism and sexism are liable to combine forces in particularly trenchant ways which can aggress the immigrant woman in her home. She may find herself at a pivot where racism and capitalism buttress each other on a support of sexism, where the three interlock to stabilise each other. One of the ways they do this is by forming a pecking-order of disempowerment. Within this pyramidal hierarchy, males who are disenfranchised by dehumanising labour within a culture of racial prejudice can still wield a compensatory sexist power within their own gender relations and in the home.

The domestic threshold of immigrants can also mark a boundary of difference inside which identity and cultural practices which refer to the country of origin may be maintained and shielded from the alien environment of the street. In this way, the domestic space of immigrants can be an intermediary dimension where the values of the original culture can be conjugated against those of the surrounding society. The maintenance of such a political space is usually the work of women. Thus, bell hooks sees the construction of 'Homeplace' as follows:

> This task of making homeplace . . . was about the construction of a safe place where black people could affirm one another and by so doing heal many of the wounds of racist domination, (by) making home a community of resistance.[51]

However, this is a complex struggle which can make of the home an arena of warring cultural practices where language, politics, accent, sexual behaviour and so on can be hotly disputed both between parents and immigrant youth who may be juggling a half-assimilated or 'double' identity.

Much of the active opposition to anglicising cultural imperialism among the Irish comes from the enduring ethnic affiliations of Irish women, their powerful role within the Irish family, and their traditional responsibility for the rearing and socialisation of children. In discussion, Irish women who have reared families in Britain typically stress the commitment they made towards instilling an Irish identity in their children. This deliberate socialisation of the second and third generations into Irishness is significant. In interview sessions, these groups often evoke the almost insistent emphasis laid on Irishness by their mothers in the home as crucial to the formation of their own identities. This contradicts the traditional perspective among those migration-specialists who have tended to suggest that women's emigration leads to a rapid and smoother assimilation into the host culture.[52] In Britain, where Irish women's immigration is particularly prevalent, their determined sense of themselves as unassimilated is revealed, both statistically in the numbers of self-declared Irish at census and in discussion with Irish women. They enrol their children in cultural activities like Irish dancing-classes and *feiseanna* at Irish centres and make a point of discussing life in Ireland. Many express regret at not having command of the native language to pass on to their children in the home, as they see Indian and Pakistani mothers can do. Observing how other ethnic women can maintain and transmit a native 'mother-tongue' to their British children, they must lament that most of themselves cannot.[53]

The main thrust of this ethnic commitment in the home seems to be the regular trips to Ireland towards which many parents save sacrificially throughout the year. These trips maintain connections with families back home and give second-generation children an experience of the Irish landscape. Adults of the second generation routinely evoke these holidays as treasured experiences of the Irishness their parents persistently told them was theirs. These trips seem to have the desired effect of anchoring the identity of the second-generation children in experiences of the Irish mainland that they can call their own. This gravitation of the ethos of the family towards Ireland can be so intense that some second-generation Irish speak of growing up within a constant sphere of oral reference to another location that was called 'home'. This dislocated sense of place meant that they grew up in the housing-estates of Kilburn and Camden, but accepted unquestioningly for the first five, six or seven years of life that home was an elsewhere they had not yet seen. Without dramatising the issue, this unshakable sense of continued belonging to their native neighbour-hood in Ireland must be recognised as a distinct feature of the Irish community in Britain, particularly those from rural areas in Ireland. Geographical proxi-mity to Ireland may foster this nostalgia with a vividness which the Irish in the United States or Australia must do without.

Another difference between Irish ethnicity in Britain and that in other countries is the assimilationist approach of Britain towards all expressions of Irishness, whether immigrant or not. This cultural-imperialist attitude affects not just immigrant Irish in Britain. It extends even to Irish people who have always lived in their own country, but who were shadowed by 'the colonisers from a culture which has always sought to appropriate Ireland and the Irish'.[54] The dominant discourse in Britain does not recognise any Irishness to be as valuably different and distinct from Britishness as the Irish typically feel them-selves to be. This long assimilationist history, extending its influence beyond immigrant locations, is clearly different from the type of assimilative pressure extended towards Asians, Blacks, Italians or Poles. It greatly complicates the task of ethnic socialisation for Irish child-raisers in their attempts to inculcate a self-concept of positive difference in Irish youth in Britain.

HOUSING AND THE IRISH COMMUNITY IN BRITAIN

Historically, large populations of Irish men and women have lived and worked in Britain long before establishing family homes there. Male Irish labourers typically boarded in cheap lodgings or in workers' hostels. The latter provided a densely homosocial environment both for single men and for married men whose families remained behind in Ireland, surviving on the earnings they sent home. Meanwhile, Irish women tended to distinguish themselves among other emigrant nationalities by migrating separately from men and establishing themselves independently with employment, accommodation and social circles.

We have seen already how labour opportunities and sexual politics dictated housing patterns for generations of Irish women, establishing them as live-in labour in hospitals, hotels and private houses. The search for private housing, however, remained particularly difficult in the decades which preceded the recent emergence of an anti-racist discourse, and it is readily evoked as a nightmare by older Irish women reminiscing about their pasts today. Because of their traditional role as single-handed family managers, many Irish women have memories of tramping the streets in search of housing for their husband and children. In the words of one woman:

> So from that night on, when Bill came in from work, the children were in bed, they were always in bed by half-past six, I'd everything done, Bill's dinner was on the table and I'd get up and go out. I'd have read the local paper for adverts. I'd have gone to shop windows but always 'No Coloured or Irish need apply'. It was Houses to Let, Flats to let, Rooms to Let, but every one of them 'No Irish or Coloured need apply'. So I thought, I'll present myself at their doors. But when they'd hear my accent some of them would say, 'It's gone'. . . .[55]

Later, in the 1980s, while Thatcherism was making racist politics socially 'acceptable', it was also introducing a newly-pervasive anxiety about housing which spread across all social classes in Britain. While homelessness escalated among poor and immigrant sub-classes at this time, many in the established middle classes also lost their homes to sudden redundancy, escalating interest rates and the 'negative-equity trap' of wildly fluctuating property values. Thus, the Conservative Party's problematisation of 'family values' extended beyond the home as a political location to a new national insecurity which now threatens the survival of the home as an actual, physical space. This generalised housing crisis has particularly heightened the difficulties of secure tenure in appropriate housing for immigrant women and mothers. During the 1980s, rents and house-prices increased faster than the cost of living. By 1990, an estimated seven out of ten people living below the 'decency threshold' wage were women.[56] Most recent surveys have found that Irish people are under-represented among those who own their own homes and over-represented among the homeless and those occupying substandard accommodation.[57] In 1991, 44 per cent of Irish-born people in London owned their homes. This figure compares unfavourably with the 59 per cent of the remaining white population who owned their own homes. Twenty nine per cent of the Irish in London at that time lived in local authority housing, compared to 22 per cent of the remaining white population in this category. In terms of housing quality, the Irish-born population was found to have 'the worst conditions' compared to other whites, Afro-Carribeans and Asians. They were particularly disadvantaged by a lack of privacy and by the lack of independently-controlled accommodation.[58] Information supplied by agencies working with the homeless in London reveals that:

> more than 30% of homeless people encountered on the street at night were Irish, . . . one in five staying in emergency accommodation were Irish, . . . one in three clients attending drop-in centres for the homeless were Irish . . . (and) the largest ethnic group using severe-weather shelters in London (since) 1991 were those of Irish origin.[59]

Another survey carried out in London in 1986 found that 'fifty-seven per cent of recent Irish immigrants had made no prior accommodation arrangements before leaving Ireland (and) seventeen per cent of the total slept rough on their first nights in the city'.[60] Under the controversial Criminal Justice and Public Order Act of 1994, sleeping rough can be prohibited now as the government targets the festivals and encampments of Britain's 'New Age Travellers'. This has had repercussions for Irish Travellers, too, as the Act criminalises their nomadic lifestyle and closes halting-sites traditionally used by this group.[61]

THE PREVENTION OF TERRORISM ACT AND IRISH WOMEN

The Prevention of Terrorism Act affected women and children particularly violently in that it targeted Irish home-life as the focus of a campaign which claimed to be concerned with pursuing terrorists. The methods in this campaign aimed quite specifically to demoralise the women of the Irish community through the detention and interrogation of ordinary mothers and children brought to police stations during armed night-raids on the home. Women were further demoralised through the institution of sexually abusive strip searches of Irish women held in custody. The home became the frontline for night-time confrontations with armed police, and often whole families were taken in and interrogated for days. One report of such raids recalls:

> For instance, (on her arrest) Kate Magee's child, aged 6, was taken away from her. Information on her child's whereabouts and health was refused for the first 6 days of her detention. . . After 66 days in prison, the prosecution dropped the major criminal charge, leaving the charge of witholding information.[62]

This became a familiar pattern throughout the late 1970s and 1980s. Of the 7,052 people arrested under the Act between 1974 and 1991, only 3 per cent were charged with any criminal offence and a quarter of those were found innocent.[63] As recently as 1986, the London Irish Women's Centre could assert that:

> Every Irish woman is aware that whenever she speaks out about our situation here in Britain or in Ireland, she is liable as a target for arrest.[64]

The Charities Evaluation Service denounced the Act in 1994 as 'institutionalised racism'.[65] Here, Sister Clarke, an Irish Catholic nun engaged in social work with Irish families, explains:

> The conditions in which women and children were held were dreadful. They refused women sanitary towels, held them for seven days without policewomen present, refused them medicines, clean blankets or washing-facilities – it was appalling. Young children were questioned about their fathers' and mothers' habits and friends, and they were bribed with sweets for information. In at least one instance, young children were kept all night in a police station, questioned for long hours and left to sleep on a window-ledge. Their mother had gone to the police station to report her husband missing and they came and arrested her and all her family.[66]

The Prevention Of Terrorism Act revealed governmental attitudes both in Ireland and in Britain which cannot lightly be forgotten. It provided insights into the actual status of Irish citizens in Britain during times of crisis, even while it repressed or refused all insight into the complexity of their actual political orientations by casting them all as potential terrorists.

The Act signalled the Irish home as an explicitly political site, a location appropriate for armed police intervention. This version of ethnic harassment by police is in contrast, for instance, to that waged at present on Britain's Black minority. For Blacks, the locus of police aggression is the street. Here, young Black males are frequently intercepted for searches and interrogation when on foot or in vehicles. The pathologising of the Black family and home, however, is achieved through a 'moral' black-listing in the press, rather than by physical intervention in domestic spaces.

The raiding of the Irish home under the PTA was an extravagant strategy and reveals aspects of governmental views towards Irishness in Britain. It would appear that under a rising, hysterical pressure from Provisional IRA operations in mainland Britain, the authorities lunged about blindly for a comprehension of what the relationship could possibly be between Irishness itself, including Irish political violence, and the millions of individuals who quietly, anonymously laboured in Britain's own cities. One report describes PTA interrogation in this way:

> the range of questions broadens and deals with family and friends – dates of birth, where they live, in-laws, number of children, political beliefs of family and relatives, political beliefs of friends . . .[67]

The very anonymity of Irish people's white skin must partly explain why their harassment was home-based while that of Blacks occurs in the street. Or perhaps it was the British government's most recent memory of direct, military antagonism with Ireland which provided the paradigm for the Prevention of Terrorism Act in Britain. The guerilla-based Irish War of Independence (1919–21) had been fought out and won upon a network of undetectable but pervasive community support, not least in urban centres like Dublin and Cork. It had been waged almost literally from the subversive, sheltering home. It may have been the shadow of that defeat which threw up a pathetic, long-outdated idiom for the Act, whereby the ordinary home would be raided in order to resolve the war with the present-day IRA. There may also have been some intuition of the extensive, covert role played by femininity throughout the history of Irish resistance. Here the issue of 'information' became central, and the charge of 'witholding' it became the sole allegation against many of those held under the Act. This left Irish women painfully sandwiched between the British authorities, on the one hand, and the Irish government, on the other. The latter made few attempts to intercede on their behalf and would themselves soon be prosecuting women in the Irish Republic for the holding of information about reproductive technologies abroad. The PTA's conflation of Irish ethnicity in Britain with involvement in the IRA reflected a complete misunderstanding of the complexities of the Irish identity there and of the political allegiances of the majority of the Irish population in Britain. It also reflected the existence of a 'hostage' mentality within establishment circles in Britain which meant that women and children would be used to somehow force paramilitaries out of the woodwork.

This often destroyed the delicate relations which Irish people were trying to maintain with neighbouring British families already alienated by IRA bombings and the propagandist press. Racist violence was at an all-time high in Britain during the early 1980s, and large-scale arrests of innocent Irish people in residential areas repeatedly shattered hopes for their complete integration into British society. Here is the testimony of Mrs Annie Maguire, who, following her wrongful arrest, spent ten years in prison in Britain for alleged participation in an IRA bombing. She describes her arrest during a night-time raid at her home by police with dogs:

> I told Anne-Marie who had started to tremble, not to cry. I told her I wouldn't be long. I'm going to help the police and I'll be back, I said . . . The next time I saw her it was five months later. They just put us away . . . After ten years when I was released, I knew that I had lost my children . . . Anne-Marie was a young woman . . . (During interrogations), I had my period and they made me stand spread-eagled against the wall . . . I hadn't changed my sanitary-towel . . . They called me names saying I wasn't a mother, I was 'a prostitute' . . . As a mother and a woman I stood up to the beatings because I knew the truth.[68]

ABUSE AND FAMILY IN THE IRISH COMMUNITY IN BRITAIN

Part of the gendering of the experience of home is the fact that the work patterns of males tend to mean that they retreat to a homespace which, however impoverished, is in opposition to the public spaces in which they labour. However, women, including even middle-class women engaged in careers outside the home, know few physical or temporal spaces which are reprieves from the call to labour. The home certainly is not one of these places. This doubling and disguising of women's labour can leave them overstretched and vulnerable in a number of ways. While raising children in the home, women may be even more firmly hedged within patriarchal control and, thus, more likely to be targeted for abuse by a male partner than a childless woman would be. In terms of finances, social stigma and physical refuge, a mother may have fewer escape options than single women have. Recent statistics about Irish immigrants in Britain bear this out. One commentator found that:

women with children were more likely to be in situations where domestic violence occurred. Twenty nine per cent of women with children said they experienced domestic violence within the last twelve months compared with 15 per cent of all women in the sample. This means that women with children are twice as likely to be facing domestic violence.[69]

The reflex of males to express crisis through various forms of gendered violence against the women of their own community is at present a major problem within Black communities in the US and Britain. The incidence of domestic abuse, addiction, absent or irresponsible fatherhood and the abandonment of Black women in favour of white women is posited in current debates as threatening the very continuance and survival of the Black family in the US. One black theorist critiques her own community in this way:

We are daily witnessing the disintegration of African-American family life . . . black people daily perpetuate sexist norms that threaten our solidarity . . .[70]

Racism seriously complicates discussion of such social problems and often encourages silence among ethnic women who are unwilling to provoke or reinforce negative stereotypes about their community perpetrated by the dominant majority. The breaking of silence erupted for Black women in the West following the release of the film *The Colour Purple* which exposed Black-against-Black sexist abuse. In reaction to this disclosure of female experience, the community itself asserted that:

the issue . . . was not accuracy but whether certain aspects of black life should be talked about (ie. revealed) in a non-black context.[71]

The tentative silence-breaking which is proceeding in Irish society at present is also a double-edged sword for many Irish people. As Ireland's intense history of child sexual abuse comes slowly to light, this welcome disclosure is exposing the pathologised sexuality of our culture to foreign eyes. The representation of this pathology in foreign media, however, can tend to simply elaborate upon a pre-existent racist text about Irish people rather than radically critiquing its causes. Irish people may therefore have ambivalent feelings about any disclosure in British contexts. An Irish psychiatric doctor, on a tea-break with English colleagues in a London hospital, reports glimpsing a TV documentary on sexual abuse among Irish clergy:

I was really interested in it and I would have liked to watch it myself but, to be honest, I turned it off because it would have been embarrassing in front of them.[72]

Before approaching Irish communities in Britain, we need firstly to acknowledge that the country from which they derive some of their social behaviour is still a long way from routine exposure or correction of sexual and child abuses. Irish society continues to normalise some social abuses, such as alcohol-addiction and punitive behaviours towards pregnant women, and has not yet reached the stage of pathologising them. Given that this whole chapter argues that the construction of silence is a pivotal, idiosyncratic dynamic within Irish social discourse even at home, it must therefore be more forceful and rooted dynamic within Irish experience in Britain.

It is clear that solidarity with their own ethnic community, as well as isolation from other forms of social support available to women in the host society, can seal Irish women in Britain into an excessive tolerance of masculine dysfunction, whereby disclosures of rape, beatings, irresponsible fatherhood and addiction threaten to evoke and affirm the original racist stereotypes of their men as 'brutish' and 'drunken'. This can leave women trying to absorb and contain the circular violence of a racism that facilitates sexism which, in turn, facilitates racism. It seems then that the roles of stretching their resources and of cushioning others, characteristic of the lives of all women, are exacerbated in women living within ethnic minority populations. They may find themselves nurturing children and socialising them into their ethnic heritage, labouring doubly, both inside the home and outside of it, in a racially disprivileging environment and absorbing abuse from frustrated, disinherited males while resolutely shielding that abuse from the surrounding society.

In terms of vulnerability to abuse, the inward-turning quality of the Irish community in Britain is a mixed blessing for women. On the one hand, close neighbourly connections are maintained, often with whole families or even neighbourhoods of people who were known at home and who have emigrated en masse. This counteracts the isolation which can be the curse of the immigrant woman marooned in the home with small children, removed from her matrilineal network of sisters and female friends and relatives in the home-country. However, the introversion and apoliticisation of the Irish community can cause the maintenance of social norms from which the woman was fleeing through her emigration. One survey explains that:

> for Irish women, leaving a violent partner or family situation is particularly hard. The cultural and religious beliefs within Irish society instil the duty of preserving the family.[73]

Dysfunctions like alcoholism, domestic violence, sexual abuse and incest, as well as traditional gender roles that are detrimental to women, can often continue to dog the family in emigration as they did at home. All of these traumas require for their healing a long process of re-education and rehabilitation in a supportive environment as they tend to be reproduced along the generations if left untreated. However, for any minority, the climate of immigrant life, with its discrimination, environmental alienation and its social, legal and financial insecurities, tends to actually heighten the sorts of pressures that can cause these abuses within the family, rather than providing a chance to heal. The options can seem stark. The large numbers of Irish women who reach Britain with memories of alcoholic family life, of sexual abuse and a harmfully repressive education, often feel obliged to flee their compatriots abroad in order to undertake treatment in a therapeutic environment. In interviews with second-generation Irish women in Britain, this author has found sexual abuse, alcoholism and male, domestic violence to be unfortunately common. These women are left with painfully mixed feelings about their Irish heritage. They long for the Ireland of their cultural and genealogical roots, but abhor the cycles of domestic dysfunction and violence which they perceive, rightly or wrongly, to be norms within Irish circles. Some recoverers from sexual abuse and incest are now forming support groups for survivors of abuse in Irish contexts. The mixed feelings of these women extend to their sense of Irish femininity. They see their Irish mothers and grandmothers as capable women who exude an earthy natural warmth and a robust integrity. However, they are shocked by what they see as the inexplicable subservience of such women to violent, drunken or irresponsible men, and they feel disinherited by these foremothers' failure to protect their children from domestic abuse. A second-generation woman recovering from sexual abuse by her immigrant Irish grandfather has this to say:

> They see their husband as some sort of God and will put up with anything from him and it makes me so angry. These guys just get really drunk and she just takes it all from them as if it's normal, as if just because he says he's sorry next day then everything is OK.[74]

Understandably, these women feel deeply torn over whether or how to call themselves Irish, because of the searing associations with abuse.

INNER CONFLICTS

The tensions and belligerence in Anglo-Irish political relations make emigration to Britain a challenge with which most other destinations cannot compare. Just being an Irish person in Britain plunges Irish people there into a dramatisation of their identity because Britain has been so thoroughly and problematically involved in the construction of what we now know as Irishness and the Irish. Whenever an Irish person enters England, or when an English person enters Ireland, a hurricane of history is blowing on them. The fact that although Irish people may condemn British exploitation of their country, they are now forced to seek financial, professional or sexual refuge there is shaming and humbling for many Irish. It requires a very thorough political education to steer oneself through the conundrum of Irish dependence on Britain. This is the testimony of an Irish woman living in Britain since 1966, whose words gave this chapter its title:

> I used to have a lot of political ideas. My father was Republican at home and I was into left-wing politics here. I used to read the 'Socialist Worker' and I had

all the terminology, you know. I took a young person's interest in politics, like. But I tell you, the propaganda in this country is just unbelievable. About India or Africa, all any English'll tell you is the good they done. Built schools and civilised them, they tell you. But I put aside all my political ideas and Irishness years ago. It gets you nowhere in this country. I just sit on it. I suppose it's being untrue to yourself but my only views these days are to have no views.[75]

The truth remains that Britain has long been salvaging Irish people from the disasters of successive Irish governments. For centuries, the Irish have poured into the belly of the British economy, assured a place below the working-class shelf of British life. And access into middle-class professions is now possible. Without a radical analysis of this dependence upon Britain, and because of their ethnic need to maintain a positive nostalgia in relation to Ireland, it is very difficult for most Irish emigrants in Britain to fault the Irish Republic's policies on economics and emigration. Yet these confusing ironies around economics, labour and imperialism are nothing compared to the ones that twist around the specifically sexual exodus of Irish women to England. The reception accorded Irish women who went to England for their illegitimate pregnancies, for the adoption of their babies, or more recently, for abortions is the hushed under-belly of the Irish tradition in Britain.

Every Irish person knows about this clandestine run between Ireland and England. Even people in very isolated parts of Ireland who have never left their own region know all about this feminine channel across the water. There is no parish in Ireland which has not produced these women. Their forbidden stories map the suppression of feminine experience across every townland of Ireland. Overtly, the relationship between the two countries is seen as being historically violent and exploitative, which has now become tamed and expedient as Britain absorbs more and more young adults from Irish dole-queues. However, the topography includes a shadowy, unofficial area where whole sectors of the Irish female population pass through a secret tunnel to sexual amnesty and asylum. These women are caught in multiple double-binds between their host communities and those of the home country. In possessiveness around territory and community resources, host communities tend to view immigrant fertility with unease. In times when the tide of racism is high, they often demonise immigrant libido and procreation as undisciplined, distasteful or threatening. Here there is a cumulative, domino-effect of painfulness and difficulty for Irish women in Britain who are often already sexual refugees from Ireland's hijacking of their fertility. For generations of Irish women, and especially for women who are politicised as anti-imperialists or nationalists on the one hand, but who have been sacrificed to Ireland's misogyny on the other, the terms invader and oppressor spin dizzyingly around Ireland and England. Such women can denounce colonisation, but on shifting from the paradigms of nation-states to those which define the intimate borders of their own bodies, they find that their own country has been up in arms against them for decades, tyrannically colonising their biology. Faced with archaic legislation concerning contraception, sex education, reproductive information and abortion at home, as well as by a fortress of punitive social attitudes which maintain Catholic sexual dogma as hegemony, the Irish woman may well find that the imperialist invader becomes her liberator, or at least a benign nurse. As Irish people, we must urgently examine how infringement of the territorial autonomy of the sexual and/or feminine body, from the microcosm of the home to the macrocosm of state legislation, relates to national experiences of territorial violation. This connection between the sexuality and the territoriality of peoples, with its massive implications for collective well-being, is not just a historical dynamic confined to the heyday of empire but is critically relevant now as increasing numbers of the world's population become migrants and refugees amidst a climate of heightening racial tensions.

Left-wing political psychiatry since the 1960s has demonstrated how colonisation causes profound pathology in the individual and collective psyche and libido and has established a clinical, diagnostic picture of the 'colonised personality' where 'successful colonisation' depends upon imposing 'a regular and important mental pathology' or a 'massive psycho-existential complex'.[76] One of its principal contributions to post-imperialist understanding has been its diagnosis of the ways in which negative introjects, framed into the colonised psyche as part of the imperial process, long outlive the official end of colonial regimes and the military decolonisation of occupied societies. It hardly needs arguing that Irish society is a text-book illustration of post-colonial libidinous trauma. What we do need, however, is for this healing awareness to become popularly available to the Irish mind and no longer to be rigorously suppressed away from the cautious, reactionary spectrum of our national discourse.

THE IRISH BODY AND SUPPRESSION OF INFORMATION

Historically at least, the Irish body was deeply pressured and problematised by colonial processes which included starvation, evictions, martial policing, mass emigrations and eugenicist, highly racist depictions of Irish people. We have already seen that the Irish body has been globally commodified as exported labour in processes contemporaneous with the colonial ones of past centuries as well as in the present and, most likely, in the future. We have also seen how the local presence and face of the Irish body on the British mainland has been registered in British national iconography only as the 'Paddy', while the female Irish body has been occluded from view, despite its daily presence as labour in service to the British public. In her unseeable, unspoken location in political space between Ireland and England, the Irish female body has been active, problematical and difficult to repress or control. The efforts to maintain hedges of silence and invisibility around her have been in no way conclusive. Rather,

they are an ever-renewed struggle, a Sisyphean task for successive Irish governments, absorbing high proportions of the energies of public and national
debates, discourses and legislative measures in Ireland.

When discussing Irish women's relationship to Britain, it must be understood that the relationship is important even to women who reside permanently
in the Republic and have no cause to see themselves as immigrants. This is
because large proportions of Irish women 'complete' their inner picture of the
reproductive life-choices available to them in Ireland by 'supplementing' them
with the possible option of availing of British social services and climates. Thus,
most Irish women know that if they needed an abortion or a non-accusatory
climate or childbirth or a relationship, one available option is to try to get to
England to find it. This means that mainland Irish women's inner mapping of
their country's relationship to Britain is silently, but urgently, different to that of
Irish men. Britain, or more usually England, fringes their experience of their
own country with a sort of virtual reality of possible escape-hatches in case of
reproductive crisis. This unofficial, inner map shades in an extra, politically-
loaded dimension which utterly differentiates their potential or actual migrations from those of their male counterparts.

Even for Irish women who for ethical or religious reasons would never
contemplate using such facilities, England features just as prominently on their
socio-sexual map as the place they would never go to do such things.
Unfortunately, such ethical positions in Irish society have up to now tended to
overwhelmingly implicate the policing of others' positions. This has meant that
the sectors which would never use the abortion route to England nonetheless
feature that location very strongly on their inner map as a place to which others
should be prevented from going for that purpose. This crucial dynamic around
ethics in modern Irish society came to an extraordinary legislative climax in
1991 with a new Irish High Court injunction ruling that:

> Irish women (who were not in imminent danger of death) did not have the right
> to travel abroad to avail of foreign abortion services.[77]

This injunction clarified that the political climate for women in Ireland is not
necessarily liberalising with the passage of the decades. This legislation emerged
from the infamous 'X' case in the same year, which provoked the passage of
emergency legislation to prevent a raped 14-year-old girl from travelling to
Britain for an abortion. Through the scapegoating of 'X', Irish women have
learnt that not-telling is not a thing of the past but the golden rule for the
future. 'X' infringed the unwritten Irish law about migration to Britain for
abortions: she wilfully provided a piece of information (by offering the police
forensic evidence to convict her rapist) and this was what brought the might of
a police state slamming around her pregnancy. The legal precedent that was set
for the future also set an injunction in concrete in Irish women's hearts which

made it safe to tell absolutely no-one – even fewer than before – if you are one of this year's thousands making the trip to England for an abortion.

The literature on Irish immigrant life in Britain often devotes an irritated line or two to the absence of information about Irish women, despite the fact that they make up about half a million of the population. According to the author of one study on race and racism in Britain:

> There is no satisfactory . . . survey of the Irish . . . the sizeable number of Irish women immigrants has remained particularly neglected in historical accounts.[78]

If foreign specialists are surprised at the lack of information surrounding Irish women, they are plainly unaware of the legislative time-warp by which Irish women are cut off from their European sisters. Words like 'information' and 'travel' may be neutral in the lexicon of migration-studies, and perhaps even within feminism, but they send a shudder down the backs of Irish women and they have no neutrality in the legal lexicon drawn up by the Irish state. 'Information' is in no way an automatic, guaranteed or integral part of Irish feminine life. Silence on the other hand is just that. If reflexive information for the Irish woman about herself is legislatively banned by her society, it should come as no surprise that the flow of expressive information emergent from her is stemmed too.

Since the debates over legislation allowing Irish women access to information about abortion abroad, the term 'information' has become a stinging legal by-word that is like a moat around women who live in the Irish Republic. This often results in farcical state-behaviour like the once-off confiscation of the section of every copy of the *Guardian* which carried abortion clinic telephone numbers for Britain. The debates around women's 'information' constitute an explicit recognition by Irish society, institutions and government that information is not a neutral, secondary term but a powerful catalytic agent in itself. It seems that foreigners looking on, even British observers, are simply not aware of the impassioned, draconian debates of the 1990s and the ensuing legislature surrounding Irish women's 'right to travel'. Here the Republic manages, not only to silence and incarcerate its women, but also to shroud its actions with impunity and invisibility. A mystical fog seems to descend around Irish legislature when convenient, cloaking it off from comparison with European mores as if normalising institutions like the European Court of Human Rights did not exist. Our European counterparts seem unaware of the extent of the convergence of (Catholic) Church and state in Ireland and of the rigour of our anti-feminine legislation.

With half an eye to Muslim immigrants, liberal European media often publish critical features on the lives of women in countries where Islamic law is legally imposed, critiquing 'the heart of the Islamic revolution – the restraint on women' with provocative titles like 'Sex, Women and Islam' and 'Hidden Agenda':

The Islamic state bore down on me . . . There is no real role for women outside of marriage . . . An Iranian woman cannot check into a hotel alone, nor can a couple get a room without proof they are married.[79]

But the Irish Republic, so much closer to home and exporting its sexual casualties wholesale into the arms of Britain, manages to escape unexamined. We really need to know how the ruling classes in Ireland achieve this sort of immunity, although it is already clear that the anti-Arab discourse and colour-racism in the international media will focus criticism on Islam while ignoring the misogynist excesses of a white-skinned European Community member like Ireland.

Right now in the 1990s, when Ireland is exporting many university-educated women, this question of women's information remains a searing political issue which divides the country almost hysterically into religious, medical, ethical and legal camps. This not only involves abortion information but also plain education for women abut their own biology and about present-day medical procedures around their reproduction. Interviews with Irish women in Britain reveal this tormenting ignorance about their own bodies and sexuality with which they faced life abroad. Many speak of attempts to get information from their mothers or teachers or from older women who had children, and of being bewilderingly rebuffed with jokes and disapproval.

One woman stated:

When it came to sex I basically went along with what men expected of me. It was something I don't think I felt I had any control over . . . If I made any decision at all, it was that I wouldn't sort out anything about contraceptives, so it was like allowing things to happen, not taking responsibility, which I think is very much connected with our lack of education to do with sex – not really knowing our own bodies, not taking any pleasure in our bodies, not knowing that women could have orgasms, not knowing that I had a clitoris until a man told me – crazy![80]

This is a testimony, not from 50 years ago, but from an educated Irish woman who emigrated to England in the late 1970s. Here is an account from Annie Maguire (see above). She describes an exchange where she seeks information from her English landlady:

'Aren't you supposed to have them every month?' She said 'Don't you think you're having a baby?' I was shocked. 'It's natural, love, when you're married', she said. I said 'I didn't know'[81]

We have to recognise that this blockade on sex education for women is a reality right now in Irish schools. Across the early 1980s, when about 4,000 Irish women were officially registered as having abortions in British clinics every year, three-quarters of these women were single, middle-class Dubliners who had been having sex without contraception.[82] This statistic is alarming in that it represents the sector which one would expect to be the most liberated in terms of reproductive technologies. It leaves us to guess at the plight of poor and isolated women in more remote, rural environments.

MIGRATIONS FOR ABORTIONS

The 1990s' debates over the banning of gynaecological information led to a saga of prosecutions of women in Ireland for possession of such information. This was the visible end of a spectrum of subversive, sexually-political activism operated by Irish women between Ireland and Britain. A clandestine network of female volunteers, feminists and psychotherapists clandestinely staff a top-secret telephone number in Ireland which pregnant women can call to obtain the number of an abortion clinic in Britain. The voice at the other end immediately offers to ring the woman back if necessary, as the coins quickly running out in a provincial phone-box is a familiar scenario. The woman is given the number of a London clinic if she wants it, along with the number of a safe guest-house near the clinic with a sympathetic family who are used to daily receiving Irish girls and women who are 'on the run' in this way. There may also be the possibility of being met and escorted by a member of a group like the Irish Women's Abortion Support Group run by Irish women in Britain, if the woman is very young, alone or traumatised.

At the British abortion clinics, there is generally an intense and supportive awareness of the traumatised condition of Irish women, who are automatically treated as a case apart from the British and other nationalities. The pre-operative counselling explores these extra layers of trauma with the woman, including the difficulty of concealing her trip abroad, the silence in which she must endure the post-operative phase on returning home and the condemnatory atmosphere in which she is forced to live on return to Ireland. Irish women are often given rooms apart from their English counterparts and are given special pamphlets on counselling information. This dimension of awareness and solicitude extended by British abortion services towards Irish women is, of course, passed over in silence by the Irish public and the Irish government. Ireland makes no acknowledgment of the assistance given by the British feminine health-care system to Irish women in their desperate migrations across the water over the past decades.

Because so many women migrate temporarily to Britain, or flee Ireland permanently in search of reproductive rights, one might expect that the misogyny of Irish legislation would be trumpeted the world over and that this constant exodus of feminine refugees out of the country would have a liberating, feedback effect. Irish women gaining reproductive rights abroad, as well as financial power and access to foreign media, could theoretically be shaming and lobbying the Irish Dáil into egalitarian legislation, thereby exercising a relentless gender-political pressure from abroad much as Irish-Americans have exerted constant pressure over Northern Ireland. However, we must consider the depressing possibility that women resolve their experience of oppression in Ireland by simply getting out as quickly as they can and by not looking back. This however is belied by the typical maintenance by Irish women abroad of as much connection as they can with the island, by their resolve not to assimilate and by their raising of their children as Irish. For such radical, liberalising feedback to operate would require a much more strongly pro-feminine atmosphere than currently exists in any western political sphere – British, American or European. For strategic reasons also, all Irish traditions of resistance and protest have tended to be secret, underground, improvised, local, spontaneous and camouflaged. Overt campaigning, exploitation of the mainstream media, flooding of the public with resistance-information, mass-demonstration . . . these are not part of the inherited Irish tradition of resistance. Instead, Irish people know in a visceral, experiential way that 'information' is not a neutral item, but the pivot between success and disaster for processes of secret resistance. Having evolved most of their sense of identity within the imperial paradigm of invasion, occupation and very long-term conflict with a formidable power, Irish people deeply understand that a gulf can lie between what appears and what is, while another related, but different, gulf lies between what happens at home and abroad.

Irish society has tended to run along these double rails, and the gulf between the actual and the articulated in Ireland runs back into a centuries-old tradition of secret resistance and subterfuge. This splitting can be traced to the effort to survive overwhelming collective trauma, to the adoption and hegemony of psychically unbearable sexual repression, to the imposition of a foreign language and the violent suppression of the native one and so on. Study into contemporary Irish society at home or abroad establishes that these are not, as neo-colonial revisionist history would have us believe, outdated or inaccurate cliches, but are rather motivations which are still shaping Irish behaviours and institutions today.

Conclusions

The next ten years should constitute a window of opportunity for the healing of Irish culture, and this will only be achieved through renewal in one of the most crucial areas of Irishness, that is in the discourses that we permit ourselves. It is clear that the silencing inherent in modern Irish society is constantly threatened by a natural, compensatory urge to divulge. This drama of contestation between the collective Irish psyche and soma, between a repressive national 'ego' and a longing, libidinous 'id', between law and the body, depicts the efforts of a repressed organism to right itself to wholeness and health. The institutionalised suppression of the history, libido and truth-telling of Irishness locks in constant struggle against the innate Irish urge to show, reveal, enquire, expose and share.

As repression squeezes more tightly in social and legislative discourse, then the body erupts ever more often, more unsparingly to the surface of the public mind. As Fintan O'Toole has commented:

> In the abortion referendum of 1983, wombs, periods, sperms and eggs, unpious ejaculations and ectopic pregnancies became the terms of political debate.[83]

This polarised tension has been heightening in the Republic in the 1990s while voices of disclosure and catharsis have been emerging. We can use the elaborate range of communication technology now available to decentralise, generate and entice this sort of proliferation. According to Betty Purcell, producer of RTE's *Questions and Answers* programme, 'radio was the real facilitator' in turning a 'culture of caution' towards a 'culture of transparency'.[84] The *Guardian* newspaper explains:

> It was radio which was largely responsible for transforming Irish newspapers . . . They had to abandon parish-hall reporting and tackle the issues – contraception, marriage break-down, clerical child abuse – which were being discussed uninhibitedly on the air.[85]

However, we need to make a further shift beyond the disembodied and faceless disclosure of confessional radio. Famous male hosts in the Republic like Gay Byrne and Gerry Ryan have innovated upon the Catholic paradigm of the confession-box by moving it onto the airwaves, stimulating radical disclosure from their overwhelmingly female listeners and encouraging a climate of desire and libido.

Now we need also to retrieve the physicality of Irishness, restoring a balance that is lost to the profuse, addictive orality of our talking and our drinking. The whole-body experience of Irish presence has been deeply undercut historically by processes of eviction, 'transportation' and emigration, where racial, legal and financial dynamics beyond individual or community control transplant, relocate or banish the Irish body in massive numbers across the globe. This causes what Seamus Heaney has described as 'a lacuna in your midriff'.[86] The 'deterritorialisation' of Irish society has made Irish people fatalistic about their physical presence, 'prepared to put up with any amount of personal discontinuity', just as hegemonic forces dictate where it is possible for the Irish body to literally exist – to be or to dwell.[87] This has led to what Cheryl Herr in her essay 'The Erotics of Irishness' calls 'a social repression of the body on a grand scale' in Irish society.[88] We are sick of it – literally, in our mentality and our physiques and metaphorically, in our discourse. When the body is repressed, the discourse emergent from it will be not an expressive depiction of reality but an anti-reality strategy which denies actual experience. This is characteristic of the spate of national 'debates' and referenda in the Republic which stretch issues of sexual politics and personal morality across the poles of demonisation and sanctification. Citizens are invited to literally assemble around the poles/polls of these 'arguments'. Clearly, 'debate' and 'argument' are inappropriate modes of discourse for such intimate territories, being more suited to the economic policies from which the state is deflecting attention. In these referenda, language is used to construct and impose neurotic, national prohibitions rather than to disclose and explore the impulses of desire and fear that emerge from the individual body.

It is important to realise that repression and silencing are recent phenomena to Irishness and will be outdistanced by our deeper passion for subtle, idiosyncratic discourse, which it is now time to restore. Our culture stands over an ancient oral tradition that delights in the telling of experience. This is a description by Seán Tom Pheats Ó Cearnaigh of the lifestyle of one of Ireland's most famous female tellers, 'Peig an Scéalaí'. In her passion for *cúntas* (giving a reckoning or narration) and *cómhrá* (giving and receiving discourse together with others), for exchanging with friends, family, strangers and foreigners personalised narrations and accounts of things which couldn't be further from fixed, hierarchical dogma, Peig Sayers was typical of her community and illustrates the withering of our discourse over the past eighty years.

> Thosnaigh na strainséirí ag teacht ansan agus, pé an diabhal cuma, bhí sí an-oiriúnach dóibh leis. Bean anshocair ab ea í. Chuadar chuichí . . . Bhí an-chúntas ar a saol ar fad, mar nuair a saolaíodh i mBaile Bhiocáire í, sin é an cuileachta a bhí acu istoíche – scéaltóireacht – agus bhí a lán lucht siúil an uair sin ag imeacht timpeall. Agus bhíodh oíche agamsa agus oíche agatsa, agus b'é a gcúram ar fad i rith na hoíche ná scéaltóireacht. Do bhíodh Peig agus cluas le héisteacht aici, agus choimead sí gach aon scéal acu ina ceann no gur chuaigh sí síos an don chré.[89]

or, in English translation:

> Then the foreigners started to come around, and whatever the devil they looked like, she'd still give them a great reception. A very calm, steady woman she was. They would go to her . . . She could give a great account of her life, because when she used to live in Baile Bhiocáire, that was the entertainment they had in the evenings – storytelling – and there was a great number of people travelling around in those days. I'd have a night (of company-keeping) at my place and then you'd have a night at yours, and their whole concern during the course of the evening was storytelling. Peig had a fine, listening ear and she kept every one of those stories in her head until she went down into the brown sod.[90]

Ireland's original, indigenous culture is known as *béaloideas*, meaning the knowing and teaching from the mouth. It sifted, celebrated and transmitted the daily experience of ordinary individuals in a neighbourhood, lovingly framing it in humour, philosophy and myth. We urgently need to revive and amplify this heritage and to launch a culture that tells of our femininity and masculinity, that celebrates personal biographies down along our matrilineages and patrilineages. This is our chance to release the pent agony of silenced emigrations, sexual abuse, adoptions and abortions as well as to promote joy and pride in our menstruations, miscarriages, abortions, pregnancies, travels, innovations and lesbian and gay culture. Perhaps mistakenly, the national fear of 'losing' Irishness to modernity, of it being dissolved by forces encroaching from abroad, is rarely directed against the Americanisation of all cultures, against modern technology nor even against mass emigration. It is often instead directed against every sign of sexual and reproductive innovation. We should take courage at least from the fact that, apart from the open wound of the loss of our language, 'modernising' forces seem to operate at another level which cannot threaten the enduring, spiritual reality which is Irishness, nor strip any more layers from it than colonisation has already done. Meanwhile, reproductive paranoia may be understandable in a people who have survived the genocidal contexts of the Cromwellian campaigns and of the Famine and who experience constant emigration. However, we need to enquire more deeply into these national concepts of territory, population and posterity and to take the pressure off our sexuality.

We certainly struggle with post-colonial trauma, but we need to direct our critiques towards the renewed colonisations we have imposed upon ourselves since the establishment of the Republic. Most importantly, we need to recognise the pattern we share with decolonising societies all over the world. With a post-independence regime which has been reactionary and non-egalitarian, with our cycles of social pathology, and with our punitive loss of solidarity between ourselves manifesting in civil wars, gender subordination and mass emigration, we are typical. The international context at this time is an unhappy one where social crisis is the norm and an apocalyptic vision is the ethos. However, as a culture which is 'emergent' in the present decade, we contrast with the climate of the day and are importantly placed to shape radical discourses which will be needed by other societies in the decades ahead. Irishness occupies a pivotal location in the world's political space. It hinges crucially between the Third World (with its colonised history, the post-imperialist war in Northern Ireland, mass emigration and loss of native language) and the First World (with white skin, EU membership, Western standards of living and autonomous access to media and education). Ireland balances on a fulcrum between punishment and privilege and this is an ideal location from which to evolve and transmit radical discourses. Wherever they end up, Irish emigrants find themselves peripheralised away from the homeland in the same way that Ireland's economy is peripheralised by larger foreign powers.[91] However, just as being outside Ireland is often the best location from which to understand our Irishness, so too Ireland's location in the international margins could be a fertile, irrepressible matrix for radical bodies and voices.

NOTES AND REFERENCES

1   From interviews conducted by the author with Irish women living in Britain, all quoted anonymously here at the speakers' request.

2   bell hooks, 'Representing Whiteness' in *Yearning – Race, Gender and Cultural Politics* (Boston, South End Press, 1990).

3   Cited in Ellen Hazelkorn, 'British Capital and Irish Labour: Evidence from the 1990's in Gearoid O'Tuathaigh (ed.), *The Emigrant Experience* (Galway, Galway Labour History Group, 1991), p. 135.

4   Jim Mac Laughlin, Ireland: *The Emigrant Nursery and the World Economy* (Cork University Press, 1994), p. 41.

5   Mary Lennon, Marie McAdam and Joanne O'Brien, *Across the Water, Irish Women's Lives in Britain,* (London, Virago, 1988), p. 9.

6   Mary Kenny, *Woman X Two,* (London, Sidgwick and Jackson, 1978), p. 20.

7   John Quinn (ed.), *A Portrait of the Artist as a Young Girl* (London: Mandarin, 1990); Julia Carson (ed.), *Banned in Ireland – Censorship and the Irish Writer* (London, Routledge, 1990); Rita Wall, *Leading Lives: Irish Women in Britain,* (Dublin, Attic Press, 1991).

8   Jonathan Rutherford (ed.), *Identity: Community, Culture, Difference,* (London, Lawrence and Wishart, 1990), Introduction.

9   Liam Ryan, 'Irish Migration to Britain since World War II' in Richard Kearney (ed.), *Migrations, the Irish at Home and Abroad,* (Dublin: Wolfhound Press, 1990), p. 55.

10   'New Irish Bury Paddy Myth', *Guardian,* 24 April 1995.

11   Marella Buckley, 'Heard about the Irish Stereotype?', *Guardian,* 30 May 1995.

12   Mary J. Hickman and Bronwen Walter, 'Deconstructing Whiteness, Irish Women in Britain' in *Feminist Review,* no. 50, Summer 1995, p. 16.

13   *Sun,* 22 January 1994.

14   Hickman and Walter, 'Deconstructing Whiteness'.

15   Ute Kowarzik, *Developing a Community Response – the Service Needs of the Irish In Britain,* (London, Action Group for Irish Youth and Federation of Irish Studies, 1994), p. 10.

16   London Irish Women's Centre Report, *Roots and Realities,* (London, 1993), p. 19.

17   London Irish Women's Centre (LIWC), 1986 Report, (London: Trojan Press, 1986), p. 11.

18   Ute Kowarzik, *Developing a Community Response,* p. 15.

19   ibid., p. 15.

20   Muhammad Anwar, *The myth of Return-Pakistanis in Britain,* (London, Heinemann, 1979), p. 19.

21   LIWC Report, 1986, p. 6.

22   ibid., p. 18.

23   Mac Laughlin, *Ireland: the Emigrant Nursery.*

24   ibid., p. 57.

25   ibid., p. 56.

26   Hazelkorn in *The Emigrant Experience,* p. 132.

27   ibid., p. 135.

28   Ryan, 'Irish Migration to Britain', p. 54.

29   Theresa Moriarty, review of 'Workers' Lives' (documentary film) in *The Emigrant Experience,* p. 35.

30   D. Blanchard, 'High Steel: the Kahnawake Mohawk and the High Construction Trade', in *Journal of Ethnic Studies,* vol. 11 no. 2, 1993, p. 41.

31   James A. Doyle, *The Male Experience,* (William C. Brown Communications Inc., 1995), p. 254.

32   hooks, *Yearning,* p. 217.

33 Hickman and Walter, 'Deconstructing Whiteness'.
34 ibid.
35 Ryan, 'Irish Migration to Britain'.
36 Cited by J. Mac Laughlin, Bronwen Walter in *Ireland: The Emigrant Nursery*, p. 71.
37 Abu Odeh, 'Postcolonial Feminism and the Veil: Thinking the Difference', in *Feminist Review* no. 43, Spring 1993, p. 27.
38 Ryan 'Irish Migration to Britain'.
39 Lennon, McAdam, O'Brien, *Across the Water*, p. 106.
40 ibid., p. 94.
41 Mac Laughlin, *Ireland: The Emigrant Nursery*, p. 69.
42 Anne Rossiter, 'Bringing the Margins into the Centre: a Review of Aspects of Irish Womens' Emigration', in Sean Hutton and Paul Stewart (eds.), *Ireland's Histories: Aspects of State, Society and Ideology*, (London, Routledge, 1991), p. 236.
43 See Ruth Fletcher, 'Silences: Irish Women and Abortion', *Feminist Review* no. 50, Summer 1995.
44 Nira Yuval-Davis, 'Gender and Nation' in *Ethnic and Racial Studies*, vol. 16, no. 4, October 1993, p. 621.
45 ibid., p. 621.
46 Bernard Canavan, 'Storytellers and Writers: Irish Identity in Emigrant Labourers' Autobiographies, 1870–1970' in Patrick O'Sullivan (ed.), *The Creative Migrant*, vol. 3, *The Irish World Wide – History, Heritage, Identity* (Leicester University Press, 1994), p. 165.
47 Ryan, 'Irish Migration to Britain'.
48 hooks, *Yearning*, p. 113.
49 LIWC Report 1986, p. 11.
50 ibid., p. 18.
51 hooks, *Yearning*, p. 214.
52 Lennon, McAdam, O'Brien, *Across the Water*, p. 15.
53 ibid., p. 86.
54 Ailbhe Smyth cited in *Roots and Realities*, p. 17.
55 Lennon, McAdam, O'Brien, op. cit., p. 42.
56 *Roots and Realities*, p. 17.
57 ibid., p. 17.
58 ibid., p. 19.
59 Mac Laughlin, *Ireland: The Emigrant Nursery*, p. 64.
60 *Roots and Realities*, p. 29.
61 Jim Mac Laughlin, *Travellers and Ireland: Whose Country, Whose History?* (Cork University Press, 1995), p. 29.
62 *Roots and Realities*, p. 26.
63 Kowarzik, *Developing a Community Response*, p. 43.
64 LIWC Report, 1986, p. 18.
65 Kowarzik, op. cit., p. 42.
66 Lennon, McAdam, O'Brien, op. cit., p. 196.
67 L. Scorer, P. Spencer and C. Hewitt, *The Prevention of Terrorism Act: the Case for Repeal*, (London, National Council for Civil Liberties, 1985), p. 7.
68 Annie Maguire cited by Rita Wall, *Leading Lives: Irish Women's Lives in Britain*, (Dublin, Attic Press, 1991), p. 25.
69 Kowarzik, *Developing a Community Response*, p. 46.
70 hooks, *Yearning*, p. 205.
71 ibid., p. 207.

72   Interview with the author.

73   Kowarzik, op. cit., p. 47.

74   Interview with the author.

75   Interview with the author.

76   Frantz Fanon, *Black Skin, White Masks*, (London, Paladin, 1990), p. 201; Frantz Fanon, *The Wretched of the Earth*, (London, Penguin, 1963), p. 11.

77   Ruth Fletcher, *Feminist Review*, no. 50, p. 64.

78   Colin Holmes, *John Bull's Island: Immigration and British Society, 1871–1971* (London: Macmillan, 1979) p. 23.

79   'Hidden Agenda', the *Guardian*, 20 March 1995.

80   Lennon, McAdam, O'Brien, op. cit., p. 189.

81   Maguire cited in *Leading Lives*, p. 22.

82   Anne Rossiter, *Ireland's Histories*, p. 236.

83   Fintan O'Toole, *A Mass for Jesse James: a Journey Through 1980's Ireland*, (Dublin, Raven Arts Press, 1990) p. 10.

84   'Airing Grievances', *Guardian*, 27 November 1995.

85   ibid.

86   Seamus Heaney, 'Correspondances: Emigrants and Inner Exiles', *Migrations*, op. cit., p. 29.

87   Fintan O'Toole, *A Mass for Jesse James*, p. 122.

88   Cheryl Herr, 'The Erotics of Irishness', *Critical Inquiry*, Autumn 1990, p. 1–34.

89   Seán Pheats Tom Ó Cearnaigh, *Fiolar an Eireaball Bháin* (Coisceim, 1992), p. 40.

90   Translated by Marella Buckley.

91   Jim Mac Laughlin, 'Emigration and the Peripheralisation of Ireland in the Global Economy', Review, *Journal of Fernand Braudel Center*, vol. XVII, no. 2 pp. 243–73.

5. The New Vanishing Irish
Social Characteristics of 'New Wave' Irish Emigration

JIM MAC LAUGHLIN

This chapter focuses on traditional and 'new wave' emigration with particular reference to the social characteristics, age structure, the professional and educational qualifications and destinations of those emigrants who left Ireland on what has been interpreted as a 'new wave' of emigration in the 1980s. It also examines changing perspectives on Irish emigration which have caused it to be interpreted as a voluntary activity, a product of Irish youth enterprise culture and an inevitable contemporary manifestation of a long-drawn out historical and cultural tradition of emigration. It suggests that, while a significant proportion of recent emigrants have undoubtedly achieved social mobility abroad, not least in Europe and in the United States, this 'emigrant aristocracy' is not so significant as to allow for the gentrification of most recent emigration. The chapter also suggests that, while Irish attitudes towards emigration have altered quite significantly since the nineteenth century, the causes and consequences of emigration have not altered all that much. To argue thus is also to caution against any premature categorisation of 'new wave' emigration as a 'European phenomenon' and a new development in Irish emigration history.

THE DE-NATIONALISATION OF IRISH EMIGRATION SINCE THE NINETEENTH CENTURY

Social and political attitudes to Irish emigration have generally been refracted through social class and ethnic lenses. They have also shaped, and been shaped by, prevailing political orthodoxies, not least by free-market economic policies and by conflicting attitudes towards nation-building and nationalism in Ireland.[1] As we have already seen, nineteenth-century Malthusians on both sides of the Irish Sea long regarded the large-scale exodus from rural Ireland as a necessary accompaniment to the modernisation of an island economy at industrial Britain's back door. By mid-century, they were advocating state support for Irish emigration and implying that those who left Ireland fared well outside it. They particularly linked emigration to revolutions in transportation which drew Ireland closer to Britain and the United States, where, it was argued, the 'troublesome Irish' properly belonged.[2] Nationalists were among the first to attack this naturalisation and sanitisation of Irish emigration, which they attributed to 'landlordism' and to 'English misrule' in Ireland. In so doing, they Anglicised the causes of Irish emigration and nationalised its solutions. They argued that emigration was a subtle exercise in social engineering which sought to make room for 'graziers and their bullocks' in rural Ireland by banishing Irish young adults abroad when they were needed to build a strong Irish nation at home.[3] Home Rule, they insisted, would put an end to large-scale involuntary emigration. Nationalists, as we have also seen, were also concerned that emigration had become so entrenched by the late nineteenth century that it was affecting the very 'bone and sinew' of the nation, attracting away too many young women, the future mothers of Ireland, and depleting the 'athletic male population' of the country.

Irish attitudes to emigration have altered significantly since independence. Particularly since the 1960s, voluntarism and opportunism have now replaced nationalist condemnations of emigration in most hegemonic discourses on the topic. Consequently, it is increasingly now suggested that those leaving Ireland are doing so voluntarily and are achieving considerable degrees of social mobility abroad.[4] This view was also rooted in popular emigration culture in the 1950s and 1960s. The families of those who had emigrated talked then of their emigrant sons and daughters in terms of their success, never in terms of their failure, abroad. Ireland's emigrant sons were 'managing' bars, supermarkets and hotels, they were never simply 'working' there. Her emigrant daughters were all typists, bank assistants and manageresses, they were never simply working in low-status female job ghettoes.

In this 'post-nationalist' literature on Irish emigration which emerged from the 1960s onwards, emigration could quite clearly no longer be attributed to 'English misrule' in Ireland. It was, instead, portrayed as a considered and rational response to restructuring processes operating at the level of Irish society and the world economy. Thus the invisible hand of *market forces* now signalled differences in income between Ireland and overseas labour markets. It indicated where opportunities existed abroad. It channelled emigrants to overseas fields of opportunity and generally determined the volume, and indeed the quality, of Irish emigration. Reflecting the neo-classical framework within which these arguments were couched, cost-benefits analysis and modernisation theory were used to portray historic and contemporary Irish emigration quite simply as a 'transfer mechanism'.[5] Emigration, it was now suggested, was merely a strategy for resolving problems of 'labour surpluses' at home by directing Irish young adults to fields of opportunity abroad. Moreover, the decision to emigrate was now posited at the level of the individual, and rarely at the level of national society and its class structure. In so doing, these new theories of emigration avoided any social-class or regional analysis of the internationalisation of Irish labour. Modernisation theorists in particular reduced emigration to strict economic causes and consequences and subjected emigrants to the compelling logic of an iron law of labour transfer.[6]

Despite the strong sense of place and sense of community, both in Irish life and in Irish history, places as the bases of real communities scarcely featured in this literature. They were, instead, reduced to the level of marketplaces and labour markets. More commonly still, Ireland was treated as a level, abstract, national plain over which the currents of emigration evenly flowed. Economists, demographers and statisticians in particular, influenced by the quantitative revolution which impacted upon the social sciences in Ireland in the late 1960s, analysed the *national* effects of emigration, and did so from a strict cost-benefit perspective. In so doing, they also largely ignored the social-class impact and the regional causes and consequences of Irish emigration. The Irish emigrant in the post-nationalist explanatory models of these theorists was simply concep-tualised as a geographically mobile *homo economicus*, moving logically from one labour market to another in a ceaseless search for economic opportunity.[7] The 'equilibrium route' to emigration, which this perspective encouraged, devalued the centrality of place to the study of emigration. It further ignored the socio-political and contextual settings of emigration and characterised as free choices decisions to emigrate that were in fact structured within, and had powerful structuring effects upon, a whole variety of regional, national and international contexts.

While attitudes to Irish emigration have altered significantly since the nine-teenth century, its causes and consequences have not altered very much. Once again emigration is being naturalised and sanitised, this time by Irish political leaders. Since the 1980s, they have been characterising recent emigration as 'new wave emigration', a 'European phenomenon', and a 'new departure' in Irish emigration history. In a now-famous statement made at the height of an upswing in youth emigration in 1987, Ireland's Minister for Foreign Affairs, Brian Lenihan, stated:

> We regard emigrants as part of our global generation of Irish people. We should be proud of them. The more they hone their skills and talents in another environment, the more they develop a work ethic in a country like Germany or the US, the better it can be applied in Ireland when they return.[8]

Another Irish senior education planner employed by the World Bank also argued that:

> If we are true EEC members and we believe in European integration, we should see the increasing manpower shortage in Europe as a fortuitous opportunity for our young people facing unemployment to think of 'mobility' and 'migration' as natural solutions.[9]

Government officials in particular have encouraged this sanitisation and voluntarisation of contemporary Irish emigration. It is increasingly now suggested that 'new wave' emigration is a voluntary activity involving well-educated young adults who are climbing social ladders abroad and are better qualified than their predecessors to compete in overseas labour markets.[10] This, in turn, has contributed to the individualisation of recent emigration. Thus, despite its volume, the tendency today is to treat emigration in composite terms, and to view it as an undifferentiated flow comprising individuals distinguished from their predecessors by their superior qualifications and distinguished from their peers by their spirit of adventure and enterprising spirit. This 'individualisation' of emigration in Ireland has clear parallels with the 'individualisation' of social problems in Britain in the 1980s. In particular it echoes Mrs Thatcher's statement which suggested that in England in the 1980s there was 'no such thing as society, there are only individuals'.[11] In Ireland also, the social class composition, as well as the social and political consequences of emigration, have largely been ignored in most recent literature on 'new wave' emigration.

WORLD-SYSTEMS THEORY AND 'NEW WAVE' IRISH EMIGRATION

The world-systems approach discussed in chapter one of this volume helps one transcend the voluntarism and behaviouralism in recent accounts of Irish emigration and is central to any structural analysis of its causes and consequences. World systems theory treats emigration not so much as a behavioural phenomenon as an intrinsically geographical relationship with clear geographical causes and consequences. However, it also insists that emigration cannot be explained away in simple geographical or locational terms. This is precisely what conventional core-periphery theory does when it attributes emigration to 'push' and 'pull' factors and when it explains it away in terms of the growing proximity of Ireland to Britain, the United States and continental Europe. In particular, it accords high explanatory values to geographical features like the 'small size' and 'openness' of the Irish economy. A world-systems approach differs from these core-periphery, nation-centered and behavioural models of Irish emigration in a number of ways. Firstly, it insists that emigration clearly is a geographical phenomenon but that it is not caused by geographical factors. Neither is it attributable to the peculiarities of the Irish, or to the exceptional geographical mobility of Irish young adults. Secondly, it suggests that emigration is not 'caused' by the social attributes and aspirations of Irish young adults. It is not the inevitable consequence of the exposure of Irish young adults to the fatal attractions of foreign fields of opportunity. These factors, it is argued, simply facilitate Irish emigration. They do not explain its volume, social composition or geographical characteristics. Thirdly, world-systems theory traces emigration to the peripheral status of the Irish state, especially its peripheral status in the international economy, rather than to the peripheral location of the Irish economy relative to Britain and mainland Europe. Fourthly, and most importantly, it suggests that emigration has its roots in the social geographical conjuncture which links Ireland to a number of core areas of the international economy. Thus, in the nineteenth century, emigrant trails linked regions in Ireland chiefly to Scotland, England, North America and Australia. Indeed, for much of the first half of the present century, Ireland and Britain practically functioned as an integrated labour field across which Irish emigrants freely flowed. More recently still, the axis of emigration has now shifted to selected urban centres in Europe, particularly in France, Belgium, Germany and the Netherlands, all of which have large immigrant Irish populations. Finally, and as we have already seen in chapter one, world-systems theory treats cores, peripheries and semi-peripheries as socio-historical and geographical *processes*, and not as locational *categories*. This means that a world-systems approach to Irish emigration allows us to avoid the national exception-alism in most historic accounts of Irish emigration. It especially focuses upon social, historical, geographical and political aspects of emigration. In particular, it emphasises the inextricable linkages between processes of core-formation and peripheralisation operating at the levels of Irish society and the global economy.[12] In other words, world-systems theory allows for a political and economic geography of emigration and treats places as the structuring and structured contexts wherein people make decisions about the world in which they live, including, in Ireland's case, decisions whether or not to emigrate. This suggests that the proper starting point for explaining the recent exodus from Ireland is less the enterprising spirit of young Irish adults than the local worlds where national and international factors that contribute to emigration regularly intersect in such a way as to 'lift' them from familiar surroundings at home and deposit them in unfamiliar surroundings abroad.[13] Unlike the individualist focus of behaviouralism, therefore, and the nation-centred focus of core-periphery theories, world-systems theory does not prioritise national over local analysis. Neither does it treat regions and places as mere containers of social behaviour. It insists, instead, that places matter to the study of emigration because they are the contexts within which decisions to emigrate are structured.[14]

RURAL FUNDAMENTALISM AND IRISH EMIGRATION, 1921–1960

A world-systems approach to modern Irish emigration not only focuses upon structural contexts of Irish emigration. It brings history back into the study of recent emigration. It suggests that, while the process of decolonisation created in Ireland the semblance of political independence, the country still retained the status of a peripheral state and was still highly dependent upon Britain for the export of agricultural produce and surplus labour. With the exception of a brief downturn in emigration in the late 1960s and early 1970s, the country has continued to function as an emigrant nursery for entire sections of Irish

TABLE 1: *Estimated Irish emigration, 1926–1966*

Years	Annual average
1926–1936	16,000
1936–1946	18,000
1946–1951	24,000
1951–1956	39,000
1956–1961	42,000
1961–1966	16,000

Source: Kennedy, 1973.

society ever since. Independence, it is argued, merely confirmed the hegemonic status of the substantial rural bourgeoisie and small farmers in the new state. Under de Valera, the prioritisation of the rural over the urban, together with the hegemonic status of rural fundamentalism, nurtured a positive view of farming, not least subsistence and small-scale mixed farming. This also cultivated a positive view of the family farm as the basic, even the natural unit of production in the Irish Republic.[15] This meant that the roots of emigration in post-Famine Ireland were now entwined in the social, political and moral structures of post-independence Ireland. Agriculture and agriculture-sustained industries were to be the basis of national prosperity from the 1930s to the late 1950s. This did nothing to stem the flow of young adults from Irish farms, or from rural and urban communities, but may, in fact, have exacerbated it. More and more young people joined emigrant trails out of Ireland and sought work and opportunities for social advancement in urban centres in Britain, the United States, Australia and other English-speaking cores of the world economy. As Commins has shown, this kind of rural fundamentalism was by no means narrowly economic in its logic. It emphasised the desirability of owner-occupancy and agricultural improvement and 'the intrinsic value of agricultural work' over all other occupations.[16] It paid scant regard to the merits of modern industrialisation and the need for economic diversification in Irish society. It particularly fostered the moral economy of substantial farmers who emerged victorious from political and social conflicts with the Anglo-Irish in post-Famine Ireland. If the modern Irish economy found its roots in this period, it owed its morality and its political outlook to Catholic social teaching which became hegemonic in post-independence Ireland.[17] This reflected the twin hegemonies of the Catholic Church and the substantial farmer in the new Ireland, while simultaneously reflecting the political and economic interests of medium to small farmers outside the richer agricultural heartlands of the country.

Commins also suggests that the most cogent expression of rural fundamentalism was contained in the Minority Report to the Commission on Emigration,

TABLE 2: *Number of Persons who Received Travel Permits, Identity Cards and Passports in 1940–51 in Order to Take Up Employment, Classified by Broad Occupation*

Occupation	(000)	%
Males		
Unskilled	113.3	53.1
Agricultural	43.2	20.3
Industrial	27.6	12.9
Other	29.3	13.7
Total	213.4	100.0
Females		
Domestic Services	85.5	57.2
Nursing	20.8	13.9
Agricultural	3.8	2.5
Clerical	3.6	2.4
Other	35.9	24.0
Total	149.6	100.0

Source: Commission on Emigration and other Population Problems, 1948–1954 (1954).

drawn up by Bishop Lucey of Cork in the early 1950s. This called for the containment of Dublin's expansion, the diffusion of owner-occupancy throughout the Republic and a prioritisation of the rural home as the optimum environment for raising the Irish Catholic family. It even went so far as to recommend that farm size be limited to between 15 and 20 acres.[18] All of this meant that, after independence, the processes of peripheralisation which characterised Ireland in the latter half of the nineteenth century continued and were compounded in the post-independence period. Thus, the Irish state was relieved of the responsibility for solving under-employment and unemployment. The safety valve of emigration created conditions of full employment, or at least approximated to these conditions, for much of the post-independence period. Thus, Crotty has argued that emigration has regularly given Ireland:

> . . . conditions approximating to 'full employment', with no large pool of unemployed labour to form a source of competing non-unionized labour, working either as self-employed persons or for non-union firms. These virtually 'full employment' conditions, brought about by mass emigration, have been fundamentally different from the normal conditions of massive growing labour surpluses in the former capitalist colonies.[19]

Cheap labour from Ireland certainly contributed to the regeneration of the British economy in the post-World War II years. This may in fact have reduced Britain's dependence on migrant labour from Third World countries to fill labour gaps in the British economy.[20] This was one reason why Britain was not as heavily dependent upon a *gastarbeiter* system of labour recruitment as Germany clearly was throughout the 1950s and early 1960s.[21] Irish emigration in these same years was exacerbated by glaring differentials in material standards and social opportunities between rural Ireland, on the one hand, and urban Britain and the United States, on the other. Reductions in the relative costs of emigrating to the urban enclaves of these countries did little to stem the flow of young adults from the Irish countryside. Indeed, Breathnach suggests that the scale of emigration and the quality of the exodus at this time threatened the very development of Ireland's industrial base. In other words, the large-scale emigration of young adults from urban and rural Ireland exacerbated the under-development of the country's indigenous industrial base while simultaneously consolidating the hegemony of rural fundamentalism, small farmers and the rural bourgeoisie. Even when political relations between Britain and Ireland were deeply 'soured' during the 'economic war' of the 1930s, the two countries were still locked together in a common labour market. The 'economic war' may, in fact, have cemented the relationship between the two labour fields, and it could be argued that population movements from Ireland to Britain at this time were merely part of a broader and more general process of rural-urban drift operating at the level of the British Isles.[22] Young adults from rural England, like their peers from rural Scotland and Wales, migrated to British cities where they filled gaps in the British labour market, particularly during the boom years of the 1950s and 1960s. Young adults from rural and urban Ireland emigrated to Britain where some found new niches in the tertiary sectors and in new sectors of industrial employment. However, the majority still gravitated to the traditional job ghettoes of Irish immigrants in urban Scotland and the south of England. As Hazelkorn succinctly puts it, thousands of the young Irish in the early decades of the new state at least voted with their feet to abandon the narrow nationalism of de Valera with its dreams of 'frugal comfort' and devotion to 'things of the spirit'.[23] They at once opted for, and were compelled instead to settle for, a life in the urban enclaves of Britain and the United States where they lived out their lives in places which could not be further removed from the Ireland they literally left behind.

Breathnach suggests that emigration characterised relations between Ireland and Britain for much of this period.[24] As Tables 1 and 2 show, emigration certainly was a diagnostic feature of Irish society throughout the 1950s and well into the 1960s. Emigration then structured social relations between Ireland and Britain. It was responsible for structuring political, social-class and gender relations within Ireland. It literally also constructed and de-constructed social space in Ireland throughout much of the post-independence period. Just as the removal of the Irish in the nineteenth century was interpreted by many as a strategy for 'making room for graziers and their bullocks' in Ireland, the large-scale emigration of Irish youth in this period made way for the development of Irish agriculture and its system of family farms and market towns.[25] Far from simply being a historical tradition generated by an emigrant culture, emigration on this scale had its roots in Ireland's economic and political system. It particularly reflected the structural dependence of post-independence Ireland on overseas labour markets to host the artificially-created labour surpluses fostered by an exclusive devotion to export-led agricultural production based upon the family farm. To argue thus is not to suggest that Ireland was *naturally* a labour surplus economy. It is merely to argue that the forms taken by Irish economic development have regularly generated surpluses of specific types of labour. This also caused emigration to be treated as an acceptable solution to the problem of labour surpluses and unemployment at home. Criticising the designation of nineteenth-century Ireland as a 'labour-surplus economy' Ó Tuathaigh has stressed that this is a highly relativistic term.[26] What is 'surplus' is only to be considered as such in the context of a specific social formation, a specific system of economic development and a specific set of hegemonic ideas, values, priorities and policies. The logic of the Irish nationalist case in the late nineteenth century implied that if the core concern of Irish government was the economic development of the country in the interests of the Irish as a people, then its capacity to retain and maintain a much larger population would be unquestionable. According to this essentially nationalist view, Ireland was a 'labour-surplus economy' only in the context of its subordinate and exploited status within the British empire. In suggesting that emigration was primarily due to the British connection, to absentee landlords, to the draining effects of rents, to under-investment, nationalists anglicised the causes of Irish emigration and nationalised its solutions. They particularly ignored the roots of emigration in Irish property relations and in the logic of Irish economic development. Emigration in the post-independence period was clearly not caused by Ireland's status in the British Empire, and the country's geographical location could not explain levels of development or account for the political institutions and the class structure in the new state. These were the products of historical processes and the result of social and political changes taking place within Irish society. They were not simply products of geography. From the 1930s onwards, they were also the product of Ireland's historically defined place in international relations.[27] Similarly the country's political institutions, like its political culture, were the inheritance from an Irish past as much as from an Anglo-Irish past. They were at once the accumulation of conflicts waged between different social classes in Ireland and structural and ideological responses to changes in an evolving Irish society.

The Post-war Period: Emigration, Social Mobility and Regional Industrial Development

World War II particularly stressed the close links between Irish and British labour markets. It also emphasised Britain's heightened dependence on Ireland for surplus labour throughout the war years and afterwards. Irish labour now, particularly Irish women workers, filled gaps in the British labour market that were directly attributable to the war. It was almost a case of Irish workers getting more and new opportunities in Britain because British workers were 'away from home'. Thus Lennon, Mc Adam and O'Brien have argued:

> During the war Britain needed to supplement its labour force and it automati-
> cally turned to its traditional source, Ireland. This dramatically underlined the
> extent to which the economic relationship between the two countries remained
> unchanged by political independence. The Irish state was officially neutral – in
> practice it was 'neutral on England's side'. Thousands of Irish men and women,
> from north and south of the border, joined the British Army. Many more left for
> Britain, directly recruited by the British authorities to fill the gaps in the labour
> force.[28]

Certainly at this time, recruitment posters appeared in labour exchanges all over the country urging Irish women, in particular, to apply for jobs and to help the war effort in Britain. Given the economic problems of the Irish economy at this time, and particularly given the high levels of unemployment and under-employment, the Irish government welcomed the option of exporting its 'surplus labour' as an alternative to the creation of new employment opportunities in Ireland. As a result, many Irish women found that the war presented them with new opportunities in nursing, factory work and clerical work that were not available at home. This pattern continued long after the war as Irish immigrants, both male and female, found new positions in the British welfare state, especially in nursing, teaching, clerical work and in low status positions in public administration.

The branch-plant industrialisation of Ireland in the 1960s temporarily reversed the flood of emigration out of the country at this time, at least in parts of the country. This did not result in any fundamental change in the peripheral status of the Irish state. Instead, the axis of dependency now shifted from Britain to more advanced cores areas in the United States, Germany, France and Japan. Ireland by then had clearly become highly dependent for industrial employment upon foreign-owned firms from these and other countries in the world economy. By the mid-1970s, these firms accounted for over a third of the entire workforce in manufacturing industry in Ireland. The country then was also notoriously dependent upon high-technology, capital intensive indus-tries which frequently fled the Republic when their 'tax-free holidays' ended.[29] Nevertheless, dependent industrialisation in Ireland had a number of important consequences. Firstly, it gave the country a more diversified economy and created a significant degree of occupational segregation and regional differentiation in the country. As Wickham has pointed out, this also mixed mastery of technology with technical awe and national pride to produce a false sense of autonomy which suggested that these industries allowed the nation to recover economic sovereignty and stem the flow of emigration.[30] Secondly, while they did alter the ownership and composition of industry and gave Ireland the image of a technologically-advanced society, new capital intensive industries did not absorb the country's sizeable labour surpluses, particularly of the long-term unemployed. Neither did it reduce Ireland's dependence on overseas labour markets for disposing of 'surplus' workers nor close the substantial gaps separating Ireland from the core areas of the world economy. This is another way of saying that the new industrialisation of Ireland did not fundamentally alter its peripheral status in the international economy.[31] It may in fact have exacerbated it. Ireland, like Greece, Scotland, Portugal, Spain and Italy, retained the status of an emigrant nursery, a geographically marginalised nation and a peripheral state. Young adults left these countries not because they were possessed of a spirit of adventure or an enterprising spirit. They left because the supply of labour exceeded demand and because more opportunities for social development existed abroad than in the restrictive economies of the home country. Thus, 'new wave' emigration from Ireland in the late 1970s and throughout the 1980s coincided with a downturn in the industrial economy which marked a turning point in Irish industrial development. Manufacturing employment dropped from 243,000 in 1980 to 201,000 by 1986. This constituted the longest sustained decline in manufacturing industry in the country since the foundation of the state.[32] This, rather than the enterprise culture of Irish emigrants, is the structural background against which 'new wave' emigration must be analysed.

THE 'NEW WAVE' – THE MODERNISATION OF IRISH EMIGRATION?

Despite the high volume of emigration in recent years, the tendency today is to treat emigrants as enterprising individuals, rather then seeing them as social class victims or benefactors of restructuring processes operating at the level of Irish society and the world economy. The exodus has been estimated at 72,000 between 1981 and 1986.[33] By 1986, net emigration had reached 28,000 or just under 8 per 1,000 of the total population. Courtney estimates that almost a quarter of a million people left the country between 1982 and 1988. The three years up to April 1989 was the period of heaviest out-migration. Record levels of over 50,000 per year were leaving the country at this time. The exodus has been estimated at approximately 14,400 per annum in the first half of the 1980s, rising to over 50,000 in 1987–8. These figures exclude the very large number of illegal Irish immigrants in the United States in the late 1980s. The

Irish Emigration Reform Movement recently estimated Irish 'illegals' in the United States alone at approximately 135,000. Upwards of 20,000 of these were living in Boston alone.[34] Estimates of the number of 'illegal Irish' in New York city vary from a low of 40,000 to a high of over 100,000.[35] It is also important to note that the number of emigrants leaving the country is much smaller than the pool of potential emigrants. Thus, for example, 120,000 Irish people applied for visas to enter Australia in 1986 but only 1,251 were successful.[36]

Results from most recent surveys of Irish emigration suggest that this 'new wave' of emigration is not that different, either in its social composition, geographical destinations and occupational profile, from traditional Irish emigration, particularly that of the 1950s. Emigration still is an employment strategy and a strategy for survival which impacts more heavily upon the rural poor and the working class than upon middle-class and suburban families. That said, however, it is important to note that these also have clearly been seriously affected both by voluntary and involuntary emigration. Once again, however, it is important to stress that this is not a new development. For much of the post-Famine period, as in the post-independence period, middle-class emigrants constituted a considerable, if neglected, element in Irish emigration.

A sample survey carried out by the Department of Labour in the mid-1980s found that 1,800 school leavers out of a total of just under 61,000 had left the country within one year of leaving school.[37] A recent survey by the National and Economic and Social Council (henceforth NESC) found that the majority of emigrants were aged between 15–24 years when they left the country.[38] This report also suggested that second-level school leavers accounted for the majority of Irish emigrants in the 1980s. This means that the traditional view of the Irish emigrant as an unskilled manual worker must be revised to include the large numbers of female emigrants and other young emigrants, both male and female, with second-, third-level and other professional qualifications. Large numbers of Irish emigrants now possess third-level and other professional qualifications. An estimated 26 per cent of the 11,300 third-level award recipients who left full-time education in 1988 had emigrated by the following spring (See also Tables 3 and 4).[39] Drawing upon data for the period 1986–8, the NESC survey found that record levels of between 19 and 29 per cent of all graduates had emigrated in search of work shortly after graduating. In the early 1980s, 8 out of 10 Irish graduates were still finding work at home. By the late 1980s, this figure had fallen to 6 out of every 10 graduates.

The authors of the NESC report raised important questions about the effects of the brain drain on Irish society and questioned the manner in which higher education is subsidised from general taxation in Ireland. Thus, they suggested that the criteria for funding Irish third-level institutions from EU revenue should be extended to include engineering and a wide range of other

TABLE 3: *Gross Migratory Outflow in 1987/88 Classified by the Social Group of the Household Head in which the Emigrant Previously Resided.*

| | Rate per 1000 Population | | |
Social Group	Males	Females	Total
Farmers	12.4	12.4	12.4
Professionals	19.3	14.4	16.8
Employers/managers	19.9	16.2	18.1
Salaried inter-mediate non-manual	15.3	13.4	14.3
Other non-manual	21.3	14.5	18.0
Skilled, semi-skilled manual	18.9	12.1	15.6
Unskilled	19.1	10.6	15.2
Unknown	48.8	9.3	22.4
Total	19.1	12.8	15.9

Source: Labour Survey (1988)

TABLE 4: *Estimated Gross Migration Outflow from Ireland to Year Ending April 1988 Classified by Sex and Age*

| | 1000 | | | % | | |
Age	M	F	Total	M	F	Total
0–14	0.5	0.5	1.0	1.5	2.2	1.8
15–24	22.0	16.8	38.8	65.3	74.0	68.8
25–44	10.3	5.0	15.3	30.6	22.0	27.1
45–64	0.9	0.3	1.2	2.6	1.3	2.1
65 +	–	0.1	0.1	–	0.4	0.2
Totals	33.7	22.7	56.4	100	99.9	100

Source: Labour Survey, 1988 (special tabulation) in Social and Economic Implications of Emigration, 1991, p. 72.

applied courses with high levels of technical skills. Until this happens, it could be argued, the brain drain will continue to contribute to the peripheralisation of Ireland. It will also represent a significant loss, not only in terms of resources invested in the education of emigrants, but also in social and political terms. This is because those leaving the country, namely well-qualified graduates and

TABLE 5: *West of Ireland Survey.*
Targeted Population and Emigrant Families per Survey Area

Survey Area	No. Families	No. Emigrant Families	Emigrant Families as %Total
Cork City	1,720	341	19.8
Limerick City	891	176	19.7
Skibbereen	437	109	24.9
Schull/Ballydehob	219	57	26.0
Waterford	429	86	20.0
Wexford	210	43	20.4
Tralee	690	174	25.2
South Limerick	179	34	18.9
South Galway	641	127	19.8
Cloughaneely	217	54	24.8
Inishowen	321	65	20.2
Raphoe	64	13	20.3
Totals	6,018	1,279	21.7

Source: Mac Laughlin, 1991.

TABLE 6: *West of Ireland Survey. Number of Emigrants per Emigrant Family*

Survey Area	No. Families	Number of Emigrants per Family			
		1	2	3	> 4
Cork City	341	65.1	25.3	6.1	3.5
Limerick City	176	63.3	21.4	7.2	8.1
Skibbereen	109	60.3	21.4	7.2	8.1
Schull/B'hob	57	59.9	21.4	11.2	6.5
Waterford	86	61.8	22.0	8.0	7.2
Wexford	43	70.1	23.6	5.8	0.5
Tralee	174	67.2	20.6	7.4	4.8
Sth Limerick	34	70.4	23.1	5.1	1.4
Sth Galway	127	64.7	25.3	4.7	5.3
Cloughaneely	54	56.3	20.1	11.7	11.9
Inishowen	65	57.1	21.2	10.3	11.4
Raphoe	13	70.3	20.4	7.3	2.0
Totals	1,279	63.9	22.2	7.7	5.8

Source: Mac Laughlin, 1991.

young adults with second-level qualifications, may well be consolidating the hegemonic status of conservative and right-of-centre parties in so doing.

Certainly in Ireland, as in peripheral economies in Europe, the Caribbean basin and Central America, the process of peripheralisation is so far advanced that many families may be classified as 'transnational households' because they have family members working abroad.[40] Accordingly, a survey of emigration from selected regions in the west and south of Ireland carried out by this author in the late 1980s (henceforth the West of Ireland Survey) found that one fifth of the 6,018 families surveyed had at least one member living abroad and 13 per cent of emigrant families had three or more emigrants (see Table 6).[41] This survey suggested that sanitised images of emigrants as individuals with impressive qualifications should be radically revised to conform to the reality of most recent emigration. Thus, it found that young emigrants of both sexes with second-level qualifications accounted for just over approximately two thirds of all emigrants. While graduate emigrants have certainly added a qualitative dimension to recent Irish emigration, this survey found that they are hardly significant enough to have contributed to its gentrification. Moreover, although university graduates attract more attention than graduate emigrants from technical colleges, the latter group may be outnumbering university graduates on emigrant trails out of Ireland in recent years. Today's emigrants are therefore not that different from those who stay at home. They certainly differ from many of their predecessors, but their superior educational and professional qualifications are best evaluated in terms of overseas labour market needs, rather than focusing on the undoubted gaps that separate today's emigrants from their predecessors. Most recent surveys also show that the urban bias in 'new wave' emigration is not simply a reflection of greater urbanisation of the Irish population in recent years. It is also due to the deterioration of urban labour markets and the lack of jobs and promotional opportunities in Irish urban centres.

Given the age structure and qualifications of recent emigrants, it is difficult to account for the gentrification of 'new wave' emigration in Irish political discourse. The NESC report found that of the estimated 56,500 emigrants who left Ireland in the year ending April 1988, almost 70 per cent were aged between 15 and 24 years. One third of all emigrants in the west of Ireland survey were still teenagers when they left the country. Of those who went to Britain, 40 per cent were in this age group. Thus, unlike their peers in the core areas of the European Union, adolescence for many Irish young adults may well be a period of considerable psychological and peer-group stress exacerbated by the stress of having to emigrate. Just under 10 per cent of emigrants in the West of Ireland Survey were under 18, and almost 45 per cent were less than 20 years when they left the country (see Table 7). In parts of Donegal and Kerry, those aged eighteen years and under were between 20 and 35 per cent of all emigrants. These figures correspond to the findings of another survey in Cork city in 1988

TABLE 7: *West of Ireland Survey. Emigrant Age at Leaving Home*
(Emigrants to UK only)

Study Area	Total	<18	18	19	20	21	≥22
Cork City	325	4.6	9.2	15.2	12.9	13.5	44.6
Limerick City	197	10.7	16.2	16.6	14.2	7.6	34.5
Skibbereen	143	10.5	11.2	9.1	12.6	17.4	39.2
Schull/B'hob	62	12.9	14.5	12.9	16.1	11.3	32.3
Waterford	132	11.4	17.4	18.9	15.9	9.1	27.3
Wexford	60	13.3	18.4	15.0	13.3	16.7	23.3
Tralee	174	6.9	11.5	16.1	12.1	16.6	36.8
S Limerick	42	9.5	9.5	28.6	7.1	7.1	38.2
S Galway	161	11.2	14.8	21.1	13.7	11.2	28.0
Cloughaneely	83	15.7	20.5	12.1	12.1	16.8	22.8
Inishowen	118	9.3	26.3	12.7	16.9	11.1	23.7
Raphoe	23	4.3	21.7	21.7	4.3	17.4	30.6
Totals	1,520	10.0	15.9	16.7	12.6	12.9	31.8

Source: Mac Laughlin, 1991.

TABLE 8: *West of Ireland Survey. Educational Qualifications of Emigrants*
(Emigrants to UK Only)

Study Area	Total	Intermediate Group Cert.	Percentage Leaving Cert.	Third Level
Cork City	325	14.8	46.4	38.8
Limerick City	197	27.4	49.2	23.4
Skibbereen	143	18.2	45.4	36.4
Schull/B'hob	62	37.1	43.5	19.4
Waterford	132	21.2	53.8	25.0
Wexford	60	18.4	58.3	23.3
Tralee	174	20.7	45.4	33.9
S Limerick	42	23.8	52.4	23.8
S Galway	161	20.5	54.1	25.4
Cloughaneely	83	50.6	34.9	14.5
Inishowen	118	34.7	42.4	22.9
Raphoe	23	0.0	69.6	30.4
Totals	1,520	23.9	49.6	26.4

Source: Mac Laughlin, 1991.

where it was found that one quarter of all recent emigrants had completed their secondary education only up to Junior Certificate level and a further 39 per cent had gone on to take their Leaving Certificate.[42] The NESC report found that two thirds of those who left the country with an Intermediate Certificate in secondary education did so without having a job arranged. This figure dropped to 40–50 per cent of those going with a Leaving Certificate or a higher qualification. These two groups, particularly the former, are the most disadvantaged recent additions to the Irish diaspora. In the West of Ireland Survey, secondary students still accounted for the majority of those emigrating, and those with third-level qualifications were only around one third of all emigrants (See Table 8).

Recent reports also suggest that Irish emigrants may also be entering virgin territory in moving to mainland Europe, Japan and a number of Third World countries. However, despite official perceptions of 'new wave' emigration as a European phenomenon, most recent surveys still point to Britain, specifically the south-east of England as the major host of most recent Irish emigrants. The NESC report found that just under 70 per cent of all those who left the state in the year ending April 1988 went to the UK. The United States accounted for an additional 14 per cent of the total.[43] These figures correspond to those in the West of Ireland Survey where it was found that about two thirds of Irish emigrants in the late 1980s were still going to Britain (see Table 9). A further one fifth went to the United States and less than 6 per cent went to mainland Europe.[44] This suggests that many 'deterritorialised' Irish young adults may now perceive London, not Dublin, as their capital. They may also see it in much the same light as their peers from the north of England and Scotland see it – a field of opportunity for those capable of adapting to the needs of the labour market, and an easy place from which to return home on a regular basis. Thus, the geography of recent Irish emigration to Britain has altered significantly in recent years. It is particularly contributing to core-formation in the south and south-east of England. Reductions in the relative costs of travel to London are reducing immediate costs for those leaving the country, and this may be encouraging Irish young adults to think only of travel costs when considering the costs of emigrating. Indeed, young emigrants today are also inventing 'new traditions' in emigration by returning home far more frequently than their predecessors did, at least in the initial years away from home. This, together with qualitative changes in recent emigrant flows, sets modern Irish emigrants apart from their predecessors. For many of the latter, emigration meant a life lived permanently abroad, in England and Scotland or in the United States, Canada or Australia. The majority of those emigrating in the late 1980s were returning home at least once a year, especially, as already indicated, in their first few years away from home. That said, however, 10–20 per cent of those who moved to Britain at that time had not been home in the twelve

TABLE 9: *West of Ireland Survey. Destinations of Emigrants*

| Survey Area | Percentage of emigrants to | | | | | |
	London	Other UK	N. America	EC	Other	Total
Cork City	46.0	17.6	18.4	11.3	7.6	511
Limerick City	51.7	16.2	16.6	4.8	10.7	290
Skibbereen	56.2	17.5	15.3	6.7	4.1	194
Schull/Bhob	45.2	28.6	21.4	1.2	3.6	84
Waterford	51.4	15.2	15.6	6.7	11.1	198
Wexford	58.3	13.2	11.9	7.1	9.5	84
Tralee	58.0	13.1	18.3	3.3	7.3	245
S Limerick	42.2	23.4	18.7	1.6	14.1	64
S Galway	56.8	11.4	22.9	3.0	5.9	236
Clough'ly	59.0	24.0	11.0	2.0	4.0	100
Inishowen	56.7	18.5	15.9	1.3	7.6	157
Raphoe	57.7	30.9	3.8	3.8	3.8	26
Totals	53.3	19.1	15.8	4.4	7.4	2,189

Source: Mac Laughlin, 1991.

TABLE 10: *West of Ireland Survey Frequency of Return Home in one 12 month Period (Emigrants to U.K. only)*

| Survey Area | Number of times returned home | | | | | |
	0	1	2	3	≥4	Total
Cork City	18.8	23.1	23.1	15.6	19.4	325
Limerick City	15.7	26.9	25.9	12.2	19.3	197
Skibbereen	21.0	18.8	26.6	18.2	15.4	143
Schull/B'hob	12.9	30.6	25.8	17.8	12.9	62
Waterford	20.5	25.8	26.5	12.8	14.4	132
Wexford	13.3	28.3	38.3	8.3	11.8	60
Tralee	12.1	23.0	32.2	21.2	11.5	174
Sth Limerick	21.4	33.3	16.7	21.4	7.2	42
Sth Galway	14.3	27.3	32.9	13.7	11.8	161
Cloughaneely	12.1	23.0	33.7	22.8	8.4	83
Inishowen	9.3	21.2	25.4	23.8	20.3	118
Raphoe	4.3	13.1	26.1	26.1	30.4	23
Totals	14.6	24.5	27.7	17.8	15.2	1,520

Source: Mac Laughlin, 1991.

months preceding the survey. In places as far apart as Cork city and the Inishowen peninsula, on the other hand, one of five emigrants were returning home four or more times per year. The results of this survey tend to suggest that contemporary Ireland is becoming an integrated field of emigration in the sense that regional variations particularly in the age structure, destinations and frequency of return home are not that significant (see Table 10). They also suggest that Ireland and England form an integrated labour field, particularly for unskilled, casual and semi-skilled labour. We may indeed be witnessing the birth of a new form of 'seasonal migration' from Ireland in recent years. In the late nineteenth and early twentieth century, large numbers of seasonal migrants from the north-west and the west of Ireland regularly worked part of the year in Scotland or the north of England and spent the rest of the year at seasonal work at home. Today, young emigrants from all over the country work for most of the year in England, particularly in the south-east, and return home on seasonal holidays, especially at Christmas. This is reflected in increases in the volume of traffic passing through Dublin and provincial airports at these times. Recent emigrants are undoubtedly also spending money saved abroad on these frequent trips back home. In this respect also they differ from their predecessors whose 'remittances' were a useful supplementary source of income for small farming families in the west of Ireland and for many working-class families throughout the country. Moreover, while frequency of return home has been used to sanitise recent emigration and to suggest that it is no longer a traumatic experience for many young Irish people, this may also indicate the involuntary nature of much recent emigration.

There are still, however, marked regional as well as social-class differences in the volume and quality of recent emigration. The enduring nature of emigration is particularly noticeable in the poorer rural areas of the country, especially in Donegal, Leitrim, Monaghan, Mayo, Roscommon, Galway, Cork, Kerry and Waterford, as well as in working-class districts of Dublin, Cork and Limerick. In the case of the north-west of Ireland, one in four families in parts of Donegal had at least one member living abroad. One quarter of all families in parts of Kerry were 'emigrant families', 12 per cent of which had three or more members living or working abroad (see Tables 5 and 6). Even in urban centres like Cork and Limerick, where one fifth of all families surveyed were 'emigrant families', just under 30 per cent of these had two or three family members living or working abroad.[45] This is not a recent development. Ever since the nineteenth century, families in Ireland have been structured by the employment needs of core areas of the world economy. The transnational nature of the Irish family has also long been intimately bound up with the changing circumstances of Irish and international capitalism. This paradox in Irish political and economic life, namely the scattering of the youth of Ireland in the interests of fostering a specific form of economic growth and political culture in Ireland, has created a profound contradiction at the very heart of Irish politics.

The Irish family has long been loaded with a double burden as a result of emigration. On the one hand, it has acted as the social terrain of personal life, a private space where mother, father and children are expected to share a healthy emotional and material life. The family in colonial Ireland was, for example, expected to fulfil the same functions as it did in mature industrial nations like Britain and the United States. On the other hand, families in Ireland were not only social arenas where the inner emotional life of the family met with the full force of the external economy – they were also places where the structuring forces of national and international capitalism intersected and helped to push young adults onto the emigrant trail.[46] Thus, in Ireland the twin forces of capitalism and emigration have had a powerful structuring effect upon the social composition of Irish families, and upon rural, working-class and middle-class communities. This, in turn, has added to the contradictions surrounding the Irish family. Ever since its institutionalisation in the 1937 Constitution, the traditional Irish patriarchal family was meant to act as an emotional retreat and a cocoon which protected its members from the *ennui* of social and economic life outside the family and outside Ireland. The degree of opposition to any amendments to family law as articulated in that Constitution shows the extent to which certain sectors in Irish society wish to cosset the Irish family against the external world, including legislative reform originating outside Ireland. However, while Church and state teach reverence for family values and respect for the sanctity of human life, political and social leaders since the nineteenth century have condoned emigration as a solution to Irish economic problems. The sanctity of the family as enshrined in the 1937 Constitution is therefore in stark contrast to a reality which sees emigration, often of quite young teenagers, embedded in the economic landscape and political system of this country. Moreover, in the very parts of this country where support for the traditional family and where opposition to divorce, abortion and family planning was strongest in recent referendums, teenagers of eighteen years and under often accounted for up to one third of total emigration. This also means that nationalism in contemporary Ireland has operated quite differently from nationalism in many other European countries. Anderson has shown how the very language of nationalism singles out the nation as the home and symbolic repository of group identity. Nations are discussed in a vocabulary of belong-ingness, kinship, motherland and fatherland and *heimat* in such a way as to denote a territory to which one is 'naturally' tied because one was naturally born there.[47] Nationalism today does not serve this important 'territorialising' function for large numbers of Irish young adults, many of whom still have to seek *lebensraum* or 'living space' abroad.

Emigration not only affects family life and emigrants but also has clearly influenced the social structure of urban and rural communities throughout the country. Large numbers of small towns and villages in rural Ireland today are in danger of 'dying' in much the same way that island communities have 'died' through 'senilisation' in the nineteenth century.[48] This aspect of community decay – the death of balanced communities through emigration and senilisation – is also evident in contemporary rural Ireland where entire communities are fading away due to the effects of emigration. Provincial cities and county towns are also be witnessing the re-opening of emigrant trails that were temporarily closed during the 'boom' years of the 1960s and 1970s, and this will undoubtedly affect their demographic structure.

Emigrants with professional qualifications undoubtedly constitute a new aristocracy in modern Irish emigration. Members of this group are also higher on the social ladder, and are probably more widely scattered around the global economy, than those from working-class and poor farming backgrounds, although these also have been entering virgin territory for poorer Irish emigrants. The pinnacle of the male emigrant aristocracy is occupied by engineers, dentists, doctors, accountants and other professionals. This group accounted for 16 per cent of male emigrants in the West of Ireland Survey. The professions accounted for significantly more male than female emigrants. Below the pinnacles of emigrant professional employment, the majority of male and female emigrants lead humbler lives and occupy the traditional occupations of the emigrant. One survey in the early 1980s found that 76 per cent of Irish men in Britain were manual workers.[49] Most male emigrants in London still gravitate to the construction industry. The West of Ireland Survey found that the construction industry accounted for more than two thirds of male emigrants from parts of Donegal, Cork county and Kerry. The corresponding figure for Cork city and Limerick was less than one third of all male emigrants.[50] This suggests that large numbers of the latter are still filling gaps in the semi-skilled, unskilled and casual labour market. It also suggests that while a minority of Irish male emigrants are climbing social ladders abroad, many more are simply climbing ladders.

Despite their neglect in most recent accounts, women still account for almost half of all emigrants since the 1980s. The NESC survey found that females accounted for almost 40 per cent of those aged between 15 and 44 who left Ireland in the year ending April, 1988.[51] Forty seven per cent of emigrants in the West of Ireland Survey were young women and many of these were teenagers when they left the country. These are among the most neglected sector in recent Irish emigration. Irish women who emigrated in the late nineteenth century were strongly represented in farm work, domestic service and factory work.[52] Large numbers of those who emigrated to Britain after World War II entered lower-middle-class positions in the welfare state. Even today,

Irish women emigrants who move to London often end up at a lower status than their non-immigrant peers, though many may have been better off than if they had remained at home.[53] A recent study of the causes and effects of emigration on Irish women argued that:

> The vast majority of women emigrate for employment-related reasons. Unemployment, lack of sufficient career opportunities and low paid, dead-end jobs in Ireland, combined with labour shortages in Britain and elsewhere and direct recruitment by these countries, provide the reasons for most emigration. Having said all that, women in particular have also emigrated because of what we may call 'social reasons', eg to escape domestic violence by travelling to Women's Aid shelters in England, to have an abortion, to conceal a pregnancy, to escape a feeling of not 'fitting in' because of beliefs or sexuality.[54]

Stressing the specificity of the female emigrant's experience since then, these authors went on to argue that:

> Many women . . . have decided that they must get out of Ireland permanently and set up home somewhere else. Their main reason for leaving was the repressive moral and social climate in Ireland. They describe how narrow social attitudes and restrictive laws which had an impact on almost every aspect of their lives contributed to their decision to leave. Many told us that for them the defeat of the 1986 referendum on divorce symbolised the intolerant nature of Irish society and drove them to emigrate . . . women emigrants repeatedly stress that the inability of Irish society to tolerate dissent or disagreement and to acknowledge difference were major factors influencing their decision to leave.[55]

As Kelly and Nic Ghoille Coille have emphasised, this feminisation of overseas labour markets, especially in the UK and the United States, has also drawn large numbers of Irish women workers abroad. As Buckley has shown in this volume, many of these have been only partially integrated into their host societies. Thus despite their numerical strength in their host societies, many Irish women are hidden from the history of recent Irish emigration. They are also widely scattered across a wide range of low income and 'invisible' employment. This category includes women working in neo-domestic service occupations like hospital orderlies, au pair work and in the catering trade. Thus, for example, Bronwen Walter has recently argued:

> Irish women in London are doubly invisible. As members of an ethnic minority whose existence is frequently unrecognised and as women whose work is scattered in various homes, hospitals and offices their contribution to London's economic and social life is largely ignored. Yet they comprise 10 per cent of all women in London. Their employment in particular sectors, notably nursing, catering and cleaning . . . virtually underpins the day to day functioning of the city.[56]

The fact that Irish communities abroad are male-dominated means, in turn, that Irish women emigrants have fewer support networks than their male counterparts. This also means that Irish women emigrants can also experience more difficulties in finding employment than men do, as many of these can rely on Irish contractors and other Irish employers to ease their entry into the labour force. As Kelly and Nic Ghoill Coille also point out:

> The pressures on women to adapt and assimilate have always been stronger than on men because women have always been more actively engaged in the cultures in which they have lived.[57]

It has also been found that women's role as primary carers of children often forces them to face decisions not only about their own ethnic identity but also about that of their children, many of whom may be brought up in multi-ethnic communities and in racially-mixed families. This strain is particularly strong in Irish communities in London where Irish women may be experiencing extra pressure due to the fact that they wish to make their children relate positively to their roots at times when political violence often makes this particularly difficult.

CONCLUSION

This chapter suggests that a world-systems approach has a number of advantages over conventional explanations of Irish emigration, not least those couched in the logic of behaviouralism and modernisation theory. Firstly, it avoids the pitfalls of exceptionalism in nationalist accounts and the cultural reductionism of behavioural accounts which over-emphasise the peculiar disposition of the Irish to emigrate. Secondly, it enables us to see Irish emigration as a social process linking core-formation within Ireland and the international economy while simultaneously contributing to the peripheralisation of the Irish state. Thirdly, it shows that, far from being untouched by the forces of industrialisation, Irish labour occupied a central position in the international division of labour and workers from Ireland have been crucial in the formation and maintenance of core areas of global capitalism.

This chapter also suggests that emigration has been as much a cause as a consequence of peripheralisation. Far from being caused by the adventurous spirit of emigrants, Irish emigration instead is a response to restructuring processes operating at the level of the national and global economy. Finally, except for short periods when emigration was halted by war, or reversed by short-term upswings in the Irish economy, Ireland has continued to function as a major emigrant nursery in the global economy. Indeed, like other world migrants, the Irish helped to establish the core areas of the world economy. They have also maintained them since then by filling labour gaps and literally regenerating their labour forces. Thus, labour has been Ireland's most consistent export and its most mobile and neglected resource.

ACKNOWLEDGEMENTS

The author wishes to acknowledge that some of the field research for this chapter was financed by a grant from the Arts Faculty Fund, University College, Cork.

NOTES AND REFERENCES

1   Robert D.C. Black, *Economic Thought and the Irish Question, 1817–1870* (Cambridge University Press, 1960); T.H. Boylan and T.P. Foley, *Political Economy and Colonial Ireland* (London, Routledge, 1992).

2   George Dangerfield, *The Damnable Question: A Study in Anglo-Irish Relations* (London, Quartet, 1979).

3   Gerard R.C. Keep, 'Official Opinion on Irish Emigration in the Later Nineteenth Century', *Irish Ecclesiastical Record*, LXXXI, pp. 412–21, 1954.

4   P. Geary and J. G. Hughes *International Migration in Ireland*. Economic and Social Research Institute, General Research Series, Paper no. 54. (Dublin, 1970); P. Geary and Cormac O'Gráda. 'Postwar Migration Between Ireland and the U.K.' in Ian Gordon and Andrew P. Thirwall (eds.), *European Mobility: Trends and Consequences* (London, Macmillan, 1989).

5   B. Walsh, 'Emigration: Some Policy Issues', *Irish Banking Review*, 2 1989 pp. 3–13.

6   Hassan Hakimian, *Labour Transfer and Economic Development: Theoretical Perspectives and Case Studies From Iran* (New York, Wheatsheaf, 1990).

7   ibid. p. 90.

8   Tom Whelan, 'The New Emigrants', *Newsweek*, 10 October 1987.

9   R. Foster, 'Young Emigrants Still Looking West', *Irish Times*, 14 April 1987.

10 John Bermingham, 'Head-hunting for top students', *Business and Finance*, May 28, 1987 pp. 13–19.

11 Cited in Scott Lash and John Urry, *Economies of Signs and Space* (London, Sage, 1994), p. 34.

12 Fernand Braudel, *The Perspective of the World* (London, Collins, 1984); I. Wallerstein, *The Modern World System* 1.(New York: Academic Press, 1979).

13 G. Hyland and R. Peet, 'Appalachian Migrants in Northern Cities', *Antipode*, vol. 5, no. 1 pp. 33–41.

14 John A. Agnew, 'The Devaluation of Place in Social Science' in John A. Agnew and James Duncan (eds.), *The Power of Place* (Boston, Unwin, 1989), pp. 17–45.

15 P. Commins, 'Rural Social Change' in P. Clancy, (ed.) *Ireland: A Sociological Profile* (Dublin, IPA and SAI Publications, 1988.

16 ibid. p. 19.

17 T. Inglis, *Moral Monopoly* (Dublin, Gill and Macmillan, 1987).

18 Commins, 'Rural Social Change', p. 21.

19 Raymond Crotty, *Ireland in Crisis* (Dingle, Brandon, 1986), pp. 84–5.

20 P. Cohen and H.S. Bains, *Multi-racist Britain* (London, Macmillan, 1988).

21 S. Castle and G. Kosack, *Immigrant Workers and Class Structure in Western Europe* (London, Oxford University Press, 1973); S. Castles et al. *Here for Good* (London, Pluto, 1984).

22 S. Glynn, 'Irish Immigration to Britain, 1911–1951', *Irish Economic and Social History*, vol. viii, 1981, pp. 50–69.

23 E. Hazelkorn, 'British Labour and Irish Capital', in *The Emigrant Experience*, Galway Labour History Group Publication, 1990, pp. 124–41.

24 P. Breathnach 'Uneven Development and Capitalist Peripheralisation: the Case of Ireland', *Antipode*, vol. 20, no. 2, 1988, pp. 122–41.

25 Brendan Kerr, 'Irish Seasonal Migration to Britain, 1800–1838', *Irish Historical Studies* 3: 1943, pp. 34–62.

26 M. A .G. O'Tuathaigh, 'The Historical Pattern of Irish Emigration: Some Labour Aspects' in *The Emigrant Experience*, op. cit., pp. 9–28.

27 Carol Coulter, *Ireland: Between the First and Third Worlds* (Dublin, Attic Press, 1994), pp. 93–116.

28 Mary Lennon, M. Mc Adam and J. O'Brien, *Across The Water* (London, Virago Press, 1988).

29 Breathnach,'Uneven Development'.

30 James Wickham, 'The Politics of Dependent Capitalism: International Capital and the Nation State', in A. Morgan and B. Purdie (eds.), *Ireland: Divided Nation, Divided Class.* (London, Macmillan, 1982).

31 J. A. Kennedy, *The Irish in Britain* (London, Routledge and Kegan Paul, 1973).

32 E. O'Malley, 'The Problem of Late Industrialisation and the Experience of the Republic of Ireland', *Cambridge Journal of Economics*, vol. 9, 1985, pp. 246–262.

33 Damian Courtney, *Recent Trends in Emigration from Ireland*, Department of Social Science, Regional Technical College, Cork, Ireland, 1989.

34 Anthony Cronin, 'The Law that Keeps the Huddled Asses out', *Irish Times*, 15 January 1988.

35 Mary Corcoran, 'Informalization of Metropolitan Labour Forces: The Case of Irish Immigrants in the New York Construction Industry', *Irish Journal of Sociology*, vol. 1, 1991, pp. 31–51.

36 Fintan O'Toole, 'Permanence and Tradition are Illusions in a Makeshift Society', *Irish Times*, 30 May 1994.

37 Cited in *The Economic and Social Implications of Emigration* (National Economic and Social Council, Dublin, 1991).

38 ibid., p. 90.

39 ibid. 87.

40 Jim Mac Laughlin, 'The Familiar Side of Emigration', *The Irish Reporter*, No. 15, p. 6; Elizabeth M. Thomas-Hope, 'Caribbean Skilled International Migration and the Transnational Household', *Geoforum*, vol. 19, no. 4, 1988, pp. 423–32.

41 Jim Mac Laughlin, *Ireland: The Emigrant Nursery and the World Economy* (Cork University Press, 1994).

42 ibid., p. 78.

43 *Economic and Social Implications of Emigration.*

44 Mac Laughlin, *The Emigrant Nursery*, p. 55.

45 ibid., p. 52.

46 Mac Laughlin, 'Familiar Side of Emigration', p. 5.

47 B. Anderson, *Imagined Communities* (London, Verso, 1983).

48 F.H. Aalen and H. Brody, H. Gola: *Life and Last Days of an Island Community* (Cork, Mercier Press, 1969); Tom Steel, *The Death of St. Kilda* (London, Fontana, 1988); John Healy, *No One Shouted Stop* (Achill, Healy House, 1988).

49 *Irish Times*, 13 July, 1988.

50 Mac Laughlin, *Emigrant Nursery*; see also Jim Mac Laughlin, 'The Social Characteristics and Destinations of Recent Emigrants from the West of Ireland', *Geoforum*, vol. XXII, no. 3, 1991, pp. 319–31.

51 *Social Implications of Emigration*, p. 88.

52 Hasia Diner, *Erin's Daughters in America* (Baltimore: Johns Hopkins University Press, 1983); J. Rudd, 'The Emigration of Irish Women', *Irish Studies*, vol. 9, no. 3, 1987, pp. 3–11.

53 K. Kelly and T. Nic Giolla Choille, *Emigration Matters for Women* (Dublin, Attic Press, 1990), p. 17.

54 ibid., p. 16.

55 ibid., p. 21.

56 Bronwen Walter, *Irish Women in London* (London Strategic Policy Unit, 1988).

57 Kelly and Nic Giolla Choille, *Emigration Matters*, p. 23.

6. The Ex-Isle of Erin
Emigration and Irish Culture

FINTAN O'TOOLE

There is an absence real as presence.
John Montague[1]

The more I see iv thim, the more I says to miself that th' rale boney fide
Irishman is no more thin a foreigner born away from home.
Mr Dooley[2]

In his memoir of growing up in the small West Virginia town of Piedmont, the
black American writer Henry Louis Gates Jnr remembers that the whole west
side of the place, where the road rises towards the Allegheny Mountains, was
called 'Arch Hill':

> I figured that it was called that because it was shaped like the arch of your foot.
> Twenty five years later, I learned that what the coloured people called 'Arch Hill'
> had all along been 'Irish Hill'. Cracked me up when Pop told me that.[3]

The trick of the tongue that turned Irish into Arch, transforming the ethnic
identity of the O'Rourkes, O'Briens, O'Reillys and O'Neills who lived there
into a human footprint was a happy one. To hear in the word 'Irish' the shape
of a foot in motion is to catch the true note of a culture that is not just marked,
but actually defined, by the perpetual motion of the people who bear it.
Emigration and exile, the journies to and from home, are the very heartbeat of
Irish culture. To imagine Ireland is to imagine a journey.

The nature of that journey has changed, however. What used to be a voyage
beyond the point of no return is now, increasingly, a series of temporary shifts.
The symbol of permanent Irish emigration is no longer the wake but the
wedding. The American Wake that used to mark the sense of passing to 'the
other side' has been replaced by the wedding, for it is only through marrying
abroad that young Irish people now declare themselves as immigrants rather
than emigrants. But even weddings are always more elusive than wakes. They
have no finality, no certainty. They are a declaration of intent rather than a
statement of immutable fact. The uncertain emigration of the 1980s that they
symbolise marks a change in the meaning of emigration for Irish culture.

One way of envisaging that change is through the familiar metaphor of margin and centre. It can be said with some confidence that historic Irish emigration marked a movement from margin to centre, in the sense that rural Irish migrants moved from a largely pre-modern society to a modern one. The shift in space could also be construed as a shift in time, or more accurately in period. But in the late twentieth century, the metaphor of margin and centre no longer works. For one thing, it is a metaphor appropriate to a flat earth and the earth is no longer, in cultural or economic terms, flat. It has become global, an increasingly integrated system that is, if not quite de-centred, at least multi-centred. Since the centre is no longer capable of being expressed in simple geographical terms, moving from one part of the globe to another no longer necessarily implies a shift from margin to centre. The nature of the transition depends much more critically on the place of the emigrant within the home society. Some Irish emigrants (for example, a computer graduate who moves from IBM in Dublin to Wall Street) are already economically, psychologically, and to a large degree culturally, a part of the centre before they leave.

Nor is the nature of marginality unchanged. The long process whereby cultures of the centre have romanticised certain cultures of the margin has itself altered the meaning of those cultures. There is now a zone, at once cultural and geographical, that belongs neither to margin nor centre, and much of Ireland belongs in it. The Australian poet Les Murray has argued that the true margin now is not on the outer edge but in the middle. It lies between the metropolitan centre, on the one side, and what Murray calls the *meta-margin*, on the other. This latter zone is 'the exotic, the wilderness, the vanishing archaic'.[4] And certain aspects of Irish culture – those that were truly marginal for most of the nineteenth century – now belong clearly to the meta-margin. Tourism has completed and commodified the process that Romanticism and Celticism started in the last century. It has made the exotic and archaic aspects of Irish culture not merely acceptable to, but desirable for, the centre. And this, in turn, has had tangible effects for Irish emigrants, particularly those going to America, where Irish emigration has been favoured by visa programmes over emigration from more truly marginal societies.

To understand this change, it is necessary first to understand just how central emigration has been to the way we understand ourselves. In Liam O'Flaherty's stark, grief-stricken story, 'Going Into Exile', for instance, you can feel how the ebbing away of human reality in the act of emigration opens up a blank space to be filled by the imagination. There is an American Wake in progress, marking the move to Boston the following day of a son and a daughter, Michael and Mary. O'Flaherty writes it like the Last Supper, a feast that is also a sombre preparation for a death. As the morning of departure dawns, the unseen, the unreal, the imagined takes a subtle grip:

The stars were growing dim. A long way off invisible sparrows were chirping in their ivied perch in some distant hill or other . . . Cocks crew, blackbirds carolled, a dog let loose from a cabin by an early riser chased madly after an imaginary robber, barking as if his tail were on fire. The people said goodbye and began to stream forth from Feeney's cabin.[5]

Eventually, at the end of the story, the mother is left in a world of desolate imaginings, 'listening foolishly for an answering cry', imagining she can 'hear the crags simmering under the hot rays of the sun. It was something in her head that was singing.' This counterpoint between an emptying house and the tightening grip of the imaginary (the invisible sparrow, the imaginary robber, the simmering crags, the singing in the head) is emblematic of modern Irish culture. Reading between the lines, discerning meaning in the empty spaces, is often the task in hand.

A later O'Flaherty story, 'The Letter', virtually a follow-up to 'Going Into Exile', can stand as a metaphor for this task. A peasant family is working in the fields. Their eldest daughter Mary has gone to America. They have had no letter from her for a long time, though a neighbour has written to say that Mary is without work. The family's two youngest daughters arrive home from school with a letter they have received from the postman. It is from Mary. The father opens it and takes out a cheque for £20, enough to buy a new horse to replace the one that died a year before. There is unbounded joy. Then the eldest son reads the letter aloud:

'Dear Parents', the son began. 'Oh mother, I am so lonely.' It's all covered with blots same as if she were crying on the paper. 'Daddy why did I . . . why did I ever . . . ever . . .' It's hard to make it out . . . yes . . . 'why did I ever come to this awful place? Say a prayer for me every night, mother. Your loving daughter Mary.'[6]

After a long silence, the whole family begins to wail and weep. Nothing has been said, nothing made explicit. There is no explanation for the £20 cheque or for the daughter's anguish. But the family fills in the blanks. Reading between the lines and making out the tear-blotched letters, they imagine an unthinkable truth. Their reading of the letter is also a kind of writing, an engagement of their creative imaginations that gives shape and meaning to the barely discernible realities that the letters on the page hint at. This is what a culture defined by emigration does – it writes itself as it reads itself.

There is, of course, a profound connection for all cultures between nationality and the fictive imagination. All national borders are, at a fundamental level, works of fiction. They separate the nation from all that is not the nation. And what they enclose is not just a physical space, but also an imaginative one. Nations are the product of history rather than geography, of culture rather than race. Like a book or a play, they are made up. As Peter Stallybrass puts it:

The nation has to be invented or written; and written, what is more, in the crucial and troubling knowledge that it could be written otherwise. It is *because* the nation could be written otherwise that the act of writing must be forgotten, transformed instead into the act of reading a pre-given past.[7]

The conflict between writing the nation and reading it lies at the heart of Irish culture in the twentieth century. It is an insoluble conflict because it arises from the most difficult contradiction of Irish politics and economics – the contradiction between place and people, between the search for a fixed national space and the existence of an unfixed, mobile population. Considered geographically, Ireland is a pre-given space, standing sharply out from the ocean that surrounds it. But considered demographically, Ireland is an unbounded sprawl, an incoherent network of memories and resentments, dreams and desperations, moving between the island itself and its diaspora in Britain, the United States, Australia, Canada and elsewhere.

The geographical Ireland, the bounded island, is a place that can be read. It can be imagined, albeit problematically, as the result of a given past, as the present form of an innate and immemorial Irishness. The second, demographic Ireland is a nation that cannot be read but must be written. And because it must be written, it could be written otherwise. Existing, as it does, imaginatively, it is always open to the possibility of being re-imagined. As such, it poses a constant threat to the first Ireland. It questions its readings by remembering that they, too, were once written, that they are inventions, that they represent, not an innate expression of the nation, but merely the one strand from a range of possibilities that happened to develop within the frame of the island of Ireland.

The great German critic, Walter Benjamin, reminds us that there are two kinds of storytellers, embodied, respectively, in the tiller of the soil and the trading seaman. The first carries 'the lore of the past, as it best reveals itself to natives of a place.' The second is imbued with 'the lore of faraway places, such as a much-travelled man brings home.'[8] Storytelling, Benjamin says, is most potent when it comes from 'the most intimate interpretation of these two archaic types.' Sometimes, at its most powerful – as in, for instance, the work of James Joyce – Irish culture combines the lore of the past and the lore of faraway places. But more often the two have been in contest with each other.

Modern Irish writing comes out of the attempt of the Irish Literary Revival to posit Ireland as a culture that could be read, and read through the lore of the past. The whole idea of a revival presupposes a belief that there is some intact inheritance from the past which can be recovered by careful reading. By clearing away the false impositions of Britishness and urban modernity, the lines of a culture implicit in the island itself could be deciphered and their meaning restored. Thus, Yeats, for instance, claimed that the modern Irish drama would be founded on a medieval poetic, and that he could track any authentic folk expression still in use back to classical times.

This was, of course, untrue. The revival is a writing that pretends to be a reading, an act of invention that pretends to be an act of restoration. The fact of emigration, the fact that the immediate past of the revival period was one of extraordinary dispersion was glossed over in the revival's emphasis on the authenticity of place. By taking place rather than people as the touchstone of Irishness, the revival was able to appeal to a sense of continuity and stability that were simply unavailable in contemporary Irish experience. But this effort involved an inevitable strain.

The worries in the early Abbey over Lady Gregory's play *Twenty Five*, for instance, give the game away. The play was originally to be called *Fifty*, referring to the number of pounds the hero Christie brings home after two years in America. The Fay brothers, who ran the acting company, originally rejected the play on the basis that if young men were shown that they could save £50 in two years, they would all be off to America. Lady Gregory had to re-write it, cutting the sum in half and changing the title to *Twenty Five*.[9] Emigration undercut the very notion that an Irish theatre could safely reflect Irish reality.

Even more emblematic of the contradictions is a paragraph in Padraic Ó Conaire's novel *Deoraíocht* (*Exile*) published in 1910 as the first major novel in the Gaelic language, that shows the fault-lines. It is striking in itself that one of the first real literary expressions of the language revival centres, not on the recovery of a fixed place and a finished past, but on the tormented wanderings in Ireland and England of a displaced man who becomes a freak in a travelling circus. Even more striking, though, is the irony of the following passage, describing social gatherings in a part of London called Little Ireland, inhabited mostly by people from Munster:

> There would be a man there who could relate the contents of Keating's *History of Ireland* as well as a man who knew nothing about it. And if somebody were to disagree with anything the savant said, he would just go to the big trunk he had brought with him from Ireland and take out a parcel wrapped in linen. He would open the parcel and take out a large book in manuscript. And how careful he was of that book! He would then show you in black and white where you had been wrong. And when he closed the book to put it away he would look at you as if to say 'Now what have you to say for yourself?' But he never said a word.[10]

Ó Conaire's image of this man with his linen-wrapped parcel of unarguable history brought from Ireland into exile is a perfect example of the act of writing being forgotten and transformed instead into the act of reading a pre-given past. The struggle to survive in England is occluded by the struggle to hang on to a fixed, finished identity. Where history and geography are confused and displaced by emigration, the appeal to the authority of an invented past becomes coercive. In the Little Irelands of the Irish diaspora, there was for a long time an overwhelming temptation to read Ireland as a closed book rather than to imagine it as a blank page waiting to be written.

Irish emigrants were removed, not merely from Ireland to elsewhere, but from the land to the city. And their absence from the landscape is what makes it possible for them to disappear from the emergent culture of modern Ireland. That invention of modern Ireland was driven by the Romantic search for a culture organically rooted in an authentic landscape. What was to be read in that cultural quest was the landscape itself. John Montague, in *The Rough Field* imagines:

> The whole landscape a manuscript
> We had lost the skill to read

and the image could stand as a summation of the nationalist project and its desire to regain the skill to scrutinise the landscape until it gave up its hidden, authentic meanings.

But emigrants were not merely, by definition, absent from this landscape. They were absent from all landscape, ensconced as they were in cities. George Russell, writing in 1912, noted the

> growing dislike of the land among the rising generation. How many Irishmen go to the land in the States? Not one in twenty, not in a hundred – hardly one in a thousand. They have been on the land in Ireland, and they go anywhere – to any crowded slum – rather than to the fields.[11]

Forty years later, the novelist and playwright Bryan MacMahon noted that 'The pattern of Irish life in the shoddy towns of industrial England is yet to reveal itself; it seems rather a pity that the rural Irish did not emigrate to rural England.'[12] What he does not note is that there is an innate connection between the first half of his sentence and the second: Irish life in industrial England could not 'reveal itself' in Irish culture precisely because it was not rural and, therefore, lay outside the dominant forms and ideologies.

This exclusion was, of course, self-perpetuating. Emigration created a vicious circle for Irish culture: the difficulty of imagining urban life robbed Irish culture of much of its capacity to embrace its emigrants; the failure to embrace emigrant experience, meanwhile, made it hard for Irish culture to develop ways of imagining urban experience. Many essential Irish stories belong, in the first instance, to other cultures. The most profound dramatisations of the Irish experience of social mobility and of the gap between parents born in poverty and children born in comfort, belong in the American theatre, in the plays of Eugene O'Neill, especially *Long Day's Journey into Night*. The most coherent narrative of Irish Catholic working-class life – James T. Farrell's Studs Lonergan novels – belong to American fiction. The most troubling exploration of the Irish as both colonised and, in the context of the genocide of Native Americans, colonisers – John Ford's film *The Searchers* – belongs to American cinema. Emigration simplified the representations of Irish experience and made it possible to imagine Ireland as a cultural monolith.

Where culture is understood as immanent in place, as it is in the Irish revival, the displaced emigrant can disappear from the culture, can suffer an almost literal loss of voice. Again, John Montague, born in Brooklyn but brought back to Ireland at the age of four, gets to the heart of the matter. In his poem 'A Flowering Absence' he recalls his experience of emigration and return as a loss of language itself, his childhood self taunted by a schoolmistress 'who hunted me publicly down/ to near speechlessness':

> Where did he get that outlandish accent?
> What do you expect, with no parents,
> sent back from some American slum:
> none of you are to speak like him!

The effect, he writes, was that 'I could no longer utter/ those magical words I had begun/ to love. . .'.[13]

In the silence left by emigration, the aesthetics of emptiness took hold. Empty wilderness is seen as innately more noble than ordinary urban existence. George Russell is explicit in his contempt for Irish towns, which he describes, significantly as 'excrescences on the face of nature':

> Our small Irish country towns, in their external characteristsics, are so arid and unlovely that one longs for a lodge in some vast wilderness as a relief from the unbearable meanness. Better look out on boundless sand and boundless sky, on two immensities, than on these mean and straggling towns, those disreputable public houses, those uncleansed footways like miry manure yards.[14]

Michael Collins also objects to urban life on aesthetic grounds, remarking that:

> the fine, splendid surface of Ireland is besmirched by our towns and villages – hideous medleys of contemptible dwellings and mean shops and squalid public houses, not as they should be in material fitness, the beautiful human expressions of what our God-given country is![15]

And Collins, too, looks to the deserted places – in his case Achill, a beautiful landscape made all the more beautiful by mass emigration – for the idealised contrast to squalid urban life.

In the conversion of depopulation into an opportunity for romantic landscape, the painter Paul Henry is perhaps the key figure. A product of urban, evangelical Belfast, his re-invention of himself as an artist involved a chosen devotion of the empty West. Belfast may not be, strictly speaking, elsewhere, but it was, for Irish nationalism, alien. As Derek Mahon has put it:

> The suburbs of Belfast have a peculiar relationship to the Irish cultural situation in as much as they're the final anathema for the traditional Irish imagination.[16]

The ability of the Irish nationalist mentality to ignore urban Ulster indeed is inextricable from its ability to ignore the Irish diaspora in the industrial cities of

Britain and the US. The Irishness that was constructed by positing a Catholic, rural identity – and thus, of course, excluding Belfast – was also one that could paint out emigrants.

The sense of absence in Paul Henry's work, the disappearance of Belfast, of city dwellers, of industrial workers – in short of precisely the kind of people emigrants became – is overwhelming and, in the end, literal. As his work develops, it becomes more and more clear that human figures are mere adjuncts to the landscape, devoid of any relationship to the economic world, and eventually the human figure disappears altogether. His subject is narrowed down to sky, sea, mountain and thatched cottages. When, in 1941, Henry has to produce a picture of Belfast to go with a guide book written by Seán O'Faolain, the image is as distant as possible and conforms as closely as possible to his Western landscapes. The picture is called *Belfast from Greencastle*, ensuring that the point-of-view is on acceptable, non-urban ground. The top three quarters of it is sky, like any Western sky. Almost the entire bottom quarter is sand and sea. Between these safe blocks of landscape runs a thin thread of urban skyline, shadowy steeples and murky chimneys belching out foul smoke that threatens to obliterate the beauties of nature. George Russell's preference for 'boundless sand and boundless sky' over the reality of urban life is expressed in pictorial form.

As a way of filling up the space left by departing emigrants, and at the same time of reading Ireland so as to elide the awkward emigrant experience, this kind of nationalist Romanticism was very potent. It is worth noting in passing that even the most heart-wrenching and immediate reminder of emigration – the ruined villages and cottages that still litter the countryside – may not necessarily have been read by Irish Romanticism as images of defeat and despair. Luke Gibbons has noted, suggestively, that the dominance of ruins – particularly of round towers – in Irish nationalist iconography marked the special set of associations which ruins evoked:

> The very survival of ruins meant that they had withstood the ravages of time and successive waves of invasion, thus attesting to the continuity between past and present and the resilience of Gaelic civilisation. It was this which fastened the link between ruin and political violence, for the affirmation of an ancient *separate* civilisation meant that a complete break with Britain was required, outside the limited confines of parliamentary reform.[17]

There is a connection between the contempt for ordinary urban buildings expressed by Michael Collins and the IRA's subsequent willingness to destroy Irish cities. George Russell makes it when, just after the passage about sand and sky quoted above, he remarks that:

> For if one has a soul and any love for beauty he must feel like an anarchist if he strays into an Irish country town, and must long for bombs to wreck and dynamite to obliterate.[18]

In this obscure sense, the process of cultural obliteration of emigrants and the campaign of violence which established the Irish state itself are connected through the image of dereliction. As one of the most self-conscious of exiles, Samuel Beckett, noted acerbically:

> What constitutes the charm of our country, apart, of course from its scant population, and this without the help of the meanest contraceptive, is that all is derelict, with the sole exception of history's ancient faeces.[19]

Daniel Corkery, the former IRA man who was the most coherent ideologue of Irish cultural nationalism, makes the obliteration most explicit. In *Synge and Anglo-Irish Literature*, he begins his argument by first winnowing out most of the best-known living Irish writers, among them Padraic Colum, Thomas McGreevy, Austin Clarke, James Joyce, James Stephens, Seán O'Casey, Liam O'Flaherty, George Moore and Bernard Shaw. Noting that all of them live outside Ireland, he performs a rhetorical sleight-of-hand in which they all disappear as Irish writers:

> Now unless one can show that the demands of the alien market are on all fours with the demands of the home market, how can this literature be Anglo-Irish? How can it be a national literature? The question is not: Can expatriates produce national literature? but: Can expatriates writing for an alien market produce national literature?[20]

The question, of course, is rhetorical, for it is entirely clear that, to Corkery, expatriates cannot produce a national literature. Note how beautifully circular this argument is. At least in part because of censorship, which Corkery does not mention, there is no home market. Because there is no home market, the writers must go abroad and write for foreign audiences. Because they write for foreign audiences, they are not Irish writers. Because they are not Irish writers, why should anyone worry if their books are banned?

In Corkery's ideology of the indigenous and the alien, which is classically nationalist in its concern with fixed opposites, its paradoxical obsession with England which can only imagine Ireland as not-England, the Abbey theatre itself may, as he puts it, be 'no more than an exotic branch of English literature'. Since there is, in his mind, no real Irish writing or Irish theatre in the English language at all, then nothing that happens within it can have any significance. This is something much more profound than censorship – it is obliteration. The point is not so much to control and to shape the work of writers as to make it disappear by constructing an ideological frame within which that work is almost literally unthinkable.

Not the least of the ironies of this willed obliteration of the vast bulk of Irish literary achievement, on the grounds that it was produced abroad, is that most of the realist tradition in Irish culture is the creation of exiles. The dominance of Romanticism in Irish culture meant that the realist project of Frank

O'Connor and Seán O'Faolain, who for the most part stayed in Ireland, was doomed. The would-be writer Michael Dempsey in Brinsley MacNamara's novel *The Clanking of Chains* is more or less forced into exile. MacNamara notes that 'He would have to be a realist dealing only with facts in whatever country he might go to, and it is part of the irony of things that he could not be this same realist in his own country.'[21]

Realism in writing is a concern with the bits and pieces of experience rather than with a grand, archetypal narrative. In writers of the diaspora like James Hanley, who doesn't appear in Hogan's *Dictionary of Irish Literature*, let alone the *Field Day Anthology of Irish Writing*, a coherent narrative itself comes to seem impossible. Towards the end of Hanley's three-novel saga of an Irish family in Liverpool, *The Furys*, Peter Fury discovers that he cannot re-assemble in memory the broken pieces of his family history:

> 'There are so many bloody fragments that you couldn't even begin to gather them up, you couldn't even begin to think about it,' and he seemed to see them fall, one after another, the members of the family to which he had once belonged. He even heard each separate thud. 'I wouldn't even know where to begin if I thought it was worth beginning.'[22]

That kind of fragmented, embattled history is what emerges in the work of exiled writers. The divisions that are suppressed at home – especially the divisions of class – emerge in full voice in the work of writers like Patrick MacGill, the Irish equivalent of Zola, and Robert Noonan (Robert Tressell), whose great work *The Ragged Trousered Philanthropist* owes infinitely more to Dickens and British socialism than to Yeats and Synge. In MacGill's work there is always the open road, in Hanley's the open sea. MacGill, in particular, manages to write about what are essentially nomadic people. Characters like Moleskin Joe in the novel of the same name and in *Children of the Dead End* belong to no fixed abode. They are part of what MacGill calls 'the migratory peoples of the road'.[23]

And equally their stories are unstable and polymorphous. Like the auto-biography of Liam O'Flaherty, the most travelled of major Irish writers, which begins with a declaration that 'Man is a born liar',[24] thereby undermining all claim to a single narrative truth, MacGill's novels acknowledge the instability of narrative. Against the Revival attempt to construct a fixed narrative of Ireland, the stories told about Moleskin Joe change their shape and meaning in transit. Because there is, in exile, no one place, neither is there any single narrative:

> These stories were, of course, distorted and magnified until the narrative spun in a Manchester 'model' had little semblance to the actuality which had footing in a Glasgow dosshouse.[25]

Such unstable stories need to be written rather than read. The remarkable thing about the exiled Irish writers, though, is how few of their stories were about exile itself. The point of departure – in Joyce's *A Portrait of the Artist as a Young Man*, for instance – is often clearly dramatised, but what happens after exile is not. Joyce most obviously conforms to John Wilson Foster's description of Irish writers taking with them 'place transformed into the memory of place and therefore transportable'[26] in his obsessive recreations of the city he had left behind. But the description applies to many other writers. Edna O'Brien's epigraph to *A Pagan Place* – Brecht's 'I carry a brick on my shoulder in order that the world may know what my house was like' – could be placed on the title page of many Irish novels written in exile.

It is, rather, in the theatre that emigration has its most profound effect on Irish writing before the contemporary period. For it might be said that the Irish theatre in the twentieth century has undergone two revivals. The first revival, that of the early Abbey, is one which keeps the reality of emigration at bay and puts itself forward as a reading of Ireland. But the second, that of the late 1950s and early 1960s, is almost entirely driven by an attempt to get to grips with emigration. Its two major playwrights, Brian Friel and Tom Murphy are writers whose work is simply unthinkable without the continual interplay of departure and return, of home and away. In their later plays, like Friel's *Faith Healer* and Murphy's *Bailegangaire*, those concepts take on large spiritual and existential resonances, but in their early work they are literal derivations from the acutely-observed reality of emigration.

It is significant that this second revival of Irish theatre, so utterly involved with emigration, begins precisely at the point at which Irish society – in the shape of the First Programme for Economic Expansion – is at last beginning to accept the ideal of urban and industrial life. The implicit acceptance of cities in the modernisation of the Irish economy, itself a desperate response to the relentless flow of emigration in the 1950s, makes it possible for the mainstream of Irish culture to begin to comprehend the urban lives of Irish emigrants.

Tom Murphy s *A Whistle in the Dark* (1961) is set among Irish emigrants in Coventry. On the surface, it might look like an archetypal story in which Bryan MacMahon's 'pattern of Irish life in the shoddy towns of industrial England' might reveal itself. The city in which the Irishmen have placed themselves is a kind of hell, full of violence and corruption. But, in fact, the play turns the archetype on its head. For the move to Coventry has meant for the Carney family only an intensification of the tribal family ties and the struggle for survival in a brutish world which they knew at home in Mayo. It is not the flight from an Irish past, but actually the failure to escape that past (embodied in the monstrous shape of Dada) that dooms them. Emigration becomes, in Murphy's vision, a relentless exposure of Irish society at home. The import of the play is clear – emigration is not a solution to Irish problems, but merely the sharpest indicator of how profound those problems are.

The same is true of the other major Irish play of the period, Brian Friel's *Philadelphia, Here I Come!* (1964), in which Gar O'Donnell's choice of staying in Donegal or emigrating to America is seen as no real choice at all, since both options are equally terrible. Friel does not set the play in America, but he does bring Irish emigrés to America onto the stage, in the shape of Gar's aunt and her husband. *Philadelphia* draws its power from the way it dramatises Ireland and America, not just as two places, but as two opposing but equally unhappy states of mind. Ireland is a place haunted by memory, America a place haunted by forgetfulness. Gar and his father are tormented by inescapable memories which may be mere inventions, showing again how emigration makes narrative unstable and untrustworthy. But Gar's American aunt is unable even to remember where she has been a few hours ago. Ireland is unbearable stasis and claustrophobia, America terrible anonymity and impermanence.

But this polarity is impossible in more recent Irish writing, where the feeling in O'Flaherty's *Going into Exile* that the emigrant and the Ireland left behind are two worlds as separate as death and life has been replaced by a strong sense of Ireland itself as a place forever on the move between different worlds. In Sebastian Barry's recent play, *Prayers of Sherkin*, Fanny Hawke, speaking of Sherkin Island, but touching on an image that serves for the bigger island of Ireland, asks her brother 'Do you not feel that this island is moored only lightly to the sea-bed, and might be off for the Americas at any moment?'[27]

Such a question arises from the profound social changes in Ireland that began in the 1960s and are still in progress. The impulse to emigration remains, of course, largely economic, and the surge of the late 1980s clearly followed from the 1979 oil crisis and the huge rise in unemployment. Economic under-development and the failure to provide work for a growing population is not the wrong answer, but it is, since the 1960s, an insufficient answer. Belgium and Britain, for example, also had very high unemployment at the same time, but there was no British or Belgian diaspora in the 1980s. There is something particular about Irish culture that makes it respond in this way to economic recession. And, more and more, it is hard to dismiss the idea that one of these particular things is the sense of internal exile, the sense that Irish people feel less and less at home in Ireland, that Ireland has become somehow unreal. In one way or another, very many Irish people have experienced a sense of the familiar becoming unknown, unrecognisable. Ireland has become so multi-layered, so much a matter of one set of images superimposed on another, that it is hard to tell home from abroad. Thirty-five years of being an offshore economic dependency of the United States have left us with a society that is seen by an increasing number of its young people as a pale imitation of the Real Thing across the Atlantic.

The Americanisation of Ireland that began with the construction of Ireland as a European base for multinational companies has fundamentally altered the meaning of emigration itself. Since Ireland has become in some respects a little America, emigration can no longer be posited as a shift from one state of being to another. A change of location no longer implies a complete change of lifestyle, as it did for, say, a farm labourer from Mayo going to Boston in the 1920s. In significant ways, America has already come to Mayo.

A place like Ballyhaunis, for instance, has clearly undergone a profound change in its cultural understanding of what is or is not foreign. In their book *The Dynamics of Irish Politics*, Paul Bew, Ellen Hazelkorn and Henry Patterson note an incident in Ballyhaunis in March 1938. A 'pitched battle' between locals and the Guards broke out when an official of the Land Commission tried to distribute land to 'people from outside the district', leading to seventeen arrests.[28] Those people fought, presumably, because they knew their own place so well, because they considered it to be so truly theirs, that they couldn't bear to think of it in the hands of strangers, even though those strangers were probably indistinguishable from themselves.

Fifty years later, what was Ballyhaunis like? It was dominated by an Islamic meat factory, where Middle Eastern mullahs intoned prayers from the Koran over the animals before they slit their throats. It had its own mosque. On Sunday nights, the locals went to the Nite Klub where a man in a light-up bow-tie hosted his own live version of an American game show, 'The Price Is Right'. It was, in other words, an almost surreal mixture of cultures within a small-town setting. The intensity of local identification, the absolute certainty that people from a few miles away were foreigners, the fierce determination to hold to a line separating native from migrant, could hardly survive in such an utterly altered cultural context.

For the generation of Irish writers that grew up after the First Programme of Economic Expansion, that process of alteration has also been a process of estrangement. Home has become as unfamiliar as abroad. Because Irish places have themselves been radically changed, it has been possible, in a sense, to emigrate without leaving the island. Everything begins to exist in a state of internal exile. The difference between home and abroad has shrunk to virtually nothing. Rosita Boland, for instance, looking at the moon in Australia, writes that:

> I was looking at a mirror image
> Of a moon I had known all my life.
> The points of its crescent faced the opposite way:
> Exactly as something does when you look at it
> From the other side.[29]

Nostalgia for a homeland has lost its meaning, not least because the images of a natural landscape that once constituted memories of home for emigrants from a predominantly rural society have been replaced by memories of a predomi-nantly urban Irish society. What can be remembered, even from exile, is no longer a lost homeland that represents a different state of being, but a place that is of essentially the same kind as the place in which the exile now lives, all the more so because memory itself is now saturated with globalised media images.

A good example is Michael O'Loughlin's poem 'The Fugitive', published in 1982.[30] The opening is conventional, evoking as it does an Irish exile in Paris:

> In the hour before the Metro opens
> I remember you . . .

But the next words are not, as might be expected, 'Ireland', or 'mother', but 'Richard Kimble'. Richard Kimble was the eponymous fugitive in the American television series of the 1960s, and the exile's memory is of watching the programme as a child at home in Dublin. An exiled Irish poet's memory of home from Paris is a memory of America:

> I can't remember the stories now
> But in the end it's only the ikons that matter,
> The silent, anonymous American city
> With the rain running down the gutter.

For a generation that grew up on American television shows, America will always be interwoven with memories of an Irish homeland and an Irish childhood:

> The muffled snarl of American accents
> Coming in loud and razor sharp
> Over the local interference.

This interplay of American accents and local interference is taken to its logical, and comic, conclusion in Roddy Doyle's *The Commitments* where identity itself, for young working-class Dubliners, is a matter of identification with American black music:

> Where are yis from? (He answered the question himself.) – Dublin. (He asked another one.) – Wha' part o' Dublin? Barrytown. Wha' class are yis? Workin' class. Are yis proud of it? Yeah, yis are. (Then a practical question.) – Who buys the most records? The workin' class. Are yis with me? (Not really.) – Your music should be abou' where you're from an' the sort o' people yeh come from. – – – Say it once, say it loud, I'm black an' I'm proud. They looked at him. – James Brown.[31]

When 'where you're from' is best expressed through the music of blacks in industrial American cities, how can you feel nostalgic for home if you're Irish and living in one of those American cities? And, furthermore, even this way of remembering is no longer distinctively Irish. It is itself an aspect of a global cultural shift, of what Frederic Jameson calls 'the cultural logic of late capitalism'. Jameson remarks that, with the collapse of the high modernist ideology of style, 'the producers of culture have nowhere else to turn but to the past: the imitation of dead styles, speech through all the masks and voices stored up in the imaginary museum of a now global culture.' But the past is itself saturated in electronic imagery: it has itself 'become a vast collection of images, a multitudinous photographic simulacrum.'[32] Culture – in the form of received images of, say, Richard Kimble or James Brown – becomes what nature used to be – a kind of second nature.

And if nostalgia in the old sense is impossible, so is return. The exile's dream of return has no meaning when the homeland is an ex-isle, a place forever gone. Dermot Bolger's poem and play, *The Lament for Arthur Cleary*,[33] harks back to Eibhlín Dubh Ní Chonaill's eighteenth-century *Caoineadh Art Uí Laoghaire*, in which a returned exile is killed because he no longer knows how to keep his place in a changed Ireland. Bolger's Arthur Cleary comes back to Dublin from Germany 'consumed with nostalgia/ For an identity irretrievably lost':

> But that world was dead
> Though you could not realise it
> A grey smudge of estates
> Charted the encroaching horizon . . .

Equally, in Deirdre Madden's *Remembering Light and Stone,* a depressed young Irish woman in Italy visits a doctor who diagnoses 'homesickness'. She should go back, he says, to her mother. 'If I went away from my own home, what could I expect, only unhappiness and loneliness.' But she knows that this diagnosis is wrong, that the unhappiness is something she has brought with her and that it would still await her were she to return: 'I thought that to go back to Ireland wouldn't help at all, because it was something that had been caused by my early life . . .' The once impossible desire to return has been replaced by a sense that returning is largely irrelevant, either because the problems are personal or because the world that was left behind has now disappeared.

Yet it is not, in contemporary Irish culture, returning exiles alone who sense that the world they knew has gone. One of the saddest but comforting things about emigration used to be the tragi-comic figure of the Returned Yank. Sad because of the sense of loss, the incomprehension at the fact that everything was different from the way it was remembered. Comforting because that incomprehension eased our sense of inferiority, told us that we were the ones who really knew, we were really on top of this place. Now we are all Returned Yanks, looking around us and saying 'gee, didn't there use to be a pub there, didn't that place look different, didn't I know that guy?' And like the Returned Yanks it is easier to go back to a place that is less complicated, less haunted by its own past, to get on the plane and go home to America, regretful but relieved.

Part of this process of estrangement is the alienation of the young from the images and icons of official Irish culture, now seen as repressive and exclusive.

Dermot Bolger's re-reading of Patrick Pearse in *I am Ireland*, makes this alienation explicit by speaking a variation on Patrick Pearse in the voice of an Irishwoman in exile in Birmingham:

> I am Ireland
> Lonelier I am than a hag on Birmingham common.[34]

When identity is understood as being a matter of class or gender or sexual orientation before it is a matter of nationality, a sense of belonging is no longer necessarily dependent on remaining within a homeland. Indeed, the former may be incompatible with the latter.

Sometimes, of course, this sense of being at home in America or in England is a mere reflection of the bland materialism of international yuppie culture. Joe O'Connor has captured the style of the NIPPLES (New Irish Professional People in London):

> Well look, Dave, I took the liberty, right, I called this little chumette of mine who runs a rather interesting little unit trust outfit, who as it happens is looking for some willing hands to do a bit of cleaning at the moment, and I mentioned your name, said we were good mates, did the whole business.[35]

But equally this sense of being more at home in exile is often rooted in the exclusions of Irish life itself. In Emma Donoghue's story 'Going Back', Cyn, an Irish lesbian in London says 'Listen, I felt more of an exile for the twenty years I was in Ireland than I ever have in the twelve I've been out of it.'[36] Conversely, many Irish people feel more culturally at home in England or America than they did in the Ireland of the 1980s, simply because those societies may be be more accomodating to their beliefs and sexual identities than the Ireland of the 1983 and 1986 referendums on abortion and divorce appeared to be.

Irish culture still wants to think of our emigrants as being in a continuous line with all those who have left since the Famine. But in fact, in some important respects, they are the exact opposite. The old Irish emigrants felt themselves in exile over there; the new feel themselves in exile over here. The old ones pined for a culture from which they felt themselves removed – Irish culture. Some of the new ones have that feeling long before they go – the culture which they pine for and from which they feel themselves removed in Ireland is American culture. The old ones sang 'Danny Boy' in Boston and the Bronx to put themselves in touch with their Irish homeland. The new ones have been singing 'New York, New York' in Bray and Belmullet, while waiting for their Green Cards to come through.

The point is that for very many young Irish people, America already is their cultural and spiritual homeland. If you've seen the movies and listened to the tapes, if you've worn the jeans and eaten the burgers, then you might as well live the life. The old Irish in Hackensack and Hell's Kitchen desperately tried to appropriate their homeland through its cultural symbols – the songs, the music, the style. The new Irish have already, in many cases, appropriated the symbols of their cultural homeland in the United States. Stuck here, they are far from the land where their young heroes sleep. The new Irish have the same yearnings as the old Irish, only in reverse and with the crucial difference that whereas their predecessors couldn't come home to Ireland, they can go to America.

In the new, shifting, ill-defined emigration of the 1980s where many Irish young Irish people found themselves in more or less constant motion, in and out of Ireland, as the fluctuations of the world economy made them alternately in demand and surplus to requirements, it was no longer possible to pretend that there was a given Irish culture to be lost or held on to. And Irish writers began to reflect much more directly a sense that Ireland was a set of questions and contests rather than a given landscape waiting to be read. The relevant difference is no longer that between home and abroad, but that between the Irish themselves. Exile becomes a prism through which the diverse social forces within Ireland are separated and revealed. The Irish abroad are now written about as people divided from each other by politics, class and sexuality rather than as a single category of humanity divided from a homogenous homeland by exile.

In Michael O'Loughlin's story 'Traditional Music', for instance, Irish 'guest workers' in Germany attending a Monster Irish Folk Festival are attacked by Germans when they throw beer cans at a man making a pro-IRA speech. The Germans think they must be English. Or in Dermot Bolger's novel *The Journey Home*, another Irish factory worker in Germany is beaten up by a fellow Irishman for supporting Turkish co-workers who go on strike.

That notion of internal exile, of an Ireland that has become, in a sense, a foreign country for many of its people, whether they stay or go, marks a profound change in the way Irish culture construes emigration. Exile is no longer a process in which a fixed idenity is traded for an anonymous and impermanent one. In *True Lines*, a play devised by John Crowley in 1994, the young emigrés already live in a world of anonymity and impermanance. All of its protagonists are Irish, yet the play never touches down in Ireland. Its Ireland is whatever they carry with them in four continents – the play is set in Berlin, in Arizona, in Australia and in Ethiopia. They travel not to escape an Ireland that is, as Gar O'Donnell's was, too numbingly continuous, but in the hope that they might find some kind of absent continuity on their journeys. The play is dominated by images of being adrift in an unbounded world where random encounters and casual partings have taken the place of certainty. Its imaginative cultural reference points are the marks of human journeys across the landscape – songlines, road markings, ancient footsteps.

True Lines is the first coherent and self-conscious attempt to replace the map of a place with a map of the journeys of its people but it is almost certainly the first of many. What is important is that such maps will depend on a sense of identity that is entirely imaginative, though not imaginary. The connections are not physical but cultural, matters not of a past that can be read but of a present and future that have to be constantly written and re-written. And in that writing and re-writing, the Irish abroad will have just as much of a claim on the creation of Irish culture as do the Irish at home.

In the 1990s, America and Ireland represent not opposites, not a dialogue of modernity and tradition, but a continual intertwining in which far from Ireland being the past and America being the future, America can constitute Ireland's past and Ireland can invent America's future. In the mid-1980s, for instance, it was an Irish rock band, U2, which embodied mythic America for the world at large, through their use of the deserts of Colorado and Arizona as a dream landscape in their photographic images, their films 'Under a Blood Red Sky' and 'Rattle and Hum', their carefully worked-out Wild West costuming, and their post-apocalyptic born-again lyrics which used the desert as the image of a world after the nuclear holocaust.

Conversely, in the mid-1990s, the international image of traditional Irish culture was constituted most powerfully by *Riverdance*, the Irish dance show that had its origins in the Eurovision Song Contest and that was essentially a product of the Irish diaspora in America, its choreographer and two principle dancers being American-born. When young Irish people can best embody an American dream, and young Americans can best represent Irish tradition to the world, we are dealing not with anything so simple as cultural domination or even so rational as cultural exchange, but with something obsessive, repetitive, continually unfinished, all the time renewing itself in old ways. We are dealing with the ways in which the notion of America itself is an Irish invention, the notion of Ireland an American invention. When we step into this divide, we step into, not an open space, but a hall of mirrors.

Irish writers have coped with this by destroying Daniel Corkery's old ideology of the indigenous and the alien. Dermot Bolger has remarked that 'Irish writers no longer go into exile, they simply commute',[37] and this is true metaphorically as well as literally. Their precursor, as it were, is not the James Joyce of *Ulysses*, obsessively re-creating the detail of Dublin streets from exile, but the Joyce of *Finnegans Wake*, for whom Dublin is but a template of all other places, linked linguistically to any other point on the globe. Just as, for the later Joyce, Dublin is also Lublin, West Munster is also Westminster and Crumlin is the Kremlin, the Ireland of the 1990s is, for its writers, also America and Europe. It is a linguistic, imaginative Ireland, an Ireland that cannot be read but must always be written.

The writer who first found this way of encompassing Irish reality is the poet Paul Durcan. He found it partly though what might otherwise be regarded as realistic description of a visible and recognisable Ireland:

> We live in a Georgian, Tudor, Classical Greek,
> Moorish, Spanish Hacienda, Regency Period
> Ranch-House, Three-Storey Bungalow
> On the edge of the edge of town:
> 'Poor Joe's Row' –
> The townspeople call it –
> But our real address is 'Ronald Reagan Hill',
> – That vulturous-looking man in the States.[38]

The movement of these lines, through a random succession of periods and places, through a landscape where even the names of places are unstable, where a woman starts to describe her home in Tipperary and ends up in the United States, is emblematic of contemporary Irish culture. Place in Durcan is unstable, permeable, unbounded. Durcan's Ireland exists, not just in familiar place-names, but in such surreal yet meaningful places as 'the east European parts of Dublin city', 'the road from Mayo into Egypt', 'Westport in the Light of Asia Minor', 'Africa on the West Coast of Kerry', 'the Kalahari, Pimlico, and the West of Ireland', 'The Dublin-Paris-Berlin-Moscow Line', 'a French Ireland'.

These are the places of a poet who asks in 'Red Arrow' of 'the history of transport – is there any other history?' For Durcan is, supremely, the poet, not just of emigration, but of a place constituted by its history of emigration. The American tourists in 'Loosestrife in Ballyferriter'[39] to whom 'Ireland is an odyssey odder than Iowa' are not too far in their sense of estrangement from a poet whose Ireland is, above all else, an odyssey, a journey, a history of transport. For not only is Durcan in his poems continually in motion around Ireland and beyond it to Russia, America, France, Italy, Catalonia and England, but the places themselves are continually shifting and melting into each other.

There are parallel universes on either edge of Europe, the Atlantic and the Caucasus. Poems placed in Ireland repeat themselves on the far side of Europe, as when 'The Girl With the Keys to Pearse's Cottage' becomes 'The Woman with the Keys to Stalin's House', and 'Going Home to Mayo' becomes 'Going Home to Russia'. 'Home' is neither Mayo nor Moscow but both and therefore neither:

> From the shores of the Aran Islands
> To the foothills the far side of the Caucasus
> These are the terraced streets
> That smell of home to us.[40]

Durcan's example has been followed, in one way or another, by almost every younger contemporary Irish writer. The most important place in recent Irish novels is Elsewhere, the foreign place through which Ireland can be reached. Thus – to give some more or less random examples – Colm Toibín's *The South* happens in Ireland and Catalonia, Hugo Hamilton's *Surrogate City* in Ireland and Germany, Eilís Ní Dhuibhne's *The Bray House* in Ireland and Sweden,

Sebastian Barry's *The Engine of Owl-Light* in Ireland and America, Joe O'Connor's *Desperadoes* in Ireland and Nicaragua. Ireland is now, in this work, more a trajectory than a place. In it we can see the lineaments of a culture that at last places the experience of emigration where it should be – at the very heart of the matter of Ireland.

NOTES AND REFERENCES

1 John Montague, *The Dead Kingdom* (Oxford University Press, 1984), p. 90.

2 Finley Peter Dunne, *Mr Dooley and the Chicago Irish* Washington D.C. (Catholic University of America Press, 1987), p. 276.

3 Henry Louis Gates Jnr., *Colored People: A Memoir* (London, Viking, 1995), p. 5.

4 Les Murray, 'Only a Flat Earth Has Margins: Footnotes on a Deadly Metaphor', *Krino*, no. 18, Dublin, 1995, p. 1–15.

5 *The Short Stories of Liam O'Flaherty* (London, New English Library, London, 1966), p. 103.

6 ibid., p. 260.

7 Peter Stallybrass, 'Time, Space and Unity: The Symbolic Discourse of The Faerie Queen' in Raphael Samuel (ed), *Patriotism*: vol. III: *National Fictions* (London, Routledge, 1989), p. 200.

8 Walter Benjamin, 'The Storyteller', in *Illuminations* (Fontana, London, 1973), pp 84–895.

9 See Brenna Katz Clarke, *The Emergence of the Irish Peasant Play at the Abbey Theatre* (Michigan, UMI Research Press, 1982), p. 144.

10 Padraic Ó Conaire, *Exile*, trans, by Gearailt MacEoin (Cló Iar-Chonnachta, 1994), p. 104.

11 George Russell (AE), *Co-Operation and Nationality* (Dublin, Academic Press, 1984), p. 22.

12 Bryan Mac Mahon in John A. O'Brien (ed.), *The Vanishing Irish*, London, 1954, p. 207.

13 John Montague, *The Dead Kingdom*, p. 91.

14 George Russell (AE), *Co-Operation and Nationality*, p. 42.

15 Michael Collins, *The Path to Freedom* (Cork, Mercier Press, 1968), p. 99.

16 Derek Mahon in an interview with Harriet Cooke, *Irish Times*, 17 January 1973.

17 Luke Gibbons, 'Romanticism in Ruins: Developments in Recent Irish Cinema', *Irish Review* no. 2, 1987, p. 62.

18 George Russell op. cit., p. 42–43.

19 Samuel Beckett, *First Love in The Expelled and Other Novellas* (London, Penguin, 1980) p. 18.

20 Daniel Corkery, *Synge and Anglo-Irish Literature* (Cork University Press, 1931), p. 4–5.

21 Brinsley MacNamara, *The Clanking of Chains* (Dublin, Maunsel and Co., 1920), p. 236.

22 James Hanley, *An End and a Beginning* (London, Andre Deutsch 1990), p. 308.

23 Patrick MacGill, *Moleskin Joe* (London, Caliban Books, 1983), p. 12.

24 Liam O'Flaherty, *Shame the Devil* (Dublin, Wolfhound Press, 1981), p. 9.

25 ibid., p. 12–3.

26 John Wilson Foster, *Colonial Consequences* (Dublin, Lilliput, 1991), p. 31.

27 Sebastian Barry, *Prayers of Sherkin* and *Boss Gready's Boys* (Methuen, London, 1991), p. 13.

28 Paul Bew, Ellen Hazlekorn and Henry Patterson, *The Dynamics of Irish Politics* (London, Lawrence and Wishart, 1989), p. 77.

29 Rosita Boland, 'Arriving', in *Ireland in Exile* op. cit., p. 114.

30 Michael O'Loughlin *Atlantic Blues* (Dublin, Raven Arts Press, 1982), p. 28–9.

31 Roddy Doyle, *The Commitments* (Dublin, King Farouk, 1987), p. 7–8.

32 Frederic Jameson, *Postmodernism or the Cultural Logic of Late Capitalism* (London and New York, Verso, 1991), pp. 17–18.

33 Dermot Bolger, *Internal Exiles* (Portlaoise, Dolmen Press, 1987), p. 67 ff.
34 ibid., p. 38.
35 Joseph O'Connor, *True Believers* (London, Sinclair-Stevenson, 1991), p. 40.
36 Emma Donoghue, 'Going Back', in Dermot Bolger (ed.), *Ireland in Exile*, (Dublin, New Island Books, 1993), p. 160.
37 Dermot Bolger, Introduction to *Ireland in Exile*, op. cit., p. 7.
38 Paul Durcan, 'The Haulier's Wife Meets Jesus on the Road Near Moone', *The Berlin Wall Cafe* (Belfast, Blackstaff Press, 1985), p. 4.
39 Paul Durcan, *Daddy, Daddy* (Belfast, Blackstaff Press, 1990), p. 32.
40 Paul Durcan, 'The Dublin-Paris-Berlin-Moscow Line', in *A Snail in My Prime*, p. 239.

7. The Devaluation of 'Nation' as 'Home' and the De-politicisation of Recent Irish Emigration

JIM MAC LAUGHLIN

Popular perceptions of nation-building and emigration in Ireland have long been refracted through the perspectives of social class and political ideology. Today, as in the nineteenth century, emigration – or as it increasingly now categorised, the 'globalisation of the Irish' – is perceived as an inevitable consequence of the modernisation of Irish society. The link between nation-building and emigration here, however, is not a peculiarity of the Irish. Third World countries, peripheral nations in Europe and now, more recently, 'Second World' nations in eastern Europe have all at one time or other functioned as 'emigrant nurseries'. As such, they supplied cheap and abundant reserves of adaptable and skilled labour to the core nations of western Europe and the world system for much of the post-World War II period.[1] Many of these nations still function as 'emigrant nurseries' for the world economy today. Thus, European colonial powers did not dispense with empire after World War II but strongly relied on labour supplies from former colonies well into the twentieth century. A central argument of this chapter suggests that racial and ethnic minorities from these countries have often functioned as internal colonies, or 'Third Worlds within', in powerful European nations and in other core nations of the world economy. Since the late nineteenth century, relationships between coloniser and colonised that were often mediated *within the colonial world* gradually gave way to new relationships between ex-colonial subjects and European employers *within Europe*. This was particularly clear in the case of post-Famine Ireland. Similarly, in the post-war western Europe ethnic minorities from the Mediterranean basin and south-eastern Europe were also transplanted to the core areas of European capitalism.[2] This exodus from the peripheries to the re-developing cores of the European economy was as much a consequence and a cause of the peripheralisation of whole regions in the sending nations. However, while the influx of 'foreign' workers meant that the under-development of ex-colonies and the European periphery was often linked to core-formation in western Europe, at other times emigration may

179

indeed have contributed to the development of sending nations. This was particularly the case in Ireland for much of the late nineteenth and early twentieth century. Here as in Turkey, Spain, Greece, Portugal and Italy, and also in Islamic societies across from Europe's southern borders, the export of 'surplus workers' and the subsequent inflows of 'emigrant remittances' contributed in a vital way to regional development and social welfare in deprived areas in the early stages of these countries' development.[3] In the case of Turkey, for example, successive post-war governments were so concerned with shedding 'surplus workers' abroad that they did not consider the negative impact of emigration on emigrants themselves.[4] Large numbers of Turkish emigrants were professional, skilled and semi-skilled workers who were expected to return to their own country and devote their enhanced skills to the development of Turkey. Many of them did not do so, but stayed behind in host societies where they became victims of racial discrimination and marginalisation. Similarly in post-war Spain, Portugal, Greece and Italy, and more recently in Ireland, it was regularly suggested that the more migrant workers 'honed' their skills and developed their work ethic in countries like Germany, France and Britain, the better they could contribute to the development of their own country when they returned home. As Minister Brian Lenihan stated:

> We regard emigrants as part of our global generation. We should be proud of them. The more they hone their skills and talents in another environment, the more they develop a work ethic in a country like Germany or the U.S., the better it can be applied in Ireland when they return.[5]

Such views are still widely held in many Islamic and Third World countries today. They were part of conventional wisdom in southern Italy, Spain, Portugal, Greece and Turkey for much of this century. It remains to be seen to what extent other peripheral economies in Europe, and in the Third World, still actively promote emigration in order to enhance the skills of their labour force and to attract emigrant remittances from abroad.[6]

IRISH EMIGRATION IN THE REVISIONIST PROJECT

While migration from the colonial to the metropolitan world clearly involved a change in the location of coloniser and colonised relationship, it did not involve any fundamental change in the nature of that relationship. This was certainly the case with Irish immigrants in Victorian Britain in the nineteenth century.[7] It is also true, though to a much lesser extent, of the Irish in Britain in the post-war period. The Irish, like racial minorities and 'unmeltable' ethnic communities, many of them from Third World countries engaged in the process of nation-building, were expected to subordinate their national identities to that of their host society. Thus, just as nationalism in the nineteenth century was the prerogative of expansionist white societies in the metropolitan world, ethno-nationalism in post-war Europe was tolerated only if it derived from Europe's indigenous minorities, not from exogenous minorities like the Irish in Britain, or from Islamic minorities in France, Germany, Belgium and Spain.

Emigration and nation-building have been so linked together in Ireland's case, both in the historical imagination, and particularly now in Irish youth enterprise culture, that the 'shedding' of large numbers of young adults through emigration is increasingly now interpreted as a rite of passage which is not only in the interests of those leaving the country, but also in the national interest. Emigration, it is argued, contributes to the health and vitality of a globalised Irish society, while simultaneously benefiting the Irish economy back home. According to this sanitised view, 'new wave' emigration from Ireland today is placing large numbers of Irish young adults on extended social ladders in the international economy.

This chapter also suggests that the sanitisation and voluntarisation of Irish emigration in recent years is testimony to the success of revisionism as an intellectual project. This not only reinterpreted the historical record to rid it of 'nationalist bias'. It also influenced Irish attitudes to a whole range of contemporary social problems that had their roots in the colonial past and whose effects were still felt in the present. Thus revisionist wisdom since the 1970s has attributed emigration to the socio-psychological attributes and aspirations of Irish young adults, rather than to the neo-colonial status and dependent structure of the Irish economy. Indeed, revisionism has so thoroughly pervaded our most crucial assumptions about Irish society in recent decades that its impact has largely gone unnoticed. This is particularly noticeable in changing attitudes towards nationalism and emigration. As Mary Holland notes, nationalism in the Republic of Ireland at least 'has come to be regarded as an embarrassment, something we have to live with but must keep decently hidden'. Both kinds of nationalism in Northern Ireland, namely Irish nationalism and 'big nation' British nationalism or Ulster Unionism, are 'seen as primitive, a disgrace to the island as a whole at a time when we are trying not only to polish up our image as a modern European state, but also to attract more and more tourists to a burgeoning heritage industry which demonstrates how tastefully an unhappy history can be turned to a pretty profit'.[8]

This chapter suggests that Holland is only half right in arguing that the violence of the IRA in the North of Ireland 'has sickened very many people to the point that they no longer know how to relate to their own history'. The radical displacement of history from Irish political discourse is also intimately bound up with the wider success of revisionism as an expansive hegemonic discourse in Ireland since the 1960s. It is also linked to a profound devaluation of nationalism that went hand in hand with the remodelling of Ireland and Irish society since then. The narrowing of nationalism to an ideology 'contaminated' through association with working-class politics and political violence in

Northern Ireland certainly rendered it a political embarrassment within hege-monic circles in the Irish Republic. This reluctance to examine the contemporary significance of nationalism is related to a heightened concern for the image of Ireland as a progressive European country and as a nation without a past. This, in turn, has meant that Irish political leaders have prioritised the modernisation and Europeanisation of Irish society over and above a wide range of other social issues ranging from unemployment to large-scale emigration. The latter, it is now suggested, is a welcome development in Irish society because it externalises solutions to an essentially Irish problem and encourages Irish young adults to consider emigration as an acceptable and normal alternative to unemployment and lack of opportunity at home.[9]

Theoretical neglect of emigration and its history contrasted sharply with a new concern to analyse the causes of rural-urban *migration* within Ireland in the 1960s and 1970s. Indeed, this was a distinctive feature of the intellectual and optimistic social climate at that time. The reversal of emigration was widely interpreted as the passing of traditional Ireland and the birth of a new Ireland. For many, it marked the end of Irish emigration history.[10] Revisionism also signalled the coming of age of a post-nationalist organic intelligentsia in Ireland. This group articulated the hopes and dreams of the new Ireland, legitimised its emergent social order and fitted Ireland into new disciplinary discourses on social change and modernisation in the global economy. Many of those belonging to the new intelligentsia had professional and academic qualifications which generally set them apart from national politicians and from founding fathers of the Irish state. They rapidly dissociated themselves from the narrow nationalism of earlier decades. They embraced, instead, the logic of cost-benefits analysis and modernisation theory, both of which were central to revisionist projects and practices and which were soon to become hegemonic and institutionalised discourses in the post-1960s Irish state.

For Ireland in the 1960s, modernisation meant technological determinism and technocratic ideology. This, in turn, meant the rapid expansion of a number of new industrial sectors in the Irish economy, particularly in fields of electronics, pharmaceuticals, computer technology and electrical engineering. This was not just a natural development which followed from the decom-position of the more traditional and labour-intensive industries that dominated Ireland's economic landscape in the first 50 years of political independence. As Wickham has shown, these very sectors were promoted as an expression of 'institutionalised ideology'. They were developed as a strategy for 'nativising' foreign technology in 'an ostentatious display of strategic planning by state agencies responsible for industrial development and manpower policy in Ireland'. This gave Ireland a more diversified economy and fostered a significant degree of occupational segregation and regional differentiation. According to Wickham, this mixed mastery of technology with technical awe and national pride in such a way as to create a false sense of autonomy which suggested that development of these sectors gave the nation back its economic sovereignty.[11] As Crowley has shown, Ireland's peripheral location in the New International Division of Labour, instead, meant that the country now occupied a new position in a global economy of flexible accumulation. Ireland at this time, she argues, was transformed into 'a primary arena for female proletarianisation' by transnational corporations operating out of these sectors of the global economy.[12]

Modernisation in the 1960s also meant regional planning, a prioritisation of the urban over the rural, and a disenchantment with the values of rural fundamentalism which permeated the Ireland of de Valera. In this new environment, there was less concern for the purity of the original nationalist ideals of state and far more concern with Ireland's image as a modern European nation. In this optimistic environment also, revisionism strongly influenced official attitudes towards a whole ranges of social issues in Irish society, including emigration, industrial policy, regional development, national identity and the relation between town and country in the new Ireland. It was not only that this was more 'politically correct' than conventional explanatory modes that were now seen to be too heavily imbued with a nationalist bias. It was also the case that revisionism allowed for a profound sanitisation and voluntarisation of a wide range of social issues, not least emigration, and fostered the hegemonic rise of the new intelligentsia in Irish society. The political project of this intelligentsia was not only revisionist. It was also hegemonic in that it advanced a wide range of institutionalised and ideological discourses and practices that reflected the thinking of new élites in Irish society who were further and further removed from the traditional centres of power in post-independence Ireland.

From the 1960s onwards, revisionism, and the instrumentalist thinking that it nurtured, mirrored changing cultural perspectives and contributed to a further devaluation of rural fundamentalism and nationality as the basis of Irish identity. Henceforth, rurality referred not so much to a territorial space, namely the 'country', as to social space and to the social production of new symbols and identities that turned the rural into an arena of intense social and ideological conflict.[13] The Irish countryside now was rediscovered by a Euro-centred agribusiness sector and by development agencies deeply engaged in processes of literally re-marketing Ireland for primarily political and commercial purposes.

Revisionism and instrumental thinking also informed the collective unconsciousness of post-nationalist Ireland. Adopting a 'blame-the-victim' approach originating in social studies of Black poverty in the United States in the 1960s, political commentators and social scientists in Ireland now traced poverty, rural decline, urban blight, emigration and unemployment to the 'cultures' and 'psychologies' of poverty, emigration and unemployment.[14] Irish economists in particular, not least those employed in the Economic and Social Research Institute, so mixed behaviouralism with modernisation theory that they avoided any structural or social-class analysis of the historical and international contexts of Irish social problems. The conventional wisdom which this approach nurtured tended to attribute emigration to geographical factors, to 'the idiocy of rural life', to the proximity of Ireland to Britain, and to the geographical location and small size of the Irish economy. It also called for closer attention to the reasons for the success of the Danish economy with which Ireland, as another geographically small European economy, was increasingly and unfavourably compared. Explanations of social problems in Ireland now were couched in the logic of behaviouralism. This caused emigration in particular to be explained away in terms of the educational qualifications and social aspirations of a new generation of Irish youth. It was also traced to the peculiarities of Irish geography and to the Irish psyche. Emigration was portrayed as an *unbudgeable* element in Irish youth enterprise culture, a historical and cultural *tradition* that had persisted for so long that it had all the characteristics of a *natural* rather than a *social* phenomenon. Thus, the current sanitisation and voluntarisation of Irish emigration has its roots in behavioural approaches to migration in the 1960s.

In the new Ireland of the post-1960s, rural-to-urban migration was explained away in terms of the aspirations of young adults frustrated with what Marx would have called 'the idiocy of rural life'.[15] Behaviouralists did much to expose the nationalist bias, as well as the economic reductionism, in conventional explanations of Irish emigration. However, they failed to relate migrant *behaviour* to the regional, national and international *contexts* within which migration and emigration were structured. This was particularly obvious in the work of Hannan, Walsh, Sexton and Mac Mahon, all of whom combined behaviouralism with core-periphery theorising and contributed to a complete revision of the causes, and indeed the consequences, of modern Irish emigration.[16] Hannan's pioneering study of migration in the 1960s was central to this revisionist project. He was the first to advocate a behavioural approach to rural migration in Ireland in the 1960s. His analysis was not only free of the nationalist bias of earlier discussions of Ireland's rural exodus; it was also free of the rural fundamentalism which had traditionally caused political leaders to bemoan the exodus from the land. His work was later to influence a number of others students of Irish emigration and demography. It was particularly popularised by the media and adapted by modernisation theorists to explain emigration away in terms that Hannan had used in the study of migration within Ireland. Hannan emphasised the progressive outlook of the new Irish youth and radical changes in transportation and communication which made rural communities in Ireland highly susceptible to the restructuring forces of migration, and his followers adopted this same logic to explain the peculiar vulnerability of Irish society to the restructuring forces of emigration.[17] In so doing, behaviouralists and core-periphery theorists reduced emigration to behavioural and geographical causes. They suggested that emigration, both in the past and in the present, was an inevitable response to these restructuring processes operating at the level of the national and the global economy. In tracing emigration to supra-national causes, they also contributed to a de-nationalisation of the causes of emigration and suggested that Irish governments could and should do nothing to prevent it.

Core-periphery models and modernisation theory also adopted spatial categories to explain Irish emigration in geographical terms. They reified place and discussed social processes and exploitative relationships in spatial rather than in social-class and political terms.[18] Accordingly, they also suggested 'supra-national', global solutions to emigration, treated it as a 'non-event', or portrayed it as a social problem that could only be resolved through more funding from the European Community. Geographical and behavioural explanations like these have become so hegemonic in recent years that, as Lee argued:

> The semantic coinage of 'peripheral' has appreciated considerably since the possibility of procuring compensation for it from Brussels has come to our attention. Now that our grievances against history are receding, we need to nurture a grievance against geography. The question is, where is the centre? We were less peripheral to Britain than were most of our European competitors. If we failed to take advantage of the relative centrality of our location, the answer should not be sought in geographical location.[19]

Indeed, Fintan O'Toole has suggested that Ireland's membership of the European Community 'increased rather than decreased the Irish sense of periphery'.[20] The country was now a minor member of a European state system comprising nations with which Ireland had little in common. The debasement and devaluation of nationalism which ensued from this is especially reflected in the current and widespread acceptance of emigration as both natural and traditional in Irish society.[21]

'NEW WAVE' EMIGRATION AND THE DISAPPEARANCE OF TRADITIONAL IRELAND

The category 'hegemony' is central to any discussion of the new theoretical discourses and political practices which have contributed to the de-nationalisation and de-politicisation of Irish emigration in recent decades. The cultural Marxist Antonio Gramsci first used this category to describe the cultural and economic modes of incorporation which allowed dominant sectors of class-structured societies to establish control over subordinate sectors and to legitimise their monopoly of the state apparatus.[22] He also extended the analysis of modes of incorporation beyond the economic to include intellectual,

ideological, theoretical, educational and legal strategies adopted by ruling
classes to prevent subordinate social classes from growing insubordinate.
Gramsci insisted that social change was not effected by individuals or ruling
élites separated from society, but rather by 'intellectuals who are conscious of
being organically linked to a national-popular mass'. Indeed the hegemony of a
political class for Gramsci meant that such a class, through control over the
political, educational and cultural modes of incorporation no less than through
ownership of the means of production, succeeded in persuading other social
classes to accept its world view, including its political, moral and cultural values,
as the sole legitimate ones for governing an entire society.[23] In a period of
political and economic crisis, such as that which beset Ireland in post-
protectionist phase of the early 1960s, and which exposed the country to new
political and economic opportunities and stresses, the apparatus of hegemony
which kept the old social order intact often breaks down. In such circumstances, parties long-accustomed to monopolistic control over state apparatuses
can split or realign, in a fundamental way, their entire political and economic
philosophies. In this situation, conditions are ripe for a shift of power, for the
creation of a new hegemony and for a fundamentally new basis of political
consensus. In Ireland's case, this contributed to a profound devaluation of
nationalism as an ideology informing the country's social and economic policy.
It also fostered a backlash against the very insularity of de Valera's Ireland and
contributed to a radical pejorativisation of rural fundamentalism and an
unthinking prioritisation of the modernisation project. Consequently, as writers
like John Waters and Kevin Whelan have so cogently argued, rural Ireland (and
one is almost tempted to add 'all those who sailed in her') became 'dislodged
from the national consciousness, marginalised, drained of meaning, pejoratively
associated with atavism and retardation'.[24] This meant that the ground shifted,
literally as well as metaphorically, for many people in Ireland in the period of
acute transition which began in the 1960s and still continues. Discussing the
crisis of identity, and the crisis between past and present in this transitional
Ireland, Noreen Collins has recently suggested that:

> The revisionist claim over history, the flight from the land, the ensuing decay of
> rural towns and villages has left many reeling, and their narratives should be read
> as an emotional response to such events . . . It would not be an exaggeration to
> say that the country is at a watershed, with two opposing forces trying to steer
> the country in different directions.[25]

This level of revisionism recently caused another commentator to argue that
there is 'a disturbing lack of proportion in the history Ireland is happy to tell
itself nowadays. Principally, it has got to do with a power élite – in politics,
business and the media – aggrandising its role in shaping our present'. History,
it is suggested, has now become 'a story', one that casts the pre-1960s 'as a dark

age of austere de Valerean idealism'. Ireland since then is 'a brave new world, peopled by young Europeans, with business degrees, who don't even have to learn history anymore'. This 'new bourgeoisie', it is argued, needs a story 'which extols Irish activism and demeans the influence of the wider world'.[26] This is the Ireland so accurately and so deftly portrayed in Waters' *Jiving at the Crossroads*.[27] It is a country where, as in the title of another of Waters' books, 'every day is like Sunday'.[28] It is also a country where the political and intellectual establishments have become 'deeply absorbed in a view of Ireland's economic condition which to most people is a fiction'. Thus, Waters condemns the self-complimentary posture which has allowed prominent political leaders to congratulate themselves on the 'success' of economic policies which give no thought to the real costs of abstract gains to 'the people who are unfortunate enough to populate [the Irish] economy'.[29] Discussing the decimation of rural Ireland through emigration he asserts:

> Each percentage point of an increase in the rate of inflation can be measured just as surely by the widening gap of the silent greyness which is enveloping rural Ireland in its cold embrace. We celebrate our 'recovery' from our recent bout of economic frostbite, softening our focus to obliterate the loss of vital limbs and organs which have resulted from our 'cure'.[30]

That Waters holds out little hope of a challenge to the ruling hegemony is particularly evident in the following passage where he also sees emigration deconstructing entire communities the length and breadth of rural Ireland.

> I don't know what is going to happen to this country, but I know there is not a vast array of choices as to the remedy. I think we can rule out the possibility of all of us coming up with the six numbers to bring us the 'Lotto Luck' windfall which would ensure our survival. But I suspect – and hope – that people power will take a hand before it's too late. If it does not, and if we continue to place ourselves at the mercy of the market forces which are destroying our towns and villages, then we are *all* destined to live in The Land Where Every Day Is Like Sunday. And if Dublin stands idly by while market forces come for the Loughlynns, the Charlestowns and the Castlereas, who will be left to stand up for Dublin when the cold winds of market forces sweep from Europe to take her as well?[31]

For Waters, the very term 'rural Ireland' is an abstract and dangerous tautology, the product of negative stereotyping which has allowed an urban-based intelligentsia to abstractly ignore the dismantling of real communities by submitting them to the harsh forces of the marketplace and emigration. He adds:

> [The] term 'rural Ireland' should be abandoned on the grounds that . . . Ireland is overwhelmingly a rural society, not merely in its culture and structure, but in its ability to maintain itself in economic terms. I suggest that, in so far as Irish society has shifted away from its rural configuration, this exercise has largely been

counter-productive and very possibly foolhardy. The most appalling social catastrophes of recent decades have resulted not from the collapse of rural society but from botched attempts at urbanisation. Not only have the modernisers failed to evoke an imaginative model of what a modern Ireland might be like; they have also failed to indicate how this 'post-rural' society might provide for itself.[32]

To understand other reasons *why* this happened, it may be useful to supplement Waters' interesting analysis with Frantz Fanon's discussion on the role of the national bourgeoisie in transition from colonial rule to political independence in post-colonial Africa.[33] This provides the wider context for a discussion on the role of the bourgeoisie in post-colonial societies in general. It also avoids the national exceptionalism which sometimes affects analyses of social and political change in Ireland since the 1960s. As Frantz Fanon has argued:

> The national bourgeoisie steps into the shoes of the former European settlement
> . . . It considers that the dignity of the country and its own welfare require that it
> should occupy these posts . . . The national middle class discovers its historic
> mission, that of intermediary.[34]

This also describes the position of the new generation of political and social leaders in Ireland's post-protectionist and post-nationalist phase. Beginning in the 1960s, new élites emerged in Irish society, and like the middle class in post-colonial Africa, they were 'quite content with the role of the western bourgeoisies' business agent, [which] it played out in a most dignified manner'. They lacked the 'dynamic, pioneer aspect, the characteristics of the inventor and of the discoverer', and followed the western bourgeoisie 'along its path of negation . . . without ever having emulated it in its first stages of exploration and invention'.[35] Because it was 'bereft of ideas', and lived cut off, or, more accurately, was disenchanted with life as lived by their predecessors and by the rank and file of Irish society, the new middle class which emerged in Ireland in the 1960s was not unlike its class peers in post-colonial Africa. Many of them adopted the role of political managers and became representatives of foreign enterprises in Ireland. However, they were destined to be completely and inevitably undermined through their 'hereditary incapacity to think in terms of all the problems of the nation as seen from the point of view of the whole nation'.[36] Instead, they used their new-found class aggressiveness to oust the older nationalist middle class from positions of power, not least in the intellectual and cultural arena. They then occupied the political space that was formerly dominated by the rural bourgeoisie and other native capitalist groupings. Dissociating themselves from the bankruptcy of the latter, and from the values and life-styles of small-farming rural Ireland, they unreservedly and with considerable enthusiasm, adopted the ways of thinking of their metropolitan 'betters'. In so doing they became, like the Algerian bourgeoisie who were the targets of Fanon's critique, 'wonderfully detached' from their own traditions and even from their own history. More importantly still, they were also detached from their own *geography*, particularly from geographical images of Ireland which carried with them images of rural decline, unemployment, poverty and persistent and high levels of involuntary emigration. Basing their consciousness instead 'upon foundations which were typically foreign', the new intelligentsia in Ireland internalised the causes of the country's social problems and externalised their solutions.[37] Where nationalist leaders of post-independence Ireland 'offered nationalism alone as food for the masses', the new generation of political leaders now substituted themselves for the older generation of leaders. They also adopted a self-conscious and Hegelian perception of themselves as the expression of the popular will of a people grown disenchanted with what Fanon called the 'sterile formalism' of the older nationalism. They were never, however, truly 'national', let alone nationalist leaders. Neither did they create government by the whole people. To quote Fanon once again, they did not foster government 'for the outcasts and by the outcasts'.[38] They ruled a *fragmented Ireland* from within a *fragmented island*. Moreover, they merely ruled a fragment of Ireland, scarcely acknowledging the existence of 'other Irelands' within, or the wider diasporic Ireland overseas.[39] The ensuing divisions which this created in political space, and in the landscape of class configuration in Ireland, were by no means uniquely Irish. Indeed, it could also be argued that divisions between urban and rural, between 'traditional' and 'modern' in Ireland, simply mirrored divisions between north and south, between landscapes of power and landscapes of powerlessness in Thatcherite Britain in the 1980s. Thatcherism was responsible for re-inventing and re-fashioning divisions between the 'two Britains' that were such a feature of the nineteenth-century political landscape. The upwardly mobile, 'thrusting and ambitious' nation in the south-east always provided Thatcherism with its landslide victories. The 'other nation', or the 'other Britain', never had that much time for Thatcherism.[40] So also in Ireland, the upwardly mobile entrepreneurial and ambitious nation living high on the abstract national plain became progressively separated from diasporic Ireland, and from a gentler Ireland nursing the values of neighbourhood, community and parish throughout the 1960s and 1970s. This 'other Ireland' has been treated as an historical abstraction at best and an embarrassing political failure at worst. Little wonder that most involuntary recent emigration still derives from this Ireland.

'IMAGERY' AND THE DE-TERRITORIALISATION OF MODERN IRELAND

In Fintan O'Toole's words, this was an Ireland which, by the 1990s, 'had escaped from itself'. O'Toole's Ireland is a place where people are both rootless in a historical and geographical sense and more attached to symbols and brand names than to real places and historical identities. By the 1990s, this Ireland was also a country where the ruling hegemony was so narrow that it was exercised by a handful of powerful individuals who were constantly inventing symbols for the country so that they could literally market Ireland in the global arena. Tony O'Reilly is the perfect representative of, and the perfect image-maker for, this Ireland. O'Toole describes how O'Reilly literally used Ireland as a backdrop in an advertisement for one of his products. This is how Ireland appears in one such advertisement which literally had the country as its logo:

> At its centre was a map of Ireland. Around the map was the distinctive triple bordered shape of a label familiar to devotees of tomato ketchup and baked beans. Within the borders were five large letters spelling HEINZ. There was nothing else – no slogan, no exhortation: just this strange map of a small island in the Atlantic. Inside the jagged contours of its coastline this country had no political boundaries, no features, no landmarks of history, none of the resonant names or contested zones of a place emerging from a dark and tangled past. It was a clear, uncomplicated space, a brand image, a label that could be stuck on a billion bottles.[41]

It could be argued that O'Toole's portrait of Tony O'Reilly also throws a new and interesting light on the inner mechanisms of the modern Irish entrepreneurial mind. It certainly illuminates central aspects of the hegemonic political discourses and practices under discussion here which have contributed to the de-nationalisation and de-teritorialisation of people and power in the post-Lemass period. He paints O'Reilly as a self-made man and a 'hero of capitalism's unheroic age'. Like the bourgeoisie in Fanon's analysis of the bourgeoisie in post-colonial Africa, his genius 'is not for making or inventing things, but [for] buying cheap and selling hard'. O'Reilly's 'story' is, O'Toole suggests, 'a parable of globalisation'. It is the account of 'a man rising from a specific time and place into a great network of world-wide power'.[42] O'Reilly himself is not only the image-maker par excellence in this new Ireland, he is also the greatest symbolic event to have happened in Ireland in recent decades. O'Reilly perfectly symbolises the highest hopes and dreams of this new Ireland, not least those of the ruling élites that we have been discussing. He is also at once a role model and source of aspiration for those managing a whole range of development agencies in Ireland, from the Industrial Development Agency to Bord Failte, from the Confederation of Irish Employers to the Irish Farmers' Association. O'Toole depicts O'Reilly thinking all the time, not about the state of democracy or the condition of the Irish nation, but about the possibilities of a real beginning for global marketing in a post-Cold War world. O'Toole also depicts O'Reilly like the political managers, the entrepreneurial élite and the 'thrusting Ireland', dreaming of 'the arrival of the new placeless consumer'. Such a consumer, he suggests, is no longer simply a citizen of the nation-state. Instead, this new citizen-as-consumer belongs 'to a world where allegiances to brand names have replaced the more dangerous and visceral loyalties of history and geography'.[43] Like the new Ireland which he has made so fashionable and so marketable, O'Reilly, like Fukuyama and the new Irish political managers, believes that history is 'over'. Politics now has no place in the world and the business of Ireland, as of the free-enterprise world, 'now and forever more, is business'.[44] Like the country itself, in other words, the new hegemonic groups in Irish society, with powerful individuals as their role models and leaders, belong to a post-modern era of high-tech capitalism.

Yet for all the superficial changes, including the comparatively high level of industrialisation in recent decades, this is an Ireland which would have been perfectly familiar to Frantz Fanon. It still is a country where imitation, both in the cultural and in the economic arena, is infinitely more important than invention. For all the emphasis upon production and industrialisation, it still is also a country where 'buying cheap' and 'selling hard' are more important than production itself. Powerful individual business leaders like Tony O'Reilly, Larry Goodman and Michael Smurfit are the perfect representatives of this Ireland. They are also the ultimate role models for other members of Ireland business and political élites. They are de-nationalised and de-territorialised Neitzschean 'supermen' who belong, not so much to the nation of Ireland, as to an *ahistorical* world and to an Ireland-as-marketplace. Thus, Goodman's control over the beef industry meant that this important sector of the national economy was now 'at an angle to the polity of modern Ireland'.[45] This polity, in turn, was now so fragmented and so incoherent that it was itself in the control of the beef trade. For O'Toole, this means that the old question posed by Edmund Spenser and William Petty, namely whether a coherent political society was possible in a country shaped by cattlemen, now returned to modern Ireland with a vengeance and 'in quite unexpected ways'. He further added:

> The nature of the beef industry has been such as to fragment and weaken national politics. Economic links between different parts of Irish society have been weakened, active co-operation has been inhibited, the population itself has been scattered. The strength of the beef industry has been such as to limit the development of the kind of coherent, confident civil and political society which could control that industry and integrate it into a working notion of the common good.[46]

In Goodman's Ireland, as in O'Reilly's world, the products and their images which business élites and development agencies created, as well as the commodities and the media through which they were sold, became 'virtually indistinguishable from each other'. In this environment, the narrow ground separating politics from business, like the distance between production and advertising, disappears completely. Thus, like so many political leaders and promotional agencies in post-Lemass Ireland today, these same powerful business magnates have been responsible for reducing Ireland to the level of a brand name. They have even transformed the country into a company logo. As such, Ireland becomes a moving shamrock on an Aer Lingus aircraft, a feature-less map devoid of regional personality and local identity in an IDA billboard and brand name for selling butter and beef in the international marketplace. Instead of being a country it becomes, instead, 'a standard' to be held aloft, literally an empty symbol 'under which the masses of Irish around the world can congregate'.[47] O'Reilly derives from an Ireland where the government jet and lavishly-refurbished government buildings are its most fitting symbols and its most potent images. The government jet is possibly the most fitting symbol of this new Ireland. It perfectly represents the priorities of its managerial politics and entrepreneurial élites. It not only signifies the close connection between Irish politics and international marketing today. It also testifies to the symbiotic relationship between a de-nationalised Irish political system and an inter-national economy where Ireland's political leaders are increasingly more 'at home' than they are *at home.*

O'Toole rightly suggests that when O'Reilly opted for a career in the Heinz corporation in preference to a political career within Ireland:

> he made a profound statement about the nature of power in the late twentieth century. He could at that stage have launched a political career that would certainly have taken him all the way to the office of taoiseach . . . Given the choice between running a multinational company and running a small European country, however, he chose the former. He had seen that once Ireland had opened itself up to American multinationals, the idea of national sovereignty, of state control, had become untenable.[48]

Thus, by the late 1980s, individual businessmen like Goodman, Smurfit and O'Reilly literally had Ireland in their pockets. Irish politics as a consequence were more and more concerned with management and marketing than with local communities and subordinate social classes. The great paradox surrounding the image of the country which these powerful élites and hegemonic institu-tions created was the fact that their prioritisation of the modernisation project seemed to offer new chances, and suggested a new Ireland, while all the time 'it embodied an embrace of the global economy in which no Ireland, old or new, could really matter'.[49]

THE DEVALUATION OF 'NATION' AND 'HOME' IN CONTEMPORARY IRELAND

Given their views on modern Ireland, it is not surprising that Irish political managers increasingly look past the structural fault-lines within the Irish economy to the search in global arenas, particularly in Europe and, more recently, in the Pacific Rim, for solutions to Irish economic problems. Their ceaseless quests for new markets for Irish goods and services take them into the narrowest recesses of the global economy. All the while, however, it could be argued that the emigrant sons and daughters of Ireland, particularly those from poor rural and working-class families, are still the most fitting symbols of the failure of this Ireland's managerial politics and its entrepreneurial culture. There is every danger, indeed, that this obsession with seeking out 'windows of opportunity' in a neo-Fordian world of global markets and in neo-Hanseastic technopoles of accumulation, may cause Ireland to be forgotten and cause places as communities in rural Ireland in particular to become further ignored in hegemonic discourses. Definitions of space as linkages, networks, flows, interaction, constituencies and fields of opportunity predominate in these hegemonic political and entrepreneurial discourses. Such categorisations of place also take precedence over the political and administrative divisions of national territory. Ireland thus becomes the spatial articulation of a larger-than-national global economy, a place where international forces fleetingly intersect and construct and de-construct places throughout the country. It is transformed into one 'node' in a dynamic international economy, a place where hegemonic *metropolitan* cultures, including the entrepreneurial and managerial cultures of a globalised bourgeoisie, frequently take precedence over *local politics and national custom*. In the geographical constructs of Ireland nurtured by the entrepreneurial discourse, places like Dublin, Shannon, Limerick, Cork and Galway, together with the richer agricultural heartlands and 'blandscapes' of the midlands and south-west, shatter the tidy congruence of polity and economy within the national territory. These places, instead, are progressively segregated from the rest of the country and occupy a hegemonic position in national political space. Like provincial cities and county towns that host large corporations, they are increasingly integrated into a global matrix of flexible accumulation and become enclaves in their own country. Thus, just as corporate capital and powerful transportation networks have re-mapped the global hierarchy and re-structured the new world order, they have also reconfigured Ireland's social and economic geography. Ever since the 1960s, they have literally turned de Valera's rural fundamentalist Ireland inside out. They have been responsible for the construction of new cores of accumulation and new constituencies of political power in the new Ireland. This has also caused entire regions of the country to be 'de-linked' from the national territory as they become more fully integrated into a new power geometry of centrality and trans-territoriality which transcends the Irish nation-state.

Places, regions and cities in the hegemonic discourse of contemporary political leaders are not only devalued. They are viewed simply, and instrumentally, as 'constituencies'. They are transformed into trans-territorial entities of 'mediascapes', 'cyberspaces', 'financescapes', 'ideoscapes', 'commodityscapes' and 'technoscapes'.[50] In this hegemonic discourse, geography goes well beyond the confines of geo-politics and geo-economics. It embraces the distribution of centres of influence, images, symbols and communications, international networks, patterns of mass consumption and global shifts in capital investment and technological frontiers. Accordingly, the new Ireland runs the risk of being reduced to a veritable 'sci-fi' geographical space, a place where regions and places constitute nodes in a world order and function simply as circuits in a global hierarchy of flexible accumulation. As such, they could eventually end up merely as 'informational' fields, arenas of accumulation, flood plains across which uncontrollable forces of global capitalism flow. If this process were to continue much longer, Ireland could well cease to function as a 'container' of 'Irishness' as it could equally well fall through the powerful grid that binds together the post-modern world-system under the hegemony of strong metropolitan nation-states. The latter, and not peripheralised nations like post-colonial Ireland, are constantly reproducing the global urban hierarchy and shaping and re-shaping the social and economic life of world regions. In Ireland's case these same forces are de-constructing local towns, villages, provincial capitals and rural communities and drawing their 'surplus' sons and daughters onto emigrant trails that lead out of the local into the global arena. These same emigrant trails are testimony to the powerlessness of local communities in the face of re-structuring processes operating at the national and global level. They are bridges between disadvantaged areas within Ireland and the core areas of a constantly-changing world economy. They are intended to bridge the gap, and simultaneously stress the linkages, between the local and the global in Irish society.

It is also important to stress that the hegemony which we have been discussing does not reside simply in the ideological arena. It has permeated every aspect of Irish society to such an extent that it has constituted the substance and limits of common sense for most Irish people since the 1960s. John Waters emphasised the dominance of the ruling hegemony in contemporary Ireland when he stated:

> Anything will seem normal if you have known no other reality. Almost all of the public discourse in this society emanates from a single generation, and this generation is the one which benefited from the boom of the Lemass era. All our political class, economists, sociologists, media managers and leading commentators emerged from the Big Lie of the 1960s. This lie was that the past was over and the future had begun, that the rising tide was lifting all boats. The rising tide lifted some boats and they remain lifted, but the tide has long departed. The crew and passengers of these artificially suspended craft continue to maintain a dialogue based on the ideological prescriptions which put them where they are. They dismiss the entire narrative of Irish history up to the 1960s as an aberration. Everything that happened before Lemass was the result of backward thought.[51]

The hegemonic status of this group is such that, in Waters' words, 'nobody can get a word in edgeways'. Yet the reality perceived by these hegemonic groups is frequently out of touch with life as it is experienced by subordinate social classes and by victims of hegemonic projects. As such, it is an aberration, a 'non-reality'. Emigration, unemployment, urban blight and rural decline still feature powerfully in the world of subordinate social classes in Irish society. However, the hegemony of power élites, not only in politics, but also in public discourse and in the media, prevents the reality of the dislocated, the experiences of the marginalised and the social issues that concern the majority from breaking through to the surface of Irish society. If this hegemony was merely based upon an abstract set of ideological notions imposed from above by the new élites in Irish society, and if socio-political and cultural ideas and ideals in modern Ireland were simply the product of ideological manipulation, then Irish society would be much easier to transform than it has proved to be in practice. That said, however, it is also important to emphasise that hegemonic projects and practices in modern Ireland are like those in peripheral societies and in many Third World countries. They have had to be renewed, revived and defended because they are open to challenge from below and subjected to stresses that, potentially at least, could tear Ireland's modernisation project apart. The ruling hegemony here simply offers what E.P. Thompson terms 'the bare architectural framework for containing relations of domination and subordination'.[52] Within that architectural form, many different scenes can be set and different dramas enacted. The sheer 'porosity' of Ireland's social, economic and political borders goes a long way towards explaining why radical challenges to the ruling hegemony have been few and far between.

'HOME' IS EVERYWHERE? THE EMIGRANT EXPERIENCE

Many of the factors which we have so far discussed, and which were responsible for bringing Third World countries closer to the core nations of the European economy, have clearly also transformed Ireland's relations to the external world for a very long period of its history. As we have already seen, this has also fundamentally altered the way the Irish have perceived themselves in relation to the international community since at least the 1960s. Unlike most other European societies, however, the abandonment of Keynesian goals of full employment has not given rise to a significant grassroots nationalism in the Irish Republic. Unlike the situation in several other European nations, for example, modernisation through globalisation has not exacerbated nationalist tensions or encouraged a racist politics of the ultra-right in the Irish Republic. There are few signs that localism and globalism in Ireland have clashed in such a way as to produce a new nationalism. Neither have they strengthened the quest for security that place always offers in the midst of a shifting world that the flexible accumulation of capital implies. As I have argued elsewhere, however, the modernisation project has nurtured new closures in Irish society.

In particular, it has fostered a local geography of closure and a politics of exclusion which have sought to exclude Irish Travellers and, more recently, New Age Travellers, from many rural and urban communities throughout the country.[53] However, unlike the situation in France, Germany and Britain in recent decades, modernisation through globalisation has not given renewed significance to traditional myths of 'blood and soil'. Neither has it cultivated a racist nationalism which excludes the 'foreigner' by preserving the 'native' and protecting traditional values.[54] This is clearly attributable to Ireland's status as an emigrant nursery. It is largely due to the fact that as a peripheralised nation with high levels of unemployment, Ireland has functioned as a *sending* country which exported labour, rather than as a *host* society for receiving immigrants. Moreover, there is nothing particularly modern about this. The openness or 'porosity' of the Irish economy and Irish society, like the encounter between the colonised and the coloniser, between the 'self' and the 'other' in Irish society, goes back a very long way indeed. However, that 'openness' was radically deepened from the latter half of the nineteenth century onwards and acquired new significance since the mid-1960s. The accelerated de-territorialisation of Irish society since then, together with the increased globalisation of Irish workers in the 1980s and 1990s, has caused some commentators to suggest that we are literally now witnessing the disappearance of Ireland 'under the pressures of economics, of geography, of the collapse of the religious monolith which was inseparable from our self-definition'.[55] Many others have inadvertently contributed to a naturalisation of this globalisation of Irish youth through 'new wave' emigration by arguing that Ireland has now become such a radically open society that it *naturally* 'lets in the great tide of international blandness and it lets out much of the life blood of the country'.[56] O'Toole attacks this view because it treats Ireland as a peculiarly exposed society, one where Leopold Bloom's definition of a nation as the 'same people' living in 'different places' is increasingly said to apply. As he also points out, and as other chapters in this volume confirm, the Europe experienced by recent Irish emigrants is not at all that of Irish artists and writers who lived in Europe in the first half of this century. It is, instead, the Europe of 'the *gasterbeiter*, the migrant worker, a shifting alienated Europe of hostels and railway stations and factories'.[57]

The 'de-territorialised thesis' which paints Ireland as a radically fragmented nation scattered across global space, is remarkably close to mainstream postmodernist arguments which suggest that 'home' today:

> . . . is no longer just one place. It is locations. Home is that place which enables and promotes varied and everchanging perspectives, a place where one discovers new ways of seeing reality, frontiers of difference. One confronts and accepts dispersal and fragmentation as part of the constructions of a new world order that reveals more fully where we are, who we can become.[58]

The problem with this 'devaluation' of home and nation, as applied to Ireland, is not just that it sanitises emigration by treating it simply as a natural dispersal of Irish young adults across a global plane. It also tells one very little about the social class and gender composition of historic or recent emigration. It sheds even less light on the factors which determine who should, and who should not, stay 'at home'. In particular, it ignores the political implications of emigration. It simply suggests that emigration is in the country's interests and implies that all those leaving Ireland today are doing well outside of it. This is clearly not the case. As most recent surveys of Irish emigration show, emigration still impacts far more forcefully upon working-class and small-farming families than it does upon middle-class and suburban families, although these also have been seriously affected by emigration, including involuntary emigration. The history of Irish emigration suggests that this is not a recent development either. The historical record shows that emigration, class configuration and state formation testify to the radical openness of Irish society since at least the eighteenth century. Since then, the twin processes of modernisation and globalisation have allowed the Irish state literally to take shape, not least by excluding very large numbers of young adults from the nation-building and modernisation project by casting them, instead, into the global arena. History also shows that the links between emigration and nation-building run deep in Irish society and in the Irish psyche. The commercialisation of relations of production in Ireland brought about through the extension of the spatial framework of interdependence which linked the country to Britain and the world economy goes back at least to the mid-eighteenth century. Since then, society, politics, culture and social landscapes in Ireland have been responding to the globalising force of a dynamic British and global capitalism. However, the axis of Irish dependency has shifted significantly since Irish independence. The Americanisation and Europeanisation of Irish society has been especially marked since the 1960s and 1970s. As a result, traditional Ireland has literally been sent 'a-spin' and a profound sense of dislocation is observable in Irish politics, in Irish society and, albeit to a much lesser extent, in Irish culture. This, in turn, has been intensified by the substitution of nationalism as a politics of 'mutual exclusiveness' for a uniformity of social standards and cultural forms emanating from outside Ireland. O'Toole has argued that Irish society has become even more permeable in recent years because so many Irish young adults suffer from a peculiar sense of internal exile which makes them feel increasingly less at home in Ireland.[59] As I have stressed here, however, this is by no means a new development. Like their nineteenth century predecessors, many young adults in Ireland today probably regard this country as 'unreal', just as many of those who have been 'away' and who then return often find it 'unrecognisable'. Unlike many of their peers in unemployment blackspots in Britain and in mainland Europe, for example, large numbers of Irish young adults apparently perceive emigration as a natural response to lack of opportunity 'at home'. This has prompted O'Toole to suggest that:

> we should stop using the word 'conservative' about ourselves. We are not a conservative people, we are a fatalistic one [because] Irish young people are prepared to put up with any amount of personal discontinuity rather than contemplate a radically altered future in their own country'.[60]

For O'Toole, indeed, emigration is the great guarantor of continuity in contemporary social and political life in Ireland. It has become 'the badge of our identity' in a post-modern world where more familiar cultural markers like the Irish language and Irish Catholicism, and where dreams of self-sufficiency, independence and national unification, have melted away since the adoption of modernisation through globalisation and Europeanisation as the hegemonic project of the state.

Recent changes in the political and territorial organisation of Irish society have also been so far-reaching that they constitute a radical discontinuity with the more traditional view of Ireland as a self-governing, organic and identifiable community linked to the national territory. John Waters succinctly described the effects of rapid modernisation on this society as follows:

> One way of describing what has been happening in Ireland in the past 20 years or so would be to say that the country has been going out of fashion. I do not mean that it has become unfashionable to be Irish, but that the realities of what it is like to live in Ireland and the aspects of Irish life which might ensure the health and stability of future life here have all been rendered unfashionable within the public imagination of the State.[61]

In our anxiety to become 'modern' or 'European', he suggests, 'we have denied ourselves the ability to survive at all'. Aptly quoting from Milan Kundera, he concludes that we have 'become the allies of our own gravediggers'.[62] As Whelan shows, the devaluation of national and local authority has also generated a political culture of dependency in peripheral regions in Ireland as elsewhere in Europe. He further elaborates:

> This creates a dependency syndrome, stifling local initiatives and responses, encouraging a grants mentality and a sense of persuasive civic apathy. At the centre, it tends to clog the administrative system with a plethora of detail more efficiently handled at the local level. It also creates a mandarin class, shielded from democratic responsibility or accountability and wrapped in what Tom Barrington has called 'a cocoon of complacent centralisation'. . . . Such a system puts immense pressure on the politician to act predominantly as a broker, a handler and a fixer, continuously interposed, like a tangler at a fair, between the state and its citizens.[63]

Thus, he adds:

The tendency has been to remove decision-making from the hands of elected officials and place it increasingly in the hands of appointed ones, making national bureaucracy the only effective link between the EC and local communities. The lack of effective local administration has created a vacuum at the regional level, which in turn has inhibited integrated approaches to economic development and encouraged sectorally-based decision making at the centre.[64]

It could be argued that Ireland was, prior to entry into Europe, a functioning geographic unit where state institutions administered, regulated and monitored a national economy, and where these was considerable, but by no means total, congruence between polity and economy within the national territory. These same institutions simultaneously presided over, and created, a moral geometry and a socio-political space that was in many respects recognisably and controllably Irish. That said, however, large numbers of young adults still had to locate in the international economy, particularly in Britain and the United States, due to lack of work and opportunity at home. Since entry to Europe, new institutions, by no means all of which are Euro-based, have emerged to classify, to regulate and to literally re-form Irish society and Ireland itself. Since then, also, the urbanisation of Irish society, the industrialisation of the Irish economy and Europeanisation of Irish agriculture have created entirely new landscapes of social and economic control in Ireland. This has particularly contributed to the radical replacement of local government with abstract national and European centres of control. This transition, from the concrete reality of the locality to the abstractions of the national and the European, not only signified a locational shift in the locus of power in Ireland – it was also a territorial strategy for shifting power from the confined fields of narrow nationalism to the wider and more impersonal world of Euro-power and corporate control. Thus, the deterioration of national politics and the new culture of dependency in Ireland have not only affected *attitudes* towards 'new wave' Irish emigration; they may also have affected *patterns* of emigration. Today, more and more Irish young adults think in terms of Europe and mobility when considering solutions to the lack of work and opportunities 'at home'. Certainly perceptions of Europe as an 'untilled field' of employment and opportunity are deeply embedded in Irish youth enterprise culture. Thus a recent handbook for young Irish emigrants stated:

Europe is now wide open, the economic borders are down, labour and money are allowed to move freely and emigration has become simply migration. The reality is somewhat different. Single market or no single market, it's clear that the majority of European states are far from ready – and won't be for a long time. In fact, the politicians are already admitting in private that it will take several years after 1993 to see a borderless Europe. Even so, all over the continent, workers, especially young people, are swotting up on foreign languages, preparing to take a leap in the dark.[65]

THE DEVALUATION OF NATION: A PECULIARITY OF THE IRISH?

There is a degree of 'national exceptionalism' in the writings of O'Toole and Waters which occasionally prevents them seeing that the devaluation of nationalism, like the de-territorialisation of power and local identities, are not a peculiarity of the Irish. These are European-wide phenomena which in Ireland's case are literally influencing the way modern Ireland sees itself in the world system. Like other small nations, particularly those on the peripheries of Europe and in large parts of the Third World, Ireland has also experienced severe curtailments on its national sovereignty as a concomitant to deeper integration into the European Union and the global economy. As elsewhere in Europe, particularly in Scotland, Wales, Portugal, Italy and Greece, this has had the effect of weakening local authority and transforming nation-states into what Whelan terms 'glorified local authorities'.[66] Ireland, like other peripheralised countries throughout Europe, also has seen a profound transformation of its political culture due to the increase in the number of 'non-territorial' actors and agencies operating within its boundaries. These include, not only multinational corporations and the transnational media, but also a whole array of political, legal and economic agencies that link peripheral regions, and peripheralised statelets like Ireland, to the decision-making cores of the European Union. As we have already seen, this has radically altered the sovereignty and the territorial status of small statelets. In the case of Ireland, it transformed national territory from a container of social, economic and cultural life into a social and economic flood-plain. Fundamental changes in the territorial organisation of modern societies have been interpreted as evidence of 'time-space compression' involving a shift from a 'space of places' to a 'space of flows'.[67] This process not only 'devalues' places through a progressive de-territorialisation of people and power; it also suggests that 'place' no longer matters in a world where people are more and more attached to 'brand names' and pursue 'lifestyles', and where nations, regions, cities, towns and places, at least in Ireland, are redundant. To argue thus is to insist that 'home' now is literally anywhere and everywhere. This also implies that we are living through such an intense period of social and economic restructuring that we are witnessing the de-construction of the nation state, the fragmentation of local identities and the violent compression of space into time. There is clear and abundant evidence, both in the form of large-scale emigration and in the form of heightened economic dependency upon Europe, that this has been occurring in Ireland since at least the late 1970s.

However, this devaluation of nation and nationalism is not a universal phenomenon. It is important to stress the geographic specificity of the processes, both within Europe and in the modern world system. The nation-state is far from marginal to the socio-political organisation of entire mega-regions in the world economy, including the former Soviet Union, the Middle East and south-east Asia. Similarly nationalism, with its capacity to 'anchor' people and root decision-making within the nation-state, is still a fundamental feature of the more powerful nations of Europe and the international community. Indeed 'big nation' nationalism shows no signs of abating either in Britain, France, Germany or Russia, or in the United States, Canada, Japan, Australia and China. To argue thus is to warn against any exaggeration of the 'devaluation thesis' and to stress its geographical and socio-political specificity. Revolutions in telecommunications, the globalisation of youth culture, the heightened mobility and flexibility of capital and the dismantling of economic and cultural borders that previously contained social practices within the delineations of the nation, all of these are often taken as evidence that the twin processes of the devaluation of the nation-state and the de-territorialisation of political power is a global phenomenon. This is not the case. Throughout the period of intense Europhoria that began with the dismantling of the Iron Curtain and ended with the fragmentation of the Soviet Union, Euro-centred political leaders, economists and globalisation theorists in particular have been making exaggerated claims about the death of the nation and the emergence of a European and truly global civilisation. The more radical globalisation theorists have even suggested that changes affecting borders between territorial communities in recent years have been so far-reaching that they have blurred traditional divisions between 'domestic affairs' and 'foreign affairs'.[68] They have argued that this, in turn, has so influenced divisions between 'domestic' and 'foreign policy' that it is radically altering distinctions between 'native' and 'foreigner', between 'home' and 'abroad'. Thus, for example, it is often suggested that the heightened mobility and transnationalisation of labour makes it increasingly difficult to determine who *belongs* and who has right of citizenship in the European Union. The ultra-right and extreme nationalists have been vociferous on the related issues of 'home', nationalism and 'the 'other', both in Britain and in mainland Europe, but also in the United States and increasingly now in Israel, Egypt, Australia and Canada.[69] These groups have extremely 'set' views on those who *do not* belong within their 'nations'.

This means that 'home' is not 'everywhere' for Europe's 'unmeltable ethnics', or for its racially and culturally-defined minorities. There is a growing body of evidence which suggests that for whole sections of the Irish population in Britain and the United States, 'home' still is in Ireland. Also, far from being made to 'feel at home', Islamic communities and coloured minorities are also frequently racialised and become targets of racial scapegoating. The French sociologist Etienne Balibar has traced the roots of this resurgent nationalism and xenophobia in western Europe to post-war changes in the relationship between the old colonial powers and metropolitan nations on the one hand, and peripheral nations and the Third World countries, on the other. Discussing the effects of these structural changes on race relations in Europe, he has argued:

> the 'two humanities' which have been culturally and socially separated by capitalist development – opposites figuring in racist ideology as 'sub men' and 'supermen', 'underdeveloped' and 'overdeveloped' – do not remain external to each other, kept apart by long distances and related only 'at the margins'. On the contrary, they interpenetrate more and more within the same space of communications, representations and life.[70]

Castles has similarly suggested that the imposition of the citizenship of the coloniser on the colonised was an ideological instrument of domination in the age of empire. European states were unwilling to abandon established citizenship legislation in the post-war period because to do so would have been 'tantamount to accepting the breakdown of colonialism, which they were still trying to resist.[71] This, it could be argued, was also the case with many of the Irish in Britain in the 1920s and 1930s. Recent research by Curtis, Greenslade, Hickman, Walter and others testifies to the continued racialisation of Britain's Irish minority and to the persistence of racist attitudes towards whole sections of the Irish in Britain today.[72] What makes such modern expressions of racism and anti-ethnic sentiment all the more significant is the fact that revolutionary developments in the organisation and functioning of communications in this period literally linked Ireland to Britain, just as they linked the peripheries of Europe and ex-colonial societies to the core areas of the European and world economy. As Wallerstein and Balibar have shown, this had the effect of transforming the world economy from a functioning amalgamation of discrete geographic units made up separate but interdependent economies, on the one hand, into a space of 'unified and monopolised communications', on the other. Potentially at least, all populations in this post-modern world were now somehow immediately visible to, and in contact with, one another.[73] The reality of such contact, however, not least the paranoia surrounding the degree of future intermingling with 'the other', whether from Ireland, from the Islamic world, or from ex-colonies in the Third World, often exacerbated racial and ethnic tensions in Britain. For the more 'unmeltable ethnics', this in turn contributed to the transformation of ethnically mixed inner-city areas into contested domains where 'foreigners' were said to have no legitimate claims, least of all claims to welfare support and state recognition of their different social, cultural and political traditions. Thus, it is not sufficient to argue that 'race' is simply a psychological 'memory', a relic from the Nazi past, or an anachronistic left-over from nineteenth-century race-thinking. As Balibar suggests, we must also explain why contemporary racism, including anti-Irish racism in Britain, has remained one of the most persistent forms of historical and political consciousness in the contemporary world. We must account for the fact that anti-Irish sentiment in Britain, like anti-immigrant sentiment elsewhere in Europe, still effects the imaginary fusion of past and present. In the case of Britain it also affects relations with the Irish in Britain, particularly with the nationalist minority in Northern Ireland. The destruction of these complexes, both in post-colonial Britain and in Europe in general, has long been predicated on the demise of racist attitudes and prejudices and on the decomposition of racist communities. This has clearly not yet occurred. The post-war racialisation of religious and ethnic minorities within Britain, as in France, Germany, Holland, Spain and Portugal, is certainly a continuation of nineteenth-century racial traditions. These same traditions nurtured national geographies of closure and political strategies for excluding the 'foreigner' from Britain and other European nations, or accepting them only on terms laid down by the latter. Then as now the central function of both these strategies was to permit national societies and local communities to organise into social, cultural and geo-political entities to better compete with 'others' for goods and services essential for social and political survival.[74] Stavenhagen has argued that the stratifications arising from such status groupings were 'social fixations'. They were created by juridical means and maintained by specific social relations of production and social class relationships.[75] Discussing the effects of large-scale immigration on these 'social fixations' in the metropolitan world, he further elaborated:

> Into these social fixations intrude other secondary, accessory factors (for example, religious, ethnic) which reinforce the stratification and which have, at the same time, the function of liberating it of its economic base changes. Consequently, stratifications can be thought of as justifications or rationalizations of the established economic system, that is to say, as ideologies. Like all phenomena of the social superstructure, stratification has a quality of inertia which maintains it even when the conditions which gave it birth have changed. As the relations between classes are modified . . . stratifications turn themselves into *fossils* of the class relations on which they were originally based.[76]

In the nineteenth century, these same racial stratifications also arose out of the need to maintain core-periphery antimony in an international order of powerful metropolitan nations and powerless colonial societies. They were, in essence, a way of keeping the people of the empire 'at bay', while all the time encouraging vast inflows of material wealth from the colonial world.

Since the 1960s, the empire has literally, and increasingly, 'struck back' at the colonising world as more and more ex-colonial subjects arrived on the shore of the old colonial powers and 'set up home' in the heartlands of modern Europe. Even today, however, nationalism still divides core and periphery in an intra-zonal formation, and national categorisations of people and territory still reflect competition between and within states in a hierarchically-structured international and intranational order. Race and racism also unify 'core zones' and 'peripheral zones' in an intra-zonal relationship which often creates conflict between them.[77] One aspect of this conflict is the gradual abandonment of the principle of *jus soli* in favour of the principle of *jus sanguinis* and the movement away from inclusive to exclusive definitions of citizenships in the European community. This has meant that the binding guarantees of citizenship and equal rights for ex-colonial subjects that were formulated in the twilight of European imperialism have often since been ignored or circumvented.[78]

While the Irish in Britain have not suffered racial victimisation to the same degree as other racial and ethnic minorities, they nevertheless still encounter significant levels of anti-Irish sentiment. As several contributors to this volume have emphasised, the social-class and gendered identities of Irish people in Britain are still strongly influenced by British attitudes towards Irish people, and towards Irish nationalism in particular. Similarly, while technical innovations in communication transformed the way the world economy functioned, and transformed relationships between Britain and Ireland in particular, this did not fundamentally transform attitudes of host nations to ex-colonial minorities in their midst. They may in fact have hardened them. Therefore, as the pace of decolonisation increased throughout the British Empire after World War II, a whole range of quite novel multi-ethnic/multi-racial spaces emerged in Britain and in other European countries. These were not only spaces where geo-political strategies were formed and where capital, technology and information circulated. These were also places wherein populations were subjected to the laws of supply and demand, and where they often came into physical and symbolic contact with each other for the first time. As a consequence of this, the equivocal interiority-exteriority configuration which formed one of the structuring dimensions of modern racism, including anti-Irish racism in Britain, was now reproduced, expanded and re-activated in the post-war period. Balibar suggests that it is a commonplace to remark upon these changes as 'Third World within' effects because they were brought about by immigration from the former colonies into the core areas of metropolitan nations. He went on to argue that:

> this form of *interiorization of the exterior* which marks out the horizon against which the representations of 'race' and 'ethnicity' are played out cannot be separated, other than abstractly, from apparently antithetical forms of *exteriorization of the interior*. And in particular it cannot be separated from those which result from the formation – after the more or less complete departure of the colonizers – of states which claim to be national (but only become so very unequally) throughout the immense periphery of the planet, with their explosive antagonisms between capitalist bourgeoisies or 'Westernized' state bourgeoisies and wretched masses, thrown back by this very fact upon 'traditionalism'.[79]

CONCLUSION

This chapter has suggested that internal changes in the social-class structure of the Irish society and transformations in the Irish economy since the 1960s have rendered Ireland more exposed to the forces of globalisation. This shifted Ireland's traditional and isolationist position in the community of nations and brought it more centrally into the world economy, particularly Europe. This, in turn, compounded Ireland's status as an emigrant nursery in the world economy. It also facilitated the emergence of a new hegemony in Irish society, including new hegemonic institutions which re-interpreted the Irish past and re-evaluated the causes and consequences of Irish social problems. The success of the revisionist project since then has been so far-reaching that it has not only influenced Irish attitudes towards the past, but has radically altered Irish perspectives on a wide range of social problems from unemployment to 'new wave' Irish emigration. The latter in particular is increasingly now 'voluntarised' and 'individualised'. It is portrayed as a welcome development in youth enterprise culture in a country where managerialism and entrepreneurialism occupy central positions both in hegemonic discourses and in institutionalised ideologies. Emigration from Ireland is now discussed in terms of the globalisation of Irish youth. The hegemony of behavioural and geographical explanations of 'new wave' emigration also means that its deeper structural causes and consequences have been seriously neglected. It seems entirely natural that Irish young adults should seek work and opportunity abroad rather than at home. Young emigrants, it is argued, are more and more 'at home' in the global economy than in the national economy. This, more than anything else, testifies to the devaluation of nation and nationalism in modern Ireland. The Irish nation-state today, like the national society in the nineteenth century, does not function as a 'container' of Irish society. It has been so porous that it has, instead, become an emigrant nursery which enterprising young adults are naturally expected to leave. The success of revisionism can therefore be measured in terms of the 'naturalness' of emigration and in the growing acceptance of a social and political hegemony which suggests that the Irish *cannot* and *should not* all live on one small island. This devaluation of 'home' and 'nation' is particularly strong in Ireland. It also sets it apart from core nations and other small countries in Europe where the nation still anchors most young adults within the national economy.

Post-war emigration from Ireland to Britain, like other large-scale emigrations form the Third World to core areas of the European and the global economy, has also shown that labour has been far more flexible and far more mobile in the world economy than capital ever was. This has not been an unproblematic development. First, there were quite substantial differences in the work-cultures of several immigrant groups, including, as Greenslade shows in this volume, the

Irish in Britain, and including especially Asian, Black, Turkish and Islamic minorities elsewhere in Europe. Like racial minorities and 'unmeltable ethnics' in the United States, these groups often have different attitudes towards work, leisure, time and community than those who have been habituated to industrial production for generations. As in the United States, so also in Britain and mainland Europe, cultural differences, including different attitudes towards work and leisure, have heightened the visibility of racial and ethnic minorities and contributed to anti-immigrant racism. The chapters by Greenslade, Grey and Buckley in this volume also testify to the effects of this on the Irish in Britain today. Here, as elsewhere in Europe, racial and ethnic minorities have regularly been 'scapegoated upon' by those who insist that 'foreigners' are not just different but dangerous, lazy, dirty and disrespectful of the hegemonic culture of their host nations. Thus the problem of racism in countries like Britain, France, Germany, Belgium and Spain today is not just that it is an expression of ultra-right and extreme nationalist politics, but that racial and ethnic explanations for social unrest and social disorder are gaining currency and acceptability in these countries. Large sections of British and European society clearly are still prepared to passively and uncritically accept separate treatment for non-indigenous workers and their descendants.

NOTES AND REFERENCES

1   Jim Mac Laughlin, 'Defending the Frontiers: The Political Geography of Race and Racism in the European Community' in C. Williams (ed.), *The Political Geography of the New World Order* (London, Bellhaven, 1993), pp. 20–45.

2   S. Castles, *Here for Good: Western Europe's New Ethnic Minorities* (London, Pluto Press, 1984).

3   S. Paine, 'Replacement of the West European Labour System by Investment in the European Periphery' in D. Seers, D. Schafer and M. Kiljunen (eds.) *Underdeveloped Europe* (Hassocks, Harvester Press, 1979).

4   S. Adler, *A Turkish Conundrum: Emigration, Politics and Development* (Geneva, ILO Press, 1982).

5   Tom Whelan, 'The New Emigrants', *Newsweek*, 10 October 1987.

6   S. H. Brandes, *Migration, Kinship and Community* (New York, Academic Press, 1975); R. Pennix, 'A Critical Review of Theory and Practice: The Case of Turkey', *International Migration Review*, vol. 16, no. 4, pp. 781–815.

7   Jim Mac Laughlin, 'Pestilence on their Backs, Famine in their Stomachs': The Racial Construction of Irishness and the Irish in Victorian Britain' forthcoming in Colin Graham and Richard Kirkland (eds.), *The Mechanics of Authenticity* (London, Macmillan, 1997).

8   Mary Holland, 'A Reluctance to Examine What Nationalism Really Means to Us', *Irish Times*, 26 August 1993.

9   Robert Foster, 'Young Emigrants Still Looking West', *Irish Times*, 14 April 1987.

10   David Fitzpatrick, *Irish Emigration, 1801–1921* (Dundalgan, Dundalgan Press, 1984).

11   Kevin Whelan, 'The Bases of Regionalism' in Prionsais O'Drisceóil (ed.), *Culture in Ireland, Regions and Identity* (Belfast, Institute of Irish Studies, 1993).

12   Ethel Crowley, *Factory Girls: The Implications of Multinational Investment for Female Employment in the Republic of Ireland.* Occasional Papers in Social Science (Queen's University, Belfast, 1993).

13 Brian Mc Grath, 'Redefining Rurality in Ireland' *Review of Postgraduate Studies*, no. 4, Spring 1995–96; M. Mormont, 'Who is Rural? or How to be Rural: Towards a Sociology of the Rural' in T. Marsden, P. Lowe and S. Whatmore (eds.), *Rural Restructuring, Global Processes and their Responses* (London, David Fulton, 1990).

14 William Ryan, *Blaming the Victim* (New York, 1971).

15 Karl Marx and Friedrick Engels, *Selected Works*, Volume One (Moscow, Progress Press, 1956).

16 Damian Hannan, *Rural Exodus: A Study of the Forces Influencing the Large-scale Migration of Irish Youth* (London, Chapman, 1970); Damian Hannan et al., *The Economic and Social Implications of Emigration*, Dublin (National Economic and Social Council, 1991).

17 Hannan, *Rural Exodus*, p. 32.

18 Richard Peet, 'Spatial Dialectics', *Area*, vol. 56, no. 2, pp. 45–9.

19 Joseph Lee, 'Ireland Today – Poor Performance from a Talented People?', *Irish Times*, 13 January, 1990.

20 Fintan O'Toole, 'Culture and Media Policy' in P. Keatinge (ed.), *Ireland and EC Membership Evaluated* (London, Pinter Press, 1991), p. 272.

21 Jim Mac Laughlin, *The Emigrant Nursery and the World Economy* (Cork University Press, 1994).

22 Antonio Gramsci, *Selections from the Prison Notebooks* (London, Lawrence and Wishart, 1971), pp. 23–27.

23 Jim Mac Laughlin and John A. Agnew, 'Hegemony and the Regional Question: The Political Geography of Regional Industrial Policy in Northern Ireland, 1945–1972', *Annals of the Association of American Geographers*, vol. 76, no. 2, pp. 248–49.

24 Noreen Collins, 'John Healy and John Waters: Putting a Human Perspective on Politics' in *Review of Postgraduate Studies*, no. 4, Spring 1995, p. 29.

25 ibid., p. 27.

26 ibid., p. 33.

27 John Waters, *Jiving at the Crossroads* (Belfast, Blackstaff Press, 1991).

28 John Waters, *Everyday Like Sunday* (Dublin, Poolbeg Press, 1995).

29 ibid., p. 69.

30 ibid., p. 71.

31 ibid., pp. 71–2.

32 ibid., p. 80.

33 F. Fanon, *The Wretched of the Earth* (Harmondsworth: Pelican, 1974).

34 ibid., p. 122.

35 ibid., p. 124.

36 ibid., p. 162.

37 ibid., p. 143.

38 ibid., p. 165.

39 Daniel Corkery, *The Hidden Ireland* (Cork, Mercier Press, 1978).

40 Vernon Bogdanor, 'One Nation Divided', *Guardian*, 13 January 1994.

41 Fintan O'Toole, ' Brand Leader', *Granta*, vol. 53, p. 47, 1996.

42 ibid., p. 50.

43 ibid., p. 53.

44 ibid., p. 51.

45 Fintan O'Toole, *Meanwhile Back at the Ranch* (London, Vintage Books, 1995), p. 20.

46 ibid., p. 20.

47 O'Toole, 'Brand Leader', p. 67.

48 ibid., p. 71.

49 ibid., p. 96.

50   S. Sassen, 'On Concentration and Centrality in the Global City' in Paul Knox and Peter Taylor (eds.), *World Cities in a World System* (Cambridge University Press, 1995), p. 65.

51   Waters, *Every Day like Sunday*, p. 82.

52   E.P. Thompson, 'Eighteenth Century English Society: Class Struggle Without Class?', *Social History*, vol. 3, no. 2, 1978 p. 119.

53   Jim Mac Laughlin, *Travellers and Ireland: Whose Country, Whose History?* (Cork University Press, 1995); Jim Mac Laughlin, 'The Evolution of Anti-Traveller Racism in Ireland', *Race and Class*, vol. 37, no. 3, 1995, pp. 47–63.

54   Jim Mac Laughlin, ' Defending the Frontiers: The Political Geography of Race and Racism in the European Community' in C. Williams (ed.) *The Political Geography of the New World Order*, (London, Bellhaven, 1991).

55   Fintan O'Toole, 'Permanence and Tradition are Illusions in a Makeshift Society', *Irish Times*, 30 May 1994.

56   Fintan O'Toole, 'Culture and Media Policy', p. 90.

57   ibid., p. 91.

58   Cited in Jim Mac Laughlin, *The Emigrant Nursery*, p. 15.

59   Fintan O'Toole, 'Strangers in Their Own Country', *Irish Times*, 28 September 1989.

60   ibid.

61   Waters, *Every Day Like Sunday*, p. 77.

62   ibid., p. 77.

63   Whelan, 'The Bases of Regionalism', p. 19.

64   ibid., p. 15.

65   E. Cobbe and S. Mac Carthaigh (eds.), *Living and Working in Europe* (Dublin, Macmillan, n.d.), p. xv.

66   Whelan, 'The Bases of Regionalism', p. 17.

67   David Harvey, *The Condition of Postmodernity* (London, Blackwell, 1992), p. 27.

68   Z. Mlinar, 'Individuation and Globalization: the Transformation of Territorial Organization' in Z. Mlinar (ed.), *Globalization and Territorial Identities* (Aldershot, Avebury, 1992).

69   Michael Ignatieff, *Journeys in the New Nationalism* (London, Phaidon, 1992); M. Ignatieff, 'France's Born-again Fascists', *Observer*, 8 November 1991; M Ignatieff, 'The Tricolour Seen in Whiter Shades of Pale', *Observer*, 21 July 1992.

70   Etienne Balibar, 'Es Gibt Keinen Staat in Europa: Racism and Politics in Europe Today', *New Left Review*, vol. 186, p. 14, 1991.

71   Castles, *Here for Good*, p. 92.

72   L. P. Curtis, *Nothing but the Same Old Story* (London, Macmillan, 1984); Mary Hickman, *Religion, Class and Identity: The State, the Catholic Church and the Education of the Irish in Britain* (Aldershot: Avebury, 1995); Liam Greenslade, *The Irish in Britain in the 1990s* (Liverpool, Centre of Irish Studies, 1993); Bronwen Walter, 'Irishness, Gender and Place', *Society and Space*, vol. 13, 1991.

73   Immanuel Wallerstein, 'The Construction of Peoplehood: Racism, Nationalism and Class' in Immanuel Wallerstein and Etienne Balibar (eds.), *Race, Nation, Class* (New York, Sage, 1992), pp. 73–84; Etienne Balibar, 'Racism and Nationalism' in *Race, Nation, Class*, pp. 37–64.

74   Castles, *Here for Good*, pp. 34–6.

75   R. Stavenhagen, *Agrarian Problems and Peasant Movements in Latin America* (Boston: Doubleday, 1970), p. 99.

76   ibid., p. 101.

77   I. Wallerstein, *Geopolitics and Geoculture* (Cambridge University Press, 1992), p. 82.

78   Z. Layton-Henry (ed.) *The Political Rights of Migrant Workers in Western Europe* (Sage, London, 1990).

79   Etienne Balibar, 'Es Gibt Keinen Staat in Europa', p. 19.

8. Unmasking Irishness
Irish Women, the Irish Nation and the Irish Diaspora

BREDA GRAY

As we move towards the end of the twentieth century, it is becoming increasingly difficult to locate Irishness either culturally or geographically. While Irish identity is now frequently represented as a globalised transnational phenomenon, it is not clear that a more global Irishness positions women any more positively than a nationally bounded Irishness.[1] In this chapter, I explore the particular contradictions that Irish women identify in relation to national and transnational ideas of Irishness. I discuss these contradictions in the particular context of on-going emigration from the Republic of Ireland in the 1980s and 1990s.

Few analyses of national identity take account of the movement of people through migration.[2] Yasemin Nuhoglu Soysal makes a connection between the nation-state and migration when she suggests that international labour migration 'has been closely tied to the unfolding of the European nation-state system and the development of the institution of citizenship'.[3] The concept of the international migrant is, she suggests, 'a product of the nation-state system and its ideologies of national membership'.[4] Whether it is national identity or emigration, these issues are mainly discussed as if both phenomena were gender neutral. My research on women, emigration and Irish national identity in the 1980s and 1990s involved group discussions and individual interviews with Irish women in Ireland and London. In the discussion groups, we explored what it meant to be Irish women whether living in Ireland or London, and how this was affected by on-going emigration. I use excerpts from these discussions in this chapter to explore issues of gender, Irish national identity, emigration and belonging. I am concerned therefore with such questions as: What kinds of national belonging do women experience? How is this affected by continuing emigration? What are the consequences of territorialising concepts of identity such as nationalism for emigrants? How does a de-territorialised transnational Irishness position Irish women emigrants and non-emigrants? What are the cultural resources out of which Irish women produce different kinds of Irishness in the 1990s? How are these affected by continuing emigration? Who carries out the practical and emotional work involved in maintaining the global Irish diaspora? I address these questions in the context of the simultaneous operation of discourses of nation and transnational diaspora in Ireland in the 1990s. Both of these tend to be all encompassing discourses which play down internal differences and inequalities.

FROM NATION-STATE TO DIASPORA: THE SHIFTING CONTEXTS OF IRISH EMIGRATION

Following the Great Famine of the mid-nineteenth century, Kerby Miller has suggested, nationalist politicians supported a view of emigration as exile – a kind of 'reluctant emigration' – 'which would cease only when Ireland was independent and so able to provide prosperity and employment for all'.[5] Emigration was linked to the lack of territorial sovereignty and was held to be symbolic of the Irish people's lack of political control over their own nation.[6] The very idea of exile assumes a bounded place/nation to which one is naturally connected. This rooting of a people in the land or soil of their national territory assumes a 'natural' connection between a people and the landscape or the place that they inhabit.[7] Emigration, or the leaving of that nation where one 'naturally belongs' is then seen as disruptive and unnatural. Kerby Miller suggests that, even after independence and right up until the World War II, most Irish Catholics still looked on emigration as exile from their national territory, caused now by the legacy of British rule and the border, rather than British 'misrule' in Ireland. The Free State government was concerned in the 1920s and 1930s with creating a stable national community within the twenty-six counties and, over time, this stability relied on a playing down of the partition of the country and a re-inscription of the Irish Catholic family as the basic unit of the nation. Women were seen as most appropriately located within the domestic sphere of the family and were actively excluded from the public processes of nation-building.[8] Those women who emigrated in the nineteenth and early twentieth centuries were constructed by commentators as potential wives and mothers of future generations. By emigrating, they were depriving the nation of its rightful national stock.[9] Women emigrants were also seen as being seduced by Hollywood's images of 'lavish and romantic American lifestyles' which 'unbalanced already flighty female minds'.[10] Women emigrants were pathologised for leaving, for being attracted or lured away from the country where they rightly belonged. While pathologising Irish women, these discourses also acknowledged, at an implicit level at least, the potential of Irish women to undermine a patriarchal and family-oriented Irish national identity. The high levels of emigration in the 1950s brought about a sense of national failure as levels of emigration had become a critical index of national performance.[11] The belief that the Irish people, particularly Irish women, should rightly be rooted to the national soil of Ireland was still a widely-held view, and belief in a territorially-bounded Irish identity fed into the expectation that the new state should provide for all the Irish people. This expectation, together with the accompanying belief in a 'natural' and 'rooted' relationship between territory and a people is reinforced, according to Lisa Malkki, 'by extending the connection via kin to the family tree, an arborescent image which is rooted in a particular place'.[12]

Thus, despite the loss and separation experienced by many Irish families through emigration in the 1950s, Irishness itself was being constructed by official state discourses as encapsulated in happy rural family life. Jenny Beale suggests that the 1950s in Ireland were a time:

> when politicians were praising family life in rural Ireland, when de Valera was exalting the countryside, 'bright with cosy homesteads', [yet] the people of the west were streaming away, leaving the traditional way of life as fast as they could.[13]

Anne McClintock argues that the family trope is important to constructions of nation and national identity because the 'family offers a "natural" figure for sanctioning social hierarchy within a putative organic unity of interests'.[14] She further elaborates:

> Since the subordination of woman to man, and child to adult, was deemed a natural fact, other forms of social hierarchy [such as the nation] could be depicted in familial terms to guarantee social difference as a category of nature.[15]

Gender inequality within the 'Catholic Irish family' was naturalised by making the family an 'authentic' source of Irishness while the class implications of the break-up of peasant families by emigration were largely obscured. Arborescent images of rootedness in a specific territory, and the idea of the family as the building block of the reproductive and productive nation, together served to 'naturalise' a sense of national belonging which rendered gender, class, religions, ethnic and other inequalities invisible. As Radhakrishnan points out, nationalism thus achieved 'the ideological effect of an inclusive and putatively macro-political discourse' that subsumed and subordinated gender, class and other identities under the hegemony of nationalist politics.[16] The national community is authorised as the most authentic form of collectivity such that any other form of collective identity, such as women, is seen as less authentic and a potential threat to the *national* collectivity. However, the popular perception picture of nation, emigration and belonging became more diffuse and complex in the decades after the foundation of the nation-state. Thus, theorists increasingly now suggest that the idea of emigration as exile from a territorially-bounded nation where one really belongs is being undermined in the 1990s by a transnational perception of migration influenced by globalised communications and market systems.[17]

The views of the Irish women taking part in my research suggest that both national and transnational perceptions of Irishness co-exist in contemporary representations of Irish identity and emigration. While some theorists suggest that the increasing globalisation of markets, communications networks and travel make the geographical location of Irishness less easy to define, Irishness continues to be connected with the nation, most notably through ideas of kin and family. The abortion and divorce referendums of the 1980s and 1990s are good examples which show how Irishness can still be firmly located within the boundaries of the nation-state and closely allied with the family trope in an effort to promote particular moral agendas.[18] Ironically, however, transnational forces were also at work here in that fundamentalist groups from the US and other countries attempted to influence Irish national political and social agendas.

National belonging and nationalist identity, while still significant aspects of people's lives, are problematised by a proliferation of images of the nation in the 1990s. One might well ask: Where is the nation? Is Ireland the rural idyll of 'the West' so fondly promoted by Bord Failte, the Irish tourist board, or is it an economy with high levels of expertise in electronic and computer technology and therefore an ideal place for high-technology industry to locate. Is it also a cultural arena capable of producing a range of popular culture ranging from U2, the Cranberries and Enya to *Riverdance*? Or is Ireland simply a brand name, the product of a promotional mentality, or an image 'in people's minds as a result of everything they know about the physical characteristics of a product. . .'[19]

Images of Ireland which are closely tied to Ireland's future economic prosperity raise many questions about what it means to be Irish in the 1990s. Which of these and many more images and constructions of Irishness do we embrace in the construction of our sense of Irishness today? How do these transnational, promotional and economically-motivated images of Ireland and Irishness represent Irish women? Are Irish women invisibly located in the rural cottage, or are they independent computer executives, dancers, singers, smiling icons of a friendly tourist destination, or are they all of these at once?

The multiplicity of images and representations of Ireland and Irishness bring about a self-consciousness of identity which undermines, to some extent at least, the apparently immanent or 'natural' nature of national identity. Yet in this allegedly self-reflexive era, the lack of attention to persistent class and gender oppression is quite remarkable. Indeed, despite a proliferation of mirrors within which we can view ourselves, only some reflections are acceptable. Wherever we locate our Irishness in the 1990s, contradictions are produced by these absences. The apparent shift in recent years from a focus on a territorially-bounded Irishness to a more transnational and culturally based identity is evident in President Mary Robinson's invocation of the term 'the Irish Diaspora'.

The Irish diaspora is represented as a transnational and inclusive idea which includes the Irish people world over. However, the discourse on diaspora, like the discourse on nation, tends to subordinate gender, class and other politics. In so doing, it frequently perpetuates a hegemonic middle-class liberal agenda. In discussing their relationships to Ireland and Irishness, the Irish women that I interviewed constantly grapple with the contradictions in their experiences of being Irish women emigrants or *non-emigrants*. The section that follows discusses this 'identity crisis' by looking at the conflicting attitudes of a number of Irish women to Ireland and the sense of Irishness

RESOLVING THE CONTRADICTION: IRELAND – 'THE BEST PLACE ON EARTH' – THAT PEOPLE LEAVE

While Ireland is represented by many of those remaining in Ireland, and by Irish women emigrants, as one of the best places in the world to live, the rituals of farewell parties continue to dominate the experiences of many young Irish people. Those who leave and those who stay struggle with the contradiction generated by a view of Ireland as 'home', as 'the only place you can belong', and 'the best place in the world' on the one hand, and the fact that many young Irish people continue to leave it, on the other.[20] Indeed, I here identify three main narratives of Irishness which may be taken as ways of reconciling this contradiction at both private and public levels. One story centres around emigrants being seen as bodily located somewhere else but at home, spiritually and emotionally, only in Ireland. A second story represents Irish emigration as a 'normal' everyday part of Irish life. A third, and most publicly articulated narrative, is that of emigration as opportunity, as the making the best of a 'good start'. These narratives reinforce the significance of arborescent notions of rootedness and kin in maintaining connections with a territorially-based national identity. They draw on historical and current media discourses on Irishness, the nation-state and Irish emigration which at first glance appear ungendered. However, these women's accounts also highlight the extent to which discourses of nation and national identity overwhelm their particular experiences as women.

EMIGRATION – A TEMPORARY BODILY RELOCATION

In one group discussion in London, Áine suggests that her parents do not think of her as really belonging in London and find it hard to relate to her actual life there. She adds:

> They see me as someone who's over here [London], who's an outsider over here. And, whereas I feel like an outsider when I go home. . . Their perception of my life here is bizarre. My dad has never come to visit me in a flat of mine here. He won't deal with the reality of my life here at all, says things like, 'So, do you have a phone in the hall?'. . . Thinks I'm in a bedsit or something. My mom has come to visit and says things like – 'Oh, the British are being very nice to me', shock. . .

While Áine may be living, working and indeed feeling more at home in London than in Ireland, as far as her parents are concerned she can only ever belong in Ireland. This denial of Áine's actual life in London enables her parents to believe that she will return and live in Ireland, *where she rightly belongs*. The idea of the phone in the hall conjures up discomfort, a sense of temporariness, and is used as a suggestion that she has not 'settled down' here in London. Her mother's view that the British are nice to her constructs Áine as a *visitor to*, rather than *a rightful resident in* the United Kingdom. Áine is thus aware of the disparity between her actual life in London and her parents view of that life. However, she is unable to bridge the distance created by the disparity in these two views. This disparity, in turn, contributes to Áine's ambivalence about both places, London and Ireland, and can at times contribute to a sense of 'homelessness'.

Jenny for her part notes that her brother finds it difficult to accept that she can belong in London. She elaborates:

> . . . my brother, for example, . . . always thinks that I should come home. And especially when my marriage broke up, he was always pressing me to come home and not to work here . . . he would not ever see me as really being here permanently. He would rather that I came home . . . he also thinks that an Irish person cannot be happy and settle down in England at all. That's his kind of prejudice. . .

Jenny's decision to remain in London, and to live out her life there, is thus in direct conflict with her brother's expectations of how and where she can be happy. Although, later on, she suggests that she feels more part of things in London now than she does in Ireland, she is also aware that at least one member of her family sees her as displaced, as not really belonging in London. She becomes doubly displaced as a consequence, by virtue of living in London rather than Ireland, on the one hand, and by the knowledge that any sense of belonging she may feel in London is denied by her brother, on the other. Áine and Jenny, therefore, are seen by members of their respective families as temporarily displaced individuals, as physically located outside of Ireland but emotionally and spiritually at home only in Ireland.

EMIGRATION – A 'NORMAL' ASPECT OF IRISH LIFE

Anne, Mary and Pauline, in a group discussion conducted in Ireland, highlight the ways in which emigration is 'naturalised' at a social level by the large numbers taking the emigration route out of Ireland, and by the many 'leaving parties' which have become such a 'normal' aspect of Irish life since the 1980s. The sense of loss and sadness is, according to Anne, confined to the 'individual's situation'. Thus for Anne:

Emigration . . . not just for women but for the Irish in general . . . it's not an unusual step, it's not an unnatural step in that if somebody says they are emigrating it can be upsetting within that individual's situation. But it is seen now as a path, or a right path, a normal path for so many Irish people. . . .

Mary on the other hand stressed the effects of emigration on Irish identities. She added:

I think it has to make us psychologically different to other people of our same generation across the world. Because it has to have an effect on you. You know, for example, every year more and more of your friends leave. . . And even your own going away and coming back. The ritual farewell parties make the fact of emigration visible while the tensions and contradictions remain unspoken.

Irish novelist and columnist Joe O'Connor characterises this complex combination of history, popular memory and culture underpinning the sense of Irishness and the 'naturalness' of Irish emigration as follows:

Famine, depopulation, the coffin ships, the ghettos of Kilburn and Hell's Kitchen, the statistics, the lists, the death of the Irish language, the way emigration became a tradition in Ireland, not just a phenomenon, but actually a way of life.[21]

This sense of a history and tradition of emigration tends to further normalise the practice of emigration. Pauline and Anne develop these ideas in the following interchange.

(Pauline) The whole idea though, when someone leaves, you know, you have a party, a big group go down to the pub, and it is made a big thing of, you know I think it reflects back to the say kind of famine days when it was for life and the person never came back, a kind of final farewell or something. And in a sense I think that's still very true, isn't it, going away?

(Anne) It's still often for life, you know you don't come back.

(Pauline) I know I don't mean you will never see them again. What I am saying, I mean like, they are not gone, that's it, you will never see them again. But I think the majority who live abroad and don't come back, not for long periods of time anyway.

Although the telephone, fax, e-mail and air transport now make the leaving of Ireland seem less final – e.g. 'I don't mean you'll never see them again' – most of those who leave *do not return* to live. They live their lives somewhere else. Leaving evokes memories of past leavings and the loss of generations of Irish emigrants from Ireland. Even in the 1990s, that sense of loss is easily evoked and those who remain have to carry on in the absence of many friends and family members. While these resonances make emigration a kind of inevitable fact, the memories and feelings evoked by emigration remain implicit rather than explicit. They are rarely discussed openly. Nevertheless, emigration affects relationships between family members, both between those at home, and between those at home and those 'away'. It often also involves an implicit re-negotiation of familial duties and responsibilities. Thus Mary, who took part in one of my group discussions in Ireland, speaks of her own experience when siblings emigrated. She said:

> But from the point of view of your family, half of my family, well there's only four of us, but half of them have gone away now, so it changed the situation for me at home . . . we've got to spend a lot of time keeping in touch, contact, and make that extra effort to keep that family together . . . you're the one at home . . . it changes the . . . relationships . . . it's just different than of we'd all stayed at home . . .

This re-configuration of relationships and responsibilities is often contained within the family, and many of the women speak of the responsibility for maintaining family relationships as falling on *their* shoulders and not on those of male family members. The loss, the pain, the absences, the memories and the new responsibilities brought about by emigration become accepted, but unarticulated, aspects of this so-called 'normal path' of emigration.

SUCCESS AND OPPORTUNITY – JUSTIFICATIONS FOR LEAVING

While high levels of unemployment make emigration the only employment option for many young Irish people, not least young Irish women, emigrants are not seen as leaving simply to find work but to be high achievers in a global economy. Thus, Jim Mac Laughlin argues that the current trend amongst politicians, economists, social scientists and other commentators in Ireland today is to portray young Irish emigrants as:

> people set apart from their peers by their spirit of adventure and enterprising spirit and to treat emigration as an integral element in Irish youth enterprise culture. This encourages a view of emigrants as upwardly-mobile individuals . . .[22]

Official discourses construct those who leave as the ambitious and brainy. By implication, those who stay are less adventurous, less ambitious and remaining only to keep the home fires burning.[23] Emigrants and their families often represent emigration in similar terms. Mary and Anne, for example, in another group discussion in Ireland, point to the power of the discourse of success and how distant that success might be from the actual experiences of some emigrants.

> (Mary) I think there is . . . a pressure on a person who is away to be successful. There is this snob value involved. You know, 'Oh my daughter is in France, and my son is in England'. And the children returning home have to prove that they have been successful. . . . There is an expectation of the people that are left behind that the people that go away have to be very successful. And it's pressure on the people that I don't know if anyone else has found that?

(Anne) But you would see, even when we were in London an awful lot of the voices were people who were homeless on the streets with Irish accents. I mean if someone got to thinking. . .' I came over and there was nothing here for me, I can't go back, I can't go back there'. It's very frightening.

The only way to justify leaving is to present emigration in terms of career and success. Leaving has to be continually justified by achievements which family members can report to relatives and friends back home as further justifications of emigration and to make good the loss brought about by the latter. If emigration does not bring success, then the emigrant is trapped outside Ireland, living out an Irish identity that is unacceptable at home as well as abroad. Mary continues the discussion:

> But you can't admit that you went away for any other reason than to be successful, why else would you leave Ireland? Surely Ireland is so wonderful that you don't want to leave. The only reason you would go is to make your life better. Which is, you know, you can't say you left Ireland because you couldn't get recognition or you weren't happy.
>
> (Pauline) Why? What's wrong with that?
>
> (Mary) I suppose, well, that you would have an idea that Ireland you know, well, people I suppose abroad, would wonder why you would ever want to leave such a place. That would be the view they would have on it. I mean why else would you leave, but to become successful.

Despite the long history of emigration, and particularly given the continuing high levels of emigration, there is still an uneasiness about leaving Ireland. Leaving can only be understood and discussed in a limited number of ways. Although Mary is aware of the many complex reasons for leaving, she cannot see how these can easily be articulated. To leave for any reason other than work or career might be seen as rejecting 'mother Ireland', the mother that fed, reared and cared for her children. Many deeply-held feelings are contained and made safe in this discourse on emigration as 'opportunity' and 'success'. Anne goes on to suggest that this need to protect oneself and the nation (mother Ireland) from how many Irish women actually experience Ireland and Irishness is true also for those who stay.

> But it is in here as well. You can't admit that Ireland is bad. You know I think that this is a general thing, we can't say there is anything wrong with Ireland. . . The thing about Ireland, you can't criticise Ireland, can't criticise the Irish you know in general.

The adage 'whatever you say, say nothing' applies equally to those who stay at home in Ireland and to those who leave. There is a pervading defensiveness that is seen to silence any critical views about Irish society, the Irish state and Irish culture. This makes 'speaking out' a potentially dangerous activity. The Irish state, Irish people and Irish politicians must be represented as blameless in relation to emigration – rejecting Ireland. Instead, individual emigrants, with the help of government and media discourses on emigration as success and opportunity, have to represent their leaving in terms of an individual quest for adventure and success. The limited ways in which Irish emigration can be represented silences the tensions that many Irish women experience in relation to being Irish and living in Ireland. Thus Sue argues:

> But apart from this whole idea of success, most of the people that I know who have left, have left for a specific reason that they are looking for anonymity. And if that's what is lurking here, if that is the problem for them, that everybody knows them, and everybody knows everybody, and everybody them and what they are doing and what they are up to.

Pauline for her part stated:

> . . . they have no sense of freedom to live their own lives whatever they may be. I mean, . . . it's that idea that they leave here and head for a big city somewhere. . . Maybe you are gay or lesbian maybe, whatever, but you can actually live the life that you want to live without, you know, your aunt sending the parish priest around.

Emigration, for Pauline, is seen as offering the opportunity to 'live the life that you want to live', a freedom that is not, as she sees it, afforded to many women in Ireland without interference or ridicule. The anonymity of the foreign city offers the opportunity for emigrants 'to find themselves'. While the potential is there to view emigration as a rejection of Ireland and Irishness, this is rarely mentioned in public or private debate about emigration. Emigrants, as well as those who remain behind in Ireland, have to find acceptable and bearable ways of understanding and discussing leave-taking from Ireland. I have suggested here that this contradiction between an idealised view of Ireland and the fact that many leave is partly resolved by the stories we tell ourselves about emigration. While economic necessity is a major factor in emigration, these women point to the many other factors influencing their decision to emigrate and the ways we perceive emigration. All of these contribute to their sense of what it means to be Irish in the 1990s.

I have identified three dominant stories arising from my research with Irish women, namely emigration as bodily relocation, emigration as a normal part of Irish life and the representation of reasons for leaving in terms of career opportunities. A striking feature of these women's stories is the power that discourses on nation, rootedness and kin have had on perceptions of Irishness, including the articulation of Irish identity. Spaces of resistance, rearticulation and expression of gendered experiences are difficult to locate within this discourse. The women quoted above highlight a fear and defensiveness which prevents a facing-up to the on-going realities of emigration from Ireland. The farewell parties and talk of success provide ways of acknowledging and justifying the practice of emigration without really asking what Irish emigration means for young Irish emigrants today. To ask more questions about emigration would involve opening up questions about Irishness, what that identity means, who is included and who is excluded; national economic, political and cultural issues; Irish families and expectations of Irish women in the domestic and public spheres. Although articulated by women, these stories of Irishness and emigration appear gender neutral. Yet, I want to suggest that while these narratives attempt to account for Irishness and emigration in the 1980s and 1990s, the women's own gendered experiences point to the silences, gaps and tensions in these narratives. They give accounts of Irishness and Irish emigration, but they also express hesitancy and point to gaps between the stories of emigration and their experiences of its realities. Áine's parents and Jenny's brother see Ireland as the only place to which they can belong, suggesting that an Irish woman's rightful place is in Ireland rather than on the move, or in England. Their actual lives in London are thus denied them, and the continuing desire on the part of their parents or other family members to locate them within Ireland further displaces them. Pauline counters the view that Irish women can only belong in Ireland when she suggests that some Irish emigrants find that they can only live the life that they want to live outside of Ireland.

These woman draw on dominant narratives of Irishness and emigration in the 1990s only to reveal the actual experiences, absences and contradictions which are glossed over by these narratives. Rather than a temporary bodily relocation, emigration in the 1980s and 1990s may enable a more fulfilling sense of belonging for some Irish women. Certainly to perceive Irish women as only ever belonging in Ireland is to deny the experiences of those who find that they can belong elsewhere. Similarly, to normalise continued Irish emigration as a historical and contemporary Irish tradition is to deny the on-going pain, loss and re-configuration of family and friendship relations that emigration brings about. Opportunity and success become euphemisms for the many complex and often gendered factors influencing emigration that cannot be publicly articulated lest they literally undermine idealised perceptions of Ireland as the only place that Irish people, and Irish women in particular, can really belong.

Although nation remains a significant reference point for Irishness, new discourses of Irishness and emigration are emerging in the Republic of Ireland in the 1990s which tentatively incorporate a de-territorialised and more global sense of belonging. This discourse is increasingly characterised in terms of 'the Irish Diaspora'. The following section unravels some of the ways in which the official and academic discourse of this Irish diaspora is employed. It particularly explores some of the ways in which women are positioned by this discourse.

THE IRISH DIASPORA – A NEW IDENTITY FOR THE TWENTY-FIRST CENTURY

The shift towards an Ireland and Irishness which is seen in terms of 'the Irish people' rather than simply in terms of territorial boundaries is evident in political, academic and media analyses of recent Irish emigration. The whole idea of 'the Irish people' beyond the territorial boundaries of the Irish Republic raises the important possibility of a 'global imagined community' of Irish people. By this, I mean a sense of Irishness which is not confined to the island of Ireland but includes those living in their mutual imaginings of an 'Irish people' both at home *and abroad*.[24] Fintan O'Toole asserts that emigration 'means, quite simply, that the people and the land are no longer coterminous'.[25] He develops the theme as follows:

> If you see a country as its people rather than its territory, then, far from being small and well-defined, Ireland has been, for at least 150 years, scattered, splintered, atomised like the windscreen of a crashed car . . . Ireland is a diaspora, and as such is both a real place and a remembered place, both the far west of Europe and the home back east of the Irish-American.[26]

Looking outside Ireland, Anne Holohan in her recent overview of the Irish in Britain suggests that 'for younger Irish people their Irishness has nothing to do with territorial sovereignty or where they live'.[27] This non-territorial concept of Irishness has been promoted by President Mary Robinson since her election in 1990. In her inaugural speech as President of Ireland in that year, she pointed out that her primary role would be to represent the State of the Republic of Ireland. However, she then went on to say that:

> the State is not the only model of community with which Irish people can and do identify. Beyond our State there is a vast community of Irish emigrants extending not only across our neighbouring island . . . but also throughout the continents of North America, Australia and of course Europe itself. There are over 70 million people living on this globe who claim Irish decent. I will be proud to represent them . . .

In this speech, the President constructs notions of an 'Irish people' and an 'Irish community' which stretch beyond the national boundaries of the state. The term Irish diaspora represents the Irish people as a national collectivity which has been broken apart by centuries of emigration, while also being enriched by transnational connections at familial, political and cultural levels. It is these interconnections and their potential for creativity that proponents of diaspora such as Mary Robinson seek to celebrate. In Mary Robinson's second speech to a joint session of the Houses of the Oireachtas in February 1995, she points to the potential for the diaspora to inform, even challenge, politics within the Republic of Ireland.

Our relation with the diaspora beyond our shores is one which can instruct our society in the values of diversity, tolerance, and fair-mindedness . . .The men and women of our diaspora represent not simply a series of departures and loss. They remain even while absent, a precious reflection of our growth and change, a precious reminder of the many strands of identity which compose our story . . . We need to accept that in their new perspectives may well be a critique of our old ones.[28]

While constructions of Ireland and Irishness have emanated from emigrants in the forms of the songs and in the literature of emigrant communities in the past, President Robinson's idea of the diaspora represents the Irish within Ireland as taking account of relationships with emigrant Irish communities elsewhere. The very term diaspora, because of its emphasis on dispersal and scattering, presumes a diversity of locations and ways of living Irishness. There is also an implication of mutual interaction and a networking of relationships in which those who remain in Ireland are actively engaged in contacts with those outside Ireland. This interactive model of the Irish diaspora, of which those remaining in Ireland are a part, is evident in the largely favourable reaction to the President's decision to place a symbolic light in the window of Aras on Uachtaráin, the official residence of the President of Ireland, for Irish emigrants.[29] Similarly, more and more organisations are being established within the Republic of Ireland which are concerned with maintaining contact with emigrants and many of these use the term diaspora in their title.[30] The section that follows analyses in more detail the meaningfulness of the category 'diaspora' as applied to the Irish situation today.

WHY THE TERM DIASPORA?

Over the past two decades, chiefly as a result of new transnational global forces such as increased global migration and the development of a globalised economy, the view that collective identities can be organised around the nation-state has come into question.[31] The term 'diaspora' is used here to designate a group of people dispersed throughout the world and was once most commonly used to describe Jewish, Greek and Armenian dispersion.[32] According to Tololyan, the category:

now shares meanings with a larger semantic domain that includes words like immigrant, expatriate, refugee, guestworker, exile community, overseas community, ethnic community.[33]

Robert Cohen places this new emphasis on diaspora in the context of advanced capitalism and global markets.[34] However, this chapter argues that the importance of the ethnic and cultural dimension of globalisation to the smooth operation of world markets cannot be underestimated. Thus, Cohen suggests that the diasporic experience is different from what he calls 'late modernity', due to a globalised world economy with 'quicker and denser transactions between its subsectors [due also to] intermittent postings abroad', and to a 'cosmopolitan and hybridised culture'. 'Gone', he suggests, are:

> the traumas of exile, the troubled relationship with the host culture and other negative aspects of the traditionally upheld diasporic condition. Instead, strong diasporas are now represented as the key to determining success in the global economy.[35]

A global network of mutual trust 'business diasporas' is seen as a means to adapt to rapid capital flows, the international market for skills and the demands of the powerful multinational corporations.[36] This suggests that Irish business networks world-wide can be profitably developed and exploited in order to maximise opportunities in a global economy. From the point of view of increasing consumption and creating new market niches, a variety of cultural identities stimulates product innovation and new consumption niches upon which 'Irishness' can capitalise. Viewed thus, the proliferation of different cultural diasporic groups expands the range of consumption niches world-wide. However, although a small number of Irish emigrants and non-emigrants will benefit from rapid capital flows, from the globalisation of business and from the expansion of diasporic networks, most Irish workers, at home and abroad, will lose out to cheaper sources of labour and the increasing use of technology to reduce numbers employed in industry and the service sector at home.

The idea of diaspora also tends to flatten out the varied experiences of migrant workers from different nations and the gender and class differences between the migrant workers from the same nation. Jim Mac Laughlin's empirical findings in the 1980s offer insights into this particular aspect of Irish migrants' experiences. Discussing the employment profiles of recent emigrants to Britain, for example, he found that most of these still gravitate to the traditional job ghettoes of the Irish emigrants. While recognising the existence of a substantial 'emigrant aristocracy' within the 'new wave' emigrant community in Britain and the United States, he also found that:

> Below the pinnacles of emigrant professional employment, the majority of male and female emigrants lead humbler lives and occupy the traditional occupations of the Irish emigrant.[37]

While diasporic networks of workers may be helpful in finding work, just as they have done in the past, the economic potential of the diaspora in the 1990s is most evident at the top levels of business. Thus, Mac Laughlin and others have increasingly acknowledged the existence of a transnationalist emigrant élite exists alongside a transnational workers' class.[38] Irish emigration in the 1980s and 1990s can easily be stratified in these terms, with some migrants contributing via their executive positions in transnational corporations or in the

European Union to the development of global capitalism, while most fall into a migrant workers' class and move to find employment.

Alongside the economic significance of diasporas, it is also important to recognise the potential political significance of diasporic communities. Advanced communications and transportation improvements enable the latter to become deeply involved in the affairs of their homeland in ways that were not hitherto possible. However, as the Irish case also shows, Irish emigrants in Britain and North America in the nineteenth century often played crucial roles in the political and economic life of their own country, and their own communities, by lobbying for Irish national self-determination and by sending substantial 'remittances' back home for the support of family members. This shows how diasporas, according to Tololyan, 'are sometimes the source of ideological, financial and political support for national movements that aim at a renewal of the homeland. . .'[39] A more recent example of this view of the Irish diaspora is the economic and political support and influence of Irish communities in the United States evident in recent Anglo-Irish negotiations about the Northern Irish peace process.[40] As long as diasporic communities abroad are seen as contributing positively to events within the nation-state, then such political influence and contribution is welcome. However, it is equally possible to imagine circumstances in which this might not be the case. For example, it would be instructive to ask what would be the response to a wealthy Irish American putting herself or himself forward for election to political office in Ireland?

Benedict Anderson, among others, has pointed to the increased significance of diasporic groups for national politics and national culture. He also draws attention to the potentially transformative effects that diasporic influence and involvements can have for the modern nation-state.[41] This chapter argues that although diasporas raise potentially disruptive possibilities for the nation-state, the whole idea of an Irish diaspora, which by definition includes a whole range of Irish people abroad, can act as a political solvent for the loosening of entrenched positions and identities within the Irish state. This means that the notion of 'diaspora' suggests an inclusiveness that allows for different geographical locations and ways of living out Irishness. Diaspora, therefore, has the potential to expand Irish identity and may contribute to a more open and fluid notion of that identity. It is however important to pose the question of the power of discourse and rhetoric and the extent to which it can transform identities. While language is an important element in the construction of national identity and influences the very understanding of that identity, the languages and rhetoric of national identity and the diaspora are never impartial. They always position nationals, meaning those living inside Ireland, and non-nationals, meaning Irish emigrants living outside it, in different ways. Therefore, the effects of the discourse of diaspora depend on its 'positioning' function and on its representations of particular national and non-national experiences. This is an important element in diasporic discourse and is one that is briefly discussed in the section that follows.

WHO ARE 'THE IRISH DIASPORA'?

While the term 'diaspora' may be seen as an inclusive one, it also has the effect of blurring the boundaries between a variety of different statuses and homogenising very different experiences. The cultural, political and economic status of the migrant worker is very different from that of a member of the emigrant aristocracy and the transnational emigrant élite. Movement itself is not an undifferentiated category. The experience, for example, of the nomadic, even 'jet-setting' business woman is very different from that of the unskilled female migrant seeking employment opportunities in a globalised job market. Similarly, as Corcoran has shown in relation to the 'new Irish' in the United States and Mac Laughlin in relation to the Irish in Britain today, recent Irish emigrants cannot be seen as an undifferentiated social mass.[42] Anne, a middle-class woman taking part in a group discussion in London, highlights the divisions in the Irish emigrant 'community' and, in so doing, questions the validity of this term as applied to contemporary Irish diaspora. She perceives the situation among Irish emigrants in London today as follows.

> I discovered huge cultural differences in so far as . . . the through flow of people from there [Ireland], were people like, I wouldn't have even come into contact with at home. You know your nice secure middle class, father a headmaster and all that, and meeting people some of the people coming over, that you'd read about, you know literally, literally, one pound fifty in their pockets. And they'd come over here with that amount of money, but . . . once you get over the shock of that the braveness or foolhardiness whatever way you look at it . . . life is just very different. And it struck me that their turn of phrase was different from mine even, you know. As an east coast person and meeting people from much more south, say, . . . I notice differences more so between myself and themselves, you know that sort of emigrant coming over.

She concluded:

> But then likewise you can identify clearly differences between ourselves as Irish people and English people. English society if you like, in terms of like language as well can be one thing, you know the way we speak . . . but . . . the Irish pubs, and being in the Irish centre as well, brought it home to me, and it was something that I actually found I backed off from, because again, I didn't do any of that at home so I certainly wasn't going to start doing it here . . .

Anne differentiates herself from the sizeable number of young Irish emigrants who arrived in London in the late 1980s and early 1990s with 'one pound fifty in their pockets'. She is a middle-class woman and, as such, does not want to have contact with 'these people' from 'home' just because she, like them, is an Irish emigrant living in London. This suggests that there is a sense in which identifying with the larger Irish community in London has the potential to undermine a hard-earned middle-class identity there.

Anne similarly identifies important regional differences amongst Irish emigrants in London today. As an east coast person, which might suggest the sophistication of a 'West Briton', she notices differences in the 'turn of phrase' used by people from the south of the country which separates their brand of Irishness from her own. She wants to maintain some continuity with her lifestyle in Ireland and to avoid any kind of ghettoisation within an Irish community with which she has little in common.

Geographical mobility has also been an important factor in the attainment and maintenance of class position for many Irish and British people in Britain since the 1980s. Thus Doreen Massey suggests that 'entry into middle-class occupations was often accompanied by movement from one region to another'.[43] Movement, therefore, involves what she calls 'different geographies of power'. She further points out that:

> the very people who are often found most strongly arguing for free trade on the basis of some unspecified, unquestioned right to global movement . . . are often also the ones who would erect barriers to the free movement of migrants. (Here, too, there is inequality: global migration is far easier for highly-skilled workers and those with capital than it is for those without training and resources.)[44]

Migration is also segregated by gender, although this has received less attention in the recent proliferation of literature on Irish emigration. Jenny, who took part in my research, points to stereotypes of the Irish woman migrant in London:

> I think Irish men in England seem to have a higher profile somehow . . . women seem to be more anonymous as to what they [do] . . . women of my own age went to train as nurses in hospitals . . . And there are people who expect all Irish people to be . . . working in domestic jobs . . . or expect Irish women to be working in domestic work, or to be a nurse. Someone asked me if I was a nurse, I said no, I was a teacher, and he said well I was nearly right. So there are those kinds of expectations . . .

While Jenny suggests that Irish migrant women are either invisible or seen primarily as working in domestic or service sector employment, Molly disassociates herself from another stereotype of the migrant Irish woman in London by locating her sense of Irishness firmly in Ireland. She adds:

> I would say I am a woman and I am from Ireland. I think people's perception of an Irish woman in London is that you're sort of involved with a lot of Irish clubs, and you belong to, you go to a lot of Irish functions, and I don't do that. So from that point of view, I would say I am more of a woman from Ireland rather than an Irish woman . . .

The above discussion shows that Irish diaspora is differentiated along class lines and in terms of gender. It also stresses the fact that the global mobility of Irish migrants varies according to gender, class and educational or other qualifications. To identify oneself as Irish is only part of the story told by these Irish emigrants. An individual's class and gender position within the global labour market affects her/his experience of Irishness as well as her/his relationship to the cultures of their host societies. This means that, far from being 'a community', the Irish diaspora is shot through with divisions of power and class that both these terms tend to obscure. The idea of 'a global Irish imagined community', or an 'Irish diaspora' therefore, like Benedict Anderson's national imagined community, suggests communal interests whereas, in fact, that community, like the Irish diaspora, is actually fractured by class, gender and other differences which in many cases reveal deep conflicts of interests among the Irish abroad and the Irish at home. One such difference is that between those who remain in Ireland and those who leave. This is particularly noticeable in the realm of voting rights, and Ireland is one of the few European countries which does not provide voting rights to its emigrants. As a result, there has been much lobbying by emigrants in recent years for the right to vote in national elections. Emigrant demands for this right, however, point to some of the potential splits in the imagined global Irish diaspora. When, as a group, Irish emigrants demand the right to participate at a political level in the affairs of the Republic of Ireland, then the different interests of emigrants and non-emigrants become visible. These differences particularly complicate any notion of an imagined community of the 'Irish diaspora'. They also highlight issues of authenticity by questioning, for example, whether or not one has to live in Ireland to be really Irish. They also raise questions about the kind of national political stance one has to adopt in order to be really Irish? By way of corollary, they also raise questions about how long one has to live outside Ireland before one should rightly lose the entitlement to vote and thereby lose one's active sense of an Irish national identity? Dave Reynolds hints at potential divisions between those who stay in Ireland and those who leave in the following terms:

> I realised that, since '88 and the success of the soccer team, you have this brand-new identity of being Irish, but this sense of being Irish is in the main brought on by the Irish abroad. And this identity has damn all to do with the Irish Republic. It's got to do with emigrants and their sons and daughters and grandchildren. This new sense, whether it's in music, in football or in literature . . . it's a positive energy.[45]

He also highlights the power of emigrants to construct their own Irishness in the 1990s. His views raise further questions about geographical location of Irishness and about those who should have the right to define that identity.

Some of the issues raised by this debate are evident in the following discussion which took place in Ireland amongst some of the participants in my research. One woman, Lorna, talked about a row she had with a good friend who had emigrated to England, about the issue of emigrants being given the right to vote in elections in the Republic of Ireland.

> The idea of someone living somewhere else, prescribing how I should live where I am . . . I'm sorry, I couldn't go along with that . . .

She goes on to say that when her friend heard her views on this matter she was very angry and, according Lorna, went on to point out that:

> she was part of the diaspora, how could we possibly exclude her and hundreds and thousands of people like her who were driven out of their own homes . . . I was really shocked that she should be so passionate about this . . .

Anne suggested:

> Well there's a certain element of . . . I'm still here suffering along with the rest of the country so, I'm entitled to say people outside the country have no say . . . there is a resentment that everyone who goes abroad is having a brilliant life and earning loads of money and it's always sunny abroad . . . there is sometimes this real sour grapes that, em, God, you know, we're suffering here in the rain and we don't earn much money, what the hell are they worried about . . .

> (Lorna) One of the things that really [upsets me] is . . . this kind of strand that the bright and the brilliant and the beautiful and the adventurous take off, you know? . . . and all the boring daisies and common, ugly ones like ourselves stay here and keep the home fires burning . . .

> (Anne) You talk to people who have left and they're sorry for you . . .

> (Everyone in the group agrees)

> (Lorna) . . . as if the geography . . . was going to change you from the inside out . . . give me one English Channel and suddenly 'I'm a new woman'.

While Lorna is sceptical about the extent to which the English Channel can enable an Irish woman to become a 'new woman', many of the women in these group discussions suggest that emigration enables some women to develop a better sense of their gender and sexual identities and, eventually, to bring their Irish and sexual identities together and to the fore. The perceptions of the women in these discussions is that those who emigrate are more career-oriented than those who stay. They also suggest that, if they wanted to identify themselves primarily as Irish, then they could make some compromises in their careers and return to Ireland. The women in these group discussions, therefore, seem to be reacting to the apparent valorisation of movement, career ambition and the search for success. John Waters links this valorisation of movement with the proliferation of de-territorialised mass media images of the Irish today. He suggests that:

the modern of form of mass-media colonisation tells us that we are only worthless if we remain where we are; it bombards us with images which devalue our own place, diminish our psychic gravity, and lure us away.[46]

Movement and adventure are associated with a masculine quest for 'mastery' and achievement, while remaining at home and stasis are more frequently identified with the feminine and with passivity. Lisa Malkki put this well when she suggested that there has always been a tendency 'to see the tourist as male and the destination as female'.[47] These characterisations of emigrants and non-emigrants could be seen as positioning women emigrants as on a masculine quest for achievement while contributing to a feminisation of those who remain at home.

DIASPORA – A TERM FOR 'EVERYWHERE AND NOWHERE'

The idea of diaspora, therefore, seems to valorise movement and depoliticise the nature of migration and the historical and economic factors that are central to understanding particular migrations and social relationships to place. David Lloyd, for example, warns against the use of the term 'diaspora' in relation to recent Irish emigration to the United States. He argues:

> The invocation of an 'Irish diaspora' has the effect of naturalising the continuing massive outflow of skilled and unskilled labour from Ireland, as if there were some given population level for the island that we have already exceeded.[48]

Lloyd also suggests that the term 'emigration' has more political connotations as it invokes 'recollections of famine, of eviction, of dispossession and of economic legacies of colonialism'.[49] His reservations surrounding the use of the category 'diaspora' in relation to the Irish here highlight the ways in which discourses of diaspora may disguise economic, political and historical factors underlying most Irish emigration over the past 50 or so years. Mark Ryan, on the other hand, suggests that the idea of diaspora constructs Ireland as 'everywhere and nowhere, the prototype of the borderless nation'.[50] Having given up a nationalist territorial basis for Irish national identity, Ryan suggests that Ireland's leaders in the 1990s are endlessly discussing the past and are particularly obsessed with the 150th anniversary of the Great Famine. The focus on the Famine, he suggests, can be seen as the beginning of the 'spatial diffuseness' of Irishness, now being defined in terms of the diaspora. Ryan also implies that constructions of Irishness as a transnational and spatially-diffuse identity have the effect of playing down specifically national issues of injustice and inequality.[51]

Noel Browne is also sceptical about the use of the term Irish diaspora and draws attention to the loss and grief that the discourse of diaspora often overlooks.[52] He further implies that the Irish state should take responsibility for its people and points to the range of social problems that many emigrants encounter in their country of destination. He calls on President Robinson in particular to switch off 'her fatuous low-watt, low-powered, "cheapest available, warmly welcoming, electrical" candle in her window' because, he suggests that it has brought 'no comfort to our diaspora'. He adds:

> In the pent-up love, pain and tear-stained faces of those leaving and those of us left behind etched in all its human reality, was 'our' diaspora, those of us with little else but our bare hands driven into exile by hunger, joblessness and poverty. We are among the Irish second highest ethnic group, sleeping rough in London's cardboard city, in the prisons, the jails, the mental hospitals, the alcoholic wards, the brothels, the kitchens of cheap labour hotels, the building sites, the dole queues, and skid rows of the world, too poor to come home for Christmas.[53]

Browne here contests the idea of an Irish diaspora as a homogenised category for the liberal and progressive goals of a modern Ireland. Instead, he draws attention to the underside of this 'free egalitarian, independent, democratic Republic' which continues to shed its 'excess labour force', and its problems, in what he calls a 'cynical ethnic cleansing'.

GENDERING THE DIASPORA

We have already seen that diasporic experience is discussed mainly in cultural, political and economic terms in such a way that it ignores the many ways in which culture, politics and economics are gendered and literally 'classified'. Cultural representations of the Irish diasporic woman are few and far between. Those images that are available to us are mainly those of the caring Irish nurses working in developing countries. The economic positioning of Irish women in global labour markets is rarely acknowledged in discussions of emigration, success and opportunity. The expectations of women emigrants, in particular, are that they will keep in touch with family and friends in Ireland as well as maintain and pass on their Irish culture in their country of destination. Many of the women taking part in my research resist the stereotypes and responsibilities which they associate with being Irish women. Mary Robinson's speech entitled 'Cherishing the Irish Diaspora' included a definition of cherish as 'to value and to nurture and support'. The word cherish is reminiscent of the marriage vows and evokes ideas of commitment and responsibilities as well as caring for and holding dear. Cherish is more often associated with the domestic sphere of the family than with the public world of national politics. The discourse of the family re-emerges even in constructing an apparently more loosely associated transnational community like the diaspora. This discourse implies gendered roles and responsibilities for maintaining community which fall heavily on the shoulders of women.

If the diaspora has to be cherished in order that it may survive, then who will do the work of cherishing? While the tasks of nourishing and supporting are usually carried out by women, in the context of President Robinson's speech about the diaspora, these activities are represented as the responsibilities of the Irish public and range from keeping in touch, to providing the political channels by means of which the voices of the Irish diaspora abroad may be heard at home. Perhaps it was the unfamiliar nature of this call that made her speech about the diaspora somewhat unpopular amongst politicians and media managers. The lack of open discussion about emigration has the potential to create divisions between women who leave and women who stay as responsibilities to family and community are re-configured. Those living in London are aware of separation from everyday life in Ireland and although they are 'not a long way away', they are very aware of not being 'there'. Irish women living in London are separated in time and space from the interconnected collectivities of nation and family. They are prevented from doing the work of maintaining collective identity in the same way as those who remain in Ireland. Although President Robinson does not explicitly discuss the gendered implications of 'cherishing' in her speech on the Irish diaspora, she does make important connections between the community-building activities of Irish women and their contributions to the development of Irish national identity in other speeches.[54] Jim Mac Laughlin made this point particularly poignantly when he suggested that the 'Telecom Eireann Mother' is the new mother-as-heroine in contemporary Ireland. Thus he adds:

> Having shown her resourcefulness in raising children . . . she is now seen as dutifully sustaining – at no inconsiderable expense – motherly interest in her far-flung children over the phone.[55]

When it comes to the maintenance of community linkages and keeping in touch with family members abroad, it is important to ask what relationship exists between imagining a community and actually maintaining a sense of community. This raises questions about how differences within the community are treated and understood. Is there, for example, yet more 'invisible work' now being carried out by Irish women in support of family members and national collectivities expanding across national boundaries which is placing more and more responsibilities on Irish women back home? Is the Irish mother becoming a global mother responsible for maintaining Irish culture, community values and a sense of family in a global, not just a local or domestic, arena?

The dominant stories of emigration and Irishness in the 1990s which help us to understand the phenomenon of on-going emigration from such a 'great place' as Ireland, divert attention away from the actual experiences of different groups. They particularly distract attention from the specificity of Irish women emigrants' experiences. For many Irish women, whether 'nationals' (i.e. living in Ireland) or 'non-nationals' (living outside Ireland), their 'Irishness' is often in conflict with their gender/sexual identity. Emigration is one way of resolving that conflict for some Irish women. The sense of defensiveness and social taboos about criticising Ireland and Irishness expressed by women in the group discussions described above highlight the extent to which an idealised view of Irishness dominates the lives of women who leave and those who stay. The apparently progressive discourse of diaspora, while acknowledging emigration in a new way, does not help to confront the factors affecting women's emigration and their relationships to Irishness in the 1990s.

CONCLUSION

If 'culture alive is always on the run, always changeful' then it will only ever be possible to partially locate Irish culture and identity.[56] We may identify structures, processes and changes but we will always be missing something. I hope, in this chapter, to have begun a process of questioning the ways in which discourses of nation and diaspora mask continuing gender and class inequalities in the Irish context. Gayatri Spivak, in her discussion of the consequences of the shift from the local to the global, asks 'in what interest, to regulate what sort of relations, is the globe evoked?'[57] Questions of how, and in whose interests, the academic and political focus is shifting from the national to the global must also be addressed in contemporary analyses of Irishness. The shift in focus from the national to the global introduces new definitions of difference, such as those based on movement and geographical location. Further questions emerge such as: What kinds of hierarchies and power dynamics are created by these differences? What are the implications for gender, class, ethnic and other differences/ structures of inequality? If Ireland is, as Declan Kiberd suggests, 'about to be re-invented for a new century', then perhaps that re-invented Ireland will produce a sense of Irishness which will provide a 'home' for the diversity of Irish womanhood in the late twentieth century.[58] While for some women, national borders might be less important than their feminist identities, women continue to live within the actual boundaries of nation-states. The geographical location of women continues to affect their rights, entitlements and duties. Women, like men, are in constant relationships with nations, whether the nation be their nation of origin or that of their host society. In relation to Irish women, perhaps the best we can hope for is that the transformation of both Irishness and the Irish diaspora will provide more heterogeneous spaces and forms of identification that will more fully incorporate feminine subjectivities and create equality of opportunity for those women who stay 'at home' in Ireland and those who go abroad.

Acknowledgements

I would like to thank Celia Lury, Jim Mac Laughlin, Bev Skeggs and Jackie Stacey for their helpful comments on earlier drafts of this chapter.

Notes and References

1   Richard Kearney, Introduction, *Thinking Otherwise* in Richard Kearney (ed.), *Across the Frontiers: Ireland and the 1990s* (Dublin, Wolfhound Press, 1988), pp. 7–29; Richard Kearney, *The Fifth Province: Between the Global and the Local* in Richard Kearney (ed.), *Migrations: the Irish at Home and Abroad* (Dublin, Wolfhound Press, 1990), pp. 109–122; FIntal O'Toole, *Black Hole, Green Card: the Disappearance of Ireland* (Dublin, New Island Books, 1994).

2   I use the terms Irish national identify and Irishness interchangeably in this chapter for variety of style. I focus on national identity because I want to incorporate issues of national borders, citizenship and nation-state within my discussion. Irish cultural or ethnic identity and the term Irish identity, could probably be claimed by a wider pool of people than those whose nationalitites are Irish.

3   Yasemin Nuhoglu Soysal, *Limits of Citizenship: Migrants and Postnational Membership in Europe* (Chicago, University of Chicago Press, 1994), p. 14.

4   Soysal, *Limits of Citizenship*, p. 14; Castles and Miller (1993, p.3–4) point to the fact that both sending and receiving countries are affected by migration.

5   Kerby A. Miller, 'Emigration, Capitalism, and Ideology in Post-Famine Ireland', in Richard Kearney (ed.), *Migrations*, op. cit., p. 97.

6   In fact the high levels of emigration among the rural lower classes were really more attributable to profit-maximisation among Catholic graziers, strong farmers . . . (Miller, *Emigration, Capitalism and Ideology*, p. 91). Malthusians in Britain and Ireland according to Mac Laughlin, regarded nineteenth-century Irish emigration as a necessary social evil brought about by the transition from tradition to modernity and revolutions in transportation. See Jim Mac Laughlin, *Historical and Recent Irish Emigration: A Critique of Core–Periphery Models* (London: University of North London Press, 1994); Jim Mac Laughlin 'Emigration and the Peripheralization of Ireland in the Global Economy', Review, *Journal of Fermar Brandel Center*, vol. xvii, 2, 1994, pp. 243–73.

7   Lisa Malkki, 'National Geographic: The Rooting of Peoples and the Territorialization of National Identity Amongst Scholars and Refugees', *Cultural Anthropology*, vol. 7, no. 1, 1992, p. 27.

8   Maryann Gialanella Valiulis, 'Power, Gender and Identity in the Irish Free State', *Journal of Womens History*, vol. 6/7, no. 4/1, 1995, pp. 117–136.

9   Catherine Nash, 'Remapping and Renaming: New Cartographies of Identity Gender and Landscape in Ireland', *Feminist Review*, no. 44, 1993, p. 49.

10 Joe J. Lee, 'Emigration: A Contemporary Perspective', in Richard Kearney (ed.), *Migrations*, op. cit., p. 34.

11 Thomas Boylan, Review Symposium, *Irish Journal of Sociology*, vol. 1, 1991, pp. 78–82.

12 Malkki, 'National Geographic', p. 28.

13 Jenny Beale, *Women in Ireland: Voices of Change* (Basingstoke, Macmillan, 1986), p. 35 Eamon de Valera became Taoiseach (Prime Minister) of Ireland in 1932. He devised the 1937 Constitution of Ireland Bunreacht na hEireann which is still the constitution today. He was elected President of Ireland in 1959 and retired as President in 1973. He died on the twenty-ninth of August 1975.

14 Anne McClintock, 'Family Feuds: Gender, Nationalism and the Family', *Feminist Review*, no. 44, 1993, p. 64.

15 ibid., p. 64.
16 R. Radhakrishnan, 'Nationalism, Gender and the Narrative of Identity' in Andrew Parker et al., (eds.), *Nationalism and Sexualities*, (New York and London, Routledge, 1992), pp. 77–95.
17 Kearney, Introduction, *Thinking Otherwise*; Kearney, *The Fifth Province: Between the Global and the Local*; O'Toole, *Black Hole, Green Card*.
18 See also Garret Fitzgerald's article 'Mass Emigration Movement Shows Strength of Family' *Irish Times*, December 6, 1995.
19 John Fanning, 'Branding Ireland Aids our Overseas Image', *Irish Times*, 4 December 1995, p. 17.
20 These phrases recur in the group discussions in relation to Ireland and how family and friends, as well as emigrants themselves, see it.
21 I use pseudonyms in the interests of confidentiality.
22 Jim Mac Laughlin, 'Outwardly Mobile: The Sanitising of Emigration', *Irish Reporter*, vol. 13, no. 1, 1994, pp. 9–10.
23 Cormac Ó Grada suggests that the notion that the millions who left Ireland to live and work elsewhere over the last two centuries were in some sense different or better than those who stayed is almost as old as movement itself; see his 'Determinants of Irish Emigration: A Note', *International Migration Review*, vol. 20, no. 3, 1986, p. 650.

The National and Economic and Social Council report, *The Economic and Social Implications of Emigration* (1991), suggests that the main factors underlying the migration process were career aspirations and perceived local opportunities of occupational achievement. The possibility is also sustained by the existence of network of family and friends who have emigrated.
24 Breda Gray, 'The Home of Our Mothers and Our Birthright for Ages? Nation, Diaspora and Irish Women', in Mary Maynard and June Purvis (eds.), *New Frontiers in Womens Studies: Knowledge, Identity and Nationalism* (London, Taylor and Francis, 1996).
25 O'Toole, *Black Hole, Green Card*, p. 18.
26 ibid., p. 27.
27 Anne Holohan, *Working Lives: The Irish in Britain*, (Hayes, Middlesex, *Irish Post*, 1995).
28 Mary Robinson, Address to both Houses of the Oireachtas, 'Cherishing the Irish Diaspora', 2 February, 1995.
29 In Mary Robinson's earlier address to the Houses of the Oireachtas in 1992 on Irish identity in Europe, she referred to Irish emigrants and the symbolic light in the window of Aras an Uachtarain: 'I had in mind all our exiles, all our emigrants – past and present – when I put the light in the window of Aras an Uachtaráin. I was not prepared for the power and meaning which a modest emblem would have . . . that light reminds us – that the community of Irish interest and talent and memory extends far beyond our boundaries, far beyond Europe's boundaries . . . Through this absent community our national constitutency and culture are present in wider ones. I put the light in the window to show that the dialogue between the absent and the present is one of remembrance at all times.'
30 The following is a selection of initiatives within the Republic of Ireland in the 1990s which focus on emigration/diaspora as an important aspect of Irish culture and identity:

President Mary Robinson's election campaign and speeches since becoming President.

In 1994 FAS (the national state-sponsored employment agency) sponsored a seminar which drew on the experiences of statutory and voluntary agencies working on emigration issues. As a result, FAS has committed itself to establishing local networks of information providers on emigration. A Trans-Frontier Committee of FAS and the UK Employment Service has been established.

The Kerry Emigrant Support Group has developed a transition year module on emigration entitled 'Emigration Awareness' edited by Sr Anne McNamara (1994).

Radio Telefís Éireann (RTE, the national television station) has broadcast a number of TV series such as the series on Irish music *A River of Sound*. Micheál Ó Súilleabháin's plans to establish an Irish World Music Centre at Limerick University which is aimed at facilitating postgraduate students from all over the world in tracing the river of sound which has streamed out of Ireland back to its source.

An International Conference entitled 'The Irish Music Diaspora' held in Limerick in February, 1995.

The decision to hold a referendum to amend the constitution so that emigrants can be represented by three representatives in the Seanad (the Upper House).

The Irish Diaspora Project was established in 1992 under the auspices of the Institute of Irish Studies, an independent organisation which provides courses on aspects of Irish life and culture. The Director of the Institute, Noelle Clery, was the initiator of the Project. The Irish Diaspora Project is a networking agency for the reputed 70 million people of Irish origin throughout the world.

'Arising from the experience of running the Institute [for Irish Studies], the conviction grew that more could be done to match Irish cultural resources . . . to needs and opportunities abroad . . . What is envisaged are exchanges of information and personnel in both directions; from other countries to Ireland as well as from Ireland outwards, facilitating short and long-term projects.' (Irish Diaspora Project publicity leaflet 1995).

The project is a non-profit making private venture and publishes a magazine called *Irish World-wide* (one in 1994 and one in 1995, a further issue is planned for 1996) and is currently preparing a database directory of the Irish diaspora containing over 3,000 relevant organisations world-wide. It aims to develop close ties between the global Irish community.

31 Khachig Tololyan, 'The Nation-State and its Others: In Lieu of a Preface', *Diaspora*, vol. 1, no. 1, 1991, pp. 3–7.
32 The diaspora is also used in relation to the dispersal of African peoples through slavery.
33 Tololyan, 'The Nation-State and its Others' op. cit., p. 4; I return later in this chapter to the danger of blurring the boundaries between very different experiences of movement and migration.
34 Robin Cohin, 'Rethinking Babylon: Iconoclastic Conceptions of the Diasporic Experience', *New Community*, vol. 21, no. 1, 1995, pp. 5–18.
35 ibid., p. 12.
36 ibid., p. 13.
37 Jim Mac Laughlin, *Historical and Recent Irish Emigration: A Critique of Core-Periphery and Behavioural Models* (University of North London Press, 1994), p. 40.
38 Leslie Sklair, *Sociology of the Global System* (Harvester and Johns Hopkins University Press, 1991); Leslie Sklair 'Going Global: Competing Models of Globalisation', *Sociology Review*, November, 1993, pp. 7–10.
39 Khachig Toloyan, *The Nation-State and Its Others*, p. 5.
40 Andrew Wilson points to the significance of Irish-American republicans' support for the IRA to declare a cessation of violence in 1994. To achieve this support Sinn Féin leaders requested that Joe Cahill be allowed into the US for this purpose. The opening of contacts between the US government and Irish republicans gave Sinn Féin a political respectability which they would not have achieved so quickly otherwise. Gerry Adams was given permission by President Clinton to fund-raise in the USA. In November 1994 the US financial contribution to the International Fund for Ireland was raised by $10 million to a total of $30 million for 1996. Much emphasis was also placed on private US investment in Ireland and a major international investment in Ireland conference was held in Washington in May 1995 to lure US business to Northern Ireland. The Mitchel Report (compiled by a US senator) has played

a significant role in more recent negotiations and in finding bridges back to peace following the breakdown of the IRA cease-fire; see Andrew Wilson, *Irish America and the Ulster Conflict 1968–1995*, (Belfast, Blackstaff Press, 1995).

It is important, however, not to appear to suggest that such diasporic political activities are a new phenomenon, as even the briefest reference to Irish history will reveal such diasporic political initiatives in the past. However, the increasing significance of globalised media networks in political events increases the speed and effects of such influence and expands the number of levels at which such diasporic involvement operates.

41 Benedict Anderson, 'Exodus', *Critical Inquiry*, vol. 20 no. 2 Winter, 1994, pp. 314–27.

42 See Mary Corcoran, 'Of Emigrants Eirepreneurs and Opportunities', *Irish Reporter*, no. 13, First Quarter, 1994, pp. 5–7.

43 Doreen Massey, 'Making Spaces: Or, Geography is Political Too', *Soundings*, vol. 1, Autumn, 1995, p. 204.

44 ibid., p. 197.

45 Dave Reynolds in Anne Holohan, *Working Lives: The Irish In Britain*, op. cit., p. 7.

46 John Waters, *Race of Angels: Ireland the Genesis of U2* (Belfast, The Blackstaff Press, 1994).

47 L. Malkki, 'Citizens of Humanity: Internationalism and the Imagined Community of Nations', *Diaspora*, vol. 3, no. 1, 1994, p. 51.

48 David Lloyd, 'Making Sense of the Dispersal', *Irish Reporter*, vol. 13, First Quarter, 1994, p. 4.

49 ibid., p. 4.

50 Mark Ryan, 'Digging up Ireland's Dead', *Living Marxism*, September, 1995, p. 21.

51 In the same article Ryan is critical of Irish feminist politics and implies that feminist criticisms of nationalism, child sexual abuse and so on emanate from a feminist imagination. His position reinforces the all-encompassing nature of nationalism which silences other interests and concerns.

52 Noel Browne, Letter to *Irish Times*, 13 January 1996.

53 ibid.

54 For example, in her Allen Land Foundation Lecture of 1992, Mary Robinson asserts that women do not possess the skills of local and international community building: 'so as to be kept at home. The fact that due recognition is not always given to women's participation in public life results in a huge loss to the local community, to the state and the international community'.

55 Jim Mac Laughlin, 'The Familiar Side of Emigration', *Irish Reporter*, no. 15, Third Quarter, 1994, p. 6.

56 Gayatri Spivak, 'Love, Cruelty, and Cultural Talks in the Hot Peace', *Parallax*, no. 1, September, 1995, p. 157.

57 ibid., p. 1.

58 Declan Kiberd, *Inventing Ireland* (London, Jonathan Cape, 1995).

9. Clandestine Destinies
The Informal Economic Sector and Irish Immigrant Incorporation

MARY P. CORCORAN

The purpose of this chapter is to provide an account of the lived experience of undocumented Irish immigrants who relocated to New York City during the late 1980s.[1] I employ the term relocation rather than emigration deliberately, because many of these 'emigrants' see themselves as *transients* rather than settlers in the United States. While they live and work in New York City, their primary identification remains bound to the sending communities in Ireland. In other words, their status as emigrants – in terms of how we in Ireland traditionally understand that designation – remains unresolved. This ambivalence is in large part a consequence of their illegal status, which results in their exclusion from mainstream social, economic and political institutions in the host society. It is also, however, a consequence of the increased flexibilisation imposed on peripheral workers in the core cities of advanced capitalist societies. Apart from the rigours of relocation from one country and culture to another, Irish illegals experience additional adjustment problems arising from their profound dislocation, not only from the sending communities, but also from the host society.

In order to contextualise the experiences of Irish illegals, I will first sketch an explanatory framework which focuses on the dynamics of advanced capitalism as a major catalyst in population flows between peripheral and core countries. Economic and political factors interact to structure the conditions of international migration. In general, migration occurs 'under the pressure of utter necessity or haphazardly under the rubric of inconsistent laws and opportunities'.[2] World-wide economic recession and restrictive immigration laws in both the United States and Europe have had the effect of producing significant populations of internationally mobile workers who are by definition 'illegal aliens' – that is, they have no legal status in the host countries. Consequently, they are exploited for their labour power, often in circumstances which would be legally and socially unacceptable to indigenous workers. I will argue that the category 'illegal alien' is fundamentally a socially constructed one. In other words, responses on the part of the host society to undocumented workers or illegal aliens vary according to the ascribed characteristics of a given individual or immigrant group, the local economic needs and the context of reception. The experiences of the Irish in New York will be examined in a comparative context as I am mindful that Irish illegals are not a unitary phenomenon but form part of a growing underclass within the international division of labour.

EXPLANATORY FRAMEWORK: THE DYNAMICS OF ADVANCED CAPITALISM

The upward trend in Irish emigration in the 1980s saw tens of thousands of Irish people quitting Ireland for the metropolises of core countries, not only in Britain and Europe, but also in the United States.[3] The numbers of Irish in London, Munich, Sydney, New York and San Francisco have grown dramatically in recent years. Similarly, there has been a massive rise in the number of legal and illegal immigrants migrating to cities in the United States and Europe from Eastern Europe, Asia and North Africa. How can we explain these cross-continent population flows which continue even in the face of exclusionary immigration policies?

Explanatory models of migration range from single/multi-variable models to those that involve complex group dynamics and structural relationships in total systems. Among the former are models that are based on rational choice theory involving the calculation of distance between the place of origin and the place of destination.[4] The spatial distribution studies were later supplanted by the push/pull factoral models which look at inducements to migrate in both the donor and host countries.[5] These orthodox theoretical perspectives are problematic. As Portes and Borocz point out, they are based on an image of the world divided by national boundaries and of immigration as an event which takes place between such self-contained political entities. Furthermore, the push/pull model imputes to sending areas attributes which are the obverse of those found at home.[6] Thus, if workers are enticed abroad by the pull of higher wages, it is assumed that there must be widespread poverty in the sending country, and to the demand for immigrant labour there must correspond an undifferentiated supply of willing-to-work applicants.

Among the more complex structural models which have challenged the push/pull model are those based on the analysis of the *dynamics of the world system*, notably those put forward by Wallerstein and elaborated in the context of international migration by Petras and Zolberg.[7] Following the latter, I begin from the premise that capital, commodities and labour move within a core, semi-periphery and periphery framework. From this perspective, patterns of immigration may be interpreted as the outcome of structural and historical rather than individual factors. As Portes and Borocz have argued:

> Immigration, like other international processes does not so much take place between compartmentalized national units as within an overarching system, itself a product of past historical development.[8]

Large-scale migration between developed and developing regions is understood in terms of the structure of job opportunities, which themselves are largely historically determined. An explanation of this movement cannot simply be found in individual motivations but is related to the differential opportunity structures of core and periphery states.[9]

According to Petras, the pressure toward migration is an expression of the inequality among nations, in particular, between the periphery and the core. At times, the core needs more labour from the world market, at times it needs less. During periods of expansion, it is beneficial for employers in the core to have easy access to cross-national labour pools:

> The tendency to import labour is a *cyclical* expression of the uneven expansion of capital accumulation among economic sectors, among nations, and within the world economy.[10]

This process is regulated by policies whereby states restrict or encourage access to the labour market located within their national territories. Borders come to define two categories of international workers: insiders – those who are legitimately present within the national boundaries and deemed assimilable, and outsiders – those who are illegally present within, or seeking to gain entry to, the host society. Within the core states, the use of imported workers has allowed capital to extend labour market recruitment beyond its legal national boundaries into poorer and weaker nations. International capital is able to move freely among nations seeking the most profitable locations for investment, markets and labour supplies. Labour, in contrast, remains governed by state boundaries and policies. Capital benefits form a flexible regulatory framework, but workers must negotiate national boundaries and legal barriers in their quest for a livable wage:

> While the products of human labour have acquired a freedom to move, their human creators have no such freedom; and in practice, the latter right operates on a differential scale closely related to the amount of money they have.[11]

International bankers, investors, entrepreneurs and professionals move relatively freely around the world; unskilled workers operate within a much more restricted and ultimately discriminatory regime.

Petras argues that core states are motivated to 'look the other way' where economic or political imperatives are in conflict with legal imperatives with regard to immigration.[12] Hence, many international migrant workers – agricultural labourers, construction and domestic workers – in Europe and in the United States are in fact illegal, a state of affairs which is known and tacitly accepted by state agencies.[13] Undocumented workers are, by definition, the most vulnerable of all immigrant groups. The vast majority of these immigrants in Europe and the United States, regardless of their prior skill levels, work predominantly in poorly-paid manual, unskilled or semi-skilled occupations vacated by 'native' workers who refuse such work, even in times of recession and unemployment. These immigrants perform tasks that are socially degrading, physically taxing and detrimental to their health.

THE RISE OF INFORMAL ECONOMIC ACTIVITY IN ADVANCED INDUSTRIAL ECONOMIES AND THE DEMAND FOR UNDOCUMENTED LABOUR

In her ground-breaking study on the mobility of labour and capital,[14] Sassen points out that considerable evidence has been accumulated on international labour migration and on the internationalisation of production. But they are mostly two separate bodies of literature. Sassen argues that there is a close articulation between the two processes which requires explication. While multinational corporations decentralise their production facilities into peripheral areas of the world, the advanced industrial countries continue to attract immigrant labour much as they did in the nineteenth and early twentieth centuries. Both production *and* labour, she contends, are organised on an international scale.

Since the late 1950s, Irish industrial policy has followed an aggressive marketing strategy of 'selling' Ireland as a location to international capital. Manufacturing subsidiaries of multi-national corporations enticed to locate in Ireland by the attractive incentive packages provided by the IDA, hire from the local indigenous community. At the same time, immigrant workers *from those same peripheral communities* also serve the needs of capitalist enterprise, through their incorporation into the informal economies newly emerged in the metropolises of core countries. In other words, internationally organised capitalism relies on flexible and (ultimately) disposable workers in *both* locations.

The capacity of global cities in the core regions of the world economy to absorb hundreds of thousands of new immigrants from peripheral areas of the globe is linked to the changing needs of advanced capitalism.[15] Specifically, Sassen has documented the decentralisation and informalisation of the work process in global cities such as New York and Los Angeles. Decentralisation occurs when a small number of large companies in an industrial sector are replaced by a large number of small companies. Informalisation occurs when companies begin to operate close to, or outside, the law in an effort to cut their cost base. These developments can be traced to three key factors:

1. The recession of the mid-1970s, triggered by the oil crisis, particularly affected developed countries causing a profit squeeze. Overnight, companies found that their costs were rising and profits fell sharply as a result. Hence, they sought strategies to reduce their cost base. Labour proved to be the one flexible ingredient in the production process whose cost can be varied considerably, particularly if one is to rely on unregulated labour such as illegal aliens, rejected asylum-seekers and refugees.

2. Increased labour costs and/or competition from cheaper foreign-produced goods has made the decentralisation of work arrangements and informalisation in the manufacturing and service sectors in global cities considerably more attractive to entrepreneurs.[16]

3. The concentration of specialised services and corporate headquarters in major cities has created an élite market for exactly the kinds of goods and services produced in the informal sector – designer clothing, gourmet food stores, fast food outlets, child-minding services and artisan, renovation/construction work. Sassen argues that the proliferation of low wage jobs to service the high income lifestyles of the top level workforce in the advanced economies is a key to the expansion of the informal sector. These factors combine to create the conditions for the demand and absorption of immigrants into the global cities, even at at a time when unemployment was rising among the indigenous population. In cities like New York, London, Paris and Munich, a relatively small number of large companies which traditionally provided secure conditions of employment operating within statutory controls, have been replaced by large numbers of small firms which frequently flaunt the regulatory apparatus governing pay and working conditions, social insurance and taxation. In such circumstances, employers increasingly turn toward immigrant workers and, in particular, undocumented workers, who are willing to 'work off the books'. Apart from the obvious savings on wages, tax and social security contributions, the flexibility of this form of labour acts as a major incentive for these employers.

To summarise, multinationals firms locate production plants around the globe in pursuit of ever cheaper labour forces. A Polish worker may be hired for a fraction of the wage demanded by a German worker; a Mexican worker will demand considerably less than his American counterpart over the border. Factories relocate accordingly. However, under the conditions of advanced capitalism, cheap labour can be exploited in much the same way, not in the far flung corners of the world, but in the immigrant ghettos now characteristic of the global cities which also house the multinational headquarters. Conditions traditionally associated with Third World economies are being reproduced in the global cities of the core economies in the world system.

LOCATING THE IRISH IN THE INTERNATIONAL DIVISION OF LABOUR

Contemporary Irish emigration is not confined to a single class grouping; it permeates the entire Irish class system. One can identify a professional educated élite (brain drain) positioned at one end of the emigration continuum, and an underclass of unskilled undocumented workers at the other. Crucially, Irish immigrants are absorbed into *both* the élite and the informal labour markets at the core. Élite jobs are associated with the primary labour market which, according to Portes, corresponds roughly to employment in government, other large-scale institutions and the oligopolistic sector of the economy.[17] A key defining characteristic of this sector is that job ladders or internal markets offer an opportunity structure within which graduate immigrants can advance their careers. According to Hanlon, for example, the Big Six international accountancy firms facilitate the emigration of Irish accountants by 'the creation of an international status hierarchy which makes certain destinations more prestigious than others – multinational firms thus appear to have created international élite labour markets that encourage people to move to the core'.[18] Immigration in this sector occurs through legal channels. Workers are hired on the basis of their technical skills and qualifications rather than their ascribed characteristics such as ethnicity. Pay, conditions and promotional opportunities are not significantly different from indigenous workers at the same level. The function of primary labour market immigration is not to undermine the domestic labour force but to 'overcome inelasticities in the domestic supply of labour'.[19]

The majority of Irish workers who relocate abroad – whether their destinations are Britain, the United States or continental Europe – are absorbed into the secondary and informal sectors of the labour market, which are characterised by low wages, menial social status, considerable employment instability or, at least, uncertainty.[20] As was pointed out above, firms in the informal sector are engaged in fierce competition with each other. The conditions of production invariably lead to a downward pressure on wages.[21] Immigrants, in particular those without documentation, find themselves in jobs which generally require little or no prior training, are clustered at the low end of the wage scale, offer little or no mobility opportunities and provide no security of tenure. Workers are hired mainly on the basis of ascribed characteristics such as their ethnicity. The function of immigrants in the secondary and informal sectors is not only to supplement the domestic labour force, but also to discipline it. Legal ambiguity surrounding the status of the workers heightens their vulnerability within the labour market.

RESTRUCTURING THE CONSTRUCTION INDUSTRY: A CASE STUDY

The construction industry in both London and New York has historically relied on immigrant Irish labour. It is an excellent example of a sector which has undergone the dual processes of decentralisation and informalisation, with a consequent diminution of the rights and benefits of workers.[22] In his analysis of the incorporation of Irish immigrants in the London labour market, Connor demonstrates the way in which that market has been transformed since the post-war boom.[23] A process of de-industrialisation has taken place with a rapid decline in the manufacturing industry, especially in inner-city areas. At the same time, there has been an expansion of jobs in higher professional and white-collar work, as well as a more limited expansion in low skilled manual service sector jobs. As a result, employment has shifted toward a more polarised and segmented labour market. On the one hand, highly qualified Irish accountants emigrate to London to enhance their career opportunities. On the other hand, poor and unskilled Irish emigrants find themselves queuing for work outside the Cricklewood cafés. The casualisation of work in the construction sector of the labour market has particularly affected Irish emigrants.

According to Connor, the construction industry in Great Britain virtually collapsed in the 1970s. The big British building firms of McAlpine, Taylor Woodrow and Laing slashed their labour forces as a result. They were replaced by sub-contractual labour, with the big firms distancing themselves from labour relations by placing the sub-contractor in between. Many Irish workers were forced to become 'self-employed'. In practice, this meant that they had to make their own arrangements for the payment of taxes, social security and pension contributions. Inevitably, the lump system in which tax and insurance payments were avoided increased dramatically. Regulations in the construction industry became open to abuse, resulting in declining standards and the erosion of good employment practices. Jobs in construction, argues Connor, are now more dangerous and insecure, are less likely to be unionised and are characterised by much tougher conditions. A large proportion of the workforce in the British construction industry is now categorised as 'self-employed'. 'Self employed' workers are generally hired by a sub-contractor, on a day-to-day basis. If the contractor has gaps between jobs, he simply lays off the 'self-employed' workers without notice or recompense. For many labourers, self-employed status has effectively undermined employment protection and employee's rights. The Union of Construction Allied Trades and Technicians (UCATT) estimates that at least 70 per cent of those workers classed as self-employed should be classed as employees under common law because they work continuously for the same employer.[24] Instead, they are forced to operate as independent agents, negotiating each day's work with their employer, often fearful of complaining because of the ever-present threat of losing their job. The situation of construction workers in London is mirrored in other core cities across the European continent. Thousands of Irish and British construction workers have sought refuge from the British building recession by looking for 'self-employed' work in Germany, where reconstruction of the old Eastern Europe has brought a jobs boom. Under a 1972 German employment law, contractors who win a job tender must include their own labour as part of the cost. Those employees are then covered by employment and safety law and can earn the going rate for the job. However, the supply of immigrant labour from the former Eastern European countries and, to a lesser extent, from Britain and Ireland has made it possible for employers to engage in the illegal practice of 'labour leasing', whereby workers are treated as 'self-employed'.[25] Wages have been driven down and many workers are no longer covered by health and safety insurance.

The construction industry in New York has been moving in a similar direction. The sector has seen a steady expansion in the past few decades. According to New York State Department of Labour statistics, New York City had over 10,000 registered construction firms in 1988.[26] The average number of workers in these firms is 11, with over 80 per cent of all firms employing fewer than 10 workers. The proliferation of small firms is relevant to the question of informality for two reasons. Firstly, small firms are the most appropriate setting for casual hiring, non-reporting of income and other informal practices. The provisions of the Immigration Reform and Control Act (1986), which provides for fines on employers who knowingly hire illegal aliens, specifically excludes from its provisions companies who hire less than ten workers. Secondly, small firms are easier to convert into totally underground enterprises.[27] It is estimated, for example, that 90 per cent of interior work in New York City is done without a legal permit.[28]

THE EXPERIENCE OF ILLEGALITY IN NEW YORK CITY IN THE 1980S

The majority of undocumented (male) workers who travelled from Ireland to New York City during the 1980s were absorbed into the construction sector. Apart from a minority who inveigled their way into the construction unions, most young Irish men found themselves working for small sub-contractors in the informal sector. The primary advantage accruing to employers in this sector is the vulnerability attached to the juridical position of undocumented employees. Irish immigrants tended to gravitate toward employers in the established Irish community in their search for jobs. While the fact of their Irishness often helped to get them hired, it also exposed them to unscrupulous employers who used the illegal status of their employees to exploit them in a number of ways. Essentially, a clientelistic relationship prevailed between employer and employee. Employers exercise autocratic forms of control and the lines of communication run along a vertical, rather than a horizontal, axis within the firm. Given the extent of clientelism and the individualistic relations which that fostered in the workplace, workers almost never organised around their own interests.

Work in construction, in particular, is generally dead-end, dirty and dangerous. One Irish worker, who was part of a team of landscape gardeners, explained the drudgery of his working day:

> It was dog work, especially when the heat came on. The guys got jealous of each other over the jobs they had to do – some people got stuck in the garage doing dirty heavy work. The trucks that they used were from 1971. No appreciation was shown for the work that we did. It was a dog's life, sleeping on the floor at night, and slaving by day.[29]

Another worker, who formed part of a team of underground construction workers recalled:

> For the last few months I really wanted to get out of the tunnels. You come off the job every morning covered in dust and dirt. Taking the subway home you see people move away from you, because of the dirt and the smell of a night's sweat. The muck runs off me in bucketfuls in the shower.[30]

Work on construction sites, which is physically demanding, is tightly controlled, with authority exercised in an almost feudal fashion. The workers, because of their illegal status, have little or no access to avenues of redress. The system of surveillance undermines any creativity which might attach to the job and locates the workers as objects rather than subjects in their work environment:

> I make things with steel. After about six months here I realised that the system was very different. You are given specific directions for every task and you are closely supervised. Basically, people are spoon fed. They are not encouraged to use their initiative and so they don't. I have had many arguments with the foreman. When you work in a situation where everything is done according to specified directions you need more overseers to get the job done.[31]

Control is generally exercised in an arbitrary fashion which further disempowers the workers. Often these men were denied any sense of security or continuity in the job:

> I was on a job up-state to do some shop front lettering. While I was there the truck broke down and it took a couple of days for someone to come and fix it. I was stranded with just a couple of dollars to my name and it wasn't a nice feeling. So when I got back I insisted on payment for the hours I was stranded up there. They paid me for the hours but then let me go. I thought that was a bit rough.[32]

Even for workers who enjoyed greater job security and benefits through their membership (generally on false premises) of a construction union, the flexibility demanded by the employer restricted access to work:

> A friend of my cousin's was a delegate for the Carpenter's Union. Through that contact I became a member of the union for $300 and got a union job in the city. It really does make a difference. You are guaranteed your wages every week, you are covered for medical benefits, dental treatment, hospital service and of course steady work. The work is hard though, and membership of the union does not confer a right to work, it just confers a right to get benefits. It is always up to the company to decide whether or not you will work. They hire on a day-to-day basis. Most of the carpenters are on a high wage so it really costs the company. They can't afford to have guys hanging around on the job. So if they need five carpenters instead of ten one day, they will simply take on five.[33]

Given the propensity of small firms to cut corners in their desire to reduce costs, injuries and dangerous practices at work are relatively commonplace:

Two of the lads were pushing a container of concrete up the tracks. They used a piece of wood to position it but they didn't wedge it in properly. The container came loose and careered down the tracks. One of the lads just missed it but the other took the full force of it in his back. The fact that the guy was large framed probably saved him as a smaller man would have fallen to the ground. The man's hand was broken and his back injured.[34]

One guy who had a bit of a drink problem came on the job drunk. He was walking near another worker who was using a power saw and accidently brushed against him. His arm was slashed and he had to go to the hospital to get stitches.[35]

On the job . . . they constantly expose the workers to hazardous substances but if you complain you are out the door. They violate the regulations by not issuing enough protective clothing and mouth filters. Since I raised objections about this, I haven't been called into work . . . There is constant pressure to get the job done quickly and cheaply and little concern about exposure to hazardous substances.[36]

Not surprisingly, there is a high degree of alienation among Irish construction workers. They complain of the lack of autonomy on the job and the necessity of 'switching-off' mentally during working hours. Work is viewed instrumentally as a means to an end. For many of them, the end constitutes a weekend of binge drinking before the treadmill starts over again on Monday morning. Construction workers regularly go straight to the bar after work on the weekends – dirty, exhausted and with a full pay packet in their pockets. The bars conveniently provide a cheque-cashing service so that their clients have plenty of ready cash enabling them to drink steadily throughout the weekend, often breaking off only to get some food or catch up on sleep. According to the workers themselves, it is the drudgery of the working week which leads to these weekend drinking-bouts. The bar is perceived as a symbolic home from home, offering the kind of social support, friendship and camaraderie absent from the job. A fractured sense of self is an integral part of the undocumented experience given the fact that illegals have of necessity to spin a repertoire of lies and subterfuges about who and what they are. The bars provide the one refuge from the inauthenticity of their lives. Here the psychological barriers employed defensively by the illegals are lowered, and they are free to simply be themselves.

THE SOCIAL CONSTRUCTION OF THE 'ILLEGAL ALIEN'

While we can identify the key characteristics which shape the work life of undocumented workers in the international division of labour, there are also significant divergences in the treatment accorded them in practice. Responses to undocumented workers or illegal aliens vary according to the ascribed characteristics of race, ethnicity and gender, variations in the local demand for skilled and unskilled labour and the general context of reception.

When people are hired on the basis of their race or ethnicity, it generates and reinforces division between workers, often along racial lines. Employers in the secondary and informal sectors hire from within their own ethnic group. Their capacity to act as patrons and brokers in their own ethnic community considerably enhances their social standing as well as maximising their control over the work process. Given the informal nature of the hiring process, especially in the sub-contracting sector, a mixed race construction crew may gradually be supplanted by a single ethnic group handpicked by a sympathetic foreman. Given the over-supply of labour in the informal sector, the power of employers to pick and choose between employees is virtually limitless. The willingness of certain ethnic groups to collude with employers by accepting less than the going rate of pay ensures that the labour force in this sector is internally stratified. While highly-skilled artisans and craft workers are always in demand, conditions for all other workers tend to deteriorate in situations of over-supply of cheap labour. New York, London and Berlin all provide examples of global cities where secondary and informal sector workers constitute a highly stratified heterogenous group. Immigrants are stratified according to race, ethnicity, skills and experience, as well as legal status, and that stratification system determines to a great extent their labour market experience. Given the nature of control in the competitive sector and the importance attached to ascriptive qualities (such as ethnicity and kin relationships), immigrants are hesitant to form solidaristic alliances as a group. Rather, they find themselves played off against each other by employers who fine-tune a stratified system of pay to maximise profits and productivity.

In the quest for a cheaper and more flexible labour force, employers engage in wage-cutting strategies. Recently, a British newspaper reported that Bosnian refugees were under-cutting Irish builders by accepting 'slave wages' to work on unsafe construction sties around south-east England.[37] The report alleged that many Irish sub-contractors are displacing Irish labourers in favour of the Bosnians who crucially are willing to work longer hours for much less pay. While some Irish labourers had formed a cartel to ensure that they would get paid £40 for a day's work, Bosnian workers are prepared to work for £25 per day or less. Immigrants from Bulgaria and Poland have also under-cut the Irish daily rate, which has been depressed downwards as a result. In Berlin, the influx of migrant workers has also exerted a downward pressure on wages. The German Department of Employment estimates a sliding pay scale depending on nationality with Germans receiving DM65 per hour, British and Irish expecting DM30 to DM38 per hour and, at the bottom of the scale, Poles earning between DM7 and DM10 per hour.[38]

Similarly in New York City, workers find that wage scales varied dramatically in accordance with their social and legal status. Workers are stratified not only on the basis of ethnicity, but also on the basis of their union membership and their legality. Rates of pay vary accordingly. Labour racketeering practices in some New York construction unions in the 1980s made it possible for some contractors to hire non-union labour in return for bribes paid to union agents. Thus, a contractor could have as many as four categories of workers under his control: unionised legals, unionised illegals, non-unionised legals and non-unionised illegals. Each group was paid a different daily rate. An Irish worker on a construction site in New York, for example, could hope to earn approximately twice as much as a worker from Central America for doing the same work. An Irish worker who is a member of a construction union could in turn earn more than his counterpart who is not in the union. Massey has argued that legal status in itself is not the principal determinant of differential wage rates:

> On average, undocumented migrants do earn lower wages than legal migrants, but they do so not because they lack legal papers, but because they compare unfavourably to legal migrants on variables that determine wage rates. U.S. wages are principally a function of English-language ability, time spent on the job, skill level and close kinship with a legal migrant.[39]

Irish illegals with good English, a high level of skill and close ties to Irish-American power brokers in the ethnic community tend to do better in the immigrant labour market in New York City than their European and Central American counterparts. As was argued above, the Third World is nowadays effectively on the doorstep of many global cities. Thus, labour can be exploited locally by small unregulated firms who seek out the least powerful and most desperate-to-stay ethnic groups. It seems inevitable that as work becomes more scarce, the Irish find themselves under-cut both in the London and New York labour markets. The long-term effect of this ethnic competition is to reduce wage rates for all immigrant groups. But for the present, the Irish in New York continue to maintain their advantage over other immigrant groups.

According to Borocz and Portes, an important consideration in delineating immigrant experiences is the context of reception in the host society. An immigrant may face a handicapped, neutral or advantaged context of reception.[40] Inability to speak English (in the US), colour of skin and low skill level indicate a relatively handicapped context of reception. A neutral context of reception is implied when individual merit and skills are the most important determinants of successful adaptation. The relative strength of ethnic networks generally indicates an advantaged context of reception. As a white, English-speaking ethnic group arriving in relatively large numbers in New York City during the 1980s, the Irish were deemed to be highly assimilable. These advantages, coupled with a relatively high skill level, a willingness to work hard and access to important ethnic networks, meant that the Irish clearly entered a privileged context of reception. A tradition of patronage and brokerage within the Irish ethnic community served newly-arrived illegals and eased their passage into employment. Such networks are not available to the same degree to other ethnic groups. The clandestine nature of their immigration, which should have resulted in a handicapped context of reception, was generally compensated for by the availability of these social networks. The Irish in New York did not have to face the kind of racial prejudice with which many immigrants (both legal and illegal) in the United States are forced to contend. In general, immigrants from Eastern Europe and South and Central America, particularly the undocumented ones, face a handicapped rather than a privileged or neutral context of reception. The differential pay rates on construction sites (and also in the restaurant and bar trades) are symptomatic of the racialisation of American society, even when statutory provisions explicitly outlaw such practices.[41] Irish illegals occupy an *intermediate* position within the New York labour market. On the one hand, they may be perceived as relatively deprived in comparison to legal immigrants. They have little or no access to the kinds of jobs for which they may be qualified and they have limited job mobility and opportunity. On the other hand, they may be perceived as relatively advantaged in comparison with both legal and illegal immigrants who are black and Hispanic. This advantage derives from the fact that the Irish are a white, English-speaking and relatively skilled group seeking opportunity in a context where racial tensions persist in both manifest and latent forms.

CONCLUSION

In the global cities, immigrant labour is sought as an alternative to workers who are highly organised and protected by state welfare legislation. Small labour-intensive industries, such as garment manufacturers, textiles and construction companies which depend on low wages to maintain profitability, are unwilling to pay the high cost of employing indigenous labour. Immigrant workers, especially illegals, can reduce labour costs because they can be more easily forced below the minimum wage levels guaranteed to indigenous workers. Employment conditions in this sector fall outside the normal regulatory apparatus of Western welfare states and lead to high levels of exploitation. Illegality confines workers to employment in small firms where ethnic brokers play a gate-keeping role. The control exercised over these workers is often of an almost feudal nature with some workers being denied even basic human rights. Illegality intensifies dependence on ethnic brokers, creating vertical rather than horizontal alliances in the workplace. In the absence of an accessible opportunity structure, work becomes a means to an end.

The function of most immigration from peripheral areas is to supplement the supply of low wage labour in core countries. There is, however, a corresponding (although much smaller) flow of highly skilled/credentialised immigrants from the peripheries to the core. The maintenance and renewal of Irish emigrant labour is taking place in two geographically seperate locations. For example, the process of renewal – raising, educating and sustaining a labour force – is organised under the auspices of the Irish state. But the maintenance of that labour force (through wage labour) is increasingly taking place elsewhere – in Great Britain, the United States and continental Europe. Both processes are interdependent. Historically, the renewal process in Ireland was dependent on income left over from maintenance which was remitted home by the Irish emigrants abroad. Today, many of Ireland's productive workers abroad require the continued support from their families at home because they tend not to have permanent legal or political status in the country where they work. The family remains an important linking institution.[42]

The structural effects of immigration, and immigrants themselves, are different depending on the sector of the economy where they become incorporated.[43] In other words, the experience and impact of the immigrants will differ depending on whether they are absorbed into the primary labour market or the secondary/informal labour markets. The overall trend in the global cities is toward income and occupational polarisation.[44] The situation of the Irish in Great Britain and the United States is a good example of this trend. Irish immigrants are represented among the élite *and* among the underclass who constitute the opposing ends of the international migratory continuum.

Many of the changes in the organisation of work in global cities are a direct result of the changing needs of international capitalism. The informalisation of global city economies has created new job opportunities in the secondary and informal labour markets which are particularly attractive to new immigrants. In particular, they attract immigrants without documentation. The influx of tens of thousands of illegals into the major cities of Western Europe and the United States during the 1980s was possible only because enough jobs had been created to absorb them. It is, therefore, structural factors, largely beyond the individual's control, which create the conditions that encourage or impede international migration. For international labour, there is no framework or international movement which formulates policies to protect its interests. The task which analysts of the migratory process face is to

> view human beings in their roles as economic, political and cultural actors, and
> [to conceptualise] the international system in a congruent manner, as structured
> into states, markets and societies.[45]

Only then can we begin to fully comprehend the complexities underlying the 'international nomadism of modern life'.[46]

Notes and References

1   People who enter the United States with the intention of working without appropriate documentation are deemed illegal aliens. Most of the Irish people who travelled to New York City to work during the 1980s were undocumented. A proportion of these subsequently regularised their status through the Donnelly and Morrison visa programmes but a residual population of Irish illegals remains today. The term undocumented is used interchangeably with the term illegal or illegal alien throughout this essay. The data on undocumented Irish immigrants presented here is based on research carried out during the period 1984 to 1990.

2   Bob Sutcliffe, 'Migration, Rights and Illogic', *Index on Censorship*, vol. 23, no. 3, 1994 p. 32.

3   Mary P. Corcoran, *Irish Illegals: Transients Between Two Societies* (Westport, CT, Greenwood Press, 1993) pp. 6–9.

4   See for example, E. G. Ravenstein, 'The Laws of Migration', *Journal of the Royal Statistical Society*, vol. 52, 1889, pp. 241–305; Samuel Stouffer, 'Intervening Opportunities: A Theory Relating Mobility and Distance', *American Sociological Review*, no. 5, 1940, pp. 845–67.

5   See *The Economic and Social Implications of Emigration* (Dublin, National Economic and Social Council, 1991).

6   Alejandro Portes and Jozsef Borocz, 'Contemporary Immigration: Theoretical Perspectives on its Determinants and Modes of Incorporation', *International Migration Review*, vol. 23, no. 3, 1989, p. 625.

7   Immanuel Wallerstein, *The Modern World System: Capitalist Agriculture and the Origins of the European World Economy in the Sixteenth Century* (New York, Cambridge University Press, 1974); Elizabeth McLean Petras, 'The Role of National Boundaries in the Cross-National Labour Market', *International Journal of Urban and Regional Research*, no. 4, 1980, pp. 157–195; Elizabeth McLean Petras, 'The Global Labour Market in the Modern World Economy', in Mary B. Kritz, Charles B. Keely and Silvano M. Tomasi (eds.), *Global Trends in Migration* (New York, Centre for Migration Studies, 1981), pp. 44–63; Aristide Zolberg, 'International Migration in Political Perspective', in Kritz et al., *Global Trends in Migration*, pp. 3–27; Aristide Zolberg, 'The Next Waves: Migration Theory for a Changing World', *International Migration Review*, vol. 23, no. 3, 1989, pp. 403–29.

8   Portes and Borocz, 'Contemporary Immigration' (Westport Connecticut, Greenwood, 1943) p. 626.

9   For a detailed application of this model to contemporary Irish emigration see Corcoran, *Irish Illegals: Transients Between Two Societies*, and Jim Mac Laughlin, *Ireland: The Emigrant Nursery and the World Economy* (Cork University Press, 1994).

10 Elizabeth McLean Petras, 'The Role of National Boundaries in the Cross-National Labour Market', p. 157.

11 Bob Sutcliffe, 'Migration, Rights and Illogic', p. 32.

12 Elizabeth McLean Petras, 'The Role of National Boundaries in the Cross-National Labour Market', p. 173.

13 Tacit acceptance of immigrants may turn to outright rejection especially during periods of economic retrenchment and rising unemployment among the indigenous labour force. This is evident in the attacks on foreigners across Europe in the wake of the economic upheaval caused by recent political changes in Eastern Europe. National governments in the EU have been instituting increasingly restrictive legislation to keep immigrants out. In 1994, in an effort to dissuade illegal immigrants from remaining in California, Californians voted overwhelmingly in support of Proposition 187 which seeks to remove welfare benefits from illegal immigrants and deny schooling to their children. This Proposition is currently under challenge in the US courts.

14 Saskia Sassen, *The Mobility of Labour and Capital: A Study in International Investment and Labour Flow* (New York, Cambridge University Press, 1988).

15 Saskia Sassen, 'New York City's Informal Economy', Paper presented at the Second Symposium on the Informal Sector, Johns Hopkins University, October 1986; Alejandro Portes and Saskia Sassen-Koob, 'Making it Underground: Comparative Material on the Informal Sector in Western Market Economies', *American Journal of Sociology*, vol. 93, no. 1, 1987, pp. 30–61; Sassen, *The Mobility of Labour and Capital*; Saskia Sassen, 'The Informal Economy', in J. H. Mollenkopf and M. Cassells (eds.), *Dual City: Restructuring New York*, (New York, Russell Sage Foundation, 1991).

16 Alejandro Portes and Saskia Sassen-Koob, 'Making it Underground' p. 54.

17 Alejandro Portes, 'Modes of Structural Incorporation and Present Theories of Labour Immigration', in M. Kritz et al. (eds.), *Global Trends in Migration*, p. 283.

18 Gerard Hanlon, *The Commercialisation of Accountancy* (London, St. Martin's Press, 1994) p. 187.

19 Alejandro Portes, 'Modes of Structural Incorporation and Present Theories of Labour Immigration', p. 283.

20 Michael Piore, 'The Shifting Grounds of Immigration', *Annals*, AAPSS 485, May 1986, p. 24.

21 Alejandro Portes, 'Modes of Structural Incorporation and Present Theories of Labour Immigration', p. 282.

22 The process of informalisation described in the construction industry is replicated in a number of other sectors, most notably in the garment trade. In 1984, for example, the proportion of French firms with fewer than 19 employees stood at 90 per cent, the majority of which had fewer than 9 employees, while almost half of all garment employees worked in firms with fewer than 19 workers. For the garment manufacturers, outsourcing to immigrant jobbers results in cheaper wages, reduction in corporation taxes, lower national insurance payments and the opportunity to circumvent labour legislation. The sub-contractors themselves outsource work to others in a chain of sub-contractors in order to further offlay risks. The sub-contracting chain is extended so that even the sewing machine operators are labelled 'self-employed'; see Scott Lash and John Urry, *The Economies of Signs and Space* (London, Sage, 1994), p. 178.

23 Tom Connor, *The London Irish* (London, London Strategic Policy Unit, 1987).

24 Martin Southwood, 'Hard Labour', *Guardian*, 19 January 1994.

25 Steve Boggan, 'Postcard from a Berlin Building Site', *Independent on Sunday*, 23 May 1993.

26 Saskia Sassen, *The Mobility of Labour and Capital*, p. 88.

27 Alejandro Portes and Saskia Sassen-Koob, 'Making it Underground, pp. 42–43.

28 ibid., p. 46.

29 Undocumented Irish construction worker, New York City, 1988.

30 ibid.

31 ibid.

32 ibid.

33 ibid.

34 ibid.

35 ibid.

36 ibid.

37 *Irish Post*, 9 July 1994.

38 Steve Boggan, 'Postcard from a Berlin Building Site'.

39 Douglas Massey, 'Do Undocumented Migrants Earn Lower Wages than Legal Migrants? New Evidence From Mexico', *International Migration Review*, vol. 21, no. 2, 1987, p. 267.

40 Alejandro Portes and Jozsef Borocz, 'Contemporary Immigration: Theoretical Perspectives on its Determinants and Modes of Incorporation', p. 622.

41 In contrast to their experience in New York City, Irish immigrants in Great Britain are not guaranteed a privileged or even neutral context of reception. In particular, Irish immigrants who are unskilled are likely to enter a handicapped context of reception given the past history between the two countries and the continuing anti-Irish racism with which the Irish in Britain must contend.

42 Michael Buroway, 'The Function and Reproduction of Migrant Labour: Comparative Material from Southern Africa and the United States', *American Journal of Sociology*, vol. 81, no. 5, 1976.

43 Alejandro Portes, 'Modes of Structural Incorporation and Present Theories of Labour Immigration'.

44 Saskia Sassen, *The Mobility of Labour and Capital*, p. 152.

45 Aristide Zolberg, 'International Migration in Political Perspective', pp. 20–21.

46 Benedict Anderson, 'Exodus', *Cultural Inquiry*, Winter 1994, p. 327.

10. Irish Immigrants in the United States' Racial System

EITHNE LUIBHEID

Irish emigrants to The United States of America in the 1980s and l990s entered a country that had grown racially and ethnically diverse. They settled primarily in urban areas that were heavily populated by US-born racial minorities, as well by immigrants from Asia, Africa, the Caribbean and Latin America. They waited on tables, painted houses and cared for children, and did all of these alongside racial minorities. This chapter asks a number of questions about the Irish experience in the US with particular reference to relations between race and immigration. It asks the following two questions in particular. Firstly, how did these experiences shape Irish immigrant adaptation to America? Secondly, what relationship can we expect to find in the future between Irish immigrants and America's expanding racial minority populations? An answer to these questions, it is argued, involves an exploration of recent literature on relationships between Irish immigration and racial attitudes in the United States. Such scholarship exists only in fragmented form at the moment. Passages from published immigration histories, footnotes in journal articles and letters to the editor in the pages of community newspapers all lend themselves to suggestive reading on the topic of race and the Irish immigrant experience in the US since the nineteenth century. This chapter, however, argues for the importance of developing a scholarship that systematically explores the interplay between race and Irish immigration across time and space.

In this chapter, lrish immigration to America is discussed within two main time periods in order to highlight ways in which race thinking affected immigrant settlement here. Firstly, I follow historian David Roediger's argument that nineteenth-century Irish immigrants in America found themselves profoundly embroiled in a politics of race.[1] How these immigrants negotiated the racial politics of the time, and how they became part of the 'white' majority rather than subordinated racial minorities, formed a legacy that has shaped subsequent Irish immigrant waves to America. Bearing this legacy in mind, the second part of the chapter focuses on contemporary Irish immigrants in

America. The chapter suggests that the social position of today's immigrants, their forms of struggle and their future prospects are all shaped by their position in the racial hierarchy and by Irish forms of race thinking. The campaign to secure a 'diversity immigrants' programme to enable many undocumented Irish immigrants to gain US residency is discussed as one example of ways that Irish immigrant communities remain shaped by, and find themselves drawing for advancement upon, their racial position in the US. The implications for Irish immigrants of their uncritical adoption of the dominant US politics of privileging whites over racial minorities are then questioned. While an alternative racial politics has yet to be articulated by most Irish immigrants, this chapter suggests that the development of scholarship which explores race as a component that systematically structures immigrant experience would assist in the formulation of alternatives, while also being of theoretical value in its own right. Such scholarship would substantially enhance the history of Irish immigration to the United States and the history of other racial and ethnic immigrations. As it stands, that history tends to ignore this dimension of the Irish experience abroad. Such scholarship would also advance world-systems theorising about emigration which links high rates of emigration to Ireland's status as a peripheral country within the global economy.[2] However, this chapter also argues that, despite its strengths, world-systems theory does not address the manner in which racial hierarchies generate divergent paths for nationals from peripheral countries who migrate to work in core countries like the US. The study of Irish immigration to America, with its broader implications for understanding transnational racial structures, can begin to unlock this question.

RACE AND IMMIGRANTS IN THE UNITED STATES

The social system of the United States is clearly and integrally structured by race, racial meanings and racial hierarchies. As Omi and Winant have argued:

> Racial meanings pervade US society, extending from the shaping of individual racial identities to the structuring of collective political action on the terrain of the state . . . race [is] a fundamental organizing principle of social relations.[3]

For immigrant newcomers, encounters with US systems of racialisation are unavoidable. These encounters can be direct, such as those that involve direct conflict and open hostility, or indirect, such as those that place constraints on where one may live or work in the US. Encounters with this system of racialisation have a profound structuring effect upon immigrant experiences in the US, and they shape the ways in which all immigrant groups adapt, or fail to adapt, to the US social system. Most recent research in this field has typically concentrated on the effects of the US racialisation system upon Asian minorities, African minorities, the Caribbean community and Latin Americans. Indeed, these groups get to be designated and treated as minorities regardless of their pre-migration status. However, the US racialisation system also affects other immigrant groups, not least those from Europe, Australia and Canada, who, far from being designated as subordinate minorities, instead are encouraged to become an integral part of the majority population. This is because, as Ruth Frankenberg explains:

> any system of differentiation shapes those on whom it bestows privilege, as well as those it oppresses. White people are 'raced', just as men are 'gendered' . . . It is crucial to look at the racialness of white experience.[4]

Frankenberg further elaborates:

> Whiteness . . . has a set of linked dimensions. First, whiteness is a location of structural advantage, of race privilege. Second, it is a 'standpoint', a place from which white people look at ourselves, others, and society. Third, whiteness refers to a set of cultural practices that are usually unmarked and unnamed.[5]

In the US, it is argued, the racial categories that exist, the meanings that attach to these categories and the ways in which race thinking organises every aspect of life are not *immediately* self-evident to immigrant newcomers. They have to be learned. This is because racial groupings are not a product of biological differences, but are socially constructed. This has caused Feagin and Feagin to explain:

> given the constant blending and interbreeding of human groups over the centuries and in the present, it is impossible to sort human groups into unambiguously distinct groups on physical grounds . . . Social scientists focus on the social definition of race and racial groups . . . From the social science perspective, characteristics such as skin color have no self evident meaning; rather they primarily have social meanings . . . A racial group is not something naturally generated as part of the self-evident order of the universe.[6]

Since race is socially constructed, racial categories and their social meanings change across national boundaries. Immigrant newcomers to the United States often encounter new racial categorisations which they never heard about before migration, but which, nevertheless, have social salience in political and social life in the US. On the other hand, they often find that racial categories and distinctions that operated in the immigrant's home country may be totally irrelevant to the situation in the US. Thus immigrants often find themselves being placed into racial groupings with which they were previously unfamiliar. They often also find themselves being treated in terms of a history and set of assumptions with which they were equally unfamiliar. Thus, for example, Martha Gimenez suggests:

> Latin Americans who immigrate to the United States should be prepared to assume a new, stigmatized identity 'Hispanics'.[7]

Moreover, even in situations where the racial labels attached to immigrant groups are the same as those operating in the country of origin, the social meanings attached to these same labels may differ in a number of ways. For example, many Haitians in the United States construct their ethnic identity around notions of 'Blackness', yet many scholars have noted that Haitian immigrants themselves often differentiate their own notions of Blackness from that of US mainstream society where Blackness is a pejorative term which is synonymous with dehumanisation and which also signifies constraints to social mobility.[8] In regard to meanings of Blackness in Haiti, for example, Charles has observed that:

> with the creation of the Haitian state as an outcome of the slave revolution of 1791–1804, race became the unifying theme in the formation of nationhood . . . the equating of race and nation conveys a sense of race-pride. Blackness is the basis for cultural nationalism in Haiti, and the Haitian revolution symbolizes the dignity and pride of the black race. Nevertheless, the equating of race-pride with blackness is complex and contradictory. While such a claim is a vindication of the race, it also disaffiliates itself from Africa and praises its ties to Western culture. At the same time, the Haitian revolution, the source of that race-pride, makes Haitians equal to whites.[9]

Racial categorisations, like racial meanings and the relationships between 'the races' in the United States have also changed over time. Thus, Mexicans who lived in territory that was subsequently conquered by the US were initially 'accorded the status of free white person'.[10] However, this status was by no means accorded to all Mexicans. People of Mexican origin were categorised as 'Other non-white' by the US census officials in 1930. In 1940 they were 'persons of Spanish mother tongue'. In 1950 and 1960 they were 'white persons of Spanish surname'. By 1970 they were 'persons of both Spanish surname and Spanish mother tongue', and by 1980 they were simply categorised as 'Spanish/ Hispanic'.[11] This group today is popularly considered a racial minority, and the Hispanic population of the US is treated as such for purposes of government affirmative action programmes.

Other groups in America, including not least the Irish, have also gone through shifts in racial categorisation and in socio-racial status. Thus, Irish immigrants today, many of whom may have experienced racial discrimination in Great Britain or elsewhere, become a definitive part of the US white racial majority in a novel (from the immigrant point of view) manner. The meanings attached to whiteness in America, for example, are not at all similar to those prevailing either in continental Europe, or indeed Ireland. As Ruth Frankenberg suggests:

> whiteness changes over time and space, and is in no way a trans-historical essence. Rather . . . it is a complexly constructed product of local, regional,

national, and global relations, past and present. Thus, the range of possible ways of living whiteness . . . is delimited by the relations of racism at that moment and in that place.[12]

As applied to the Irish in America today, this suggests that the experiences of this group continue to be shaped by their position in the racial hierarchy, newcomers from Ireland rapidly learn what whiteness means in America and capitalise upon these different meanings. This, in turn, means that they become part of the forces that shape the complex racial hierarchy of America, rather than being victimised by its system of race thinking and racial categorisation.

However, Irish immigrants have not always occupied such a privileged position in the social and political system of the United States. The origins of their present position can be traced to the nineteenth century when Irish immigrants underwent a shift from minority to majority status mainly by '[winning] acceptance as whites among the larger American population'.[13] The story of how the Irish became part of the US white racial majority is a history whose legacy crucially still shapes the position of Irish immigrants in the American racial order today.

NINETEENTH-CENTURY IRISH IMMIGRANTS AND THE UNITED STATES' RACIAL SYSTEM

The racialisation of Irish immigrants in nineteenth-century America has been well documented. Racialisation fixed on attributes like the bodies, occupations, religion and cultural practices of Irish immigrants, and suggested these were signs of immutable biological inferiority. In newspapers and popular magazines especially, the bodies of Irish immigrants were portrayed with simianised features, suggesting a direct link between the Irish and apes.[14] Irish mental abilities were also questioned. Thus, for example, the editors of *Harper's Monthly* wrote that immigrant pauperism, a trait associated with the Irish in particular, should properly be understood as 'mental pauperism'.[15] Brute-like bodies and limited intelligence, however, did make the Irish suitable, in the eyes of dominant sectors of American society at least, for occupations that were scorned by the white middle class. Thus, George Templeton Strong, a New York patrician Whig, described a crew of Irishmen who were sent to excavate his cellar as:

twenty sons of toil with prehensile paws supplied to them by nature with evident reference to the handling of the spade and the welding of the pickax, and congenital hollows in their shoulders wonderfully adapted to make carrying of the hod a luxury instead of a labor.[16]

H. Giles, a writer for the *Christian Examiner*, put the matter more bluntly when he wrote 'Irish means to us a class of human beings, whose women do our housework, and whose men dig our railroads'.[17] However, though the labour of Irish immigrants was wanted, there was concern about the impact of including them in American social and political institutions. Catholicism was taken as one sign of Irish inability to become good American citizens. Thus, Philip Gleason argued that 'it was generally accepted that Protestantism was the natural religious expression of the freedom-loving, independent-thinking Anglo Saxons, while Catholicism was best suited to the more servile.[18] 'Servile peoples', on the other hand, were believed to threaten American political and social institutions, which required participation from 'independent' and 'freedom-loving' individuals in order to function properly. Anti-Irish racism was also scientifically legitimated through an ethnological distinction between Saxon and Celt. This distinction was first institutionalised in Great Britain with the publication of John Pinkerton's works and, by 1860, a similar Saxon-Celtic dichotomy was taken for granted in the United States. Dr Robert Knox, a contemporary of racial theorist Count Arthur de Gobineau, suggested that:

> the effect of political ideology, system, or leadership is slight compared to the impact of 'race' upon government. The Celtic race, for instance, could never be made to comprehend the meaning of the word liberty. How then could the distinctively Anglo-Saxon concept of representative government ever be made workable among an American populace grown increasingly Celtic?[19]

James Nourse asserted that 'the key to the supremacy of England and America was that in those countries there were few Celts'.[20] An article in the in the *New York Independent* characterised the Irish immigrant as 'a creature with all the brutal passions and instincts of a man in the first savage state'.[21] American children learned in their geography classes that:

> New Zealand is emerging – Otaheite [Tahiti] is emerging – Ireland is not emerging – she is still veiled in darkness – her children, safe under no law, live in the very shadow of death . . . How is the wealth of Ireland proved? Is it by the naked, idle, suffering savages who are slumbering on the mud floors of her cabins?[22]

Not surprisingly, the result of such 'scientific' racialised imagery was that Irish immigrants often found themselves compared to Blacks in the America's racial hierarchy in the nineteenth century.[23] David Roediger summarises many of the reputed points of comparison between the two groups: nativist folk wisdom held that an Irish man was a 'nigger' turned inside out; a variety of writers suggested that the Irish were part of a dark race that was possibly of African descent; racial comparisons of Blacks and Irish were often flattering to Blacks, and Irish workers were associated with servile labour because they were sometimes used as substitutes for slave labour in the south.[24] Furthermore, there were indeed strong parallels between Black and Irish experiences and life circumstances. These included the fact that Blacks and the Irish often lived side by side in the teeming slums. Both groups were poor and often vilified. Both had experience of racial oppression and had been wrenched from a homeland.

They both did America's hard work. Members of neither group were ever likely to return home again. In 1829, Blacks and Irish were co-victims of a Boston 'race' riot.[25] For all these reasons, it was by no means clear that the Irish were considered 'white' by mainstream society in nineteenth-century America. Nativist opposition generated a political party that dedicated itself to the cause of political and social exclusion of these inferior immigrants. The Know-Nothings was one such party which was vehemently opposed to the integration of the Irish in the US political system. Known officially as the American Party, it developed as an offshoot of a secret patriotic society called the Order of the Star Spangled Banner. Dedicated to extending the naturalisation requirement to twenty-one years and to the exclusion of Catholics and the 'foreign-born' from political office, the Know-Nothings reached the peak of their influence in 1855 when they controlled six states (Massachusetts, Connecticut, Rhode Island, New Hampshire, Maryland and Kentucky) and sent some 75 representatives to Congress.[26] The US at this time had already shown itself more than interested in keeping Blacks and Native Americans marginalised and disenfranchised. The nativist movement suggested similar treatment might also become institutionalised and used against the 'foreign-born' and Catholics in particular.

THE IRISH AND THE DOMINANT RACIAL GROUP IN THE NINETEENTH CENTURY

Corcoran has argued that 'research on Irish immigrants is generally informed by either an assimilationist perspective or a pluralist perspective'.[27] How Irish immigrants became part of the dominant racial group in nineteenth-century America is most commonly explained by using the assimilation model. This model, developed by Robert Park in the 1920s, suggests that immigrants become progressively incorporated into the dominant culture through a combination of struggle, hard work and growing familiarity with the norms of the dominant culture. In a similar assimilationist vein, Thomas Sowell suggests that 'the Irish were the first great ethnic "minority" in American cities . . . they began at the bottom . . . with painful slowness, the Irish rose over the generations'.[28] However, a significant shortcoming of the assimilation model is its failure to treat racial difference as anything except as equivalent to cultural difference. Racial differences in this model, like the cultural distinctness of immigrant newcomers, are expected to wither away with time. However, in a society structured by racial hierarchies, this is often impossible. Omi and Winant cogently summarise the shortcomings of the assimilation model as applied to social groups that are considered not just cultural minorities but also racial minorities. They particularly suggest that distinctness from the white racial majority 'is often not appreciably altered by the adoption of the norms and values of the white majority'.[29] Assimilation as an explanation for how Irish immigrants challenged negative racialisation is, therefore, incomplete because it fails to theorise how race, not just culture, structured the Irish immigrant experience and settlement process.

David Roediger's work, however, does consider the role of racial stratification in explaining how nineteenth-century Irish immigrants challenged negative racialisation. Roediger suggests that Irish immigrants relied not just on growing familiarity with the dominant culture, and hard work, as is suggested by the assimilation model, but crucially also used the US racial system itself as a means to challenge their victimisation. Roediger suggests that the social and historical similarities between Blacks and Irish, combined with persistent attacks on the character of Irish immigrants by American nativists, spurred Irish efforts to distance themselves from Blacks so they would not share the fate of the Black minority of a caste-like institutionalised subordination. However, the existence of Black-Irish similarities meant that the primary basis from which the Irish could appeal for access to US constitutional rights, citizenship, jobs and housing was by insisting on their racial identity as 'white'. Thus, Roediger observes:

> Had the Irish tried to assert a right to work because they were Irish, rather than because they were white, they would have provoked a fierce backlash from native born artisans . . . [It was much easier] for the Irish to defend jobs and rights as 'white' entitlements instead of as Irish ones.[30]

This strategy for Irish advancement might have been unsuccessful had not others also invested in asserting that Irish immigrants were 'white' and were therefore entitled to certain privileges, even though their national origin remained subject to scurrilous comment. Roediger draws particular attention to the role of the Democratic Party in this regard. The Democratic Party asserted Irish immigrants' whiteness, not out of any particular concern for the Irish, but because as whites, they could vote. The size of the immigrant vote was very substantial indeed in the latter half of the nineteenth century. By 1845, for example, it has been estimated that one ballot in seven came from the foreign-born. Irish immigrants comprised a substantial portion of this group and their numbers continued to grow throughout the latter half of the century. In Philadelphia in 1850, for example, it has been estimated that 21 per cent of the population was Irish-born. In New York City in 1855, the Irish formed 28 per cent of the population and comprised no less than 34 per cent of the electorate.[31] The Democratic Party's championing of the whiteness of Irish immigrants was also part of a broader programme in which the Democrats 're-invented whiteness in a manner that refurbished their party's traditional links to the people'.[32] Omi and Winant connect this Irish immigrant history to a broad re-making of racial categories that took place in nineteenth-century America:

> Particularly during the nineteenth century, the racial category 'white' was subject to challenges that brought about the influx of diverse groups who were not of

the same Anglo-Saxon stock as the founding immigrants. In the nineteenth century, political and ideological struggles emerged concerning the proper classification of Southern Europeans, the Irish and Jews. Nativist opposition to the inclusion of these groups in mainstream white society was only effectively curbed by the institutionalisation of a racial order that drew the color line around, rather than within, Europe. By stopping short of racialising immigrants from Europe after the Civil War, and by subsequently allowing their assimilation into mainstream society,the American racial order was re-consolidated in the wake of the tremendous challenge placed before it by the abolition of racial slavery.[33]

This means that Irish immigrants in America in the latter half of the nineteenth century moved from minority to majority status within a newly reconstructed racial order. Irish immigrants actively participated in bringing about this racial reconstruction. Unlike Blacks and many any other racial minorities in the US today, they became part of the privileged white society. In the process, Irish immigrants also reinforced racial hierarchies as the 'American way', rather than looking upon it as something to be resisted and fought against. As newcomers to white society, nineteenth-century Irish immigrants developed a notorious record of mob violence against Black Americans. Irish immigrants, under the leadership of one Dennis Kearney, also led the fight against Chinese immigrants in California. Some Irish immigrant groups even suggested that Southern and Eastern European newcomers to the United States did not merit the legal rights associated with white racial status, since they were not 'white'.[34] The Irish also went on to prosper in the United States at this time to such an extent that 'Irish Catholics' are now ranked 'above the national average for all whites on a number of important socio-economic dimensions'.[35] This assessment, of course, reveals the tendency in much US writing to treat 'Irish' as synonymous with 'Catholic' which is obviously inaccurate. But Irish Protestants have clearly also fared well in the United States, though by some measures they did not fare quite so well as Catholics have done despite the historic strong anti-Catholic bias in the United States.[36] The continued privileging of whiteness in America which, as we have seen, the Irish themselves reinforced, has had a definite part to play in the successful social advancement of Irish Americans in recent decades. The bitterness of attitudes of other racial minorities towards the Irish in the US is the product of a long history which saw Irish Americans actively engaged in the victimization of the 'racially inferior' there.

NEW IRISH IMMIGRANTS AND RACIAL HIERARCHIES IN CONTEMPORARY AMERICA

Recent Irish immigrants in the United States find that their reception by minority and majority groups there is shaped by the history of earlier Irish immigrant action in relation to the US racial system. However, the legacy of that history is now being played out on complex new terrain. America is clearly undergoing rapid changes which are transforming social, political, and economic relationships between a wide variety of social groups and racial and ethnic minorities in the United States. De-industrialisation which is causing an increasing volume of manufacturing to be exported overseas, including Ireland and other parts of Europe, Asia, the Caribbean and Latin America, has created a declining middle class, widening income disparities, further erosion of union power and escalating informal and service sectors.[37] Attacks on social welfare programmes, and the retreat from commitments made to racial minorities in earlier decades, have also exacerbated social cleavages in the US.[38] At the same time, however, unprecedented numbers of immigrants and refugees, recently estimated at over eight million individuals, have been flooding into the US during the 1980s.

The fact that the vast majority of newcomers were Asian, Latin American and Caribbean, rather than European, fuelled racial and ethnic tensions. The concentrated settlement patterns of particular immigrant groups has heightened concern about their social and economic impact on US society. Thus six cities, namely New York, Los Angeles, Miami, Chicago, Washington DC and San Francisco, received over 42 per cent of all newcomers in 1987.[39] These concentrated settlement patterns have been maintained throughout the 1980s. In 1987 the immigration and naturalisation service began, for the first time, to fine employers who hired undocumented immigrants. Militarisation of the US-Mexico border was also substantially increased at this time. Immigrants increasingly now also became public scapegoats for a wide range of social and economic problems besetting US society.[40] Individual political leaders, including Governor Wilson of California, have capitalised upon anti-immigrant sentiment and gained political office through campaigning against the 'invasion' of the US by 'foreign immigrants'. These social forces have also intersected with, and in turn propelled, a new re-drawing of racial lines in the US in a complex fashion. Exactly where Irish immigrants fit into this re-drawn social hierarchy has yet to be established. Nonetheless, the 1980s has been characterised as a decade of 'racial reaction' in which white Americans have reacted strongly against demands for racial equality by the Civil Rights Movement. The arrival of Irish immigrants coincided with, and played a role in, this white racial reaction.

THE NEW IRISH AMERICANS AND WHITE RACIAL REACTION IN THE US IN THE 1980s

Omi and Winant suggest that white reaction against racial equality demands was enacted through a process of 're-articulation'. Re-articulation, they suggest, involves:

a practice of discursive reorganization or re-interpretation of ideological themes and interests . . . such that these elements obtain new meaning or coherence.[41]

Omi and Winant have suggested that in the US in the 1980s 'the forces of racial reaction . . . seized upon the notion of racial equality advanced by the racial minority movements and re-articulated its meaning for the contemporary period.[42] Racial equality was re-articulated in such a way as to preserve, and to even sharpen, the prevailing racial hierarchy. A 'white ethnicity revival' occurred which became one vehicle for conservative re-articulations of ideals of racial equality. Within this white ethnicity revival, various European-origin groups in America 're-discovered' their culture, history and roots, and suggested these deserved the same protective measures as those being extended, albeit for a brief time, to other racial minorities through programmes of affirmative action. However, the suggestion that white ethnic differences were equivalent to racial differences ignored the fact that racially differentiated groups are also ethnically heterogeneous. In addition to this, the focus of the Civil Rights demands centred, not on questions of benign varieties of culture, but on the fact that significant occupational, educational and income disparities generally do not exist between white ethnic groups in America – but they do exist between whites and racial minorities.[43] US understandings of the meaning of white ethnicity now are also commonly formed around the model of the third-generation white ethnics who have achieved middle-class status. Mary Waters has captured the difference between these white ethnics and racial minorities from other diverse ethnicities and different generations by arguing that 'the ways in which ethnicity is flexible and symbolic and voluntary for white middle-class Americans are the very ways in which it is not so for non-white and Hispanic Americans'.[44] But ethnicity is not symbolic for new Irish immigrants, either, in the way that it is for third-generation (and later) white Americans who spearheaded the white ethnicity revival. The relationship between contemporary white immigrants and later-generation white Americans, who are now re-articulating a conservative version of racial equality by galvanising white ethnicity, has yet to be theorized.

The white ethnic revival gave rise to a number of other forms of conservative re-articulation of demands for racial equality. For instance, once it became acceptable to speak of white ethnic difference as equivalent to racial difference, the idea of 'reverse discrimination' against white people emerged. This concept effectively 'appropriates the demand for equality presented by minority movements of the 1960s and stands it on its head'.[45] White ethnic concerns with 'culture' also enabled racist opinions to be expressed by cloaking them in a discourse of 'culture'. It was within this context, where notions of European ethnic difference were used to undercut demands for racial equality, that the arrival of new Irish immigrants was to play a role. The struggle to secure 'diversity immigrant' visas offers one visible example of the role played by the Irish in this field. The origin of the diversity immigrant visa struggle lies in the fact that 1980s' Irish immigration to America involved substantial numbers of 'illegals' who technically did not have the right to live and work in America. Prior to their arrival, Irish immigration to America was not that significant. The enormous Irish migration to America that began with the Famine had continued through the 1920s, but by the 1930s, Great Britain became the primary destination for a vast majority of Irish immigrants. By the 1970s, Irish immigration to America numbered less than a thousand a year. During that decade, people actually began returning to Ireland which was enjoying a period of unexpected, and short-lived, economic prosperity.

In the 1980s, as prosperity turned into recession, large-scale emigration to the United States re-commenced. It was at this juncture that the impact of a 1965 amendment to US immigration law became clear. In 1965, US immigration authorities abolished national origin quotas and opened up immigration to anyone with either immediate family ties or with a skill that was in demand in the US. But 1980s' Irish immigrants generally lacked family ties to America. Although some were skilled, the wait for legal permanent residence based on skill took years. The result was that most Irish immigrants in the 1980s entered the US on a tourist or short-term visa. Many overstayed their legal entitlement to do so and joined the ranks of America's 'illegals'. The suggestion that American immigration law essentially cut off the possibility of legal immigration from Ireland was voiced with increasing loudness at this time. As a result, Irish immigrants were among the first recipients of special immigration visas which were acquired by lottery in the late 1980s. First, there were Donnelly visas, named after their Congressional sponsor. The Donnelly programme provided for 10,000 visas annually for 2 years to be awarded by lottery to 36 countries whose numbers of immigrants to the US had decreased significantly as a result of the 1965 reform of the Immigration and Nationality Act.[46] Ireland was included in this list. The Donnelly programme was subsequently extended for a further 2 years and 30,000 more visas were granted under the Legal Immigration Amendments Act of 1988. A small number of Irish also won Berman visas in a one-time lottery for 20,000 visas, for which residents of 128 nations applied. The Morrison visa lottery, however, which was enacted as part of the Immigration Act of 1990, provided the greatest boon for Irish immigrants. Morrison visas were distributed under a 'Diversity Immigrants' programme that had two phases. The first, the transitional phase, lasted for 3 years and provided 40,000 visas a year to countries that were 'adversely affected' by the 1965 Immigration Act. A minimum of 40 per cent of these visas were reserved for Ireland. The second, the permanent phase of the programme began in 1995 and provided 55,000 visas a year for nationals of 'low admission states'. Ireland is likely to remain a low admission state for the foreseeable future. Limited numbers of non-European countries, including Japan, also benefited from the transitional phase of the diversity immigrants programme. Non-European beneficiaries, unfortunately, did not include Haitians fleeing Duvalier and Haiti's subsequent military rulers. Neither did it include refugees from Central America nor Central Americans who were fleeing war, repression and violence at home. However, increasing numbers of non-European countries will benefit from the permanent phase. The diversity visa programme did not reduce the numbers of visas available for immigrants with family ties or desired skills; instead, total numbers of available annual immigrant visas were increased. Nonetheless, racial minority communities sarcastically characterised the programme as a 'white list' and labelled it 'affirmative action for the Irish'.[47] These characterisations are significant for a number of reasons. First, they point to the very visible role of Irish immigrants in the 1980s in securing the diversity immigrants programme. Walter Jacob notes that there was 'universal agreement . . . that the Irish . . . community was primarily responsible for the creation of the diversity immigrants section of the Immigration Act of 1990'.[48] Second, the characterisation of the diversity immigrants programme as 'affirmative action for the Irish' pointedly refers to the way that an initiative aimed primarily at white Europeans, and calling itself a 'diversity' programme, plays into dominant white reactions against efforts to achieve racial equality for other much harder-pressed minority groups. The linking of new Irish immigrants to this latest articulation of white reaction positioned them as insensitive, if not hostile, to concerns of US-born and immigrant racial minorities. Thus, it is important to examine how the diversity immigrants programme came to pass.

In raising critical questions about the programme, I do not intend to suggest that the Irish should not have benefited from the liberalisation of immigration controls at this time. Neither do I mean to imply that all Irish immigrants knew about, or fully agreed with, the strategy used for securing these visas. Nonetheless, the strategy that was used ended up being widely seen as representative of the racial politics of the Irish immigrant community as a whole, with troubling implications for relationships with racial minorities in the United States. Testimony submitted by the Irish Immigration Reform Movement to Congress about the need for such a programme to assist Irish immigrants drew on and extended, rather than challenged white reaction against racial minorities. Thomas J. Flatley, for example, submitted:

> Despite the basic injustices of our current immigration law, they [Irish immigrants] continue to come, as they are unable or unwilling to believe that this land of the free which welcomed and harbored so many of their forefathers, would persist in giving them the cold shoulder. And yet, like those other nationalities, documented or otherwise, I am proud to state that despite all the burdens and difficulties they endure, the rank and file of these young Irish men and women have steadfastly presented themselves as models of all the virtues that we in this society seek of our citizens: honesty, a commitment to hard work and a strong

desire to be productive and law abiding. Furthermore, in a modern society like ours, burdened by drugs and other illicit activities, these young people, their status nonewithstanding, have focused their energies constructively. Let it be emphasized that the many thousands of young Irish people we have read about as new arrivals did not come to break any laws. They came here for a better life. And, if given the opportunity to participate as members of this society, I am convinced, based upon their education and work experience, that their contribution to the betterment of the United States will be even greater than that of the generations which came before them.[49]

Flatley makes a creditable case for Irish visas. But how he builds that case is significant because of the way in which he plays upon white beliefs and fears. We see that he first appeals to a long history of Irish immigration to America as grounds for creating a diversity immigrants programme that will enable Irish immigration to continue. Already a subtle racial element is at play here. The US has a history of allowing in whites, but not racial minorities, as acceptable immigrants who will become good Americans. White groups like the Irish have a long history of immigration to America, partly because their entry was not barred due to race. Chinese Americans, by contrast, cannot appeal to a history of forefathers who were 'welcomed and harbored' as the basis for gaining special visas because the Chinese were racially excluded from even entering the US between 1882 and 1943.[50] Flatley's testimony also glosses over the undocumented status of the Irish in the US, as if it were but a minor detail that needs to be corrected. This ability to minimise the illegal status of Irish immigrants relies upon, and affirms, a white racial identity in the US. Undocumented racial-minority immigrants, by contrast, have been vilified by the media and in Congressional debates as criminals. This is because their undocumented status intersects with the majority tendency to presume that racial minorities are natural criminals anyway. In San Diego in California, for example, a candidate for county supervisor referred to undocumented Mexicans and Central Americans in the following terms:

> Nowhere else in San Diego County do you find the huge gangs of illegal aliens that line our streets, shake down our schoolchildren, spread diseases like malaria, and roam our neighbourhoods looking for work or homes to rob. We are under siege in North County, and we have been deserted by those whose job it is to protect us from this flood of illegal aliens.[51]

The idea of government desertion of the people has resulted in formation of vigilante groups who have attacked, shot at and, in some cases, killed Mexicans who sought illegal entry into the United States. Clearly, public perception of the meaning of 'an undocumented immigrant' is differentially shaped by race in a way that is to the advantage of Irish and other white immigrants. Flatley attributes a set of desirable virtues to new Irish immigrants, which he makes consonant with 'American' values. Whether or not Irish immigrants possess these virtues is immaterial; more important is the fact that, in the US, it is seen as credible that white people would have such virtues. The happy convergence between putative Irish immigrant moral qualities and 'American' values is also connected to a long racial history here that sees racial minorities as not properly 'American'. Thus, a white immigrant today is still considered a virtual American (which brings its own problems, but is advantageous) simply because of his or her colour. Flatley suggests that the virtues attributed to Irish immigrants will serve as a corrective to the drug use and illegal activity that pervades America. It is racial minorities who are associated in the public mind with drug use and crime; thus, Irish immigrants, their illegal status not-withstanding, apparently will serve as a corrective to US social problems that are blamed on racial minorities.

Flatley's message finally uses effective politicking. Yet much of the effectiveness has to do with the white racial anxieties to which the speech successfully appeals. Rather than challenging racist beliefs, like the assumptions that whites make and, indeed, define good Americans, or that racial minorities are the source of social disorder that must be challenged by virtuous white people, Flatley implicitly affirms these beliefs as a way to build a strong and convincing case for legalising white Irish immigrants. His success, and the success of the Irish Immigration Reform Movement more generally, is evident by the fact that Irish immigrants to the United States in the 1980s and 1990s were able to legalise their status through diversity immigrant visas. But, at the same time, they were widely perceived as willing to use their status as members of the white race in a manner that yet again reinforced and legitimated US racial hierarchies. The struggle to secure the diversity immigrants programme is the most high profile of new Irish immigrant political activities, and the most visible in its use of race. However, we must also enquire how white race has shaped new Irish immigrant access to jobs, housing and education, as well as how it re-shapes immigrant Irish identity in a direction toward white 'American-ness'. When exploring these questions, it is important to grasp how race structures every level of experience in the US. Even undocumented Irish immigrants, who are greatly exploited, still enjoy an occupational advantage relative to other racial minority groups and other undocumented immigrants. This situation is captured by Corcoran's notion of 'unequal illegals'. Thus Corcoran writes:

> Irish construction workers . . . occupy a relatively privileged position in the informal economy . . . Similarly, Irish workers in the restaurant and bar trade occupy the highest-paid positions as waiters/waitresses and bar tenders.

> While they deal with the customers, the kitchen and janitorial jobs are reserved almost exclusively for Central and South Americans. Even in domestic work, Irish immigrant women report that an American family enhances their prestige by having a white nanny rather than a black nanny in their service.[52]

Racial minorities do, of course, occupy positions in economic sectors above those of Irish illegals in the informal sector, but these minorities still find their opportunities are affected by racism in a way that is not the case for whites in that sector.[53] Race thinking similarly structures new Irish immigrants' access to housing and education. Discussion of the diversity immigrants programme, therefore, offers only a preliminary example of the substantial amount of research that remains to be done about how recent Irish immigrant lives and actions become refracted, and have consequences, within the US racial order. The conditions of new immigrant lives must be treated with seriousness in arriving at an analysis of recent Irish immigrants within the US racial order. For example, how did circumstances of new immigrant lives inform the drive for diversity immigrant visas and shape the manner in which the campaign was organised? Being a new immigrant is often difficult. According to one Executive Director of the Irish Immigration Center in Boston: 'Many people, when they come new to this country, they're anxious to get a job, they're anxious to get housing, and they've bitten off an awful lot'. New immigrants also often have to accept jobs that are below their educational and skill levels, just as they often have to live in overcrowded housing. In addition to culture shock, loneliness and depression are common because most immigrants do not have close relatives in America. When problems do occur, immigrants have nowhere to turn. Being 'undocumented' compounds these difficulties. Undocumented immigrants are afraid to make friends, or to talk honestly about themselves, in case the immigration service learns of their unauthorised presence and deports them. At work, many undocumented immigrants suffer blocked mobility, exploitation, underpayment and sexual harassment. Educational opportunities are also blocked to illegal immigrants unless, of course, they lie about their status. Accessing health care, even in cases of serious emergencies, also becomes fraught with difficulty. When they are victims of crime, undocumented people rarely report it. Simple things become difficult. As a woman who had lived for seven years in Boston without papers told a reporter, a Green Card would mean:

> opening a bank account, getting a credit card, basic things like that. It would mean knowing you can leave the country and not worry about coming back. [My husband and I] have two children who were born here, and my parents unfortunately have seen very little of them.[54]

Linda Dowling Almeida's survey of 247 Irish newcomers in New York City in the late 1980s showed that those without documents had difficulty getting such basics as a phone, a driver's license and credit.[55] Almedia's survey also highlighted the extent to which Irish newcomers had 'insulate[d] themselves within a migrant community', with fewer than 20 per cent of the sample having any American friends.[56] Though they had established a way of life in the United States that was unavailable to them in Ireland, Irish newcomers nonetheless resisted 'the notion that their adopted country will become their permanent home'.[57] How do these immigrant circumstances interact with the US racial system (where whiteness confers systematic advantage, even while Irishness confers stereotyping, immigration confers insecurity but new possibilities, and undocumented status confers endless problems)? Furthermore, how can new Irish immigrants come to understand this interplay in a critical manner? The difficulty for anyone who is socially positioned as a racial majority to grasp the experiences and perspectives of racial minorities is captured by Peggy Mackintosh, who states:

> I have come to see white privilege as an invisible package of unearned assets which I can count on cashing in each day, but about which I was meant to remain oblivious.[58]

The fact that neighbourhoods, workplaces, schools and playgrounds remain heavily divided by race further ensures that immigrants who are designated as white will rarely learn in-depth and critically about America's racial minorities through daily experiences. The media does not promote such an understanding either. All these circumstances make it difficult for Irish immigrant newcomers – who are often preoccupied by securing basics like jobs and housing – to critically understand the interplay of race in America, and where they fit in. Yet, a critical understanding is vital for the future of the Irish in America.

IRISH IMMIGRANTS AND RACIAL MINORITIES IN THE UNITED STATES: WHAT WILL BE THEIR RELATION?

Toni Morrison has argued:

> It doesn't matter anymore what shade the newcomer's skin is. A hostile posture toward resident blacks must be struck at the Americanizing door before it will open . . . [the] most enduring and efficient rite of passage into American culture [is]: negative appraisals of the native born black population. Only when the lesson of racial estrangement is learned is assimilation complete. Whatever the lived experience of immigrants with African Americans – pleasant, beneficial or bruising – the rhetorical experience renders blacks as non-citizens, already discredited outlaws. People think, we had to leave home. We had to come here, we had to set up new roots, set up new networks and stuff. We had to get a job, get accommodation. How come so many Black people can't get jobs? They grew up here, they went to school here. And it's basically a lack of knowledge about the system that these young African American people have grown up in, and the situation that prevails, that means they don't have access to as many jobs, or to similar jobs, or that they don't have the same access we would have, even though we are immigrants. And that's to do with colour. A lot of people don't understand that, have no perception of that.[59]

Cora Flood, Anti-Racism and Immigrant Outreach Co-ordinator of the Irish Immigration Center recently stated:

Our people are one of the groups that caused pain to Black people. They're one of the groups, they're not the only group. I've spoken with African Americans who left Boston because of the Irish. I've spoken with African Americans who were denied jobs because of the Irish. . . if you're part of the problem, you have to become part of the solution.[60]

There are many reasons why Irish immigrants have to learn about, and develop positive relationships with, racial minorities in America. For one thing, Irish newcomers share some social and economic circumstances with other racial minorities, though this situation could change. Irish, Philippine, Caribbean, Black and Latin American women do much of America's child-care and care for the elderly. Irish nurses, alongside Korean, Filipina and Black nurses, staff urban hospitals all over the United States. Irish men lay bricks and erect drywall with Central American, Caribbean and Black men. Irish newcomers stand in line at the immigration office with Asians, Africans, Caribbeans and Latin Americans. The groups share common problems associated with the status of immigrants, including especially 'illegal' immigrants. Can these common circumstances translate into the development of a politics that does not re-inscribe racist hierarchies here? Ireland's national history has points of commonality that also overlap with other racial minority histories. These points of commonality are worth exploring even while we acknowledge that racial positioning keeps the Irish separated, in critical ways, from racial minorities (both immigrant and US-born) in America. Concern with suffering, injustice and inequality that is rooted in understanding Ireland's history, should easily translate into concern about US racism 'as a very key human rights issue'.[61] If Ireland's history includes the diaspora, past and present, then Ireland and the Irish abroad share responsibility for racial stratification in America. This does not make the Irish particularly worse-off compared to other nationalities, but it does suggest that 'if you're part of the problem, you have to become part of the solution'.[62]

Becoming part of the solution is important for today's immigrants who inherit the troubled racial legacy of earlier Irish immigrant generations in America. Today's immigrants must be particularly careful not to repeat nineteenth-century history by taking jobs to which long-time racial minority Americans still do not have access because of racism, or by participating in negative appraisals of Blacks (and other minorities) in order to advance more quickly into the American middle class or in other ways.[63] America is already beset by deep racial strife (of which the 1992 Los Angeles 'riots' were only one example) to which new immigrants must be sensitive. Improved understanding of racial minority concerns is also important because Irish immigrants enter into relationships and marriages with racial minorities. Although this phenomenon has not been formally documented in the US, Marie McAdam notes that 'the largest group of inter-racial marriages among immigrants in Britain is between Irish women and Afro-Caribbean men'.[64] Most Irish immigrants in inter-racial relationships in America drop quietly out of Irish institutions, activities and political groupings, rather than be faced with bewilderment and racism by their co-nationals. But what is the cost to the Irish community in America of such dropping out? And what place do mixed marriages, and racially-mixed children, have in the Irish diaspora so eloquently invoked by President Mary Robinson in her February 1995 address to the Oireachtas.[65] What is the place of the '(small) indigenous black Irish population . . . [that] is not usually recognised' in the Irish nation?[66]

Today's Irish immigrants in America can repeat nineteenth-century history by viewing their interests as opposed, or unconnected, to those of racial minorities. Or they can envision and create new democratic relationships that include minority communities through transforming their assigned roles in the US racial structure. Scholarship that explores Ireland and the Irish in relation to the complexities of racial hierarchies in different locations and time periods will generate the critical knowledge necessary for such a transformation to occur.

ACKNOWLEDGEMENTS

I would like to acknowledge the Irish Immigration Center in Boston for their inspiring and on-going work which has sought to build bridges between new Irish immigrants and other racial and ethnic groups in the city. Perhaps the model they offer will be copied by many others. Particular thanks to Lena Deevy and Cora Flood for friendly cups of tea and allowing me to interview them. Thanks to Jill Esbenshade, Alison Heather, Michael Omi, and Alberto Perez, for reading drafts of this chapter and providing critical feedback. The shortcomings are all my own.

NOTES AND REFERENCES

1 David Roediger, *The Wages of Whiteness: Race and the Making of the American Working Class* (London and New York, Verso, 1991).

2 Saskia Sassen, *The Mobility of Capital and Labour* (Cambridge University Press, 1988); Saskia Sassen, 'Why Migration?' Report on the Americas, xxvi, no. 1, July, 1992; Jim Mac Laughlin, 'Ireland: An "Emigrant Nursery" in the World Economy', *International Migration*, xxvi, no. 1, 1993, pp. 149–70.

3 Michael Omi and Howard Winant, *Racial Formation in the United States* (New York and London, Routledge, 1986), p. 66.

4 Ruth Frankenberg, *White Women, Race Matters: The Social Construction of Whiteness* (Minneapolis, University of Minnesota Press, 1993), p. 1.

5 ibid., p. 1.

6 Joe Feagin and Clairece Booher Feagin, *Racial and Ethnic Relations*, 4th ed. (Eaglewood Cliffs, New Jersey, Prentice Hall, 1993), pp. 6–7.

7 Martha Giminez, 'US Ethnic Politics: Implications for Latin American', *Latin American Perspectives*, vol. 19, no. 4, p. 15.

8   Carolle Charles, 'Transnationalism in the Construct of Haitian Migrants' Racial Categories of Identity in New York City', in Nina Glick Schiller, Linda Basch and Cristina Blanc Szanton (eds.), *Towards a Transnational Perspective on Migration: Race, Class, Ethnicity, and Nationalism Reconsidered*, Annals of the New York Academy of Sciences, vol. 645, pp. 108.

9   ibid., p. 108.

10 Omi and Winant, *Racial Formation in the United States*, p. 75.

11 Yen Le Espiritu, *Asian American Panethnicity: Bridging Institutions and Identities* (Philadelphia, Temple University Press, 1992) p. 114.

12 Frankenberg, *White Women, Race Matters*, p. 236.

13 Roediger, *The Wages of Whiteness*, p. 137.

14 L.P. Curtis, *Apes and Angels: The Irishman in Victorian Caricature* (Washington DC, Smithsonian Institute Press, 1971), p. 29.

15 Dale Knobel, *Paddy and the Republic* (Middletown, CT, Wesleyan University Press, 1986), p. 86.

16 George Templeton Strong, *The Diary of George Templeton Strong: The Civil War, 1860–1865*, (eds.) Allan Nevins and Milton Hasley Thomas (New York, Macmillan, 1952), p. 342.

17 H. Giles, 'The Present Condition of Ireland', *The Christian Examiner* 45 (July 1848), pp. 113–4.

18 Philip Gleason, 'American Identity and Americanization', in William Peterson et al., (eds.) *Concepts of Ethnicity* (Cambridge MA and London, Bellknap Press, 1980), p. 91.

19 Cited in Knobel, *Paddy and the Republic*, p. 109.

20 Cited in Reginald Horsman, *Race and Manifest Destiny* (Cambridge MA and London, Harvard University Press, 1981), p. 170.

21 Ronald Takaki, *Iron Cages* (New York and Oxford, Oxford University Press, 1990), p. 116.

22 B. D. Emerson, *The Academical Speaker: A Selection of Extracts in Prose and Verse, From Ancient and Modern Authors, Adapted for Exercises in Elocution* (Boston, Richardson, Lord and Holbrook, 1830), pp. 261–2.

23 Takaki, *Iron Cages*, p. 149.

24 Roediger, *The Wages of Whiteness*, p. 133.

25 ibid., p. 134.

26 Gleason, 'American Identity and Americanization', p. 71.

27 Mary Corcoran, *Irish Illegals: Transients Between Two Societies* (Westport, Connecticut, and London, Greenwood Press, 1993), p. 15.

28 Thomas Sowell, *Ethnic America: A History* (New York, Basic Books, 1981), p. 17.

29 Omi and Winant, *Racial Formation in the United States*, p. 22.

30 Roediger, *The Wages of Whiteness*, p. 148.

31 Marjorie Fallows, *Irish Americans: Identity and Assimilation* (Englewood Cliffs, N.J., Prentice Hall, 1979), p. 32, p. 34.

32 Roediger, *The Wages of Whiteness*, p. 140.

33 Omi and Winant, *Racial Formation in the United States*, p. 64–5.

34 Michael Novak, *The Rise of the Unmeltable Ethnics* (New York, Macmillan, 1971).

35 Feagin and Feagin, *Racial and Ethnic Relations*, p. 111.

36 Donald Harman Akenson, *The Irish Diaspora* (Belfast, Institute of Irish Studies, 1993), p. 243.

37 Paul Ong, Edna Bonacich and Lucie Cheng, 'The Political Economy of Capitalist Restructuring and the New Asian Immigration', in R. Ong, E. Bonacich and L. Cheng (eds.) *The New Asian Immigration in Los Angeles and Global Restructuring* (Philadelphia, Temple University Press, 1994), pp. 3–31.

38 ibid., Omi and Winant, *Racial Formation in the United States*.

39 Alejandro Portes and Ruben Rumbaut, *Immigrant America: A Portrait* (Berkeley, Los Angeles, Oxford, University of California Press, 1990), p. 32.

40 America's Watch, *Brutality Unchecked: Human Rights Abuses Along the US Border with Mexico* (New York, Human Rights' Watch, 1992); Maria Jiminez, 'War – in the Borderlands', *Report on the Americas*, xxvi, no. 1, July 1992, pp. 29–33.

41 Omi and Winant, *Racial Formation in the United States*, p. 173.

42 ibid., p. 114.

43 Richard Alba, *Ethnic Identity: The Transformation of White America* (New Haven and London, Yale University Press, 1990), p. 5–10.

44 Mary Waters, *Ethnic Options: Later Generation Ethnicity in America* (Berkeley, University of California Press, 1990), p. 156.

45 Omi and Winant, *Racial Formation in the United States*, p. 129.

46 Project Irish Outreach, *Immigrating USA: A Guide for Irish Immigrants* (New York, Catholic Charities, 1990), p. 32.

47 Patricia Folan Stebben, 'US Immigration Law, Irish Immigration and Diversity: Cead Mile Failte (A Hundred Thousand Welcomes)?' *Georgetown Immigration Law Journal*, vol. 6, December 1992, p. 766.

48 Walter Jacob, 'Diversity Visas: Muddled Thinking and Pork Barrel Politics? *Georgetown Law Review*, vol. 6, n. 10, June 1992, p. 298.

49 House Committee of the Judiciary, Subcommittee on Immigrants, Refugees, and International Law, Reform of Legal Immigration: Hearings on H.R. 5115 and S. 2104, 100th Cong., 2nd Sess., 7 and 16 September 1988, p. 274.

50 Sucheng Chang, *Asian Americans: An Interpretive History* (Boston, Twayne Publishers, 1991).

51 Leo Chavez, *Shadowed Lives: Undocumented Immigrants in American Society* (Fort Worth, Texas, Harcourt Brace Jovanovich College Publishers, 1992), p. 17.

52 Corcoran, *Irish Illegals*, p. 185.

53 Joe R. Feagin, 'The Continuing Significance of Race: Anti Black Discrimination in Public Places', *American Sociological Review*, vol. 56, pp. 101–16.

54 Philip Bennet, 'Visa Lottery for Irish Ends This Month', *Boston Globe*, 17 March 1993.

55 Linda Dowling Almeida, '"And They Still Haven't Found What They're Looking For" A Survey of the New Irish in New York City', in Patrick O'Sullivan (ed.), *Patterns of Migration* (Leicester and New York, Leicester University Press, 1992), p. 217.

56 ibid., p. 208.

57 ibid., p. 207.

58 Peggy Mackintosh, *White Privilege and Male Privilege: A Personal Account of Coming to See Correspondence Through Work in Women's Studies*, Working Paper no. 189, Wellesley College Center for Research on Women, (Wellesley, Ma, 1988), p. 1.

59 Toni Morrison, 'On the Backs of Blacks', *Time Special Issue: America's Immigrant Challenge*, vol. 142, no. 21, Fall 1993, p. 57.

60 Lena Deevy, Executive Director, Irish Immigration Center, interviewed by Eithne Luibheid, 17 January 1995, Boston MA.

61 ibid.

62 ibid.

63 Cora Flood, Anti-Racism and Immigrant Outreach Co-ordinator, Irish Immigration Center, interviewed by Eithne Luibheid, 27 January 1995, Boston, MA; Morrison, 'On the Backs of Blacks'.

64 Marie McAdams, 'Hidden From History: Women's Experiences of Emigration', *Irish Reporter*, 13, 1st Quarter, 1994, pp. 12–3.

65 Mary Robinson, 'Cherishing The Irish Diaspora: An Address to the Houses of the Oireachtas', reprinted in the *Boston Irish Reporter*, March 1995, pp. 18–9.

66 Gretchen Fitzgerald, 'Repulsing Racism: Reflections on Racism and the Irish', *A Dozen Lips* (Dublin, Attic Press, 1994).

11. Traditionalism and Homelessness in Contemporary Irish Music

Kieran Keohane

What lies, or stirs, at the heart of emigration? What is at the heart of the matter? To begin to answer this, we need to go on a journey, a journey to the heartland – into the heart of the Irish emigrant, and the heart of Irish culture, to try to find out what makes us tick. What is it that makes our hearts leap high with joy, or sink and ache with heavy melancholy? What scalds the emigrant heart, pierces and skewers it? What makes it glow with pride, flutter with delight, giddily stand still and leave us gasping? What makes our emigrant heart swell, thicken and overflow with emotion? If we are to try to understand the culture of contemporary Irish emigration, then we must take this journey into what Yeats calls 'the deep heart's core'.[1] For we *feel* emigration, with the fullness of our hearts. This fullness and overflowing, the pulsing excesses of pain and pleasure, sorrow and delight, joy and terror, loneliness and belongingness, is the heartbeat of Irish emigration. Our journey will be a search for the unifying principle, the spirit, of this heartbeat.

I will show that the inspiration at the heart of Irish emigrant culture is a profound and irreconcilable ambivalence. On the one hand, the culture of emigration is animated by desire to be anchored, temporally and spatially, by the particularity of tradition. We desire security and familiarity in the face of fearsome forces of globalisation that uproot, scatter, and threaten to disembody us. On the other hand, what we fear about the processes of globalisation – loss of coherence of place and time, homelessness – we simultaneously desire. We feel that emigration liberates us from the tyranny of the local, from the narrow-mindedness of the particular, that as Marx famously argued, the cosmopolitanism of modernity 'rescues us from the idiocy of rural life'.[2] The emigrant heart is torn: torn between love of the local and fear of the global and, simultaneously, hatred of the particular and desire for the cosmopolitan. In this fullness to overflowing of conflicting emotions, the heart is torn assunder and, paradoxically, sutured together again in the same moment by the double action of ambivalent desires. Thus, we experience the anguish of emigration as the thing that it is impossible to live with, the heart-break that is killing us, and also as the very thing that keeps us with our hearts in our fists, the source of our vitality, our *jouissance*. (Jouissance or 'enjoyment' is a term employed by the French existential psychoanalyst Jacques Lacan to designate the source of animation of the subject, the feeling of being alive, which often takes the form of pleasure in unpleasure.)[3]

On our journey to the heartland, we will begin with what is near at hand.[4] To take emigration's pulse, as it were, we will attune to the rhythm of contemporary music. We will approach music as a pathway, a superficial manifestation of an underlying malaise of the spirit; a symptom, as it were, of a deeper trauma. My choice of musical markers to guide us toward this trauma will be somewhat arbitrary and limited, as choice unavoidably implies that it be. I have written elsewhere of Shane MacGowan and the Pogues and, though they are not treated at length here, they are central to the rhythm of the text and they will have the final word.[5] Similarly, John Waters' excellent interpretation of the deep processes of Irish culture through an analysis of U2 helps to form part of the map for our journey, and our paths will cross on several occasions.[6] My choice of music is not arbitrary, though, insofar as we are interpellated on this occasion. Our interest in journeying to the heart is called for by, firstly, a song about a particular road, the N17, that links the heartland to the international airport; the Saw Doctors' road from Tuam, to U2's Zooropa, as it were, and by two albums which explicitly designate themselves to be 'from the heart' and 'of the heart', namely, *A Woman's Heart* and *Irish Heartbeat*.

'THE STORY OF SHATTERED LIFE CAN BE TOLD ONLY IN BITS AND PIECES' (RILKE)

A lot of odd things seem to come out of Tuam: Johnny Rotten's dad; Tom Murphy's plays; Supermac's burger chain, and the N17, the road to Shannon airport sung about by the Saw Doctors and now on the Irish Leaving Certificate syllabus. Mary brought me the Saw Doctors. I was living in Toronto, she and Robby were driving around North America in an old Chrysler pick-up truck. Mary makes a career out of being the Irish diaspora; London, Sidney, San Francisco, New York, work a few months, travel, work again, off again. This was her third North American tour. She was concentrating on the mid-west. I was a stop-over. 'The Sawdoctors are brilliant craic,' she said, 'they've really got the spirit.'

We headed for the Vic, my local. The barman's name is Dermot, from Dublin, no papers. He used to deal in Amsterdam but he had to get away. He's been in Toronto five years. He'd love to go home because his ma is sick, but if he went, 'there'd be no gettin' back, Jack', so he stays. He's playing Black 47, Celtic rappers, on the CD and the pints are flying. Another friend of Mary's is telling us how she worked for nearly a year for the Ontario Provincial Police, using a false name, illegal herself, and she working for the department responsible for deporting illegal aliens! Carlos gets a kick out of that. He does maintenance at the Canada Immigration building. They've been writing him for the past six months. He sends the letters back unopened with 'Carlos has returned to Ecuador' written on the envelope. Fernando and Souryan are getting into the craic. I'm legal, a 'Landed Immigrant', I got my papers three months ago. I'm Canadianised and I love it. I find myself, as usual, explaining figures of speech to Don and Jimmy. I called them to come out, to show off my friends from home, to show them off to my friends from home. They tell me that they like to get into the spirit of being Irish for the evening. For me, the spirit of the evening is very mixed. I'm enjoying recollecting my Irishness with fellow ex-pats. I'm also enjoying my state of transcendental homelessness, in the company of multicultural cosmopolitan travellers, we're at home anywhere, friends with everyone. My feelings are ambivalent. Simultaneously enjoying my rootlessness while also enjoying recollecting my roots, resenting having to (try to) explain the joke to my Canadian friends, and at the same time reassured that they'll be around next week when this little Paddy-fest is over.

What can we say about the Irish spirit these days? To begin with, how are we to get a handle on such a thing as 'spirit'? It's not an impossible question. In fact, it's a very ordinary one, pursued conversationally by people when we are trying to make sense of our lives and our times. Talking about the Irish spirit, we might start, as Wittgenstein suggests, with the language games we play with an entity like 'spirit'. Wittgenstein calls 'language and the actions into which it is woven, the language game'. We 'make up the rules [ie. what we mean by something] as we go along'. Wittgenstein's concept of 'language game' provides us with a way of grasping the many different meanings which something like 'spirit' may have: 'Phenomena have no one thing in common which makes us use the same word for all, but they are all related to one another in many different ways.' The different meanings which we give to something bear 'family resemblances' to one another, Wittgenstein says, and thus we can build up a picture of the phenomenon, develop our understanding of it, by exploring the reflective equilibrium amongst various meanings which bear family resemblances to one another.[7] In other words, rather than looking for the clear, singular definition – for there isn't one – we can approach the spirit with questions like: What inspires us? What do we aspire to? What spirits are we under the influence of, intoxicate us, make us numb? What lifts our spirits? What spirits haunt and terrify us? Getting a bead on the spirit of the times, the *Zeitgeist*, is what we're always trying to do. We try to read and interpret 'the signs of the times' so as to enable us to make sense of the forces that animate and vivify our lives at a particular moment, the forces that bring us together, that push us apart, that make us friends, enemies or strangers to one another, that make us feel at home in the world and contented with ourselves, or alienated and embittered, or that make us, more often than not, many of these things at the same time. Freud calls this currency of forces the playing out and unfolding of social antagonism, 'the libidinal economy' or 'the economy of desire' in society.[8] By this, Freud means that our emotions are always more or less mixed and conflictual, paradoxical and ambivalent. Social relations and the entire edifice of culture, 'civilization' for Freud, is infused with this tension, and thus the spirit of society is always more or less troubled and turbulent. But there is an 'economy' to this mixture, by which Freud means there is a discernible system of patterned distribution arising from the work of our mental apparatus to manage conflicting emotions, and it is the art of analysis to bring this economy into view. So let's begin our exploration of the libidinal economy in Tuam with the Saw Doctors and see what spirits animate their music.

'COME BACK PADDY REILLY TO BALLYJAMESDUFF'

The Garden of Eden has vanished they say / but I know the lie of it still /
just turn to the left at the cross of Finea / and stop when half way to Cootehill.
'tis there you will find it, I know sure enough / . . .
Come back Paddy Reilly to Ballyjamesduff / come home Paddy Reilly to me.

The Saw Doctors are lads, or should I say, they play at being a pack of lads from small-town Ireland. They sing about the itchiness of FCA uniforms, the camaraderie and rivalry of inter-parish hurling and football matches, pride in the green and red county colours of Mayo, watching the arses of the girls from the convent school on their way up to Holy Communion, and they sing about the painful inevitability of emigration at the end of Irish teenage innocence. Their music is Irish country and western rock 'n roll; boom-diggy-diggy, boom-diggy-diggy, 'Jamsey, throw us the keys of the Cortina for a half an hour. I'm after shiftin' yer wan!' Boyzone meets the Fianna Fail Cummann, it's the sort of stuff hip young Irish hate to love, mostly because it's a bit too close to home. But it plays a crude melody on Irish heartstrings none the less:

Well, the ould fella left me to Shannon / was the last time I travelled that road / and as we turned left at Claregalway / I could feel a lump in my throat / as I pictured the thousands of times / that I travelled that well worn track / and I know that things will be different / if I ever decide to go back / And I wish I was on that N17 / Stone walls and the grasses green . . .'[9]

The Saw Doctors articulate one polarity of the economy of desire in the Irish spirit: the desire to be connected with the local and the familiar. They voice the desire for the certainty of knowing every twist and turn in a road that always leads towards home; the desire for the strength and security of sturdy stone walls that protect us, hold us within and keep the infinity of the rest of the world outside; the desire for innocence, for fresh green grass. The Saw Doctors' music is inspired by desire for an existential reconciliation with the various parts of ourselves from which we feel separated and alienated by the processes of growing up, modernisation and emigration. Desire for unity and integrity of subjective identity when the process of individuation demands that familial bonds are torn asunder; desire for a feeling of solidarity, for a sense of belongingness to a collective, when modernisation unravels the fabric of traditional life and ensures that things will be changed and gone the next time we look for them; desire for a sense of historicity, for coherence of being in time and place when unimaginable forces suddenly send you hurtling across the globe into places where your shirts are shamefully out of style.[10] And the other side of this desire is a fear and a hatred of that which stands between desire and its object – fear and hatred of what is not familial, common to us, and of our earth. The Saw Doctors' hero is travelling alone, 'with just my thoughts and dreams', fearful and closed to the differences he encounters. He perceives the world as 'filthy' and 'overcrowded'.[11] He is open to no one, despite the throng, 'there's no one to talk to in transit' about 'the muddled up problems of living on a foreign soil', so he sits alone and dreams of the green fields and stone walls of Tuam.

We have in the Saw Doctors some of the elements of an Irish proto-fascist traditionalism: the uncritical valuation of all that is connoted by 'blood, race and soil', a response to historical and political social and emotional complexity, not in terms of a reflexive and adaptive growing openness to the world, but in a retentive/defensive attitude. A retreat to simplicity, the simple 'natural' truths of order in the home world. Familiarity. Let's have nothing strange here! A well-worn, well-known road in life; Mother behind us and Father(land) to drive us. Solid stone walls to surround and protect us. We'll wear the uniform and give our allegiance to the institutions of benign dictatorship; the Christian Brothers' school, the Local Defence Force and the Catholic Church. What's 'out there' is an Other, alien world, filthy and overcrowded, it has nothing to say to us and we refuse to converse with it. The construction of a world of 'dirty articles' can have sinister undertones. It can become, or it can be made into, an occasion for a social hygiene crusade. As I heard it expressed in a bar in Galway one night, 'a bit of ethnic cleansing wouldn't go astray, if we were up to the job!'[12]

But of course I'm being unfair, for all we have, for the most part, in the Saw Doctors' communitarian traditionalism is the expression of desire for an ease to existential anxiety, reconciliation of the chaos and complexities of modern life by the (re?)constitution and imposition of an order of unity and simplicity. While the Saw Doctors are a far cry from the extreme forms of this desire (fascism and ultra-nationalism), that are presently resurgent from Russia through Bosnia and into the heartland of the EU, they do express the stirrings of this nostalgic desire in an Irish idiom. Such desire should be seen for the moment in terms of potentiality, albeit a sinister potentiality, desire which could be mobilised by a conservative or reactionary political project which would seek to resist change and expunge difference, projects which would seek to protect the sanctity of the Irish family from 'foreign' influences like divorce and feminism, which would be intolerant of 'strangers coming over here and disrupting our way of life', and 'dirty' travellers 'overcrowding' our parishes and townlands.

A nostalgic yearning for an Irish lost Eden of Tuam (an earlier generation of crooners felt the Garden was in nearby Ballyjamesduff) is the predominant spirit animating the Sawdoctors' music, but there are also traces (though I stress traces) of an ambivalence that may provide a buffer to extremist articulations. For a start, there is a playfully blasphemous and sacrilegious streak to the Sawdoctors. The official function of the institutions of the Catholic Church, communion and confession, are subverted and re-articulated as sites of erotic fantasy and provide occasions for flirtation. On the other hand, this blasphemous eroticisation of Catholic ritual is haunted by sin and guilt ('Oh the thoughts and dreams that I had of her / would take six months in confession').[13] The risk that should accompany any real subversion of the normative order is alleviated always by the promise of confession, penance and ultimate atonement with the omniscient and omnipotent Father. Thus it is not subversive at all, but rather affirmative of the ultimately benevolent totalised order of the Catholic Church. Nevertheless, it might be argued that the catholic, that is to say, the universal/ promiscuous/permissive nature of this order would make it somewhat resistant to the elements of ascetic fundamentalism in fascistic discourse. But Irish Catholicism has historically proved no different from the peasant Catholicisms of Bavaria, Poland, Italy and Spain in its romance with the Fascist project of the Kingdom of God on Earth.

The evident xenophobia of the desire-given symbolic expression in the music of the Saw Doctors is not so apparent on closer examination either. The pain of the 'N17' song stems not so much from the problems of the encounter with Otherness and difference; the Sawdoctors' Irish emigrant is to a large extent impervious, indifferent to the Other. The Other's foreign world is reduced; it exists in its entirety as a dirty external object. The greater pain is the confused pain of betrayal. It is, after all, his father (a symbolic representation of distant emotionless discourses of economic and political 'realities') that drove him to the airport and dropped him there to face the world alone, and his mother (a symbolic representation of the nurturing culture which failed to prepare him for this) is at home with Gaybo on the wireless making the dinner for the next generation of naive fledglings who will be betrayed in their turn. Alone and betrayed, he loses himself and protects himself in the nostalgic fantasy world of the daydream, but he isn't stupidly lost in this fantasy, he knows that it's 'in vain'. He is disillusioned, free of the fantasy insofar as he recognises it as fantasy, he is reminiscing of things and times that are lost and gone, for good, as it were. For with their loss, he is free of them in the sense that, for the first time, he can choose to take them as happy memories or leave them. The decision is his: 'For I know that things will be different / if I ever decide to go back'.

The mood of the Irish spirit that is here as an underlying trace in the Saw Doctors, masked, as it were, by the noisy, superficially jovial, back-slapping and yahooing of Irish country and western culture, is melancholy. Melancholia is that state of the spirit, described by Kristeva[14] and others, as the deep existential depression and sadness that accompanies the realisation that even nostalgia isn't what it used to be. Whereas nostalgia, a yearning for a fantasised lost Eden, is one of the sustaining moods of the post-modern condition, melancholia describes the moment when the nostalgic yearning for a lost Eden comes to realise that Eden was just a fantasy, that Eden is lost and gone forever, and with the dissolution of this fantasy comes profound sadness. There can be no homecoming, for home is changed, utterly – in fact there never even was a home. Melancholy mourns for this existential loss, but is not necessarily debilitated by it. In fact, life begins anew when dreamy nostalgia begins to give way to melancholia, for after the wake life goes on. If there can be no return to Eden, then at least we are free to begin to imagine a future.

I think that this is what my friend Mary meant when she said that the Sawdoctors had the 'spirit', that they have a touch of melancholy about them. But it's only a touch, a trace. The impossibility of the desire to return to Eden is only barely glimpsed, but even as it is just glimpsed it is too painful to be confronted: a traumatic loss that they (we) are incapable of symbolising and expressing, exploring and transcending. Instead, it is masked and repressed, sublimated into the forms of carry-on that we call 'brilliant craic'. Brilliant craic is a florid symptom of a deeper, real crack that runs through the Irish spirit, a crack we desire desperately to suture, but cannot. The craic, at least allows us to carry on, and this is why as Lacan says, 'we love our symptom more than ourselves.'[15]

Let's go further west now, into the heartland of the Irish cultural renaissance. We'll go into Galway and try to catch a session with Dolores Keane or Sharon Shannon in Neachtan's or Rosin Dubh's, The Quays or Busker Brown's. Not that they'd be seen dead in those places! (Well, Neachtan's maybe, still.) Galway is home to a new phenomenon, the 1990s' equivalent of the Suburban Lounge Bar of the 1960s, namely the 'superpub', the post-modern 'traditional Oirish', faux pub, with a quarter-mile bar, festooned with 'repro' antique fittings and bric-a-brac. Like a holodeck on Star Trek, behind the wood panelling on these *Enterprises* you would more likely find blinking lights and plasma-flow gizmos than any substantial history. 'Established 1855' over the front door means that the electrician turned on the power yesterday evening at five to seven. The Traditional Irish Pub is now a commodity that can now be bought, literally, by the tonne, packed in crates and shipped out to Barcelona, Frankfurt and Saint Petersburg, where punters are gasping with thirst for a sup of genuine 'Oirish' craic.

Places like Dingle, Doolin, Miltown Malbay and Achill come and go as mini Meccas, where devout pilgrims seek to commune with the spirit of Irish Tradition, but Galway is the Rome of the Irish cultural renaissance. Jaded modern Ireland in search of a bit of the 'real thing' find it in Galway (occasionally) if they hit the right spot, and they're away again, rejuvenated. Down to Galway for the weekend, for the bit of culture, and for the craic, of course. Galway is the silicon valley of Ireland's culture industry; home to the Arts Festival, Macnas, Druid and Michael D. Higgins (socialist, socialite, would-be poet and government Minister for Culture). If not employed directly in the production of culture, people are gainfully occupied purveying craic (freely, or otherwise available in most pubs, or so the signs reading 'Ceol, Ol agus Craic' might lead one to believe). Ancillary fields include hostelling, busking, full-time boozing and, less frequently, working at Northern Telecom, Digital or a Supermac's, of which there are several in Galway. And there is the University, where one may even study culture, with field-trips downtown at the weekends when everyone piles in from Dublin, Cork and the rest of the world. Galway is the place of pilgrimage for the Celtophile equivalent of the à-la-carte Catholic; a few grand pints and a bit of the auld diddle-dee-da, or for the more middle-brow, a nice hand-knit and the latest Tom Murphy at the Druid theatre. And, of course, *A Woman's Heart* on cassette or CD for the journey back to Dublin.

A Melancholy Irishwoman's Heart

A Woman's Heart is a two-album collection by Ireland's premier women musicians, Mary Black, Maura O'Connell, Sinead Lohan, Sharon Shannon, Francis Black, Dolores Keane and others. Critically acclaimed and a 'chart-topper', along with *Riverdance* and the like, it is a showcase of the talent at the heart of the Irish cultural renaissance. The title track, 'A Woman's Heart' is a new song, but it sounds familiar, a melancholy lament on a traditional theme: 'Alone, my heart is so alone / as only a woman's heart can be'. Mother Ireland, left behind by her children, the lovelorn spinster left on the shelf by a prudish priest-ridden culture; women as lovers and mothers separated from their men and their sons. Irish women's culture has historically been a culture of abandonment, inspired by loss and destitution, a culture of being left behind minding the house. Women are neglected while men are 'out' – out making history fighting the Brits, out in the fields and the factories making money, out foreign, making out as best they can and, of course, very often, out in the pub. Women's culture is haunted by the ghosts of absent men. Here is Mary Black's contribution to *A Woman's Heart*, 'Sonny': 'Sonny, don't go away / I'm here all alone / Your daddy's a sailor, he never comes home / Night's are so long / feelings go on . . .' and so on.

What is celebrated here is a moment of Irish women's culture that corresponds to a long-standing traditional stereotype: the Irish woman as the long-suffering victim of abandonment. The Irish mother, keening for Sonny, her child/lover leaving her, alone in her frustrated bed, and the Bantry Girl's Lament for her young love, who like the beau of her friend up the country is gone 'to the shores of Amer-i-kay'. What are we to make of this contemporary re-inscription of a familiar trope? I would suggest that it may be interpreted as being inspired by a conservative desire. Most obviously this is a desire to conserve power. Power resides in tradition; that is, tradition constitutes an inheritance, a repertoire, utilised in playing power games. The discursive manipulation of themes of abandonment has been the currency of Irish women's power. This power is manifest in the unique idiom of emotional management in Irish culture, namely the 'guilt trip'. For example, on the practice of Irish mothering, Tom Inglis shows that the Irish Catholic mother made men dependent on her by doing everything for her sons, while at the same time, by limiting and controlling the physical expression of her affection. Irish men are socialised to be emotionally awkward and inarticulate about their feelings.[16] It follows that Irish men are ill-prepared for living independently from Mother, and incapable of expressing and working out the emotional basis for relations changed by maturation and/or emigration. In comparison to 'all that she has done for him', he 'owes her an awful lot', and there is always 'so much he wants to tell her' but somehow, not surprisingly, he's 'never able to find the words'. Consequently, the Irishman has always some unfinished business with his mother and a sob of abandonment will awaken his guilt and quickly bring him to heel. *A Woman's Heart* is a powerful piece of work precisely for this reason; it is primarily an aestheticisation of Irish women's traditional power. At a deeper level, *A Woman's Heart* is an expression of a desire for the conservation of the security offered by the familiar, even when what is familiar is painful and heart-scalding. The melancholy spirit languishing in an Irish woman's heart, at least as it is expressed here, is the spirit that takes pleasure in unpleasure, the latest expression of a worn and hackneyed Irish woman's *jouissance*, resigned to a melancholic eroticism; the horr-orgasm of the victim/martyr. The necrophilic ecstasy in the agony of the 'Auld Woman' down by the glenside singing 'Glory O, to the (dead) bold Fenian men', and the 'Fine Old Woman' who used to have 'Four green fields' until 'the strangers' came to 'plunder rape and pillage', and her children's 'wailing cries filled the very heavens / and her four green fields ran red with their blood'.

Like the Saw Doctors, *A Woman's Heart* is inspired by a traditionalist nostalgia. The romance with the ideal of the rural community, desire of simplicity and natural order, and the melancholy eroticism voiced by Irish country and western singers Maura O'Connell, Frances Black and Eleanor McEvoy, are Irish idiomatic expressions of neo-conservatism in American global culture, expressed symptomatically as the virulent contagion of the C&W aesthetic. Cowboys and 'gals' re-inscribe traditional gender roles eroded by feminism. Blacks are again erased from American history, the West was won by the white man, goddamnit! How could we have forgotten that? And line-dancing, the ritualistic re-enactment of *gemeinschaft*, traditional order, mechanical solidarity, evokes a spirit of belongingness based on enforced similarity – look the same, move the same, think the same. It is the manifestation of a dense – thick, if you like – conscience collective.[17] Line-dancing is the civilian equivalent of the parade ground military ballet. The resurgence of fascism in Europe is complimented in America by the hegemony of the Republican right and the Moral Majority and, thanks to MTV Country, we are also happily marching/dancing along to the post-modern military two-step.

ABANDONING THE CULTURE OF ABANDONMENT

It is interesting that it is this moment of suffering by loss and abandonment that is chosen to be celebrated on *A Woman's Heart* when alternative moments of the spirit of Irish women are available in the traditional repertoire, or at least imaginable. The moment of self-assertive, raunchy eroticism of Irish women's culture is a minor key represented by Mary Coughlan on the second album of *A Woman's Heart*, drowned out by the wail of abandonment. Women's active role in Irish revolutionary struggle might be voiced, for instance, but here women are mournful onlookers. Dolores Keane, about whom a reviewer in London's *Time Out* once said, 'when God sings in the shower She sounds like Dolores Keane', sings 'The Island', a beautiful romantic anti-violence song written by Paul Brady:

> . . . and we're still at it in our own place
> still trying to reach the future
> through the past
> trying to carve tomorrow from a tombstone . . . but hey,
> don't listen to me, this wasn't meant to be a sad song
> we've sung too much of that before
> right now I only want to be here with you
> til the morning dew comes falling
> I want to take you to the Island
> and trace your footprints in the sand
> and in the evening when there's no-one around,
> we'll make love to the sound of the ocean.

In *Unfinished Revolution* Christy Moore responded to what he identified as a conservative moment in Brady's poetry and, more generally, in the re-articulation of the 1960s' principle 'make love, not war' by such groups as the Peace People in Northern Ireland. Christy Moore's response, 'The Island', is a critical parody of Brady's song, where dreaming of making love on the beach is rudely awakened by the disruptive juxtaposition of images of continuing violence and injustice. Christy sings of prisoners in Long Kesh dreaming of making love on the beach some day, and of women being strip-searched in Armagh and Brixton jails. To an articulation of 'peace without politics' as it were, Christy Moore responds 'No justice, no peace'. With 'Moving Hearts', Christy Moore tried to awaken an Irish spirit to be critical and reflexive and move it to encompass environmental politics, feminism and awareness of global issues. Now, as Christy becomes a Grand Old Man of Irish culture, or a Boring Old Fart, depending on your perspective, it is the spirit of Brady's island that is nostalgically re-animated by Keane in *A Woman's Heart*.

The moment in melancholy where sadness expresses its wisdom, only a trace in the Saw Doctors, is more developed here. *A Woman's Heart* knows that Eden is lost and gone forever. That is not to say that an Irish woman's Eden is the same as the Saw Doctors' Eden of Tuam, nor even that an Irishwoman's Eden is a lovely place. Eden is home, and home is where the heart(h) is, the familiar, what we are used to, what means something to us. An Irishwoman's Eden, expressed in *A Woman's Heart*, is the familiar feeling of abandonment, a feeling that Irish women are used to, that means something to other Irish women who know the feeling also. The loss of the familiar is painful and frightening, even if what is familiar is the pain and despair of abandonment. Abandoning the culture of abandonment is extremely difficult, for it is haunted by the fear that with the loss of a culture of abandonment an Irishwoman's heart is left with an even more terrible emptiness. Something, however terrible, can be less fearful than nothing at all. The re-inscription of the familiar theme of the culture of abandonment in *A Woman's Heart* is a response to the anomie experienced by a contemporary generation of Irish women whose traditional roles as mothers and housewifes are breaking down, and who find themselves confronted with a myriad of emerging roles that have not as yet developed traditions that make sustaining them bearable. In the face of normative confusion, an Irishwoman's heart finds a moment of relief in traditionalism.

We can distinguish a moment of conservative traditionalism from working within a tradition and, as Mouffe says, tradition forms us and makes all political action possible.[18] What we find alongside traditionalism in *A Woman's Heart* is an effort to transcend the strictures of a traditionalism, the conservative identification with a culture of abandonment, not by abandoning that tradition (melancholia knows that isn't even possible, let alone desirable) but, rather, by re-modelling it so that it may sustain contemporary Irish women in emerging roles. Sharon Shannon's contribution to *A Woman's Heart* gives us an intimation of the possibility of re-working tradition. She takes one of the most traditional of Irish traditional instruments, moreover, a man's instrument, the button accordion or melodeon, and plays with it, innovates, decorates, begins with familiar traditional tunes and then runs away with them and makes them strange, brings them back to us transformed but still familiar. She doesn't give us 'the pure drop', the sup from the Irish holy grail that we think we all need so badly; she gives us a heady spirit of her own concoction instead. Derrida says that we cannot leave the Master's house, that there is nothing outside the text, no Eden to return to, or new place outside the discourses of tradition and history to which we can escape in order to make a fresh start. Rather, we have to live within the master's house, de-construct it and re-build it. This is precisely what Sharon Shannon is doing. She is using the master's tools and the master's language to take apart and re-model the master's house of Irish tradition so that it is more accommodating for Irish women.

Sharon Shannon's mischievous poltergeist breathes new life into the master's instruments and makes the furniture dance in his house; she also opens doors for angrier and more potent spirits. Sinéad O'Connor takes possession of the body of an Irishwoman's culture of abandonment. Sinéad picks up on the intimation of anger in the sorrowful culture of abandonment, but rather than mourn her abandonment by her lover, and her betrayal by her father, she refuses the sackcloth and ashes and rises, as she says, 'like the Phoenix from the flames'. She turns the discourse of the victim into the discourse of the survivor. The form seems unchanged, but the familiar woman of Irish tradition has a new and disturbing demonic intensity. In Sinéad O'Connor, the Irishwoman's spirit manifests itself by disrupting the normalising panoptical gaze of the surveillant collective.[19] Foucault has shown that power takes the form of the abstract gaze of society, internalised by the individual such that we 'subject ourselves'. In other words, we participate in turning ourselves into disciplined, normal subjects to the generalised gaze of the collective. Sinéad O'Connor refuses to look how she is supposed to look, she refuses to sound as she is supposed to sound. She is the spectre of 'the madwoman in the attic' of the master's house run amok. Sinéad represents the disruption of tradition by the intrusion of the discourse of the marginalised and repressed. She is the hysterical woman who refuses the normalising imperative to contain her emotions and get a grip on herself, or to reconcile the chaos of her fears and desires and to resign herself to the numbing mediocrity of being a traditional Irish woman. She expresses this, not only in her performance of subjectivity, her schizoid and emotionally disturbed (and disturbing) public personae, but musically in her abrupt shifts of tone, jumping octaves, changing pitch from a whisper to a roar, from fury to tenderness, expressing irreconcilable emotional polarities in the same utterance.

The public condemnation of Sinéad O'Connor's hysteria, her excess ('she's too much', 'over the top', 'out of control', and so on) is more than mere begrudgery. It is an expression of a conservative backlash against her bucking the traditional normative order that has parallels with the fate of Annie Murphy, the ex-lover of the former Bishop of Galway, Eamonn Casey, and mother of his son. Nothing at all unusual about that, or nothing unusual in her subsequent neglect by His Grace. Annie Murphy is a typical Irishwoman/ victim of abandonment. What is unusual though, is her public disclosure, her articulation of abandonment as unjust and her demand for recognition. Annie Murphy is reviled for 'making too much' of her status of victim of abandonment. She should have been content to be melancholic, sadly the wiser, resigned to her pain. Consequently, she is systematically placed outside the discourse of an Irishwoman's culture of abandonment ('she's a bloody loud-mouthed American'), whereas Casey himself is quickly rehabilitated in the Irish tradition: ironically he becomes the victim of persecution, exiled to the shores of South Amer-i-kay, and the hero, 'a bit of a boyo, more power to him!' and 'a dacent man with human weaknesses like the rest of us'. What Sinéad O'Connor shares with Annie Murphy is a refusal to harmonise, to settle down and fit in, to become part of the beautiful pattern of tradition.

Traditionalism scavenges on the carcass of tradition, or keens like a Banshee for its passing. Its intellectually rationalised and institutionalised counterpart is the study of culture as autopsy. *Riverdance* and *River of Sound* are among the most recent exercises in such ghoulishness and profanity. By contrast, Sinéad O'Connor is a vampire feeding on the body of a living tradition and seducing it with the promise of eternal life. Sinéad's expression of the emotional cracks in an Irishwoman's heart represents a deep existential ambivalence that cannot be quieted and smoothened into a beautiful tradition. If beauty is to be understood as the resolution and containment of conflicting desires in the continuity and harmony of pattern, and Sublime as the disruption of the pattern, a hole punched through to infinity by resurgent elemental conflict, Sinéad O'Connor's contribution to *A Woman's Heart* is less beautiful than it is sublime.[20] She disrupts the harmony of tradition by expressing something that the tradition cannot accommodate. The emotional cracking she expresses is a symbolic representation of opening the windows in the house of tradition to let in a breath of fresh air and to let some of the spirits stifled inside soar out ecstatically. She shows the contingency and mutability of the tradition, she shows that it is open to change, that it is still alive.

THE SONG OF HEART'S DESIRE

Let's explore this crack in the Irish spirit and the ambivalence of desire more thoroughly. One of the very best evocations, in an Irish idiom, of the sublime, teeming vortex of desire, is surely Van Morrison's rendition of 'My Lagan Love' in *Irish Heartbeat* (Morrison and the Chieftains, 1988). The song begins with a poiesis of the desired object: 'Where Lagan streams sing lullabyes / there blows a lily fair'. The object(s) of desire emerge, take form, fade mirage-like, to re-emerge transformed: woman, fair and virginal, yet richly sexualised, symbolised by the lily with its connotations of purity, its associations with Easter, the horror of the crucifixion and mystery of the resurrection, and equally associated with the blossoming perennial fecundity of spring and the pagan, carnal eroticism in the lily's resemblance to the vulva. The purified/eroticised object of desire is also a maternal object, connoted by the 'lullabyes', and clearly more than simply 'mother' but also (m)Other Nature (the streams, the wind, flowers) and also, unmistakably, Mother Ireland, the Nation. And here, desire, that has to this point been articulated in the register of the feminine, merges with the discourse of the father: to do one's duty, to fight and die for the Fatherland, for the cause, symbolized again by the green, white and orange of the Easter lily/flag of the Republic and the Easter rising (rebellion), a resurgent potency sanctified by Christ's rising from the tomb.

So many objects of desire are brought to light and slip away from view again, so much is desired and so much eludes desire. Desire is boundless and knows no limit. It can be focused on one or several objects, from the carnal to the ethereal, in varying degrees of intensity, simultaneously. Desire is mobile and insatiable, and insatiability, as Durkheim observed about the human condition, is a sign of morbidity.[21] Desire's insatiability is our sickness unto death, symbolised here by the trace of death (twilight, night) attaching to the object domain of desire: 'the twilight's gleam is in her eye / the night is on her hair'. Our desire will be the death of us. We can't live away for love of home, but there's no life worth living at home. The insatiable desire for unity and reconciliation with the object of desire from which we are separated, the elusive or indifferent or forbidden lover, mother, nature, nation, renders us lovesick, enslaved and the objects of history: 'And like a lovesick lenashee / she has my heart in thrall. / No life have I, no liberty / for love is Lord of all'. The object of desire enslaves us, but we love our enslavement as it keeps us in touch with the object we desire.

And yet, though we desire our enslavement, our being bound to the familial, our tradition, our native soil, our nation, we also desire freedom from them: individuation, rootlessness, liberty. The song goes on: 'And often when the beetles horn / has lulled the eve to sleep / I steal into her sheeling lorn / and through the doorway creep'. Here, we have a representation of the desire of the child (emigrant) to return in search of reconciliation with the parental dis-courses of tradition and place; the desire of the secret lover or stealthy revolutionary awaiting a chance that may never come. Most clearly, perhaps, it is a symbolic representation of the voyeuristic desire to watch the forbidden sexual act, (lighting the fire) and especially the desire to view the 'primal scene' of the parental copulation. 'There on the cricket's singing stone / she makes the bogwood fire / and sings in sweet and undertone / the song of hearts desire'. The desire to witness the primal scene, the act of our creation, is a desire articulated from an impossible, disembodied gaze of pure identity – spirit existing prior to human conception. It is the desire to be an angel witnessing its own incorporation in human form. It is also the desire of pure reason, to view the world from the hypothesised fantasy of the Archimedian point; to see with a God's eye view, with unencumbered objectivity the sheer fact; to have unmitigated proof. This dream of reason is our modern secularised religion. What is expressed here is the trace attaching to reason of the desire for the sacred in the liberal secular discourses of modernity: our desire for rootlessness, to be the disembodied gaze, to be above the affairs of the flesh. Reason frees us from passion: the feelings, pleasures, ecstasies and yearnings, the disappointments, terrors and tortures of ordinary life. It is a symbolisation of our desire for a state of transcendental homelessness; our desire to be of a race of angels.

To be present at the primal scene is the thing that is most desired and most feared. It is desired as it would constitute the absolute confirmation of the integrity of identity. It is feared, for to be present at the primal scene would entail death; to exist as pure gaze prior to incorporation would be in-human. Pure identity, the integrity of the spirit, reason, comes only at the cost of our alienation from the world. We feel nothing. The warmth of the fire, the familiar smell of turf, the sweet, soothing music are separated from us. We can only watch them from a distance. The angel's gaze is terribly lonely – life seen from the outside, through the cottage window, from the corner of the room, under the cold illumination of the microscope. Thus, our desire for the transcendental homelessness of the angel is terrifying, for the death that this entails may be a fate worse than life; to be painfully, eternally always too 'out of touch', too far away from the warmth of the homefires. Our hearts' desire is profoundly ambivalent. We want to be bound to the object of our desire and, simultaneously, we want to be above it. Our mixture of desire and horror, the profound ambivalence that we have toward our primal scene, is what Morrison expresses so eloquently in 'My Lagan Love / The song of heart's desire'; he articulates desire as broken and tortured, torn between voracious ravening for consummation with (M) Other, nature, nation, lover, all simultaneously. To consume, to fuck, to be fucked by, to negate (the distance between) the subject and the object desired and, to be a magnificent, alien creature of reason, elevated from all that squalor, to soar like a lonely angel above it.

ANGELS AND CREATURES MADE OF CLAY

Patrick Kavanagh's 'The Great Hunger' is a tremendously powerful poetic evocation of the awakening of desire to transcend the constraints of Irish tradition.[22] Kavanagh hungers to be a modern angel, to live the life of the mind, to be a free spirit giving timeless witness through his art to the eternal beauty and truth of life. But to his dismay his feet are bogged down in the stony grey soil of Monaghan. He cannot fly. Time stands still. Instead of an angel, there is a mechanised scarecrow, fumbling in the mud gathering potatoes. 'Watch him, watch him', Kavanagh exclaims in desperation, 'That man on a hill whose spirit / is a wet sack flapping around the knees of time'. The spirits that might soar here are yet 'crows gabbling over worms and frogs, gulls like old newspapers, blown clear of the hedges, luckily'. The spirit of the Irish peasant is caught by 'the grip of irregular fields' the brambles and thorn bushes. He cannot imagine 'that back of the hills love was free'. In the crushing, stagnant monotony of Irish rural life in the 1940s the spirit 'darts like a frightened robin' through an occasional opening, but 'in the gap there's a bush weighed with boulders like morality'. Too tied to the earth, a life that is 'half a vegetable' the spirit is repressed and distorted, torn out and thrown away:

> Nobody will ever know how much tortured poetry the pulled
> weeds on the ridge wrote
> Before they withered in the July sun.
> Nobody will ever read the wild, sprawling, scrawling mad
> woman's signature
> The hysteria and boredom of the enclosed nun of his thought.
> Like the afterbirth of a cow stretched on a branch in the wind
> Life dried in the veins of these women and men:
> The grey and grief and unlove,
> The bones in the backs of their hands,
> And the chapel pressing its low ceiling over them.

Nostalgic traditionalism idealises the peasant's world, imagines the peasant's world as where we may drink from the holy grail of the authentic. The travellers stop their cars and gape over the banks into his fields:

> There is the source from which all cultures rise,
> And all religions,
> There is the pool in which the poet dips,
> And the musician.
> Without the peasant base civilization must die,
> Unless the clay is in the mouth the singer's singing is useless

Kavanagh knows that this cup of everlasting life is full of clay and cowshit, and that if you drink it, you will surely choke. Kavanagh has enough clay in his mouth. He wants to spit it out so that he can speak like Apollo and not in a thick-tongued mumble.[23] So 'He rubbed the dust off his knees with his palm, and then / Coughed the prayer phlegm up from his throat', and made his way to Dublin.

'WHEN THE ANGEL WOOS, THE CLAY HEEL LOOSE HIS WINGS'

Kavanagh's hunger to be an angel drags his arse to Dublin. But to his dismay, rather than flying high, he finds himself flapping clumsily around the bars with the literati. He still cannot fly, but the problem is not only that his heels are in the clay, but that his wings are too big. Paradoxically, he discovers that he must both clip his wings and become a better creature of the flesh before he can be really angelic. This is Kavanagh's dilemma in 'On Raglan Road', as sung by Van Morrison on *Irish Heartbeat*. He has to come to terms with irreconcilable ambivalent feelings. He wants to get away from the earth and speak with the voice of an angel, and yet the angel is aloof and passionless and has nothing of substance to say.

> On Raglan road on an Autumn day
> I saw her first and knew
> that her dark hair would weave a snare
> that I may one day rue
> I saw the danger, yet I walked
> along the enchanted way
> and I said let grief be a fallen leaf
> at the dawning of the day.

Is the woman, the object of his desire, the muse, the spirit who inspires his poetry, or is she the mortal woman on the street? She is both. The muse is the mortal woman on the street. Unless he gives himself over to the seduction of earthly passion, Kavanagh can never be angelic. He has to pursue earthly corporeal love, because the unique and peculiar way in which his spirit is repressed and distorted in traditional holy Catholic Ireland is in the idiom of repression and containment of emotions grounded in sexuality. If the normative regulation of sexuality in Irish peasant morality form the boulders that crush him, the brambles and thorn bushes that entangle him and the clay that bogs him down and chokes him, he must work his way through these if he is ever to fly. The enchanted way is the path where angels fear to tread; the path through the world of passion. 'On Grafton St in November, / we tripped lightly along the ledge / of a deep ravine where can be seen / the world of passion pledge'. Kavanagh knows that to be truly an angel he must be fully of the flesh. The angel must live life ordinarily, in the streets of the city amid the mundane passions of other ordinary people, and achieve something there that raises him above the mundane. To be an angel, a man must dance lightly on a tightrope over the abyss of his own mediocrity.

The object of Kavanagh's desire is simultaneously the woman in the street, and the muse – the angel who doesn't live in the lowly life at street level at all, the angel who led him away from the garden in Monaghan. Kavanagh conceitedly thinks that he speaks with the voice of such an angel. 'I gave her the gifts of the mind / I gave her the secret sign / that's known to all the artists who have / known true Gods of Sound and Time'. He deceives himself that his poetry elevates him over the mediocrity of ordinary life and that he communes with the Gods, but it does not free him. As well as the muse of poesy, he should be pursuing a creature made of clay, for unless he can be successful at being fully human, in profane, incarnate human love, his attempts to fly with the angels on the wings of poesy are doomed. The reams of poetry he produces will be fatuous and pretentious. Flying with the angels he will always be reminded of his clay Achilles heel; that he has never felt love or lived passionately. Reminded of this, he will lose his wings and come crashing back to earth.

> On a quiet street where old ghosts meet
> I see her walking now away from me
> so hurriedly my reason must allow
> that I have wooed not as I should a creature made of clay.
> When the angel woos, the clay heel loose his wings
> at the dawning of the day.

When the angel (the muse) seduces him away from the world, it is then that the clay heel loose his wings. Great poetry cannot be written by the peasant with his mouth full of dung, nor by the passionless angel so far removed from it all. Poetry is written by the man strung out between Heaven and Earth, struggling to free himself from the Earth. But if he flies too far from the Earth, wooed by the angels, it is then that he loose his wings. His clay heel – the bit of him that grounds him, that ties him to place and time, the part of him that is not Godly, but Earthly, vulnerable and weak – is what gives the rest of him wings. What dawns on Kavanagh 'at the dawning of the day' is, that as Nietzsche puts it, 'you must have chaos in you if you are to give birth to the dancing star'.[24] Chaos is the ambivalent desire to be both at home, grounded by tradition, and simultaneously to be homeless and transcendent of tradition. And what is the spirit that enables him to dance on the tightrope between Heaven and Earth? Mephistopheles, the Earth spirit, the spirit of chaos. The fallen angel who walks the Earth; Satan, the prince of darkness, who is also Lucifer, the bringer of light.

> I have spoken with the tongue of an angel,
> I have held the hand of the devil
> but I still haven't found what I'm looking for . . . (U2)

Bono knows Kavanagh's dilemma; the working out of this ambivalence, the chaos of the desire to be both angelic and creatures made of clay, is what inspires U2's musical odyssey. The dancing star that is U2 is born of desire to give witness to the *zeitgeist* and still be in touch with Irish roots. This is the chaotic desire of a creature of clay that aspires to be angelic, and the angel that aspires to be a creature of clay. Rootlessness, transcendental homelessness, to live in the stratosphere of stardom, or to be a Zuropean, to have 'gotten over' one's (problem with) Irishness and Irish tradition, to be post-modern (that is to have a post-national sense of identification), is still existentially unsatisfying. These are the themes animating U2's work since *The Joshua Tree*, especially *Achtung Baby* and *Zooropa*. But rather than go over ground already covered by John Waters[25] and others, I want instead to draw out the connection between Kavanagh's ambivalence, his (impossible?) desire to be simultaneously both an angel and a creature made of clay, by visiting Berlin with the angels of Vim Venders' 1990 film *Wings of Desire*.

Wings of Desire tells the story of two angels watching over Berlin, watching life unfold around Zoo station. From the pillar of the Golden Elise statue of the angel of History, they are silent witnesses to life in Zurope. One of the angels says: 'Sometimes I get tired of existing only as a spirit. I wish I could grow a weight to bind me to Earth.' The angel's desires are mundane: 'To feed the cat. To blacken my fingers reading the newspaper. To be excited by roast lamb, or by the line of a neck.' This angel takes a particular interest in a woman trapeze artist in a travelling circus, a terrestrial creature, but one who enjoys mobility, transience and a sort of flight. He says to his companion: 'I've stood outside long enough. I want to enter the history of the world, if only to hold an apple in my hand. I'll plunge into life. Into death. I'll descend to be born, to see life at eye level.' He knows that by doing this he will lose his God's eye view; his perspective on the world will have human dimensions, and he is anxious about this. His companion reassures him: 'There are other suns than the one in the sky. New wings will replace the old ones. In the deepest night Spring will begin.' The angel loses his wings and falls to Earth, he pawns off his breast-plate, his protective armour, once shiny, now tarnished. It's worth only a few marks. He buys a coffee and deliciously scalds his tongue. He goes in search of the woman and finds her troubled with ambivalence also. On the one hand, she enjoys her transience as a circus performer travelling around from city to city. She is a symbolic representation of diaspora in the EU. To use a current idiom, she is 'Eurotrash', a representative of an emerging bohemian sub-culture whose sense of identity is post-national and mobile. She is comfortable with her transcendental homelessness: 'I couldn't say who I am. I haven't the slightest idea. I have no roots, no country, no history, and I like it that way. I can imagine anything. Everything is possible. I only need to raise my eyes and once again I become the world, now, in this place. The greatest feeling of joy I have ever known.' On the other hand, she is terrified by the loneliness and emptiness of her condition and desperately needs to feel grounded. 'I feel emptied out, inadequate. Fear. Fear. Fear. This evening everything scares me. How should I live? How should I think? I think as though I were talking to someone.' Emptied of the substance bestowed by the particularity of tradition she is existentially exposed and vulnerable to dissolution in the universal. She finds a kindred spirit in the fallen angel who is content to hold the tightrope on which she performs. He says: 'This amazement at the two of us has made me a human being. I know now what no angel knows.' But is he helping her to fly, or is he tying her down?

UNCERTAINTY CAN BE A GUIDING LIGHT

U2's albums *Achtung Baby* and *Zooropa* draw heavily for their influence from the depiction of the dilemma of the angel in *Wings of Desire*. To be fully an angel, the angel must trade in his wings to feel emotion, to taste the mustard on the frankfurter, to be part of lived experience. But in doing so, he risks being only clay: stupid, awkward, fumbling, clodhopping Kavanagh, who frightens the woman and disappoints the muse. He might become insular, narrow, trapped and entrapping. Similarly U2's *Zooropa* explores the paradoxical existential conditions of our contemporary interpellation within the organising discourses of the EU. 'Stay (Faraway, So Close)' is the theme music of the sequel to *Wings of Desire*. The song takes the same form as the films, a commentary on street-life of Zooropa, from above, from the point of view of the angel, as it were. It expresses a perspective, articulated from 'up with the static and the radio / with satellite television / you can go anywhere / Miami New Orleans London Belfast and Berlin'. But this cosmopolitan form of life made possible by globalising technology and the supra-national institutions of the EU can be an alienated existence where people look through one another without seeing each other, talk without communicating, are pushed together without touching or feeling – a world where people are made so close but yet far away from one another. The title track of the album, *Zooropa*, expresses this alienating form of interpellation: 'Zooropa . . . voorsprung durch technik / Zooropa . . . be all that you can be / Be a winner / Eat to get slimmer'. The integrating discourses of Zurope are the advertising slogans of Audi (progress through technology) and Colgate (the ring of confidence in a blue whiteness assured by EU immigration policy). The swarming discourses of commerce and the administrative and security apparatus merge imperceptibly ('be all that you can be' is the recruitment slogan for the British Army). We are interpellated as consumers and as defenders of the realm of mass consumption, complicit in our own domination by an authoritarian regulatory apparatus, as expressed in 'Numb':

> Don't move
> Don't talk out of time
> Don't think
> Don't worry everything's just fine
> Just fine.

>> I feel numb
>> I feel numb
>> Too much is not enough
>> Gimme some more.

For some a returning home, being bound to the earth by our clay heels may save us from the heartlessness of transcendental homelessness. The Saw Doctors are part of this movement. U2 are more intelligent. They see the impossibility and undesirability of returning to the Garden. 'And I have no compass / And I have no map / And I have no reasons / No reasons to get back'. Instead, they prefer to make the most of the opportunity presented by the dissolution of the markers of old certainties:

> No particular place names
> No particular song
> I've been hiding
> What am I hiding from?
> Zooropa . . .
> Don't worry baby. It'll be alright
> Zooropa . . .
> Uncertainty . . .
> can be a guiding light.

Despite all the processes of numbing, in the space of uncertainty represented by the advent of post-national institutions and discourses of identification, they see the possibility to 'dream up the world she wants to live in'.

There is a world of difference between the Saw Doctors and U2, but they are both inspired by the same irreconcilable ambivalence. In the space of this ambivalence many temptations are possible, and fallen angels have to work through these. There is the temptation to return to the Garden, and the temptation to live in the stratosphere, but fallen angels do not have these simple options open to them. Lucifer is the angel who has to try to live in two worlds. Fallen angels know that to desire to return to the Garden of Eden depends on mis-recognising the nature of the garden; that it is really clay and cowshit. That it is death. That there is no life in the Garden, that eternal life coincides with death. The Kingdom of God on Earth promised by Brussels and the Bundesbank is similarly deathly; a techno-pastoralist inversion of the New Age movement of returning. The Reich that would last for a thousand years was built on sharp black uniforms, the glitter of *kristalnacht*, the mechanised symphony of the *blitzkrieg* and the deafening silence of Auschwitz. The current dominant discourse shaping the building of the tower of Babel is Fortress Europe, and the conversation of Zurope is becoming the ominous hum of administration, the white noise of commerce and MTV, and the shrieking of road-kill on the information superhighway.

The artist(s) who more powerfully and more poignantly than any others have given expression to the ambivalent spirit of the Irish heartbeat in recent times are Shane MacGowan and the Pogues.[26] In the Pogues we can discern a text, a subtext, written in the cracks produced by the slippage and displacement of cultures. Their texts are, in a sense, notes from the underground: subtexts or in-between texts of the official texts of Ireland, Britain and America; a maggot's view from inside the Big Apple, a sewer rat's view of London. I would like to suggest that what the Pogues are about is putting together a pastiche, or a bricolage. In their text, we can see a piecing together of fragments of experience, a juxtaposition and superimposition of images of practices, dreams and metaphors, drawn from two worlds, which combine to give form to immigrant culture. I want to examine this pastiche and identify some of the fragments of the imaginary which the Pogues have pulled together. I believe that we can see the development of some central themes which express a degree of unification, a transcendence of fragmentation and, thereby, the development of the basis on which a more coherent, post-modern identity may develop. This identity incorporates an essential ambivalence in an unresolved but no longer destructive and debilitating way – a way which allows for the development of reflexive, critical, assertive, celebrational, and hence emancipatory, cultural forms.

The pastiche which the Pogues piece together is one composed of fragments of the historical and contemporary experiences of the Irish diaspora. We find, for example, images of work, travel, religion, fighting, boozing, fucking, gambling, politics, superstitions, whores, saints, heroes and outlaws, tales from bars in rural Ireland, from Germany, from Spain during the civil war, and from a fiesta in the 1980s. From the Wild West, from New York at Christmas, from Soho and from Kilburn, from the trenches of World War I, from a United Nations' forces camp in Lebanon, from Belfast, Australia and from Greenland. There are dreamscapes and broken dreams, the joys of love, and the bitterness and sadness of loves left behind and love's labours lost. There are potato famines and frenzied beer feasts. There are songs about past and present filled with warmth and sensitivity, others charged with enthusiasm and fun, and others bristling with anger and delivered with breath-taking ferocity. In the Pogues, we meet James Joyce and Jessie James, Brendan Behan and the Banshee, labourers and intellectuals, God, the devil, some angels and a scattering of saints; Paddy the builder, Paddy the boozer, the soldier, the dreamer, the brawler; Paddy the racist, sexist, bigoted, bastard; Paddy the socialist idealist; the rebellious, the broken-spirited, the dead and the resurrected. Terrorists and the unjustly imprisoned have a voice, as do child prostitutes, mothers, fathers, sons and daughters who are affected in whatever way, in whatever time, in whichever place, by the experience of immigration.

Frederic Jameson has argued that the feeling of bewilderment characteristic of post-modern culture is the result of the loss of a sense of history.[27] Post-modern culture takes the form of an incoherent and meaningless pastiche of temporally instantaneous and disjointed experiences of images and surfaces which the de-centred subject is left up to his/her own devices to deal with. At a historical juncture where universal truths and totalising interpretive frameworks are, it seems, being abandoned, political agency is ascribed to de-centred subjects, who identify, define and develop tactics and strategies to tackle oppressive structures and discourses of power and become the architects and agents of their own emancipation. Jameson suggests that they might approach this task by 'undo(ing) post-modernism by the methods of post-modernism: To work at dissolving the pastiche by using the instruments of pastiche itself to reconquer some genuine historical sense'.[28] I believe that this is precisely what the Pogues are about.

With regard to reconquering some genuine historical sense, the most striking aspect of the Pogues' text is its historical form and content. It is largely traditional Irish music, played in punk rock style, with instruments taken from both genres. Some songs and tunes are reworked versions of nineteenth- and even eighteenth-century folk songs. Many of their original works retain the form of a ballad, a narrative with an explicit temporally coherent structure. The content of the Pogues' text is loaded with historical references and images which are carefully pieced together and linked to contemporary experiences, lending coherence and historical sense to the culture of the diaspora. More specifically, historical coherence is achieved by the juxtaposition of historical images with contemporary ones. For example, 'Poor Paddy' is a nineteenth-century navvies' ditty about immigrant workers fleeing the famine in Ireland to work on railroad construction in England. This is juxtaposed with 'The Boys from the County Hell', a song about the working life of a contemporary immigrant. Songs about Irishmen fighting in the First World War, 'Brown Eyes' and 'Waltzing Matilda', are balanced with 'Billy's Bones', an ironic comment on Irish soldiers serving with the United Nations forces in the Middle East. 'Wild times' songs of drunken debauchery from the past, for example 'Waxies Dargle' (Dublin, *circa* 1900) are juxtaposed with similar contemporary images from London, New York and Frankfurt, in songs like 'Fiesta', and 'Fairytale of New York'.

Historical continuity is also forged by the superimposition of images of present on past within individual songs. 'Thousands are Sailing' for example, first addresses the ghosts which haunt Ellis Island, and then speaks to their living contemporaries in New York, pointing to the similarities of their plights.

Songs such as this, dealing with the contemporary experiences of Irish immigrants in the United States, are juxtaposed with 'Jessie James', about a Wild West outlaw, whose family came originally from Oola, County Tipperary. On the Pogues' album *Peace and Love*, a piece entitled 'The Boat Train' superimposes contemporary images on a ballad about the 1798 Wexford rebellion, 'The Wearing of the Green'. What the Pogues are doing here is bringing out the tradition in immigrant experience. They are pointing out that there is a history behind the bewildering experience of immigration, and that young people today are not the first ones, nor the only ones, to be feeling what they are feeling. This is a crucially important political project in the context of postmodernism, according to Chantal Mouffe, because:

> tradition allows us to think of our own insertion into historicity, the fact that we are constructed as subjects through a series of already existing discourses, and that it is through this tradition which forms us that the world is given to us and all political action made possible.[29]

The Pogues' pastiche is more than simply a historically-informed text relating past with present. It is, more importantly, a medium and a device which subjects history and experience to a thoroughgoing radical critical examination. 'Sickbed of Cuchulainn', for example, is a biting critique of a dying drunken Ireland, confused ideally, morally bankrupt, politically corrupted. God is opting out, the Devil is in control and Paddy is drunk, at Mass, or down by the bay, emigrating as always. Those 'lazy drunken bastards' who stay home, die and are replaced by equals. Those who go, even idealists like Frank Ryan who fought with the International Brigades in Spain, and depicted by the Pogues as boozing in a brothel in Madrid, are hardly better. The Pogues challenge historically-distorting idealising myths in favour of a realistic and critical examination of the immigrant heritage.

Irish politicians persistently tout the myth that young Irish emigrants today are educated people who leave by choice, who 'do well' overseas, who come home when they are wealthy and experienced and contribute to national development. This is true of some though not of the majority. They are illegal aliens in the US, au pairs, gardeners, English teachers and dope dealers in Paris, Madrid and Munich, and bar staff, tele-marketers, builders, labourers and prostitutes in London, Boston and Sidney. This is the reality which the Pogues' text reveals. The Pogues do more than tear up the flimsy legitimations and excuses for ineptitude of successive Irish governments. They also penetrate the gleaming surfaces of London and America. 'The Old Main Drag' and 'Fairytale of New York', which deal with juvenile prostitution, violence and drug addiction, are among numerous songs from the streets, or rather from the backstreets and alleys, in which the Pogues use ugly images from the guts of the metropolis – images of squalor, poverty, violence and depravity – to smash the

mythically-constructed, glittering surfaces of affluent post-modern sophisticated urban culture and reveal some of the realities hidden beneath.

The disillusioning and (in this sense alone) emancipatory content of the
Pogues' critique is balanced by the presence of a celebrational, affirmative
theme. Terrifying, panic-inducing and bewildering though the experience of
immigration may be, it is equally a lot of fun, 'a mighty crack', in colloquial
terms. This is affirmed with great delight by the Pogues. Images of harsh times,
grim lonely existences and demeaning work are juxtaposed with images of wild
parties, warm friendships and, rich vibrant communities exuberantly embrac-
ing romantic sexy cities. 'Fiesta' expresses this mood and, despite the evident
squalor, New York at Christmas-time does have a genuine fairytale quality. The
warmth of the immigrant community is beautifully captured in 'The Broad
Majestic Shannon', while the enthusiasm, light-heartedness and 'let's do it'
attitude of young immigrants charges songs like 'Transmetropolitan' and 'Sally
Mclennane'.

The myth of a green, innocent, romantic Ireland is radically de-constructed
and scathingly critiqued by the Pogues, but it is equally nostalgically, lovingly,
longingly affirmed and celebrated. The Pogues affirm positive aspects of Irish
'community': family, friendships, games, ritual cultural practices centred on
village pubs, carnivals like the Galway Races, lazy summer days in the fields and
in the streets of small towns – far from the madding crowds of the metropolis.
They celebrate the presence of a vibrant fun-filled, musical, lyrical culture living
despite (and arguably partly in response to) rampant unemployment, material
destitution and repressive Catholic hegemony. A history of resistance to
colonial oppression is also explored and, appropriately, simultaneously ennobled
and denounced. Songs such as 'Kitty' and 'Young Ned of the Hill' draw on
images of 400 years of colonial history, while the contemporary conflict in
Northern Ireland is explored in 'Streets of Sorrow/The Birmingham Six'. The
latter speaks of the pain of violence in a divided community, and of continued
British injustice evidenced by the cases of the Guildford Four and the
Birmingham Six.

The Pogues address the political and emotional 'hot potato' of Northern
Ireland not simply to score 'Brownie points' for 'being political'. Living under
suspicion of being a 'mindless Fenian terrorist', hassle from the police and being
grilled by Customs and Immigration every time one travels is part and parcel of
the life-world experience of Irish immigrants in England. By piecing these
experiences into a temporally themeatised pastiche, the Pogues contextualise
them, pose them as generalised problems facing the Irish community, make
them historically and politically meaningful, and identify them as contestable
sites of oppression and points of potential resistance.

Following Edward Said, one might argue that by idealising to some extent
the traditional past, Irish 'community' and the nationalist struggle, the Pogues'

project is regressive.[30] That it reifies Irish culture: that it identifies it, seals it off and posits a discourse of 'Irishness' as an ideal or pure culture, set diametrically, contradistinctually, against metropolitan foreign cultures, and serves as a vehicle for xenophobic quasi-fascist nationalism. This is clearly not the case. The Pogues are not in the cultural purist tradition of Eamon de Valera, Siamsa Tíre or Comhaltas Ceoltorí Éireann. Unlike such people and organisations who propose a partial focus on an ideal mythically-constructed traditional past, the Pogues deal with Ireland and Irishness 'warts and all'. Their pastiche, while drawing on the past, is more concerned with the lived, everyday present. It challenges that we be critically, not idealistically, aware of our past, such that it might inform, rather than mis-inform, our coming to terms with the present. Rather than close off and reify Irish culture, which Said quite rightly warns post-colonial societies against, the Pogues project is to keep it open, alive and self-reflexive.

The Pogues text is soaked in alcohol. Their songs are filled with references to bars, boozing and drunkenness. They frequently perform drunk, or at least appear to. Images of alcohol consumption are associated equally with their joyous affirmative themes and with their angry critical themes. What is significant in this is that just as 'the lying Arab' is a central stereotype in prejudicial Orientalism, 'the drunken Irish' is the central reference point of anti-Irishness, the prejudicial practice of what one might call (in the manner of Said) 'Irishism'. In other words, prejudicial cultural stereotypes are built and are practiced around central negative signifiers, giving rise to widely-held racist characterisations like 'lying Arabs', 'stupid niggers', 'money-grasping Jews', 'dirty Pakkis' and 'drunken Irish'. Irish institutions, organisations and artists respond to this prejudicial cultural stereotype in a number of ways. Frequently, they deny it. Comhaltas Ceoltorí Éireann, for example, deliberately exclude it from their text, hosting dry (no booze) céilis (dances/concerts). Other groups seek to refute it and counteract it by demonstrating that the Irish drink no more than other ethnic groups. Various other organisations and some writers deal with Irish alcohol consumption exclusively in terms of its negative qualities, while others (folk singers, and especially stand-up comics) idealise it and play up 'drunken Paddy' as jolly and funny.

The Pogues, by contrast, deal with the good and the bad simultaneously. They pull together positive images of alcohol use; as a sedative for the treatment of post-modern shock syndrome, and as a stimulant used in Ireland to counteract (economic) depression. They affirm its use as a social lubricant *par excellence*, and the role its ritualised consumption practices play in cultural reproduction. Equally, they employ images of the horrors of alcohol abuse: social and self-destructiveness, the sordidness and social impotence associated with alcohol dependency, and the political and creative ineptitude which results from numbed minds and dulled senses. Here the Pogues are attempting to expose and to clarify the discursive structure and practice of Irish drunkenness. Rather than adopting a standpoint on the issue based on partial perceptions, their purpose appears to be to open it up, to expose it for critical examination. The Pogues are declaring the 'drunken Irish' stereotype, and with it the whole of prejudicial Irishism, to be a problematic complex open to contestation.

While the Pogues present the problem of a discourse of prejudicial Irishism as an issue to be addressed in an English social and political context, I think that it is important to emphasize that this questioning of Irishism is largely reflexively oriented. It is directed towards having Irish people, both in Ireland and (especially) as immigrants, question their Irishness. Addressing in a critically-reflective manner aspects of Irish culture, the status of various sacred cows and heroic historical figures, the purity or innocence of certain cultural practices, the traditions associated with rural life, Catholicism and so on places the Pogues at the forefront of the avant garde cultural movement in Ireland.

By dragging together, and ironically juxtaposing, fragments of images of Irish emigrant culture ranging from the sacred to the profane, the squalid and stupefied to the glorious and heroic, the Pogues cobble together a pastiche of Irish identity appropriate to the conditions of post-modernity. 'Fairytale of New York', for example, confronts us with the polarities of the broken, half-dead body of the emigrant, taken to the limit of existence through the joyous/painful self-indulgent immersion in the culture of the metropolis; drunk, strung out, utterly fucked up, almost dead but still never more alive, passionately fighting, raging against the dying of the light, called back from the brink of oblivion by the echo, the trace of a half-remembered, half-forgotten, tradition, refracted and modulated but still clear in the NYPD choir singing 'Galway Bay'. The bells are ringing out for Christmas Day, the heart beats on, there is always redemption and salvation in the birth of a new day, a day that will be lived out somewhere in between New York and Galway. Life is possible only while we are torn between the binding power of particular tradition and the cosmopolitan forces which promise the dissolution of the strictures of tradition and that promise us fresh air to breathe. This ambivalent tension, contradictory but complimentary, desires to ground identity in the local and particular and, simultaneously, to shake off the soil and fly free but no sooner free than yearning for the earth again, is a perpetually-renewed torture that inspired MacGowan and the Pogues. In 'USA' in *Peace and Love*, MacGowan wishes that his 'heart would turn to stone' to escape the torture of living between two 'graveyards': the deathly, stifling tomb of parental Irish tradition and the culture of the US which, promising boundlessness, lacks sufficient existential purchase to sustain the integrity of identity.

I met the Pogues, appropriately enough, in a brewery in Toronto, at the moment of this heartbreak. Shane MacGowan had quit/was thrown out (who knows?). MacGowan says that the Pogues were being pulled into MTV and stadium rock. They told me that MacGowan was drowning in booze. They played their hearts out, but even with Joe Strummer of The Clash as a stand-in for MacGowan, there was no heart in it. Empty and aimless, the Pogues drifted, lacking a weight to tie them to the earth. Spider Stacey, who fronted the Pogues towards the end, was reminded by an interviewer after one of their last performances that it was 17th March, Saint Patrick's Day, and was asked what did that mean for the Pogues? He said, 'What? Is it? Oh, I dunno. I'm fucking English, ain't I!' As the Pogues vanished into the dissolving vapour of MTV cyberspace, Shane MacGowan, like Sinéad O'Connor who shortly afterwards flew too close to the flame and had her wings singed too, returned 'home' (not to London where he had lived most of his life, but to Ireland where his parents were from) to make atonement with 'The Church of the Holy Spook'.

The spirit of Irish tradition was, he says, good enough to sustain his father and mother, so he 'don't need nothing new'. But while MacGowan survives by returning to the heartland, the local and the particular threatens to stifle him. Many of the songs on his recent album *The Snake* are parody and self-caricature. 'Donegal Express' seems little more than a nostalgic paean to gratuitous debauchery, and 'That Woman's Got Me Drinking (look at the state I'm in)' hardly seems to need interpretation. The rendition of the old Fenian song 'The Rising of the Moon', like Sinéad O'Connor's recent reanimation of 'The Foggy Dew', seems strangely out of synch with the new politics of post cease-fire Sinn Féin. Tragically, it seems, the elixir of life in the church of the holy spook may turn out to be just another stale pint.

But MacGowan is far too brilliant and subtle an artist to be merely the prodigal son singing the praises of a half-forgotten, recently-rediscovered Mother culture. On the contrary. True to the form of the constitutively-unfaithful ambivalent heart of the emigrant, no sooner is he 'home' than his desire is restless again. The song 'Aisling', for example, is a subtle inversion of a traditional form, which represents a re-turning and dis-location of desire from the local and particular. The *Aisling* is a form used by Gaelic poets in the eighteenth century to represent Ireland as a woman who appears in a dream and tells a tale of her woes to the poet (*Aisling* means 'dream' and is also a woman's proper name). The *Aisling* tells how she suffers under the yoke of England, that her sons have deserted her, and she calls on them to return to her and restore her pride and dignity. But here, in MacGowan's Aisling, the woman who is the object of his desire is not an idealised dream of (restored) Irish tradition. But neither is she simply a representation of desire for the cosmopolitan as in, for example, 'My London Girl' in *Poguetry in Motion* (1988). Aisling appears rather as the elusive/allusive, obscure but ideal object of desire: 'the wind that shakes the barley'. MacGowan is thus able to reconstruct his identity in terms of an identification of his ambivalent desires with motion, change and transformation. He begins with the question of his 'true' identity: 'Faded pictures in the hallway / Which of these brown ghosts is me?' Then, through the self-understanding of his desire in its representation in his Aisling, as 'the wind that blows from the north to the south', as insatiable, perpetual restlessness, he discovers that he doesn't have to settle for a particular ghost, either a local ancestor or a distant uncle. He can, instead, be himself 'just like that wind my love', restless, but self-conscious that the restlessness of his ambivalent desire is not an obstacle to identification, but is in fact constitutive of his identity.

(IN)CONCLUSIVE (POST-SCRIPT)

Aesthetic political representations of the Irish spirit currently fluctuate between discourses of communitarian essentialism and the transcendental homelessness of a race of angels. There is a desire for post-national, cosmopolitan identification, to escape from the bonds of tradition to a free, but fearfully lonely, existential condition of rootlessness and, at the same time, a desire to return to, to re-collect and re-live in the tradition(s) of 'real' (that is to say imagined) Ireland(s). Irish desire is torn between the object domains of Zooropa and the rusty bicycle leaning against the wall of the pub in County Galway. Fearing that in Zooropa 'too much is not enough', Irish desire, Janus-like, also faces toward home in search of the holy grail of the authentic, but fears finding it also to be too much, too much that we may choke on it.

NOTES AND REFERENCES

1 W. B. Yeats, 'The Lake Isle of Innisfree', *W. B. Yeats Selected Poetry*, N. Jeffares (ed.) (London, Pan, 1974).

2 K. Marx and F. Engels, *The Communist Manifesto* (London, Penguin, 1985), p. 84.

3 See J. Lacan, *The Four Fundamental Concepts of Psychoanalysis*, (London, Hogarth, 1977). For an elaboration of *jouissance* and its usage in cultural analysis see S. Zizek, *The Sublime Object of Ideology* (London, Verso, 1989).

4 See M. Heidegger, 'The Way Back into the Ground of Metaphysics', in M. Kaufman (ed.), *Existentialism from Dostoevsky to Sartre*, (New York, Meridian, 1975), pp. 242–79.

5 K. Keohane, 'Unifying the Fragmented Imaginary of the Young Immigrant: Making a Home in the Postmodern with the Pogues', *Irish Review*, no. 9, Autumn 1990, pp. 71–9.

6 J. Waters, *Race of Angels: Ireland and the Genesis of U2* (Belfast, Blackstaff, 1994).

7 For a discussion of the analogy between language and a game, and meaning as an effect of the 'family resemblances' amongst/between language games see L. Wittgenstein, *Philosophical Investigations*, (Oxford, Blackwell, 1994). This is Wittgenstein's argument throughout the Investigations, but see in particular passages 7, 65, 83.

8 S. Freud, *Civilisation and its Discontents* (New York, Norton, 1961), pp. 27-29, and footnote on p. 29.

9 'N17' (L. Moran / D. Carton © 1987). Taken from *If This is Rock 'n' Roll I Want My Old Job Back* (Shamtown Records, 13 St Mary's Terrace, Taylor's Hill, Galway, 1991).

10 For a discussion of cultural schizophrenia, alienation and disintegration associated with global culture in the late 20th century, see F. Jameson, *Postmodernism: or the Cultural Logic of Late Capitalism?* (Durham, Duke University Press, 1993).

11 For a Lacanian discussion of fear and hatred of the Other because of their projected 'excess', see S. Zizek, 'Eastern Europe's Republics of Gilead', *New Left Review* 183, September/October 1990.

12 From a conversation overheard in a bar in Galway. A group of people were discussing the presence of 'crusties', i.e. New Age Travellers in the city. Among other things it was suggested that 'the Corporation should sweep them up off the streets', and that 'they should be sand blasted'. The fact that the exchange was jovial shows not so much a trivialisation of the issue, but rather what Hanna Arendt identifies in Adolf Eichmann as 'the banality of evil'.

13 'I Uesta Lover' (P. Cunniffe / D. Carton / L. Moran / P. Stevens © 1979/1987). Taken from *If This is Rock 'n' Roll . . .*, op. cit.

14 See Julia Kristeva, *Powers of Horror* (New York, Columbia, 1982).

15 See S. Zizek, *Looking Awry: an Introduction to Jacques Lacan through Popular Culture*, (Boston, MIT press, 1991), pp. 130–2.

16 Tom Inglis, *The Irish Mother*, (Dublin, Gill and Macmillan, 1987).

17 See Emile Durkheim, *The Division of Labour in Society* (New York, Macmillan, 1933), chapters 2, 5 and 6, especially pp. 174–81.

18 Chantal Mouffe, 'Radical Democracy: Modern or Postmodern?' in Andrew Ross (ed.), *Universal Abandon? The Politics of Postmodernism* (Minneapolis, University of Minnesota Press, 1989).

19 See Michel Foucault, 'Panopticism', in *Discipline and Punish* (London, Penguin, 1991).

20 For a discussion of the relation of beauty to sublimity in the conditions of postmodernity see D. Hebdidge, 'Staking out the Posts', in *Hiding in the Light* (London, Routledge, 1988).

21 Emile Durkheim, *Sociology and Philosophy* (New York, Free Press, 1974).

22 Patrick Kavanagh, 'The Great Hunger', in *Patrick Kavanagh: The Complete Poems* (Peter Kavanagh Hand Press, New York, 1974).

23 Patrick Kavanagh, 'Stony Grey Soil of Monaghan', ibid., p. 73.

24 F. Nietzsche, *Thus Spoke Zarathustra*, (London, Penguin, 1986).

25 John Waters, *Race of Angels* (Belfast, Blackstaff, 1994).

26 For a lengthier discussion of the Pogues see K. Keohane, 'Unifying the Fragmented Identity of the Young Immigrant'.

27 F. Jameson, 'An interview with Frederic Jameson', in A. Ross (ed.), *Universal Abandon?* (Minneapolis, Minnesota University Press, 1988).

28 ibid.

29 C. Mouffe, 'Postmodernism and Politics', in A. Ross, *Universal Abandon?*

30 E. Said, *Orientalism* (New York, Pantheon, 1978).

12. Graduate Emigrants
A 'New Wave' in Irish Emigration?

IAN SHUTTLEWORTH

Interpretations of the wave of Irish emigration that began in the 1980s, following the decade of return of the 1970s, are highly contested. Several commentators have claimed that recent emigration is 'new' because of the changed skill, educational, geographical and class composition of recent Irish migratory flows in comparison with those of earlier decades.[1] Whereas earlier emigration waves were characterised as being unskilled or low-skilled, it is argued that contemporary outflows include very significant proportions of educated individuals who seek high-status occupations abroad. It is also suggested that the more urbanised and industrialised east coast has had the greatest rate of out-migration in recent years.[2] As Mac Laughlin and others have pointed out, this perspective on Irish emigration is also associated with the view, often expressed by government officials in particular, that recent population outflows are largely a voluntary activity of well-educated young people with a spirit of enterprise that enables them to take advantage of overseas opportunities.[3] This interpretation suggests that recent emigration is new in its social and educational composition. Mac Laughlin has also argued that the emphasis placed on education, voluntarism and enterprise have contributed to the sanitisation and gentrification of recent Irish emigration.[4] Far from being a voluntary movement of the highly educated, this interpretation of contemporary Irish emigration stresses the continued importance of the emigration of the poorly-skilled and the unqualified in response to a lack of job opportunities at home, the part played by emigration in the peripheralisation of Ireland in the global economy and the unpreparedness of many young adults for the traumas of emigration. Contemporary emigration from this perspective is therefore 'new' in that it is a comparatively recent phenomenon but, it is argued, it is not qualitatively different from previous population outflows because its highly-educated and highly-skilled component has been exaggerated.

The categorisation of recent interpretations of contemporary Irish emigration into these two opposing views is problematic. Broadly speaking, however, one important dimension in the debate is between those who argue that recent Irish emigration is substantially 'new' and those who argue that its novelty has been exaggerated at the expense of the many continuities with population outflows in the past and the often grim social reality of emigration in the 1980s and 1990s.

Graduate emigrants have an important symbolic role in this interchange. This is because they have been seen as the epitomy of the 'new wave' of emigration by those commentators who have perceived graduates as leading members of Ireland's global generation.[5] They are a specialised sub-group of emigrants, and cannot therefore be considered to be representative of recent Irish emigration as a whole because of their high levels of education and access to specialised labour markets. But for this very reason, they should also provide a rigorous test of the hypothesis of a 'new wave' of Irish emigration; they possess high-level educational qualifications and, as young people who are products of recent Irish modernisation, would be the one segment of the population that could be assumed to be most imbued with an enterprise culture. These factors suggest that graduates should be at the leading edge of any 'new wave' of emigration by virtue of their educational achievements and social class background. Therefore, if it can be shown that graduate emigration has many traditional features, and is in fact very similar in its characteristics to either past emigration or to the contemporary emigration of working-class youth, then severe doubts must be raised about the extent to which 'new wave' Irish emigration is really qualitatively new either in ethos or in form.

This chapter attempts such an examination by using evidence from a series of surveys of university graduates undertaken in the late 1980s by the author. It looks at three dimensions of the graduate emigrant which might differentiate recent graduate emigrants from both past emigrants and from their contemporary peers. Firstly, the form of graduate emigration is considered. This includes the channels used to regulate the migratory flow and the duration of emigration. Secondly, the motives for emigration are examined, including the extent to which graduates appear to be differentiated from other emigrants in terms of motives for emigrating. Thirdly, there is a discussion of the structural context of graduate emigration. This section considers both the extent to which Irish graduate emigrants really appear to be taking advantage of overseas opportunities and the changed position of Ireland in the global economy.

The chapter begins by considering evidence which suggests that graduate migration is 'new' and differs substantially from past population outflows. It then moves to a discussion of data which suggest that graduate emigration has many traditional characteristics and shares much in common with Irish emigration in general. Following this, it then weighs the evidence and concludes that descriptions of graduate emigration as an important symptom of a 'new wave' of emigration are exaggerated and misrepresent the reality of the exodus since the mid-1980s. In these sections, there is a narrow empirical focus on graduate emigration which does not question the significance of graduates as a component of contemporary Irish population outflows. For example, no attempt is made to place graduate emigrants in their wider context, nor to estimate their numerical importance as a segment of modern Irish emigration. To redress this imbalance, the chapter attempts to develop a broader critique of graduate emigrants as an important part of the 'new wave' of Irish emigration by considering graduate emigration in a wider arena which includes the ideological and political factors that have led to the emphasis on skilled migration in debates about recent Irish emigration.

ARGUMENTS THAT GRADUATE EMIGRATION IS A QUALITATIVELY NEW DEVELOPMENT

The argument that recent graduate emigration is symbolic of a new type of skilled emigration from Ireland is derived from structural changes both in Irish society and in the Irish economy. The accelerated pace of socio-economic change in the last 30 years has effectively restructured emigration, both in terms of the opportunities for spatial mobility and also in terms of social opportunity. It is impossible to grasp all aspects of these developments which range from the encroachment of secularisation to the growth of unskilled, female and part-time employment in Ireland in recent decades.[6] The two most relevant features of the discussion, however, are the expansion of higher education and the penetration of the Irish labour market by foreign-owned companies.

In common with many nations, Ireland in the 1970s and 1980s saw an expansion in third-level education.[7] Although serious problems remain in ensuring access to third-level education for all social classes, particularly young adults from working-class and small-farming communities, Ireland now has a much greater proportion of its population in third-level education than in the recent past. The reasons for this expansion are complex. To some extent, the demand for third-level education has been created by a state-directed modernisation policy which has stressed the availability of educated labour as a means for achieving economic competitiveness and for attracting the 'right kind' of multinational enterprise which is prepared to invest in its workforce in Ireland.[8]

Other factors such as demographic change and changes in the social structure of Irish society have also contributed to the increased demand for third-level education in Ireland. As a country with one of the youngest populations in the European Union, Ireland naturally has a large number of people exiting the education system with third-level qualifications. The rising demand for third-level education here may be a consequence of changing social-class structures in Ireland. It may also be a 'last resort' for 'discouraged workers' who are unable to gain work on leaving compulsory education in a highly-polarised and over-subscribed labour market.[9] In some cases, it could even be argued that some young people seek access to third-level education with emigration already in mind. Alternatively, as Mac Laughlin also suggests, large numbers of Irish young adults may now view third-level education, including years spent in post-graduate research, as a strategy for postponing emigration, or for at least better preparing themselves for life in the international labour market.[10] However, even these alternative perspectives place third-level education in a nexus of socio-economic inequalities resulting from the co-existence of a large and growing middle class with increased poverty and a collapse of the youth labour market.

The expansion of education took place during a period when the Irish labour market was radically opened to foreign-owned companies and at a time when dependent industrialism took root in Ireland.[11] Rather than being a source of unskilled labour, as it clearly was in the nineteenth and early twentieth centuries, it might be argued that Ireland now became a reservoir of skilled and educated labour created as a result of socio-economic modernisation and that this labour is now exploited in the global economy. In the most benign interpretation of these changes, Ireland shares equally with other states in 'brain exchanges'. Hyperbolic claims about the quality of Irish graduates are made by state agencies in efforts to entice multinational companies to locate in Ireland, and to explain graduate emigration as the natural consequence of education and broadening outlooks.[12] Less 'rosy' scenarios are more credible, however, and these suggest that Ireland's position in the global economy has not fundamentally changed and that the recent emigration of highly-educated graduates is one aspect of Ireland's on-going peripheralisation.

The net effect of modernisation has been the restructuring of Irish society. This has affected the quality of recent emigration by fostering a 'new type' of Irish emigrant. Graduates are assumed to fit into this picture. They are perceived as a 'new breed' of Irish emigrant, as young adults equipped to take advantage of the opportunities offered by Ireland's new role as a 'human resource warehouse' in the global economy. Graduate emigration is said to be 'new' in the sense that it results from a novel conjunction of social and economic forces both nationally and internationally; 'new' in the sense that graduates are going to work for multinational companies, and 'new' in the sense that graduates are assumed to be moving abroad within the internal labour markets of large multinational organisations, rather than by the unstructured and informal mechanisms which were supposed to have guided previous population flows.

Some empirical evidence does exist to support these general interpretations. Firstly, Irish graduates, for example, are highly mobile and fit into the category of the transient skilled emigrant defined by Findlay.[13] Table 1 shows this with reference to the residential moves between 1986 and 1990 of a cohort of graduates who left Irish universities in 1986. Irish graduates appear to be highly

TABLE 1: *Residential moves of a 1986 graduate cohort*

Time of move	Within Ireland	From Ireland	Moves outside Ireland	Returns to Ireland	Total moves	Net Irish migration
June 1986–87	42	17	2	0	61	–17
June 1987–88	41	25	7	1	74	–24
June 1988–89	24	20	12	5	61	–15
June 1989–90	13	12	5	2	32	–10

Source: R. King and I. Shuttleworth, 'The Emigration and Employment of Irish Graduates: The Export of High-Quality Labour from the Periphery of Europe', *European Urban and Regional Studies*, vol. 2. no. 1, 1995, pp. 21–40

mobile. Though return to Ireland does not feature as being of major importance, there are many to-and-fro movements between third countries (for example, moves from North America to Europe), and this appears to conform to expectations of Irish graduates as a migratory élite.

Secondly, it can be argued that the destinations of graduate emigrants are different, to some extent, from those of Irish emigrants as a whole. They are more likely, for example, to go to mainland Europe. There is little direct evidence about what happens to these graduates once they have left Ireland. However, it appears that new Irish communities have grown in many European cities and that many of these 'new' emigrants are graduates.[14] The breakaway from the traditional destinations of the English-speaking world can be used to claim that graduates are part of a wave of emigration that fundamentally differs from those of the past in social origin, educational status and motivation. It also, perhaps, reflects the changed position of Ireland in the global economy which results from a process of modernisation and Europeanisation. Although no research has yet been conducted which is as thorough as Jackson's research on the status of the Irish in post-war Britain, some smaller-scale studies of new Irish emigration to Europe have been conducted.[15] There is sufficient consistency in these studies to outline the broad features of this emigration and to identify its traditional as well as its 'new' features.[16] That these new European emigrant communities are led by graduates and the middle class is significant because these groups have not usually led mass Irish emigrations in the recent past. This is also significant because university-educated emigrants have been easily assimilated, as in the case of the Irish in Paris, where there have been few cultural barriers to the integration of the new Irish.[17] These features seem to accord with the concept of young people emigrating in search of opportunities. They also fit with a new view of Irish emigrants as part of a global, or at least a European, migratory élite. Despite this, however, there are complexities which suggest that this assumption is too simplistic.

Alongside those characteristics which seem to define graduate emigrants as 'new', there are other features of the recent exodus which suggest that nothing much has really changed in the pattern of recent Irish emigration. Among these are the mechanisms by which emigration is reproduced and managed. These are traditional and very much like those of long-established Irish communities in the English-speaking world. Firstly, for example, the networking process in Paris, with friends helping to find suitable work and accommodation, and the existence of social contacts with young adults in the overseas diaspora, are strong factors in favour of emigration to mainland Europe and to France in particular, and are again very much like those observed amongst Irish emigrants to England or to the United States.[18] Secondly, many of the jobs taken as au pairs, nurses and teachers mean that there are now many contacts with host communities in Europe, particularly in France and Germany, and this enables graduates to assimilate into these host societies. However, it should be noted that many of the jobs taken up by recent graduate emigrants to Europe are not high-ranking professional occupations and certainly do not sit well with suggestions that most emigrants today are a migratory élite in search of high-grade employment. Thirdly, some European graduate emigrants do not assimilate simply because they are highly transient workers. Kockel, discussing Irish emigrants working in Munich, categorises these as a 'travelling group'.[19] As Mac Laughlin also suggests, they resemble earlier transient Irish emigrants, including seasonal harvest workers in the late nineteenth century. However, it should be noted that, unlike the latter, their stated motives for emigration, that it would be 'interesting' or a 'good thing', differ from the push forces and the *need* to emigrate that characterised most outflows in the late nineteenth century and in the post-war years.[20] It is therefore possible to claim that graduate emigration is new, both in its forms and economic context. There are, however, empirical problems with the uncritical acceptance of these notions. There are also problems with the concept of modernisation as the key to understanding the novelty of Irish graduate emigration. This is because the concept of modernisation itself has its own ideology, although interpretations of its exact meaning vary significantly. At its most favourable, graduate emigration can be perceived as the ultimate outcome of a process of modernisation. In this scenario, Ireland has ceased to supply unskilled labourers to vulnerable sectors of the world economy and has, instead, made the transition to a mature economy with a strong skills and education base in which graduate emigrants are part of an international élite who move abroad on the same terms as emigrants from other European countries. This was a feature of popular and academic discourse about the 'new wave' of emigration in the 1980s, particularly that which pointed to the emigration of skilled and educated young people in terms of opportunities, investment in human capital, upward social mobility and a thriving enterprise culture amongst Irish young adults who are assumed to be responding to a situation in which there is, as Brian Lenihan famously commented, insufficient room for us all to make a living. In this way, the ideology of modernisation can be used to sanitise emigration in such a way as to make it acceptable to Ireland's business and political élites. The latter see themselves as managing a developed post-industrial economy that is taking part on the same terms as other nations in a process of global skill interchange.

Less favourable interpretations would stress that the modernisation project in Ireland has been beset by socio-economic contradictions. They would also point to evidence which shows that the Irish labour market is characterised by de-skilled, low paid and increasingly feminised employment opportunities.[21] Graduate emigration is not, in this interpretation, a sign of a vigorous entre-preneurial culture. Neither is it indicative of the constructive integration of Ireland into the global economy. It is, instead, a symptom of the mis-match between manpower planning, political rhetoric and the realities of a truncated and peripheral economy that cannot offer meaningful employment opportunities to the young people in whom it has invested political and educational capital. This interpretation of the outcomes of socio-economic change suggests that the ideology of modernisation, as applied to Irish graduate emigrants, places the experience of Irish emigration behind a veneer of post-industrial sophistication. This ignores the extent to which graduate emigration is shaped by disadvantage and by economic failure, rather than a strategy which produces upward social mobility for emigrants seeking career paths in the international economy.[22]

Accepted uncritically, much of the evidence discussed in this section suggests that Irish graduate emigrants are part of a 'new wave' of emigration, and that a case can be made for qualitative changes in the structure and composition of Irish emigration as represented by the experience of graduates. However, the next section will approach the question of whether graduate emigration is 'new' in a more critical manner by examining the experience of emigrants, their motives for emigrating, the forms taken by emigration and some of the social patterns resulting from 'new wave' emigration since the 1980s.

ARGUMENTS THAT GRADUATE EMIGRATION IS NOT A QUALITATIVELY NEW DEVELOPMENT

Despite plausible claims that graduate emigration is 'new', other features that appear 'old' and traditional can be discerned. This section of the chapter concentrates on these and suggests alternative interpretations of graduate emigration to those advanced in the preceding section. Firstly, it looks at patterns of emigration in terms of destinations, duration and types of move, and the means by which graduate emigration is channelled overseas. Secondly, the reasons that graduates have advanced to explain their decision to emigrate will be considered. The central theme here is the extent to which graduate emigration appears to be 'new' in the types of moves that are made and in terms of the motivations that are suggested. If graduate emigration is radically new, then it should be very different in all these aspects from Irish emigration in general, particularly from past trends in Irish emigration. Irish graduates can be described as 'transients' and this accords with contemporary conceptions of skilled emigration. But what sorts of jobs do they take? How do they arrange to move overseas? What motivates them? Where do they move to? The answers to these questions may challenge the notion of a 'new wave' of emigration discussed above.

The first stage towards the testing of the claim that graduate emigration is representative of a new emigration phase is shown in Table 2 which details the destinations of graduates and all other emigrants in the late 1980s.

TABLE 2: *Overseas Locations of Irish Emigrants and of Graduates' First Destinations (percentage rates)*

Destination	Graduates 1990	All Irish graduate emigrants 1989	All Irish emigrants 1987–88
Britain	58.3	68.4	68.6
Other EC	19.3	11.9	5.3
North America	13.3	10.2	13.8
Other	9.1	9.5	12.8

Source: R. King and I. Shuttleworth, 'Education, Identity and Migration: The Case of Young Highly-Educated Irish Migrants', *Studi Emigrazione,* vol. 117, 1995, pp. 159–174

Based on information from the Higher Education Authority (HEA), the Labour Force Survey (LFS) and a survey conducted by the authors themselves, this table shows that graduate destinations do not differ that much from those of other emigrants. This suggests that there are many similarities between graduates and other emigrants in that graduates go to approximately the same destinations as all other emigrants, although they were marginally more likely to go to continental Europe. Graduates plainly, therefore, do not appear to be a divergent group with a new type of emigration behaviour since they seem to be like most other Irish emigrants in that they go to what are perceived as being 'traditional Irish' locations.[23]

It is dangerous to argue from these geographical similarities to social structures and experience as it is rare that social phenomena can be 'read off' in such a simplistic way. The evidence on location, moreover, is not conclusive on its own. Taken together with information on the means by which emigration occurs and the socio-economic experience of graduate emigration, however, it can be used as a component of a broader argument.

Table 3 shows the relative importance of various channels by which information about job opportunities is disseminated and through which graduate migration is structured.

TABLE 3: *Means by which Jobs are Found Outside Ireland*

	Direct approach	Careers office	Private agency	Public agency	Press advert	Other
1st job	6	17	10	4	22	23
2nd job	3	3	11	7	11	14
3rd job	3	1	4	3	6	3
All jobs	12	21	25	14	39	40

Source: I. Shuttleworth, *Irish Graduate Migration in the 1980s: A Case Study of Core-Periphery Relations in the Mobility of Qualified Manpower* (Trinity College Dublin: Unpublished PhD Thesis, 1991)

Given the emphasis on the changed role of Ireland in the global economy, and the belief that graduate emigration takes place in the context of social mobility within an international career, it might be expected that graduate emigrant flows would be regulated by international companies and that graduates would not find themselves in emigrant job ghettoes abroad. Table 3 shows that comparatively traditional channels of emigration are used to obtain jobs by Irish graduate emigrants. Private employment agencies, which are often assumed to be of key importance in managing skilled migratory flows, are the third most important source of information in this table.[24] In contrast to this, 'press adverts' and 'other' sources of information head the list. 'Other' means personal contacts, and this type of social network has often been associated with the growth of Irish migrant communities in many different nations.[25] The informality that is associated with this is made clear by fieldwork amongst a small group of Irish graduates in London; less than 50 per cent of these had found a job before leaving Ireland. It is also reinforced by survey evidence which suggests that only 9 graduates out of the 383 who responded stated that the reason they had left Ireland was because of a transfer abroad within a multi-national company.[26]

Informality is not necessarily a sign that Irish graduates are not part of a 'new' phase of emigration. However, it tends to suggest that Irish graduate emigration flows are structured by 'traditional' means, and this evidence does not accord with concepts of a skilled emigration flow that is structured by the institutions of an international skilled labour market. This suggestion is confirmed when the activities of Irish graduates abroad are examined more carefully. As a working hypothesis, for example, it might be assumed that if graduates are, indeed, part of a 'new breed' of global emigrants, they would work in knowledge-based and élite employment after leaving Ireland. However, this is not the case.

Looking more carefully at graduate employment abroad, survey evidence suggests that most Irish graduate emigrants are not as much a part of a 'new wave' of emigration as some commentators would suggest. A substantial group of graduates is employed in what might be termed 'graduate occupations' such as management and engineering. However, a sizeable group is also 'under-achieving' in lower-grade occupations such as clerical work, craft occupations and low level management support. Moreover, many Irish graduate emigrants are not employed in knowledge-based industries but in sectors such as retailing and catering, manufacturing and other services (excluding banking and finance) which are not considered to be the high-technology occupations planned for Irish graduates nor the type of employment which would be taken up by Ireland's 'global generation'. At the very least, this suggests that the idea that graduate emigrants from Ireland are part of a movement of 'Young Europeans' should certainly be qualified. Some graduates are in graduate-level employment abroad but a sizeable minority are 'Young Europeans' in name only; they work there but, as was the case with one respondent who was a domestic decorator in Berlin, in rather low-grade work.

The weakness of the concept of graduate emigration as a highly-skilled and highly-educated population flow becomes more apparent when the motives for graduate migration are examined as in Table 4. This shows the most important reasons that survey respondents gave for leaving Ireland under three main headings (employment and career, education and personal/other). Economic and career factors are the most important and the leading position of 'job offer abroad' shows that Irish graduates are in demand in the international labour market. But many of the economic/career factors do not reflect the existence of a modernised, high-technology economy in Ireland as 'higher wages abroad' and 'no challenging work' in Ireland are also of major importance. Educational factors are negligible; few graduates left Ireland for educational reasons. The importance of personal/other factors is, however, startling and suggests that many graduates are not moving for reasons of careers, education or as part of a post-industrial migratory élite, but for the very traditional reasons of curiosity about lifestyles outside Ireland, problems with moral restrictions in Irish society and the migratory attraction of friends and relatives who are resident outside Ireland.

TABLE 4: *Ranked Individual Reasons for Leaving Ireland of a Sample of Graduates*

Reason	First	Second	Third	Total
Employment group				
Job offer abroad	35	25	5	65
Problems in finding work in Ireland	31	24	10	65
Higher wages abroad	11	19	22	52
No challenging work in Ireland	18	20	13	51
High taxation in Ireland	9	16	21	46
Transfer abroad by firm	8	1	0	9
Other	25	3	27	55
Education group				
Offer of post-graduate place abroad	9	9	3	21
No course available in Ireland	4	4	8	16
Broaden outlook	4	4	8	16
Reputation of foreign institution	6	4	5	15
No funds for research in Ireland	4	2	1	7
Other	5	2	5	12
Personal/other group				
Lifestyle abroad	49	13	8	70
Restrictive society in Ireland	5	15	9	29
Friends and relatives abroad	5	10	12	27
Spouse moved	6	2	1	9
Other	12	14	8	34

Source: R. King and I. Shuttleworth, 'The Emigration and Employment of Irish Graduates: The Export of High-Quality Labour from the Periphery of Europe', *European Urban and Regional Studies,* vol. 2. no. 1, 1995, pp. 21–40

The motives for migration stated by graduates are very much like those seen amongst waves of migrants in the past.[27] Lack of employment opportunities, a lack of challenging work in Ireland and a desire to escape from the restrictions of Irish life are the main 'push factors' in this table, whereas higher wages abroad, job offers and the prospect of a more cosmopolitan lifestyle are still the leading 'pull factors'. In citing these general factors, recent Irish graduates seem no different from emigrants in general and from emigrants in the past.

Some insights into the motivations for emigration set out in Table 4 can also be drawn from remarks that were invited in a survey of graduates undertaken by the author. These remarks are chosen not only for their 'articulacy' and nice turn of phrase, but because they were representative of the opinions expressed by many respondents. Since much emigration is associated with career/employment reasons, remarks dealing with this issue will be presented first:

> We cannot be expected to take Mickey Mouse jobs when real work (R and D etc) is available overseas
>
> Work available outside Ireland, especially in London, offers work experience of large national and multinational companies. It also allows for a variety of methods of work to be experienced because of the ease of getting employment not only in a particular field but in the development of a career.[28]

These remarks serve several purposes. Firstly, they confirm the responses outlined in Table 4 which suggest some of the positive sides of emigration rather than the negative push factor of high taxation. Secondly, they offer a way in which hypotheses about Ireland's relationship with the global economy can be tested in a non-quantitative way. This theme will be returned to later in the chapter.

The second theme is socio-cultural and personal factors as a motive for emigration. These point to the widespread dislocation of social networks by emigration, problems in accepting sexual and political norms in Ireland and the desire to escape from the restrictions of a rural environment as major factors in the decision to emigrate. Some of these socio-cultural factors, particularly those relating to the issues of abortion and contraception, appeared to be most important to young female emigrants.[29] Economic forces are, therefore, not the only motives for emigration; socio-cultural factors and social networks are important in structuring graduate emigration and their relative significance appears to vary by gender.

DISCUSSION

The data presented suggest that Irish graduate emigration is ambiguous with a duality between its 'old' and 'new' aspects. At the level of the individual, one aspect of the discourse of modernisation, as applied to recent graduate emigration, is that graduates have left Ireland by choice, that they are part of a new wave of 'Young European'-style emigration, and that they take high-status jobs. To some extent, this perception is accurate, but the survey research undertaken on graduates by the other writers suggests that the key phrases to describe this emigration flow are informality and the search for experience. In many ways, these aspects imply that graduate emigration is very similar to other types of Irish emigration both past and present.

For example, with regard to the labour market, less than 1 in 40 graduate emigrations were structured by the internal labour markets of large companies. Formal job-search methods such as private or public employment agencies had some importance, but many emigrants relied on informal networks, personal arrangements and simply 'trying their luck'. This suggests that recent graduate emigration is in the tradition of Irish emigration as a whole. Furthermore, the jobs that graduates took whilst outside Ireland were not always 'graduate' in quality. For some, especially for the transient graduate population that moved to and fro between several countries, construction work, retailing and personal service employment (such as 'nannying') were the rule rather than the exception.

The 'search for experience' was important as a motive for emigration, in either a specific career-related sense or in terms of the broader socio-cultural context of 'life experience'. Again, however, this type of motive does not appear to be so different from those voiced by other emigrant groups. Conventional wisdom points to high taxation and career factors as being the most important themes motivating graduate emigration. This emphasis was true to some extent, but personal and cultural factors in their broadest sense, particularly for female graduates who felt constrained by the limitations of Irish society, were also important. The remarks above that pointed to the desire to escape provincialism, to get away from a restrictive Irish moral environment, together with the fact that graduate emigration is deeply embedded in the social milieu of many graduates, suggests that, in these aspects, graduate emigration has many traditional or 'old' characteristics.

At a more abstract level of analysis, graduate emigration is in other ways new. It has occurred in response to changed structural relationships within the Irish and global economies which have 'manufactured' a new and highly-educated social group and provided a context for their emigration. These developments have clearly altered the socio-economic context in which recent emigration has taken place. The most generous interpretation of the ideology of modernisation is that these graduates are now part of an international élite and the product of a high-technology, high-education economy.

This position, however, is untenable given the evidence that Ireland has merely exchanged one type of peripherality for another. Indigenous firms, for example, tend to be too small and weak to be significant graduate employers. Meanwhile, foreign-owned companies arriving in Ireland tend to locate low-grade assembly functions there, keeping their main graduate-employing functions in metropolitan centres.[30] It might, indeed, be argued that Ireland has a truncated labour market because of its lowly position in the global economy and that it is reliant on world cities for managerial and research functions.[31] Considered in this way, graduate emigration might be thought of as 'new' because it is an expression of a relatively new form of peripherality, but it is 'old' in the sense that it is as much a response to socio-economic marginalisation as the population outflows of the past.

Looking at graduate emigration in its own narrow terms, it therefore appears that there is no clear evidence that it is a qualitatively different representative of the 'new wave' of a 'global generation' of emigrants. This modernistic concept of recent emigration, particularly with reference to graduates, has stressed its voluntarism, its high-technology background, its search for opportunities and the search for a low taxation regime.

However, many of the features of graduate emigration observed empirically, such as the motivations for emigration, duration of time spent abroad, the low grade of much overseas graduate employment and the informal methods by which emigration is arranged, suggests that graduate emigration has much in common with the general Irish emigrant experience. The scenario for graduate emigration that seems most likely is not one of 'brain-exchange' with Ireland as an equal partner in a high-technology global economy, but rather one of Ireland in a highly dependent role. Furthermore, many graduates do not fit the model of well-educated young professionals who take advantage of the opportunities offered by the international corporate economy. In their moves, in their experience of employment and in their motives for emigrating, they resemble most other Irish emigrants.

These criticisms of the notion of graduate emigrants as being qualitatively different from other emigrants take as given the assumption that graduate emigration has been an important component of population outflows from Ireland since 1980. They have also assumed that graduate emigration is a relatively recent development. However, these assumptions cannot be justified and a number of more fundamental points can be made that question the importance of graduate emigration.

The idea that graduate emigration is a novel feature of recent Irish migratory experience that served to define this wave of emigration as 'new' can be questioned on two further counts. Firstly, there is evidence that graduate emigration from Ireland is not really new. Graduate emigration from Ireland was observed during the late nineteenth century.[32] Naturally, this emigration of graduates within the British Imperial system, to serve, for example, as engineers in India, was different in social composition, destination and context to the experience of contemporary Irish graduate emigrants, but it demonstrates that Ireland has been a source of highly-educated labour for a considerable time. Nearer the present day, and rather more similar to the experience of the 1980s, was the graduate outflow of the 1950s which attracted newspaper headlines very similar to those of the recent past which referred to Irish emigration as a 'brain-drain'.[33] Again, this demonstrates that Ireland was not suddenly perceived as a source of skilled and highly-qualified manpower in the 1980s. It is a country with a relatively long history of graduate emigration. The concerns in the 1980s about the activities of multinational companies 'poaching' Ireland's graduates also find an echo in the past when British companies were active recruiters on Irish campuses, particularly at Trinity College, Dublin, but also at other Irish colleges and universities. From this perspective, graduate emigration is not particularly new. Perhaps it has attracted so much recent attention because the comparative 'lull' in graduate outflow in the 1970s and early 1980s was succeeded by the high rates of graduate emigration in the late 1980s. Following the expansion of third-level education at this time, this meant that graduate emigration had a wider social and geographical impact. However, reductions in the rate of graduate out-migration since its peak in 1988 suggest that graduate emigration is cyclical. It may also be the result of changing conditions prevailing in the Irish and British economies, rather than the product of fundamental social restructuring processes operating within Irish society.

A similar scepticism may be extended to those scenarios that stress the numerical contribution of graduates to recent population outflows. The lack of national-level data makes it difficult to be certain about exactly who is leaving Ireland. Despite this caveat, the data that are available suggest that graduate emigration is not a major component of contemporary population outflows and that there is still a substantial number of unskilled young emigrants.

It is difficult to estimate the social composition of emigrant communities on several counts. Firstly, since emigrants have left, the sending country is usually unable to provide precise estimates of emigration because emigrants are in different jurisdictions and their locations are often unknown. Secondly, surveys based on localities in the sending country may be unrepresentative of the national experience as a whole simply because of local or regional variations. Finally, national-level sample surveys are also problematic, especially since they often have small sampling fractions, the population of emigrants from which the samples are drawn are unknown and, in the case of many government surveys, data collected on emigration are incidental to the central topics of the surveys. Beyond these difficulties lie problems of non-response and recall which plague all attempts to get a clear picture of emigrants.

Estimates of the precise nature and social composition of recent Irish emigration flows in this situation, which is fraught with data difficulties, are obviously difficult and should be treated with caution. However, some conclusions that appear reliable can be drawn by considering a variety of data sources. On the one hand, some data suggest that educated and highly-qualified people form a significant part of gross inflows and gross outflows to and from Ireland.[34] On the other hand, information taken from Mac Laughlin's survey-based fieldwork, and confirmed by the experiences of workers with Irish immigrants in the United Kingdom, suggests that graduate emigration is not so significant that we can now talk of the modernisation or gentrification of recent Irish emigration. Thus Mac Laughlin shows that most recent emigrants were not highly-qualified university graduates. A very significant proportion were young emigrants with second-level educational qualifications, and very large numbers were 'still gravitating to the traditional low-status job ghettoes of the Irish emigrant.'[35] On balance, the weight of this evidence suggests that many vulnerable and under-prepared young people are still leaving Ireland following the collapse of rural and urban labour markets. This hardly appears to be an emigration induced by attractive 'opportunities' abroad. In this context, the emphasis placed on highly-educated graduates appears to be inappropriate and exaggerated. The proportion of emigrants with third-level qualifications, however, appears to have increased in recent years, though the proportion of graduates who leave at 'first destination', nine months after graduation, is probably less than 10 per cent of the gross outflow of population from Ireland. These developments do not outweigh the experiences of the young and relatively unskilled emigrants who form, as they always did, a large proportion of Irish emigrants. This group still is a very important component in the 'new wave' of emigration from Ireland since the 1980s.

CONCLUSION

This concluding discussion evaluates the evidence presented in the chapter in terms of the question posed by its title. Firstly, graduate emigration can be categorised as part of a qualitatively new wave of emigration because it has introduced a highly-educated component that differentiates contemporary experience from many outflows of the past. Secondly, it may also be considered 'new' because it is the outcome of a process of modernisation that expanded educational opportunities, saw an increase in foreign-owned investment and that had a vision of Ireland as a high-technology, high-education country. The highly-educated also form a greater proportion of contemporary population outflows than in the past.

The case that graduate emigration is 'new', however, should not be overstated. Firstly, the destinations of graduate emigrants, their motivations, their social behaviour abroad and the means by which emigration information is managed suggest a strong degree of continuity with past waves of out-migration from Ireland. Graduates go to the same destinations as other emigrants. They do so as a result of social networking and cultural fatalism which tacitly accepts emigration as a social norm in Irish society. Thus, graduate emigration from Ireland also resembles previous emigrations in that it is a response to forces of social conservatism which view emigration as entirely 'natural' and 'traditional' solutions to lack of work and opportunity at home. Secondly, there has been a long tradition of graduate emigration from Ireland in the past, and although the graduate emigration of the 1980s appeared to be new, this was only true in comparison with the situation in the 1960s and 1970s. Thirdly, the emigration of graduates certainly is not new at a more abstract level. It is still caused by the same forces that have contributed to the marginalisation of Ireland in the global economy. These conditioned past population outflows and still condition recent Irish emigration, including graduate emigration.

The modernisation project initiated in Ireland since the 1960s was supposed to increase labour market opportunities within the country, reduce unemployment and facilitate the transition to a high-technology economy.[36] It is possible to rationalise the failure to achieve these objectives in terms of Ireland's status as the 'Human Resource Warehouse of Europe', to view graduates as mobile 'Young Europeans' and to portray Ireland as an 'overcrowded island' from which emigration is inevitable. However this discourse masks the obvious weaknesses in the modernisation project.[37] This might also explain the symbolic importance attached to graduate emigrants, especially by government sources, in the debate about emigration. It is, after all, much more acceptable to couch the discussion about recent emigration in terms of opportunities, high skills and the globalisation of Irish youth, than to portray emigration as a response on the part of disadvantaged young people to the lack of opportunity arising from unemployment and the collapse of labour markets at home.

Unemployment in Ireland remains high for many social groups. As was shown by the evidence cited in this chapter, there still remains a shortage of graduate employment of a suitable kind in Ireland. Therefore, even in its own terms, there remain some problems with the concept of modernisation as applied to the Irish situation. In the mismatch between political rhetoric, state policies and labour market outcomes, the experience of Irish graduate emigration is not a break from the historical experience of Irish emigration. To some extent, arguments that graduate emigration is 'new' therefore hide many similarities with past emigration flows. They also disguise the likelihood that modernisation in Ireland has failed to transform the prospects both for the Irish economy and for Irish graduate labour. It may simply have moved Ireland to a 'new' position of dependency in the global economy.

Finally, an answer must be sought to the question of whether graduate emigration is a harbinger of a future new wave of Irish emigration. King and Shuttleworth suggest that the argument that graduate emigration is a product of long-term structural forces should not be overstated.[38] This is because the 1980s' outflow of graduates can be interpreted as a cyclical phenomenon. Rates of outflow reached their peak in 1988, but as the global economy, and particularly that of Ireland's nearest neighbour Britain, moved into recession rates of emigration have since then declined. This indicates that graduate emigration is often motivated by short-term factors and that it is very difficult to predict as it responds to the volatility of the business cycle. As it falls, comment on graduate emigration as a new type of emigration may appear to be irrelevant, but it could again appear as a new type of emigration when the global economic environment changes.

Graduate emigration therefore appears to have a dual nature; the extent to which it is possible to say that it is 'new' depends upon the analytical scale within which it is considered. The new social and educational forces that created it support the claims that it is qualitatively different from emigration flows in the past. But the balance of evidence suggests that graduate emigration is just another part of the Irish emigration experience that is caused by the same forces as for other social groups, that it is closely comparable with previous waves of emigration and may only be a short-term phenomenon.

NOTES AND REFERENCES

1 J. Sexton, 'Recent Changes in the Irish Population and the Pattern of Emigration', *Irish Banking Review*, Autumn, 1987; Jim Mac Laughlin, *Ireland: The Emigrant Nursery and the World Economy* (Cork: Cork University Press, 1994); R. King and I. Shuttleworth, 'Ireland: New Wave Emigration in the 1980s', *Irish Geography*, vol. 21, 1988, pp. 104–08.

2 D. Garvey and M. McGuire, *Structure of Gross Migration Flows* (Dublin, Central Statistics Office, 1989).

3 J. Bermingham, 'Head-Hunting for Top Students', *Business and Finance*, 28 May 1987, pp. 13–19; F. O'Toole, 'Getting Out', *Irish Times*, 16 October 1988.

4 Jim Mac Laughlin, *Ireland: The Emigrant Nursery and the World Economy* (Cork, University Press, 1994); Jim Mac Laughlin, 'Emigration and the Peripheralisation of Ireland in the Global Economy', *Review of the Fernand Braudel Center*, vol. 27, no. 2, 1994, pp. 243–73.

5 Tom Whelan, 'The New Emigrants', *Newsweek*, 10 October, 1987.

6 P. Breathnach, 'Women's Employment and Peripheralisation: the Case of Ireland's Branch-Plant Economy', *Geoforum*, vol. 24, no. 1, 1993, pp. 19–29.

7 P. Clancy, *Who Goes to College?* (Dublin, Higher Education Authority, 1986).

8 P. Danagher et al., *Manpower Policy in Ireland* (Dublin, National Economic and Social Council, 1985).

9 I. Shuttleworth, 'Graduate Emigration from Ireland: a Symptom of Peripherality?', in R. King (ed.), *Contemporary Irish Migration* (Dublin, Geographical Society of Ireland, 1991), pp. 83–95.

10 Jim Mac Laughlin, 'Social Characteristics and Destinations of Recent Emigrants from the West of Ireland', *Geoforum*, vol. 22, no. 3, 1991, pp. 319–331; Mac Laughlin, *Ireland: The Emigrant Nursery*.

11 Peter Shirlow and Ian Shuttleworth, 'Training, Migration and the Changing World Order: a Case Study of Foreign Capital Restructuring and Training Policy in the Republic of Ireland', in M.W. Gould and A. Findlay (eds.), *Population Migration and the Changing World Order* (London, Belhaven, 1994), pp. 91–111.

12 The Industrial Development Authority (IDA) which in the 1980s described Irish graduates as 'Young Europeans' who were by implication prepared to work anywhere.

13 A. Findlay, 'From Settlers to Skilled Transients: the Changing Structure of British International Migration', *Geoforum*, vol. 19, no. 4, 1988, pp. 401–10.

14   U. Kockel, 'Irish Migration to Mainland Europe: Observations from Southern Germany', in R. King (ed.), *Ireland, Europe and the Single Market* (Dublin, Geographical Society of Ireland, 1993), pp. 128–136; P. MacEinri, 'The New Europeans: the Irish in Paris Today', in J. Mulholland and D. Keogh (eds.), *Emigration, Employment and Enterprise* (Cork, Hibernian University Press, 1989), pp. 58–80.

15   J. Jackson, *The Irish in Britain* (London, Routledge and Kegan Paul, 1963).

16   P. MacEinri, 'The Irish in Paris: an Aberrant Community', in R. King (ed.), *Contemporary Irish Migration*, 32–41; U. Kockel, 'Irish Migration to Mainland Europe'.

17   P. MacEinri, 'The New Europeans: the Irish in Paris Today'.

18   ibid.

19   U. Kockel, 'Irish Migration to Mainland Europe'.

20   J. Johnson, 'Harvest Migration from Nineteenth Century Ireland', *Transactions and Papers*, Institute of British Geographers, vol. xli, 1967.

21   P. Breathnach, 'Women's Employment and Peripheralisation'.

22   Jim Mac Laughlin, 'Social Characteristics and Destinations of Recent Emigrants from Selected Regions in the West of Ireland', *Geoforum*, vol. 22, no. 3, 1991, pp. 319–331.

23   K. Miller, *Emigrants and Exiles: Ireland and the Irish Exodus to North America* (New York, Oxford University Press, 1985); J. Jackson, *The Irish in Britain*.

24   A. Findlay and L. Garrick, 'Scottish Emigration in the 1980s: a Migration Channels Approach to the Study of Skilled International Migration', *Transactions*, Institute of British Geographers, vol. 15, no. 2, 1990, pp. 177–192.

25   R. King, I. Shuttleworth, and A. Strachan, 'The Irish in Coventry: the Social Geography of a Relict Community', *Irish Geography*, vol. 21, no. 2, 1989, pp. 64–78; J. Jackson, *The Irish in Britain*; P. MacEinri, 'The New Europeans: The Irish in Paris Today'.

26   I. Shuttleworth, 'Irish Graduate Migration in the 1980s: a Case Study of Core-Periphery Relations in the Mobility of Qualified Manpower', (Trinity College Dublin, Unpublished PhD Thesis, 1991).

27   J. Jackson, *The Irish in Britain*; B. Walter, 'Ethnicity and Irish Residential Distribution', *Transactions*, Institute of British Geographers, vol. 11. no. 2, 1986, pp. 131–146.

28   R. King and I. Shuttleworth, 'The Emigration and Employment of Irish Graduates: the Export of High-Quality Labour from the Periphery of Europe', European Urban and Regional Studies, vol. 2. no. 1, 1995, pp. 21–40.

29   ibid.

30   P. Breathnach, 'Uneven Development and Capitalist Peripheralisation: the Case of Ireland', Antipode, vol. 20, 1988, pp. 122–141; R. King and I. Shuttleworth, 'Education, Identity and Migration: the Case of Young Highly-Educated Irish Migrants', *Studi Emigrazione*, vol. 117, 1995, pp. 159–174.

31   R. Hayter, 'Truncating the International Firm and Regional Policy', *Area*, vol. 14, no. 4, 1982, pp. 277–282; J. Friedmann, 'The world-City Hypothesis', *Development and Change*, vol. 17, no. 1, 1986, pp. 69–83.

32   Ian Shuttleworth, Irish Graduate Migration in the 1980s.

33   ibid.

34   D. Garvey and M. McGuire, *Structure of Gross Migration Flows*.

35   Jim Mac Laughlin, 'Social Characteristics and Destinations of Recent Emigrants from the West of Ireland', p. 328; D. Hannan et al., *The Economic and Social Implications of Emigration*, (Dublin: National Economic and Social Council, 1991).

36   Peter Shirlow, *Development Ireland* (London, Pluto Press, 1995).

37   *Irish Times*, 3 March 1989.

38   R. King and I. Shuttleworth, 'The Emigration and Employment of Irish Graduates'.

13. Technical Experience or Social Myth
Ireland and the International Professional Labour Market[1]

Gerard Hanlon

This chapter examines the emergence of an international labour market within accountancy. This market is currently being created by the Big Six (these are the six multinational accountancy practices that dominate the profession globally). What appears to be emerging is a far from uniform picture about the validity and usefulness of these markets. What follows is based upon research carried out at various times between 1990 and 1993 in Ireland and the United States of America. Amongst other things, this research entailed interviewing approximately 55 accountants on a variety of topics, one such topic being the role of international labour markets upon the career strategies of accountants. These accountants were at different stages in their careers: some were partners in large firms whereas others had just qualified and were beginning their careers. Of these interviewees, 15 were based in America. For the sake of confidentiality, the names of people have been changed. This work attempts to address the differences in opinion that surfaced between American and Irish accountants. Hopefully, some of the points made here can be used when other professional or expert groups are examined in the light of increasing internationalisation.

Before examining the issues of globalisation and international labour markets, it is necessary to comment on the nature of the accountancy firms and the profession. The Big Six accountancy firms dominate the accountancy profession internationally. Originally these firms were Anglo-American but they are now exceptionally international with offices in every developed economic region of the global.[2] For example, between them, they employ 10,272 professionals in France, 8,137 in Germany, and 2,303 in Italy.[3] This presence is not, however, confined to Europe. Between 1975–85 the largest twenty accounting firms (which the Big Six overwhelmingly dominate) expanded their total number of offices by 115 per cent up from 2,323 offices internationally to 4,991 offices.[4] The largest relative increase was in Asia which grew by 29 per cent. In terms of revenues generated, these organisations are also very large entities. In the UK, the Big Six have an annual turnover of £2.5 billion and in Ireland the Big Six accountancy market was worth roughly £90 million in 1988.[5] These firms also dominate the international market for auditing services. They control 56 per cent of this global market in terms of Fortune 500 company audits, 65 per cent of such audits in terms of company sales or 74 per cent of this market in terms of company assets.[6] Whatever criteria one wants to use, these firms are the really significant players in global accountancy.

The Big Six have become international entities for two reasons. Firstly, they pursued a policy of merger and, secondly, they grew due to the importance of auditing and the accountant within the Anglo-American world.[7] Auditing, and hence the accountant, came to occupy an important role in the U.S. and the UK due to the individualist nature of Anglo-American capitalism and its prioritising of the rights of the shareholder and/or owner above all other rights. In contrast to this, other states, e.g. Sweden and Germany, evolved differently and gave greater importance, or as great an importance, to the rights of *all* stakeholders in the economy rather than limiting such rights to the shareholder. As a result, these countries evolved differently, with less of an emphasis on shareholders and more emphasis on the role of capital formation and/or public well-being.[8] It was from their base in Anglo-American capitalism, with its emphasis on auditing, that the Big Six firms globalised.

The audit allowed these firms a regular income and a springboard from which to establish overseas. In essence these firms expanded geographically as their clients extended their operations. Thus, as the large UK and US firms moved overseas, their accountants did likewise. Their close relationship with their clients facilitated such a move. Clients like to use the same accountancy firms where possible in different regions of the globe, so much so that spatial networks are now an important factor in landing international clients.

Elsewhere, I have highlighted how these firms came to Ireland.[9] They entered Ireland *en masse* in the late 1960s and early 1970s in response to economic development. They penetrated the Irish market via mergers with indigenous firms as they appear to have done throughout the globe. The exact details of these mergers are difficult to ascertain but it appears to be the case that the indigenous firm uses the Big Six name, pays a percentage of its fees to the central Big Six fund and adheres to Big Six accounting standards.[10] In day-to-day operational matters, however, the indigenous firm is run by the Irish partners. In essence, this operational autonomy is limited by the fact that if the Irish firm opts out of a Big Six partnership it will lose some of its current international clients and any future work that the Big Six firm would have referred to it. Given that the Irish wing of the Big Six firms depend on this international network for between 15–30 per cent of their business, such a move would have very serious consequences.[11] In the past ten years, however, the Big Six have been moving towards a 'world firm' strategy where the organisation offers the exact same service globally, trades under a unified logo, develops international networks internally via regular conferences, exchanges and so on, and generally attempts to centralise its organisational structure.[12] The reason for this is that the Big Six want their clients to feel that, once they go abroad, their accountancy firm will offer the same quality of service and advice regardless of what other difficulties the clients may encounter. In Big Six terms, international homogeneity equals profitability. One of the means by which centralisation and 'world firm' status is achieved is through an international internal labour market.

THE CREATION OF AN INTERNATIONAL LABOUR MARKET IN ACCOUNTANCY

That there has emerged (or is emerging) an international labour market within the accountancy profession has been argued before.[13] This market is largely internal in that the Big Six move people across borders within their internal organisational structures. For a peripheral economy like Ireland, this can have serious consequences. For example, 20 per cent of Irish chartered accountants are overseas, 40 per cent of accountants under 30 years of age are overseas and half of this latter group are in the Big Six. As a trend amongst Irish accountants, this pattern appears to be intensifying. In 1984, 14.3 per cent of accountants were overseas whereas, by 1989, 22.3 per cent had left despite the fact that there was a shortage of accountants in Ireland throughout much of the 1980s.[14] These people did not leave because they had a deep loathing of Irish society. Indeed, 36.6 per cent stated they definitely wanted to return home and a further 39.8 per cent stated that returning home was a possibility.[15] However, the likelihood of such a mass return is remote given that NESC estimates only one in four actually do so.[16]

Such a migratory process has emerged within a variety of 'elite' economic spheres and is usually marketed to the individuals concerned as a means of enhancing one's career.[17] This chapter will suggest that the growth of these labour markets is tied to the development of multinational organisations. There are various reasons as to why firms would want to pursue such a strategy of internationalising their labour markets. These range from the desire to enhance the international exposure of staff, to satisfying the desire of staff to travel. Within accountancy, Beaverstock has argued the primary reasons are: seconding personnel to meet staff shortages in overseas offices; to use a global network as a means of exposing junior staff to international experience, overseas transfers allow firms to promote certain personnel further up the firm hierarchy, and this market allows the Big Six to retain staff who are seeking to go abroad.[18] I would also suggest that the firms use this internationalisation process as a means of further selling themselves as 'world firms' to clients. The first three reasons above relate to the career paths of those who are selected for an international transfer. Reasons two and three, international experience and promotion, are obviously reserved for those who are deemed to be suitable for 'better things'. But even secondment to another office to help relieve staff shortages should also enhance one's career, as one will either be seconded to a position of responsibility or one will go to an office where the labour supply is limited, thus giving one greater opportunities for possible promotion. If all of the above is accurate, then one could suppose an international transfer is a good career move? Unfortunately, the answer is not quite this straightforward.

ACCOUNTANCY AND THE HIERARCHY OF INTERNATIONAL DESTINATIONS

One of the reasons for this lack of straightforwardness is to be found in the hierarchy which has emerged as regards places to go and places not to go in terms of a career strategy. For an ambitious chartered accountant, the choice of destination is fraught with danger. There are three types of destination; the experience market; the money market and the leisure market. Accountants at all levels within the Big Six, in both Ireland and the US perceive the world as being divided into these three.

> There are three different answers when one is thinking of going abroad. If you want for example to go off and build up a nest egg quickly without thinking of improving your professional skills you might go to somewhere that is perceived to be a hardship posting, somewhere like the Middle East. If you want to go somewhere where you get sun and sand and an easy sort of life you go to somewhere like the Bahamas or Bermuda where the work isn't too taxing but is highly specialised in banking and insurance. If you want to go somewhere you are going to be stretched professionally with very demanding work you might go to somewhere like New York, or Hong Kong, or London. (Kenneth Byrne, Irish Big Six Partner)

> Cayman Islands, it's a holiday . . . you'd lose whatever links you had plus whatever experience you'd get in a place like that is very narrow . . . so it may not have a lot of application in the place you go back to. (Frank Rogers, U.S. Big Six Manager)

The key viewpoint in both of the comments above is that the level or the type of technical knowledge one would get from somewhere like the Cayman Islands (large off-shore banking centre) or Saudi Arabia (lack of industrial development and a very short accountancy tradition) would limit one' s marketability upon returning to Ireland, the US or the UK.

In the light of this, it would appear that exposure to international labour markets is about gaining increasingly sophisticated technical knowledge which can then be exploited upon one's return. Considering the new international division of labour which resulted from the recent globalisation of non-accounting firms, this it is quite a legitimate assumption. For example,

Wickham has highlighted how in the electronic engineering sector, Irish engineers emigrate in search of what he terms 'hi-tech' work.[19] This is work that is more highly skilled than the work available in Ireland due to the way in which large multinational electronics organisations divide the labour process globally. These firms concentrate the research and development work in core economies such as the US and export the labour-intensive low-skilled elements of production. Within such an international division of labour, Ireland holds a mid-table position. Ireland is not a low skilled off-shore production unit for these firms, but neither does it have the very high-skilled work of the core economies. As such, Irish engineers emigrate in search of this work. For example, Wickham found that although the taxation system was cited as the biggest single reason for emigration amongst engineers, 40. 1 per cent of engineers gave work-related categories as the main reason for considering emigration. The global division of labour and the creation of an international labour market appear to have had a real impact upon the career and migration patterns of engineers. Wickham found that one in three Irish engineering graduates emigrated in the 1980s. One of the key factors in this process is the search for a higher level of technical work.

Such views are also held by the majority of Irish accountants.[20] Irish accountants perceive an international division of labour within accountancy. This division is based on two pillars. One, it is felt that technically the work in certain places (e.g. London) is more difficult and two, it is also felt that the work in places like London has more status. When talking about entering the international labour market, newly qualified Irish accountants highlight the advantages of the greater scale of business in the economic heartlands of the US or the UK, the greater responsibility one is given overseas, the performing of larger technical jobs. However, there are a number of difficulties with these 'technical experience' arguments, all of which were highlighted by the US-based interviewees. These difficulties largely relate to two issues, trust and relevance. It is to these areas that we now turn.

THE SUPERFICIALITY OF TECHNICAL EXPERIENCE

As suggested there are two areas within which the technical experience logic for going overseas falls down. The first concerns the technical level of the work given to recently-arrived migrants.

TRUST

Irish accountants who had recently qualified (called seniors) suggested that they went overseas because they would achieve higher levels of responsibility in a larger more dynamic economy

> . . . if salaries continue at their present level and trends continue leaning as they seem to do because there is such a shortage of labour, people will just be attracted by the lifestyle and the relative responsibility which they are given quite easily. (Peter Daniels, Irish Big Six senior)

> . . . if you come back from abroad, from London, looking for a job here, say, say you want a manager's job and you said oh I've worked on this and I've worked on that, yeah it goes down well. The bigger the better you know. It is the level of responsibility rather than any size, you know I was a supervisor on this job with so many staff. It's the number of staff on the audit as well as the turnover, it's kind of the two things. They'd say how many people did you supervise? And you'd say two or whatever, seven people on a large job. That goes down well. (Jean Devoy, Irish Big Six supervisor)

Thus there is the assumption that, when one moves overseas on an international transfer, the net result will be increased responsibility. One will be dealing with client staff at a higher level, one will control larger audits, one will be given more prestigious jobs.[21]

However, the American perception is very different. Accountants in the US felt that responsibility would not be forthcoming as people would not trust a new arrival. This was exacerbated by the fact that migrants were only going to be overseas for a short period (18 months is the standard time-frame on these transfers). This means that they are not going to be based in the office in the long term and hence it was a disadvantage for the host office to build them into that office's future plans. If this were the case, why should migrants receive responsible posts? If people were only going to be there for 18 months, they would spend six months settling in and maybe one or two months 'winding down' before returning to their country of origin thereby leaving 10 to 12 months to develop, and this was deemed too short a time.

> I am not going to give some guy anything really big until I know who he is and you're not going to put him on anything big if he's going to leave in the middle, so you have a year. How do you know you just won't be doing accounts payable? I mean that's not to say that there aren't exciting things to do. If I was to do something that was broadening me I'd pick something like a national residency in some particular area. I would try to get onto some really big client and see if they would transfer me down on that client. Just to move to a city? I've moved you know. Some of these guys that come here come from non-English speaking countries and they're interned here and they're managers and probably extremely competent but if they're not strong English speakers what are you going to do? Assign them as a staff one or a staff two and he could be the most brilliant guy in the world but you're not going to give him anything that's got a lot of judgement in it because you can't talk to him about it and I kind of wonder what the perceived benefit is? (Debra Harding, US Big Six manager)

We, therefore, run into two problems. Firstly, language, although it is a difficulty that Irish accountants do not face in the US or the UK, it is one that emerges when they go to continental Europe, and increasingly continental Europe is deemed a very suitable location as the EU becomes more and more integrated. Secondly, and perhaps more worryingly from the point of view of the individual migrant, is the general reluctance of staff in the host office to trust the competence of migrants. This was found across the board. All of this leads one to be suspicious about the quality of experience to be gained by going overseas:

> . . . and when people do come here from other countries, they're not, I see what they're doing they're not getting great experience here. They're not getting the best clients and it seems like there may be one or two partners like that even know they exist. (Mike Sinclair, US Big Six manager)

It may be suggested that such opinions are parochial. However, this appears not to be the case; even those who had already been, or are currently, on an international transfer have their reservations about the level of technical experience to be gained:

> I went up to Montreal to help them get their US tax practice started. When I got up there they had a partner and a Canadian senior manager. Through their own palace intrigue the partner was booted out soon after I arrived so it was just me and the senior manager. She was a lovely person but not very good at managing people and she was very difficult to work with and very focused on her own potential promotion to partnership and so she, to the extent that she possibly could, kept all the good work to herself and gave me all the shit. We were the only two senior American tax people in the office and I was a manager and I was filling out tax returns. It was extremely frustrating. I learned a lot simply because there were issues you don't see this side of the border and I was able to soak them up but I was really treated like a junior you know more than I expected. (Frank Rogers, US Big Six manager)

> It is the most difficult issue we face and unfortunately it has a lot of the hallmarks of the X process. First you make the glossy book, tell everyone how great it's going to be, send them out there, and then we don't want to hear from them again and so the only way to find out how it's going to be is to talk to other people who've done it. And you know when I came here it was a huge cultural shock because you know the profession here is much more detail orientated, much more risk adverse, we won't work on that that's too risky, procedures are different, the internal control procedures are different, culturally the firm is very different to London, the expectation level is different, and you have come from another office to the Boston office, which is somewhat parochial in itself, and they didn't quite know what to make of you. So they're not going to give you anything good because you hadn't been here that long anyway and coming from London your perception is that they don't have anything good anyway and so now you're kicking your heels saying Jesus what have I done? But slowly you do

the classic X thing – you shut your mouth, knock on doors and demonstrate you can do it and I think you're right a year and a half is just not long enough. I was on a two year rotation and I stayed a year at their request and then they said do you want to stay another year and I've got to the point where I don't want to go back to London. (John Bames, British US-based Big Six Senior manager)

Hence the idea of going overseas to higher levels of responsibility and exposure to technical expertise needs to be treated with a great deal of caution, if not rejected out of hand. Even if one is invited overseas because of one's technical expertise one may, like the Frank Rogers quote highlighted earlier, be held back by the 'palace intrigue' of the destination office. Hence the reasons as to why going overseas is an advantage must lie elsewhere. One such possible answer is that by being overseas one is exposed to different accountancy techniques. But this thesis runs into concerns over the relevance of such know-how.

RELEVANCE

The general argument given about why going overseas is an advantage will often concern the issue of developing new technical skills in a variety of areas. When accountants who had just recently arrived in the US from Ireland and the UK (these were in the US for a period of less than one month) spoke, they spoke about technical advantages:

> Specifically I was thinking about my future in Ireland and the job opportunities there. A year ago things were on the downturn, the recessions in the UK and the US were impacting upon Ireland and it didn't look like there were going to be a lot of opportunities outside the profession and I wanted to advance to managerial status within the organisation and that was very tight. I had a problem in the fact that I was based in a general audit group although luckily enough I was specialising to a small degree in investment companies. So I was looking at Australia and I was footloose having been away, so this opportunity came up and I got a phone call saying I could go to the States and work in an investment company practice. It was an area I was interested in and it was a growing area in Ireland so I took the plunge. (Phil Doyle, Irish US-based Big Six senior)

Doyle went on to say

> The Mutual Fund industry is based in Boston and New York. The level of specialism in the States that's probably the one thing that hits one about the States straight away, it's a huge industry here where it's just kind of small, minuscule in Ireland.

There is an incongruity between the two comments and indeed within the whole technical skills argument at this level. The incongruity is as follows. The Mutual Funds industry is minuscule in Ireland because the Irish economy is too small to sustain such a huge specialist industry at the same level as the US. It may also be assumed that in Ireland many of the areas of growth in this industry are in the tax-free financial services development zone recently created in Dublin. Much of this would require off-shore financial expertise which is more likely to be developed in the Bahamas or Grand Cayman, so why go to Boston or New York? Hence people go to places like the US to develop skills in specialisms which do not exist in Ireland, in the hope that these skills will then make them more marketable when they return to *a state that currently does not use them and will be unlikely to develop them on a significant scale in the future.* There may be some limited benefit if the numbers were small, but in Ireland the rate of migration amongst accountants has increased dramatically, leading one to argue that the cost in human capital is too high for the benefits gained. As stated, roughly 75% per cent of accountancy migrants wish to return to Ireland whereas the actual figure will probably be closer to 25 per cent. This means that of all emigrants, the cost of producing qualified accountants is wasted by the Irish state and Irish Big Six firms in approximately three in four cases.

Similar issues also arise in auditing and tax. If one carries out an audit or tax work in the US one does so to American Accounting Standards or US tax law which are inapplicable in Ireland, hence there is little advantage in having them. Similar reservations were expressed by accountants in the US by both Europeans based there for a considerable length of time and Americans.

> To the extent that it [technical knowledge] is specific to the country you go to, or the extent it has to do with cross-border trade not necessarily so much [in terms of relevance] but then again they haven't utilised the knowledge I picked up. The other problem with international tax rotations is that there doesn't seem to be such a demand for international corporate people. Many international tax rotations have to do with individual taxation. So you go there and you do individual tax returns for Americans living in foreign countries cause as you may be aware our tax system unlike anyone else's is based on citizenship, so tax wise you can run but you can't hide, so no matter what country you're living in you still have to file US tax returns. All of this is not really career enhancing. (Frank Rogers, US Big Six manager)

> That's the question (will the technical knowledge be of use upon returning home). It's okay to say you're learning something about US healthcare but what use is that? Maybe that's the specific that you have US healthcare which is not of much use but I am also working on NEC which is obviously Japanese and massive. We audit it in London as well, I mean the ideal would be for me to audit it back in London having seen the US side of things, how the US operations work, how we report over there. Even so I think just different ways of doing things and you say we do it this way over here or I saw this in the States. I mean there has got to be so much you can learn, just the whole seeing how business operates over here, I mean I can't believe anyone is saying they're not bringing home a lot of useful information even if you're not going to use the technical stuff so much. (Peter Davis, British US-based Big Six senior)

Hence, how useful and applicable is the technical know-how learned overseas? The two technical advantages which an international transfer can give appear to be highly dubious. If this is the case, then what, if any, are the merits of a move abroad? I will suggest that the answer lies within the realm of social and commercial factors.

THE SOCIAL AND COMMERCIAL BENEFITS OF CROSS-BORDER MOVEMENT

It is my contention that the real benefits of going overseas are not technical, but social and commercial. In terms of migration, what is meant by social and commercial is the development of overseas contacts, the development of personal flexibility and resourcefulness, the building of 'character' (these are only a subset of such skills). In light of the increasing importance of commercial and social skills within accountancy in the past decade or so, this is perhaps unsurprising.[22] More generally, what is implied by commercial skill in accountancy is the ability to manage, i.e. the capacity to control budgets, to assign staff who will perform the job to budget, to actually get the fees in from clients, not to antagonise the client, and so on. These skills have increased in importance in the past 20 years as the profession has redefined itself and shifted from a social service ethos to a commercialised or managerialist once. Today, promotion above the rank of senior within a large accountancy firm is dependent upon having these commercial skills.

Social skill has a different meaning and implies the ability to bring in new business. This is dependent upon networks, social background, contacts and so forth. Being able to bring in business is probably the most important skill one needs to become a partner in a Big Six firm. One will only make partnership if one can enlarge the cake from which one is taking a slice. Again this factor is relatively new. It emerged during the 1980s as the Big Six became more entrepreneurial and business-like. As these firms expanded and took advantage of the market, they increasingly demanded that their partners and future partners did likewise. Hence, partners came to be seen as entrepreneurs rather than as traditional non-business oriented professionals.[23] These social and commercial factors were highlighted by US accountants and by senior personnel within the Irish firms.

> On the whole emigration benefits a person's career yes . . . most people leaving would go to us abroad . . . that sort of thing is very beneficial to a person's future. I think it means an opportunity at an early stage to apply your skills in a different arena, to develop personal qualities of self-reliance, independence, maturity, to learn how to cope with different situations, with different people, and in many cases to benefit professionally from, for example in the States the typical job is much larger and in many cases more complex, you also have a different work ethic in the States good or bad. (Peter O'Neill, Irish Big Six director)

Personally you have to work extremely hard and it's sometimes very depressing and sometimes you wonder why on earth you didn't stay at home with the people that knew you and the clients who knew you but it gives you an aspect that other people don't have and that's a degree of flexibility. If you can pick up something you didn't know and improve your worth in a year and then go back I think that's a great sign rather than staying amongst people who've always known you and clients who've always known you, I think you've shown your flexibility. (Andrea Simpson, British US-based Big Six senior manager)

I think people question it [overseas experience being technically beneficial] a lot more than that. At first blush people say he's gone abroad he's got some special skills but once you get down to it the question always comes up who did you work on, what did you do abroad? And eventually the proof is in the performance. If you've got an issue where a US company is trying to relocate to Reading and the manager says Jesus I know such and such over there and calls them up and sets the contact – all of a sudden we know a person over there and we put our client in contact with them that's invaluable and whether because this guy's an incredible golfer and played golf with everyone in the firm and met some good technical people or whether the guy's a technical guy and met them that way it doesn't matter he's given us the contact, the open door. (Tom Wallace, US Big Six manager)

None of these comments relate simply to technical expertise. Technical experience does not appear to be high on the list of benefits amongst those who hold power within the evaluation process. What is valued as much, if not more, than technical qualities are the social and personal resources which accrue to the individual simply from being overseas.

But if it is simply a matter of social and personal resources, surely they can be got anywhere? Yet again the answer is not so straightforward. As highlighted, there is an international hierarchy. This hierarchy values places like New York or London over Grand Cayman or Burma. Yet one could reasonably assume that for an Irish person a place such as Burma would prove more testing in terms of one's character and flexibility than somewhere like London. However, such an assumption misunderstands the process that is taking place. The character-building process being enacted gives one a number of advantages that can only be got from core economic centres. These advantages are networking and commercialisation.

When one goes overseas, it is important to go to a place that the sending office has, or will have, a lot of contact with. Hence the preference for places like the UK, the US and, increasingly, Continental Europe. Spending time in these states is advantageous because one can possibly work on, say, the American audit of a large multinational firm that is also a client or a possible client in Ireland (see Peter Davis earlier).

> What it [emigration] does do is give you, I mean for me coming from the UK to the US a lot of clients that we do here report under UK standards because of their parents and vice versa so this was a very healthy transition to make. To actually go and make yourself more technically marketable back home, I would say, if I had gone back which was my original intention it would have added more strings to my bow if I had a good working knowledge of US issues when they came up with US subsidiaries or companies I had dealt with there, I would have been able to have some real input there. But I don't think you have anything technically to take back and use on our own clients back home. (Andrea Simpson, British US-based Big Six senior manager)

This point assumes, of course, that the UK firm would put her on these jobs and make use of her expertise. However, this is not always the case (see Frank Rogers' quotes above). This international networking also allows one to establish contacts for clients who wish to expand overseas or better understand what is happening to one of their operations overseas. Thus an Irish accountant having been abroad can put his or her client in touch with a person whom he or she has worked with in, say, the X office; this enables the firm to look truly international. The idea of international resources and a sophisticated international workforce can enhance a professional firm's reputation, and it is this reputation that is the key marketing device used by these firms in their dealings with international clients and international trade.[24]

There is one difficulty, in terms of networking, for the individuals concerned with an international move. By going abroad to develop international networking contacts, one may lose one's local or national contacts both within the national firm itself and in terms of clients. Dirsmith and Covaleski, Harper, and Hanlon have all suggested that within accountancy firms, senior partners mentor certain staff for promotion.[25] This appears to be a key, although under-researched, factor in the promotional process to partnership. If one goes overseas one may weaken or lose this relationship. Thus Frank Rogers, US Big Six manager, commented:

> However, my experience is that this office has not exploited this experience [of being abroad] at all and there have been situations where it could have and in addition I found that what was far more important in terms of my career was that my continuity with the X office was broken and so in a sense I lost quite a bit of seniority and lost a good deal of what had been a good reputation and lost what turned out to be a very important mentor relationship so that it was really almost as if I was starting over when I got back.

This process can also entail the loss of client relationships, so that one may come back and find that somebody else is working on what had been your client base, thereby negating the value of any knowledge you may have gained about the client's global organisation.

My perception is if I want to make partner the best thing I can do is cultivate X because moving around isn't going to help me with my relationships. If I move I lose my network and then I am starting from ground zero again. As a matter of fact its a real concern of mine. My husband has an academic job and his Fellowship is over in a year and I don't know what he's going to do after that. So he's got a job change coming up and if it takes us out of X it's like oh what do I do? You know I got a farm here, I've been cultivating a little farm here and what am I going to do walk away and start a new farm? It will take years to get anything new going. So the way I see it moving around wouldn't help me much. (Debra Heinz, US Big Six manager)

. . . So long as you're sustaining work and getting experience that's fine but it's a fact of life every time you move you're going to lose your current clients and every time you come back sometimes you'll fit in with them, sometimes with others. But in terms of getting just the jobs other people don't want, you should be able to walk back in and get a good job if everybody's expectation was you were going away to get good experience. (Andrea Simpson, British US-based Big Six senior manager)

Not everyone will be expected to get good experience, so whether or not accountants get good jobs upon returning is a contentious point. But what is certain is that there is no guarantee that they will be returned to their former clients.

Having briefly examined the potential advantages and disadvantages of networking it is time to look at the commercialisation issue. It has been argued by McNair, Steven, and Hanlon that the accountancy profession has become much more commercial in the past 15 years or so.[26] One consequence of this has been that accountants are evaluated much more on issues of costs and profitability than on technical issues, although these obviously play a part. This commercialism, the development of elaborate controls, the pervasiveness of 'industriousness', 'efficiency', tight budgets, the 'less parochial view' is perceived to exist at the core. Whether or not it actually exists is irrelevant; it is the perception which is important.

What is being argued is that for peripheral accountants, a move to the core is highly symbolic. Such an argument is not new. Gellner has suggested that when national groups and nation-states are being created, language and communication take on a huge symbolic importance.[27] One indicates which group – 'nationalists' or 'others' – one identifies with through one's attitude to such symbols. Harvey has also suggested that within late twentieth-century capitalism, post-modem culture (a concept he rejects) is ephemeral, throwaway, based on appearance, but it is also rooted in the more concrete economic transition from Fordism to Flexible Accumulation.[28] Bourdieu has also outlined how symbols and symbolic capital are intimately interwoven with, and reinforce, material capital.[29] He suggests that the relationship between the two allows societal élites to portray the social world and its construction as natural.

Using Bourdieu's analysis, accountants from the periphery appear to view the international labour market as part of the 'natural' world of a young professional in an international firm. This market has achieved the status of orthodoxy, in Bourdieu's terms, wherein to question the benefits of such a market is possible but considered slightly blasphemous. Thus for Bourdieu, Harvey, Gellner and many others, symbols have an underlying concrete meaning. The same, I would suggest, is true within accountancy's professional labour markets. Going to the core proves that one is prepared to make the ultimate gesture to the Irish firm that one is 'trustworthy' and, therefore, suitable for promotion because one has gone to the core and become familiar with, and endorsed, the commercial values that it represents. A move to the periphery does not convey the same meaning. One goes to the Bahamas for a holiday but not to develop the appropriate values for business (although often these values are referred to in terms of skills).

> I've friends who left London. One now who has gone to Bangkok and another who's just gone to Wellington in New Zealand and I don't think that's going to be perceived as great experience coming back and they know that – though they're probably going to have a lot more fun. One of the partners told one of them to bring his deck chair 'cause he's not going to be overworked type thing. I mean you know that when you go there, so you go there for perhaps more of a cultural experience. I wanted to go somewhere like here where I could bring back experience as well. (Peter Daniels, British US-based Big Six senior)

Yet, as highlighted, the actual extent of the experience gained and/or its relevance is very much open to question. Or is it? It appears to be the case that the actual degree of communication between the sending and receiving offices is limited, thus allowing migrants to mystify the nature of their experiences:

> Yeah definitely. From a London point of view if you go to New York they think you've had amazing experience. I mean I think there's a big lack of information flowing back to London in terms of what you really do and I think the perception is you've been to New York you've had the best experience whereas you might of been working on special practice clients the whole time, on Mutual Funds and not really got a lot of valuable experience. (Peter Daniels, British US-based Big Six senior)

> Yeah its cultural. I tell everybody that, I shouldn't tell them but I do. I tell them look don't come here thinking you're going to get the level of work you get now, it is going to be lower. Unless you're very lucky you're going to be frustrated in your technical progress because you'll probably not get the dream clients, you'll probably not get active clients. But the cultural experience to me outweighs all that and you go home anyway and no one knows what you did for two years. Use it on your CV its a CV builder. (John Barnes, British US-based Big Six senior manager)

Thus migrants can return and perpetuate the perception that they have gained excellent experience which should enhance their careers. People who have gone to the periphery, even if they have gained worthwhile experience, are hampered in this process because the perception people have of the periphery is negative. Hence it appears that the whole international labour market within accountancy is founded on a mythology.

CONCLUSION

It has been argued that there are at least two views on the need for international experience. These appear to differ along the core-periphery axis, although admittedly the evidence for this is limited due to the fact that only two countries were studied (with some limited contribution from UK accountants). Those in the US reject out of hand the need for global experience as part of an individual career strategy. In contrast, Irish-based accountants are strongly of the opinion that it is an advantage. They suggest that there are technical advantages to be gained from going overseas. However, these have been seriously questioned on two fronts: one, the level of technical exposure does not seem to be that high and two, even if one gets good technical experience it may be of a kind that is of no relevance when one returns home.

But there are other aspects to going abroad; these are networking and commercialisation. It can be argued that one develops contacts when one is abroad which may be of use to one upon returning, and/or one may work on a client both at home and abroad which will increase one's usefulness. Yet again, there are reservations which need to be expressed about these justifications. One may lose important contacts in one's original base by going abroad and there are no guarantees that one will be working on the same clients when one returns home. This potentially negates the usefulness of any exposure given by a move overseas. At the level of commercial skills there are also concerns. These skills can only be developed in the core economies according to those interviewed; however, in reality they appear to be mythologised. Commercial skills are more imaginary than real. But this is to miss the point somewhat; it is the symbolism of such a move which is important because it communicates to one's superiors back in the periphery that one endorses the views of the core, i.e. industriousness, profitability, etc.

It appears to be the case that Americans find none of these advantages really beneficial. This leads me to suggest that these attitudes are subject to core-periphery influences and that, because of the cultural climate in a Dublin Big Six office, a trip to London, New York and so on makes sense whereas, for an American, it could actually prove to be a disadvantage because, for the two offices concerned, such a move carries different symbolic meanings. In the light of the dominance of the US both economically and within accountancy, this is perhaps not such a great shock. For Ireland, and the periphery generally, the emergence of these international labour markets is worrying. Such markets have operated within manufacturing for quite some time where they could possibly be justified due to the international division of labour. This division of labour means that the highest skilled work is based at the core and hence a move to the core will probably expose one to significant experience. However, within the professional service sector, these advantages do not seem to accrue as peripheral professionals are being encouraged to go to the core for symbolic reasons.

Whether or not what has happened in accountancy will spread to the broader professional service area is a point for speculation. Such a creation appears to require the formation of multinational organisations. For example, in law, only 6.3 per cent of practising Irish solicitors are based in the UK – the primary overseas destination for Irish solicitors – and only two Irish firms have as many as three offices overseas.[30] Hence the lack of international organisations may well hamper the formation of global labour markets as people have to leave one organisation to get a job overseas and then join another organisation if they wish to return. On top of this, they also have to convince people that they picked up experience that was advantageous; this is more difficult when one is joining a new, non-international organisation. How, and if, other professional areas such as law, architecture. advertising and science are impacted by these issues remains to be researched, but the evidence from accountancy indicates that one of the crucial factors in this process is the penetration of a profession by multinational organisations.

NOTES AND REFERENCES

1   An earlier version of this paper appeared as 'The Parallax View – Images from the Core and the Periphery on the International Labour Market in Professional Expertise', European Institute Working Paper September 1994, London School of Economics.
2   Gerard Hanlon, *The Commercialisation of Accountancy: Flexible Accumulation and the Transformation of the Service Class* (London, Macmillan, 1994).
3   Hanlon, op. cit., p. 6.
4   A. Leyshon, P.W. Daniels and N. Thrift, *Large Accounting Firms in the UK: Operational Adaptation and Spatial Development*, Working Paper on Producer Services No. 2, 1987, University of Bristol and the Services Industries Research Centre, Portsmouth Polytechnic.
5   Hanlon, op. cit., Fig. 2.4.
6   Leyshon, Daniels and Thrift, op. cit., Table 3.
7   Hanlon, op. cit., p. 48.
8   S. Gallhofer and J. Haslam, 'The Aura of Accounting in the Context of a Crisis: Germany and the First World War', *Accounting, Organisations and Society*, vol. 16, no 5/6, 1991, pp. 487–520; Sten Jonsson, 'Role Making in Accounting while the State is Watching', *Accounting, Organisations and Society*, vol. 16, no 5/6, 1991.
9   Hanlon, op. cit., pp. 50–76.

10   H.W. Robinson, *A History of Accountants in Ireland*, 2nd ed., ICAI (Dublin, ICAI, 1983); Hanlon, op. cit.

11   See Hanlon, op. cit., pp. 50–76, for a further discussion of these issues.

12   Leyshon, Daniels and Thrift, op. cit.; Hanlon, op. cit.

13   J.V. Beaverstock, *Highly Skilled Professional and Managerial Labour Migration: the Case of Large Accounting Firms*, Working paper on Producer Services 9, 1989, University of Bristol and The Services Industries Research Centre, Portsmouth Polytechnic; J.V. Beaverstock, 'New International Labour Markets: The Case of Professional and Managerial Migration Within Large Accounting Firms', *Area*, vol. 22, no. 2 pp. 151–8; Gerard Hanlon, 'The Emigration of Irish Accountants: Economic Restructuring and Producer Services in the Periphery', *Irish Journal of Sociology*, 1, pp. 52–65; Gerard Hanlon 'Graduate Emigration: a Continuation or a Break with the Past?', in Patrick O'Sullivan (ed.), *The Irish World Wide*, vol. 1 (Leicester University Press, 1992).

14   Hanlon, 'The Emigration of Irish Accountants'.

15   Hanlon, *The Commercialisation of Accountancy*, p. 247, n. 4.

16   National Economic and Social Council, *The Economic and Social Implications of Emigration* (Dublin, NESC, 1991).

17   J. Salt, 'International Migration: a Spatial Theoretical Approach' in Michael Pacione (ed.), *Population Geography: Progress and Prospects* (Kent, Croom Helm, 1986), pp. 166–93.

18   Beaverstock, 'Highly Skilled Professional and Managerial Labour Migration?, p. 13.

19   James Wickham, 'The Over Educated Engineer? The Work, Education, and Careers of Irish Electronic Engineers', *IBAR-Journal of Irish Business and Administrative Research* 10, 1989, pp. 19–33.

20   Hanlon, 'The Emigration of Irish Accountants'; Hanlon 'Graduate Emigration'.

21   Anecdotal evidence from law appears to suggest the same is true of this profession. Informal conversations with the Irish Solicitors and Bar Association in London.

22   Hanlon, *The Commercialisation of Accountancy*; Hanlon 'Casino Capitalism and the Rise of the Commercialised Service Class: an Examination of the Accountant', *Critical Perspectives on Accounting*, vol. 7, 1996.

23   For a further description of this latter image see T. H. Marshall, 'The Present History of Professionalism', *Canadian Journal of Economics and Political Science*, vol. 5, no. 3, 1939, pp. 325–40.

24   Evan Davis, Gerard Hanlon and John Kay, 'What Internationalisation in Services Means: the Case of Accountancy in the UK and Ireland', in Howard Cox, Jeremy Clegg and Grazia Ietto–Gilles (eds.), *The Growth of Global Business New Strategies* (London, Routledge, 1993).

25   Mark W. Dirsmith and Mark A. Covaleski, 'Informal Communications, Nonformal Communications, and Mentioning in Public Accounting Firms', *Accounting, Organisations, and Society*, vol. 10, no. 2, 1985, pp. 149–69; Richard Harper, 'An Ethnography of Accountants', (PhD dissertation, Manchester University, 1989); Hanlon, *The Commercialisation of Accounting*.

26   C. J. McNair, 'Proper Compromises: the Management Control Dilemma in Public Accounting and its Impact on Auditor Independence', *Accounting, Organisations, and Society*, vol. 16, no. 7, 1991, pp. 635–53; Mark Stevens, *The Big Eight* (New York, Collier Press, 1984); Hanlon, *The Commercialisation of Accountancy*.

27   E. A. Gellner, *Thought and Change* (London, Wiedenfeld and Nicholson, 1964).

28   David Harvey, *The Condition of Postmodernity* (Oxford, Basil Blackwell, 1989).

29   Pierce Bourdieu, *Outline of a Theory of Practice* (Cambridge University Press, 1977).

30   'Irish Law Firms', *The Lawyer* 26 January 1993, pp. 11–5.

Index

341